RACE RELATIONS

Harry H. L. Kitano
University of California, Los Angeles

RACE
RELATIONS

second edition

PRENTICE-HALL, INC., ENGLEWOOD CLIFFS, NEW JERSEY 07632

Library of Congress Cataloging in Publication Data

KITANO, HARRY H. L.
  Race relations.

  Includes bibliographies and index.
  1. United States—Race relations. 2. Prejudices
and antipathies. I. Title.
E184.A1K47 1980   301.45′1′0420973   79-22629
ISBN 0-13-750091-2

Editorial/production supervision
and interior design by Serena Hoffman
Cover design by Jayne Conte
Manufacturing buyer: Ray Keating

PHOTO CREDITS

Chapter 11: *Filipino Reporter*, New York
Chapter 13: Monkmeyer
Chapter 14: Puerto Rican Community Development Project
All others from Wide World Photo

PRENTICE-HALL SERIES IN SOCIOLOGY
Neil J. Smelser, Editor

PRINTED IN THE UNITED STATES OF AMERICA

10 9 8 7 6 5 4 3 2 1

PRENTICE-HALL INTERNATIONAL, INC., *London*
PRENTICE-HALL OF AUSTRALIA PTY. LIMITED, *Sydney*
PRENTICE-HALL OF CANADA, LTD., *Toronto*
PRENTICE-HALL OF INDIA PRIVATE LIMITED, *New Delhi*
PRENTICE-HALL OF JAPAN, INC., *Tokyo*
PRENTICE-HALL OF SOUTHEAST ASIA PTE. LTD., *Singapore*
WHITEHALL BOOKS LIMITED, *Wellington, New Zealand*

CONTENTS

3

4

5

PREFACE

Most textbooks on race relations have been written from the point of view of the dominant white majority. In general they have advocated a universalistic view: there is one truth; there are clear standards; there are "normal" and "abnormal" behaviors. Most authors of such books, no matter how sympathetic to the minorities, skirt the fact that these "universals" were prescribed by those in a dominant position and are maintained and enforced by that power.

I look at race relations from another position—that of a minority-group member. I experienced racism from my very early days. I spent my adolescent years behind barbed wire with 110,000 other Japanese Americans for the "crime" of being of Japanese ancestry. Like countless others of all colors, races, nationalities, and religions, I was the victim of "national security." Illegal wiretaps, bribery, and outright lying are minor or nonexistent crimes when "national security" is at stake.

I changed my name to Lee in order to find employment. I became the only Asian in all-white dance orchestras performing throughout the Midwest. I later joined black bands to become the only nonblack in such groups. I have taught at the University of Hawaii (Manoa and Hilo), and the International Christian University in Tokyo, and at the University of California at Los Angeles.

I have found that what is assumed in Tokyo is debatable in Hawaii, and that interpretations of racism vary, depending on time, place, position, and situation. But several observations concerning dominant and dominated groups apply universally, no matter when and where the interaction takes place. Majority groups are for law and order and for a calm and rational approach to racial problems. They call for brotherly love, understanding, and patience, but it is important to realize that it is the dominated group that feels the hurt and that they are forced to "adapt" to discriminatory conditions. The gravest threats to a social system occur when one group feels so trapped, frustrated, and hopeless that any extreme behavior is deemed appropriate.

It is the aim of this book to analyze our racial practices so that we can prevent such a threat from materializing and can push ahead to achieve the full goals of racial equality and justice.

I would like to thank my publisher and my editor at Prentice-Hall, Ed Stanford, for support and encouragement. I would also like to thank the students at UCLA, both in Sociology and Social Welfare, for helping in the development of ideas and for raising appropriate questions.

H. H. L. Kitano
University of California at Los Angeles

RACE RELATIONS

May 17, 1954 THE SUPREME COURT OUTLAWED SEGREGATED SCHOOLS. WHY DO THEY STILL EXIST?? NAACP

WE WANT BLACK POWER

part 1

BACKGROUND OF RACE RELATIONS

The purpose of this book is to provide ways of looking at the relationships among different racial groups in the United States. It analyzes the adaptive patterns of various immigrants after their entrance into the country and discusses the importance of the early Europeans in shaping the basic character of American race relations.

It was the early European immigrants who determined who should belong to their ''world.'' They gave preference, privilege, and power to immigrants from the ''better classes'' of northern Europe, and especially England, and assigned subordinate positions to the others, especially to native Americans, slaves from Africa and their descendants, and later to immigrants from Asia. American citizenship and the benefits of American capitalism and democracy thus came to mean one thing to white people and another to people of color.

Against this background, Part I of the book examines theories of racial interaction and the effects of prejudice, discrimination, segregation, and power. It analyzes the adaptation of dominated groups to their position and formulates their patterns of interaction with the dominant culture, so that questions of goals and relative success can be addressed. Part I closes with a chapter on identity that focuses upon the difficulties that ethnic groups have faced in forming positive self-images in a white-oriented society.

Part II amplifies these perspectives by presenting the experiences of selected ethnic groups. Their culture, power, life styles, and goals are analyzed within the context of their acceptability and desirability to the group in power. The interrelationship between the ethnic group and the dominant group is established as a basis for explaining where minority groups were in the past, where they are now, and where they may be in the future. The power relationships between whites and nonwhites have significantly altered some ethnic societies so that cultures of ''poverty, powerlessness, and deprivation'' have developed and replaced relatively intact social systems.

Most textbooks on race relations have been written from the point of view of the dominant white majority. However, there is no one *white* point of view, just as there is no one *minority* perspective. For example, some majority-group scholars establish what they assume to be universal definitions of what is normal, so that they can talk about deviant or problem minorities. Others question the use of such categoric value terms and instead rely upon more relativistic perspectives. Despite these differences of approach, the importance of social scientists should not be underestimated, for as Gordon (1978:23) reminded us, it was such people as social psychologist Otto Kleinberg, and sociologists Robert McIver, E. Franklin Frazier (a black), and Gunnar Myrdal (a Swede), who helped refute the doctrine of ''pure'' races and of scientific racism that had such a strong influence on academia and national policy up to World War II.

It is appropriate that we focus upon race relations from positions not primarily majority-group oriented. This text will look at race relations from a minority perspective. From this perspective, many explanations and programs advocated by some majority-group social scientists seem inappropriate. For example, "good adaptation" from a dominant-group perspective might mean that only those individuals and minorities who look, act, or identify with those in power are acceptable and are labeled successful, or that those who can answer test questions on the basis of standardized norms are not deviant. In extreme cases, the minority culture that deviates widely from the prescribed standards becomes the target for attack. One common solution, couched in gentler terms, may be the destruction of that culture. We still are not fully aware of the consequences of cultural genocide but can hypothesize that alienation and problem social behavior are highly likely outcomes.

MAY 17, 1954
THE
SUPREME COURT
OUTLAWED
SEGREGATED
SCHOOLS.
WHY DO THEY
STILL EXIST??
NAACP

RACE RELATIONS IN THE UNITED STATES

THE MISUSE OF HUMAN RESOURCES

The United States is a vast country blessed with an abundance of natural and human resources. At one time it was thought that our natural resources were inexhaustible, and only recently have ecologists and conservationists been able to make us conscious that we have misused, wasted, polluted, and destroyed much of what nature has provided.

A tragedy of even greater proportion has been the misuse and destruction of our human resources. Perhaps there was a time when these resources were also considered to be inexhaustible, but prejudice, discrimination, segregation, exile, and extermination have caused such damage in terms of human lives that their effects can never be fully measured. We can only hope that, as our consciousness of the conservation of nature's resources heightens, our consciousness of human resources will also grow.

This is not to say that stressful race relations is peculiar to the United States. Nations more homogeneous than ours in terms of race use stratification systems other than those based on color: religion, social class, nationality, age, birth, family name, or sex. The reasons that are given for such inequalities have a familiar ring: "Those people are just lazy and backward." "They are an inferior people and culture." "The group itself is responsible for its low position in society."

The usual American solution is to work actively toward equality of opportunity and fair play and to maximize the potential capacities of each individual. At least these are the values promulgated in the Constitution and in American slogans such as "with liberty and justice for all." If we wish to live up to American ideals, the goals are clear, but the task is admittedly difficult. The United States is a heterogeneous nation with a diverse population, and emotional appeals that pit one group against another and give one group advantages over the other are apt to find willing followers.

There is a popular belief that racism is primarily associated with totalitarian regimes. In any discussion of "final solutions" and extreme racism, the name of Hitler and the Nazi party comes to mind. Organizations such as the Ku Klux Klan and the John Birch Society reinforce this perspective. But racist solutions are not the sole province of autocratic systems, nor of any one racial group. All societies appear capable of such actions. Groups have been expelled, denied equality, and prevented from full participation because they looked different. Instances of extermination and genocide dot our history books. It might be comforting to think that only "they" are the villains, but it is apparent that there is little immunity to using race or other means to gain an advantage over others, no matter what the political system.

OPPOSING VIEWS OF HUMAN BEINGS

A study of race relations is related to various views of human beings. One view emphasizes that humans are conscious agents striving after goals. From this view, concepts such as motivation, desire, and rewards are an important part of any explanation of race relations. Prejudice and discrimination, then, are aspects of consciousness and remain as a part of people's attitudinal systems that can be altered and changed under appropriate conditions. In other words, men and women do what they do because they think it will bring them closer to what they want or will enable them to avoid what they dislike. From this perspective, programs affecting race relations *focus on the individual,* with emphasis on changing the prejudiced person to become more tolerant and accepting of other racial groups.

Other perspectives emphasize the role of societal structures, so that such concepts as individual desires, beliefs, and motives play a less important part, when compared to the organizational and institutional structures of society. From this perspective, variables such as role, position, status, and institutional policies shape behavior more than individual will and desire do. Programs to combat racism at this level *focus on changing institutions* instead of individuals.

Historically, psychiatry, psychology, and social work have concentrated on the individual perspective, while sociology and social psychology have focused more on the institutions, but there appears to be a growing rapprochement among professions toward viewing the problem in multi-dimensional terms.

DIRECT AND INDIRECT RACISM

Pettigrew (1973), in discussing racism, distinguished between direct racial discrimination and indirect discrimination, in which restrictions in one area are shaped by racial discrimination in another area. One of the difficulties in attempting to eradicate racism is tied to its hypothesized explanations. For example, if racism were a phenomenon between people of different colors, then the most reasonable solution would be for the groups to meet each other, become acquainted, and eventually work together. Confrontation techniques, discussion, education, counseling, and therapy might be appropriate techniques for bringing about the desired change.

But if racism is viewed as indirect and as linked with other concerns, then programs attempting to bring different racial groups together may be less appropriate. For example, there are views of racism as an outcome of the economic and political system, urbanization, industrialization, and technological advances. Unfortunately, linkages between large societal variables and racism are difficult to unravel, and specific suggestions to implement changes are lacking. It can be hypothesized that programs leading to full employment and more equitable income distribution also can lead to more harmonious race relations.

ROLE OF SOCIAL SCIENTISTS

There is little consensus or agreement among social scientists on racial conflicts. Some respond by advocating action now, feeling that further research and planning will only tend to make things worse. Others emphasize the premature nature of any intervention and feel that unless scientific and objective procedures are rigorously practiced, action programs will be futile.

Both approaches, including their multiple variations and constant overlap, are not necessarily antagonistic (unless their adherents wish them to be). An adversary point of view is developing, which means that there are heated debates, personal attacks, impressive erudition, but questionable illumination. Current favorite areas for polarized positions are affirmative action, school busing, and the effects of the Bakke case.

The issues often are related to the position of the writer. Most minority-group researchers are likely to write with great emotion and little patience, and to advocate action that will change the status quo. Conversely, majority-group researchers are more likely to look beyond the immediate conflicts for broader and more "scientific" generalizations. Many question the notion that racism is the critical issue; social class, personality, and other variables may be viewed as more important. A more detached, objective approach with less emphasis on practical application is advocated.

THE RASHOMON PERSPECTIVE

We do not subscribe to a "one valid truth" model but prefer to respect the perceptions of reality from various positions. Some have referred to this as the *Rashomon model,* named after the famous Japanese movie in which various characters give their own interpretations of a single incident. The basic point here is an important one: views of reality are shaped by position, experiences, emotions, and needs, with variations in time, place, and situation. An explanation from one position may be valid from that view, whereas another observation from a different angle may have an equal validity. The notion that only one view represents the truth is difficult to accept, unless one assumes either that one actor has a monopoly on veracity or, more likely, is powerful enough to impose his or her point of view on the others.

One way of handling some of these problems is to rely on the scientific method, so that the observations are systematic and objective, the studies replicable, the researchers well trained, and the data carefully recorded. Up to now, however, the use of the scientific method has not significantly affected our racial problems; in fact, social scientists have probably contributed as much to the confusion and hysteria surrounding the issue as any other source.

Part of the problem lies with social scientists. Their expectations, needs, experiences, racial background, personality, training, class position, reference group, status, and position all shape their research efforts, no matter how faithfully they adhere to scientific techniques. In the arena of race relations, they are constantly challenged by value references, such as a "good," "functional" culture or "conflict-free" interaction. These value judgments are impossible to avoid in any serious effort, and social scientists of various identifications will hold different positions on these issues.

For example, a "good" minority, from the majority perspective, might be one that would accept dominant-group prescriptions with a minimum of disruptive behavior, while a "bad" group would be one that constantly would challenge majority-group authority. The case of the Indian is illustrative: the "good" Indians were peaceful, accepted their lot, and cooperated with the white authorities, while the "bad" Indians were warlike and cunning, like the "savage" Apache. Terrell (1972) wrote that the Apache were similar to other tribes living in the area, but because they resisted the white man's authority, often quite successfully, they were given these pejorative labels. And of course there was the ultimate definition of what a good Indian was—a dead one.

The issue remains the same today—a "successful" minority might adapt to a "less than equal citizen" status through passivity, humility, and acceptance. Conversely, a "bad" minority might be dissatisfied with their pariah status and be openly motivated to change the status quo.

It seems clear that the criteria for success depend on whether one takes a majority-group or minority-group perspective. Social scientists of one persuasion may objectively assess the facts, conduct their own observations, check the validity and reliability of their results and deliver one conclusion. Others may check the same facts and arrive at a different interpretation. Up to now, the most dominant (and often the sole) perspective has come from the white majority.

The Rashomon perspective calls for an analysis of a phenomenon from different viewpoints. The principle of *triangulation* used in surveying and navigation is one appropriate model. It stresses the importance of using a number of different sightings in order to gain a fix. Admittedly, gaining such a perspective is much more complicated in the social sciences, especially when dealing with ethnic relations, since there is the constant problem of the "insider-outsider," as mentioned by Merton (1972). Each side feels that it has exclusive access to the truth that the other side can only approximate, and terms like bias, objectivity, distance, and the like are used to discredit positions.

WHY THE PROBLEM?

The reasons behind the problem should be mentioned. Science as a technique, methodology, or philosophy is not the primary issue, but rather, the problem arises from the social scientist, politician, and others who write, use, interpret, and act upon the material. In the past, majority-group researchers came into minority communities to conduct "scientific" studies. Many ethnics felt that they were used and exploited by the researchers, first as subjects, then as objects of the findings. It was analogous to a colonial situation: the ethnics were the raw material from whom data could be extracted; the information was shipped to universities and research institutions to be processed, then returned to the ghettos in the form of advice and recommendations. The feelings of the ethnic groups were generally ignored; majority-group researchers learned their trade and made their reputations on these studies without any subsequent benefit to the minority communities.

There also are serious questions about the interpretations and applications of these findings. Minorities have been told that they are disadvantaged; that their family structure is pathological; that their personality patterns are neurotic; that their "culture" is the reason for their low position and status in the American social system. They have felt the sting of prejudice through studies that emphasized both their unassimilability and their general undesirability. Probably most of these findings ended up in research archives with other unused material, but because there have been enough instances in which "scientific findings of inferiority" were used to support racist arguments, ethnic communities remain wary.

One current "scientific" issue that will be discussed later is genetic inferiority and the uneducability of the black. It should be noted that only a small handful of researchers advocate this point of view, but its publicity and reaction have given it prominence. The notion of an IQ deficiency based on genetic factors has widespread lay appeal, even though most social scientists assume that the idea of "pure races" has been laid to rest. Although the Rashomon perspective welcomes various viewpoints, those who support theories of genetic inferiority should be aware of the possible tragic consequences of translating their beliefs into large-scale programs. As history shows, it is not a long step from a belief in genetic inferiority to the advocacy of the elimination of the "inferior" group.

ETHNICS TO STUDY ETHNICS?

Ethnics have reacted to research with a slogan of their own: "Only ethnics should study ethnics." Most studies of minorities in the past were conducted by majority-group researchers who often ignored the fact that whites have played the pivotal role in shaping the interaction between the races.

Sloganeering aside, an ethnic individual has several advantages over the white researcher. First, the mood of many ethnic communities currently will not allow a white researcher (or researchers) to come in to conduct a study. Or studies may call for deep community involvement and a positive relationship between the researcher and the target community (Cromwell and others, 1975). Second, the experiences of an individual growing up as an ethnic are different from those of a majority-group member, with the result that critical and relevant questions may be ignored or incorrectly assessed. Finally, there can be a black, yellow, brown, red, and white point of view, and an ethnic researcher might be in a position to bring out the heretofore ignored ethnic perspective.

An example of a differential perspective is the assessment by various researchers of the effect of the California Alien Land Law of 1920. The law forbade ownership of agricultural land by Japanese aliens. (Most of the Japanese in California were aliens at that time.) White scholars sympathetic to the plight of the Japanese, such as Daniels (1962) and Modell (1969), using hard data (land-ownership figures), wrote that the Japanese in California agriculture were not adversely affected by the law.

However, ethnic scholars such as Iwata (1962) and Kitano (1976) disagreed and pointed out some of the damaging effects on the Japanese community. They claimed that it lowered expectations, raised serious questions about the future of the Japanese in California, and heightened feelings of inferiority and difference at a time when the "melting pot" ethos was a part of the American dream. The ethnic researchers, having grown up in the Japanese community, were sensitive to the moods and feelings of the population in a way that would have been difficult for a majority-group professional. As Peterson (1972) remarked, this issue clearly separated the nonethnic from the ethnic researcher, with the former interpreting from hard but perhaps less pertinent data.

BETTER STUDIES?

Whether an ethnic will provide "better" studies than a nonethnic will is beside the point. The problem is exacerbated by the limited supply of nonwhite researchers, although this problem will disappear in the near future as more and more ethnic researchers become available.

The perspective advocated in this text encourages a variety of approaches to research, of which ethnicity is but one. Ethnic groups often go through a developmental process and at certain stages "want to do it themselves." They want to use only their own talent, researchers, and resources, and their plea is often nonnegotiable. They want to make their own errors, and at this stage it would take a highly insensitive majority-group researcher, no matter what his or her status, not to listen to their message.

How researchers deal with their own ethnicity is also important. Their degree of ethnic identification, their feelings about self, and their motivations for conducting studies of ethnic groups are healthier when addressed as conscious factors.

How ethnic researchers are used should be considered. Often they are considered as a part of an integrated research team and even given prestigious titles, but their decision-making power is limited. The name and the ethnic background are prominently displayed, but the amount of actual power would probably be more appropriate if written in small print or placed in a footnote.

As studies are conducted, research findings published, and more knowledge uncovered, the sloganeering and tokenism usually are discarded. Rather, questions of the competence of the researcher, the validity and reliability of the data, and the logic of the design and analysis become more important, and various points of view are welcomed. This is the stage when cooperative research studies can be undertaken.

DEFINITIONS

In order to discuss race, racism, and ethnic identity, we must first define our terms:

Ethnic group refers to any group "which is defined or set off by race, religion, or national origin, or some combination of these categories" (Gordon, 1964:27).

Race refers to differential concentrations of "gene frequencies responsible for traits which, so far as we know are confined to physical manifestations such as skin color or hair form; it has no intrinsic connection with cultural patterns or institutions" (Gordon, 1964:27). There are no "pure races," and our definition will coincide with a social usage of the term.

Nationality refers to being American, whereas national origin refers to the country of birth of one's ancestors, such as England, Japan, or Mexico. *Religion* means the preferred denomination, such as Catholic, Protestant, Jewish, or Buddhist.

Racism is the belief that some races are demonstrably superior to others and that there is no such thing as racial equality. Racists fear interracial marriage or "mongrelization" because of the mixing of "inferior" blood, which is thought to lead to the decline of civilization. There is presumed a physical, mental, and cultural superiority of one race over another. These tenets are central to any racist perspective. White racism would be the perspective that the white or European culture is superior to all others; people of color also would be considered racists if they held similar beliefs about the superiority of their own groups.

We shall define other commonly used terms such as prejudice and discrimination as they appear.

STUDY OF CHANGE

Finally, a study of race relations reflects the importance of *change*—time, place, and conditions all shape explanations and actions. Although we may deplore the current state of practice and research in this area, the racial models of yesterday were vastly more frightening. It was not that long ago that such reputable sources as the *Encyclopaedia Britannica* published blatantly racist explanations of white superiority, that our immigration policies were overt reflections of our views of colored inferiority, and that the only permissible public portrayal of nonwhites, such as in motion pictures, was that of servile, less than equal people.

Neither does the current state of affairs warrant wild enthusiasm. There are many, including some in academia, who believe in biological and racial inferiority and who are willing to limit equal opportunity based on these assumptions. There also are institutions that eagerly, willingly, or unconsciously perpetuate the inequalities of the past so that their repressive programs can be carried into the future. Therefore it is our view that the central problem of our era is that of the relationship between people of different colors and cultures.

BIBLIOGRAPHY

CROMWELL, RONALD, EDWIN VAUGHAN, and CHARLES MENDELL (1975). "Ethnic Minority Family Research in an Urban Setting," *American Sociologist,* 10 (3):141–150.

DANIELS, ROGER (1962). *The Politics of Prejudice: The Anti-Japanese Movement in California and the Struggle for Japanese Exclusion.* Berkeley: University of California Press.

DANIELS, ROGER AND HARRY H. L. KITANO (1970). *American Racism: Exploration of the Nature of Prejudice.* Englewood Cliffs, N.J.: Prentice-Hall, Inc.

GORDON, MILTON (1964). *Assimilation in American Life.* New York: Oxford University Press.

GORDON, MILTON (1978). *Human Nature, Class and Ethnicity.* New York: Oxford University Press.

IWATA, MASAKAZU (1962). "The Japanese Immigrants in California Agriculture," *Agricultural History,* 36:27–37.

KITANO, HARRY H. L. (1976). *Japanese Americans: The Evolution of a Subculture.* Englewood Cliffs, N.J.: Prentice-Hall, Inc.

MERTON, ROBERT (1972). "Insiders and Outsiders: A Chapter in the Sociology of Knowledge," *American Journal of Sociology,* 72 (2):9–47.

MODELL, JOHN (1969). "The Japanese in Los Angeles: A Study in Growth and Accommodation, 1900–1946" (unpublished doctoral dissertation, Columbia University).

PETERSEN, WILLIAM (1971). *Japanese Americans.* New York: Random House, Inc.

PETTIGREW, THOMAS (1973). "Racism and the Mental Health of White Americans: A Social Psychological View," in *Racism and Mental Health,* eds. Charles Wilie, Bernard Kramer, and Bertram Brown. Pittsburgh: University of Pittsburgh Press.

TERRELL, JOHN UPTON (1972). *Apache Chronicle.* New York: World Publishing Co.

2

PATTERNƒ
OF
RACIAL INTERACTION

When different racial groups meet, there can be a variety of outcomes. They may prefer to remain apart, or they may engage in conflict until one side conquers the other. Or there may be other results, each dependent on such factors as group size and power, motives, barriers, support from other groups, or time, place, and situation.

Similarly, the encounter of different groups entering the United States can be analyzed into a variety of adaptations. Sociologist Robert Park (1950) suggested that there were a number of stages such as contact, competition, adjustment, and accommodation, leading eventually to assimilation and amalgamation. For example, Park studied the case of Hawaii in 1926 and predicted that the native races would disappear as new peoples came into existence, that individual races and cultures would die but that the majority civilization would live on. The idea of all groups ultimately being absorbed into the American mainstream underscores Park's initial observations of the inevitability of assimilation. Because of his experiences in Hawaii, however, Park modified his original position and saw that the race relations cycle could also result in a caste system or in a majority-minority arrangement (Hraba, 1979:37).

Bogardus (1930), focusing primarily on the experiences of the Chinese, Japanese, Pilipino,[1] and Mexican immigrants in California, saw sufficient recurrences to propose a race relations cycle whose stages were: curiosity, economic welcome, industrial and social antagonism,

15

legislative antagonism, fair-play tendencies, quiescence, and second-generation difficulties.

Shibutani and Kwan (1965:21) wrote that assimilation is a phenomenon found in all cases of interethnic contact in which one group does not exterminate the other: "In the United States one need only to review the history of various immigrant groups—the Irish, the Poles, the Jews, the Italians, the Chinese, the Mexicans—to see the regularity with which many of them have become incorporated into the mainstream of American life." Shibutani and Kwan defined assimilation as a change of mental perspective in which the immigrant eventually perceives the world from an American point of view, rather than from that of his or her previous national background.

Cyclical perspectives give a broad picture of the relationship between an immigrant group and the host culture. These progressions should not be mistaken for evolutionary phenomena following natural laws of biological inevitability, but rather, the cycles are influenced by social variables such as welcome, contact, competition, power, discrimination, and prejudice. Therefore, there is no inevitability to the process; individuals and groups will be at different points of contact, although it is probably valid to assume that assimilation will occur if given enough time, and if there are also changes in the social variables.

BANTON'S SIX ORDERS OF RACE RELATIONS

A more sophisticated presentation of interracial contacts (Banton, 1967:68–76) describes what happens to members of two different societies when they begin to have dealings with one another. Banton pictured six orders of race relations, with the plausible hypothesis that there may be several kinds of contact with different sequences of stages.

We have modified his theory by treating each of his stages as separate models and by including the saliency of the variable of power. Power in this context determines the direction in which groups will move, so that when we speak of acculturation,[2] defined as the process of giving up one culture and acquiring another, it will be the culture of the more powerful group that will be learned. We also would like to emphasize

[1] We will use the current spelling, Pilipino, rather than the more traditional term and spelling, Filipino. Many of the younger ethnic scholars prefer P, since they argue that there is no F in their native tongue.
[2] We shall define and discuss power and acculturation in more detail in later sections and chapters.

that acculturation is seldom a linear, one-way process, and learning a new way is not necessarily linked to totally discarding the old.

THE MODELS

We shall differentiate each of the models under conditions of relative equality, and one in which the relationships are clearly unequal. Positions between the two extremes can be extrapolated. The models are based on the interaction between two groups; the addition of other groups will complicate the interation but will not necessarily alter the basic generalizations.

A. Equal power. Peripheral contact between groups with equal power is the stage in which transactions between two societies have no real influence on each other (Figure 1A). There is little change in outlook, and both groups remain independent.

Model 1: Peripheral Contact

One example of equal status contact given by Banton is that between the pygmies of the Ituri forest of central Africa and some nearby black settlements. One group places piles of goods such as game and forest products at a trading place, then retires. The other group places piles of agricultural and other goods as its exchange. The first group returns and, if the terms are acceptable, picks up what it desires; the second group goes through a similar procedure. Such transactions require little intimate contact and minimal mutual knowledge of customs, habits, and language. Nevertheless, certain logical questions arise: What if one group feels that it has been cheated? How are misunderstandings resolved? What if one group decides that it would be easier just to take over the other? The questions pinpoint one generalization about peripheral contacts: they are usually short-lived or maintained in extremely restricted circumstances.

In the United States, an example of peripheral contact was that between the early settlers and Indian tribes. Neither group had intimate contact with each other (one familiar stereotype is that of the Indians concealed in the bushes peering out at the white people), nor were there concerted attempts to learn the language and the culture of the other.

FIGURE 1A

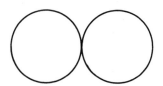

Peripheral contact
Source: Banton (1967:69)

The peripheral contact was short-lived, because in time the settlers began to desire the land held by the Indians and negotiations were started. It is possible that peripheral contact can exist for a long period if the groups are relatively equal in power, can retain their autonomy and independence, or do not covet some resource held by the other. Distance can also be a factor in maintaining peripheral relationships.

B. Unequal power. Another variation of the peripheral contact model is shown in Figure 1B, in which one group is more powerful than the other. The concept of power is fully covered in Chapters 4 and 5; the definition used here equates power with the group that has access to and control of more resources. As in the equal power model, contact remains peripheral, but it is clear that if there are further interactions between the groups, the direction of adaptation and learning will be primarily from the weaker to the more powerful. Since most American immigrant groups did not have the resources to develop and maintain an autonomous existence, their period of peripheral contact was short. Most had to learn something about the American system in order to survive.

FIGURE 1B

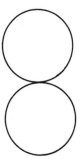

Peripheral contact

It would be difficult to visualize any group in the United States today maintaining only peripheral contact with the dominant culture. The effects of the mass communications media in the form of television, movies, radio, and newspapers are such that even the most isolated groups are exposed to American culture, for better or worse.

Model 2: Institutionalized Contact

A. Equal power. Equal-status, institutionalized contact (Figure 2A), according to Banton, is most apt to develop under the following conditions:

1.   When one of the two groups has a centralized political structure in which a few leaders control the action of their own members and use their power to dominate the other group.

2.   When two societies enter into contact principally through their outlying members and there is no strong competition for resources.

People who live on the social boundaries of the groups are most apt to exchange with each other. These people may begin to occupy positions in both systems, and a new system of interrelations develops between the groups. The roles may be rather ambiguous because the languages and the cultures may be different; but no matter how undeveloped, it is a closer system of interrelations than that of peripheral contact.

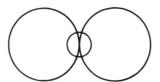

FIGURE 2A

Institutionalized contact
Source: Banton (1967:69)

There is no common political order or integral social system in institutional contact. Racial awareness occurs only at the point of overlap; the initial relations are important in determining subsequent steps. For example, if the first contact came in the form of trade, the interrelationships probably developed through interpersonal contacts, individual by individual. Expectations are formed by initial individual experiences, and insofar as the expectations continue to be realized, roles are created. If power relationships remain relatively stable, this type of institutional contact (in which only a few members from each group interact) may remain for some time.

One example used by Banton (1967:99) to illustrate institutionalized contact was drawn from Gluckman. Gluckman described the following ceremony that brought together twenty-four Europeans and four hundred Zulus. The opening formalities were followed by a carefully prepared round of speeches. Although they were brought together for the common purpose of opening a bridge, the two groups assembled in separate places. Each was bound to his own group; and although a European officer could talk with a Zulu on a common problem, he could not sit down and eat with him. Nonprofessional socialization was kept to a minimum.

The illustration "brings out the way in which the participants all occupied basic racial roles, as Europeans and Africans, but at the same time they had more independent roles to play which brought them together in other respects." Those Europeans most involved with the Zulus alternated between roles that permitted them to associate with Zulus and those that required them to keep a distance. Within these institutionalized patterns, a person's dress, stance, location, and form of greeting all are facets of the controlled intergroup interactions (Banton, 1967:99).

The most common examples of institutionalized contact between relatively equal power groups are those between independent nation states. Embassies and consular offices provide a degree of formal interaction, but this relationship leaves the majority of each group autonomous and independent of each other.

B. Unequal power. Institutionalized contact between unequal power groups (Figure 2B) is labelled as paternalism or colonialism by Banton (1967:72). When subordinates are subject to some control by a home government (for example, England), there is a high probability that paternalism (colonialism) will become the established order (see Figure 4).

Paternalism is a special form of institutionalized contact that maintains the distinctiveness of the interacting societies. Banton observed:

> It is exemplified in some forms of colonial rule, such as those that sanctioned and often reinforced the control tribal chiefs exercised over their peoples. In the pure form of paternalism, the only representatives of the metropolitan society who have dealings with the indigenous society are approved agents responsible for their action to authorities in their homeland. (1967:72).

Race, career, education, and training are important in determining specific official roles, and the influx of immigrants and new settlers strains the paternalistic order. In paternalistic orders, roles are determined by the desire of the upper group to maintain control over all significant spheres of activity.

Van den Berghe (1967) found that the paternalistic system follows a

FIGURE 2B

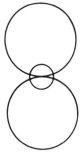

Institutionalized contact

master-servant model. The master group may be few in number but is able to dominate the subordinates. The subordinates are looked upon as childish, immature, irresponsible, and improvident, but are lovable as long as they remain in their place. Subordinated groups often internalize these inferiority feelings through self-deprecation.

Under paternalism, role and status are sharply defined. Social distance is maintained through etiquette, regulations, and repeated demonstrations of power by the dominant group. There may be high rates of sexual encounters between men of the ruling group with women of the subordinated population, but very few of these relationships end in marriage. Van den Berghe remarked that racial prejudice on the part of the ruling group is present but appears more related to economic and social position rather than to any deep psychodynamic feelings.

The paternalistic model is often found in relatively complex, preindustrial societies in which agriculture and handicraft production constitute the main economic base (Van den Berghe, 1967:28). Examples of this model include the southern United States, the West Indies, and the preabolition regimes in northeastern Brazil.

Paternalistic societies are rigidly stratified into racial castes. The caste barrier is the most important; although class distinctions do exist, the color line limits mobility between castes. Race remains the major dividing factor, and elaborate ideologies of the inferiority and superiority of races are developed to maintain the system.

Because there are more servants than masters, part of the longevity and stability of this model comes from the acquiescence of the subordinated. Although there have been constant conflicts engendered by revolting servants, peaceful coexistence is often achieved, especially in the economic area. In addition, sexual relations and other forms of unequal, but often intimate social relations (for example, a black woman mothering white children) may create affective bonds across caste lines.

DOMESTIC COLONIALISM

A special form of paternalism called internal, or domestic colonialism, was hypothesized by Blauner (1971). Rather than limiting the dominant-subordinate relationship to colonized countries, Blauner emphasized the appropriateness of this model to race relations in the United States.

This colonization complex has four components. The first concerns the racial group's forced, involuntary entry into the country. Black slaves were in this group. Second, the impact of the interaction is much more dramatic than the slower and perhaps more natural processes of acculturation. The colonizing power "carries out a policy which constrains, transforms, or destroys indigenous values, orientations, and ways of life," such as those of the native Indians and conquered Mexicans. Third, colonization "involves a relationship by which members of the colonized group tend to be administered by representatives of the dominant power. There is the experience of being managed and manipulated by outsiders in terms of ethnic status" (Blauner, 1971:396). Finally, there is racism. Since one group is seen as inferior, it is exploited, controlled, and oppressed by the dominating group. It is also important to note that the initial contact of the groups was between "inferior" and "superior."

The colonization concept helps to explain the differences between various immigrant groups. Blauner wrote:

> The crucial difference between the colonized Americans and the ethnic immigrant minorities is that the latter have always been able to operate fairly competitively within that relatively open section of the social and economic order because they came voluntarily in search of a better life, because their movements in society were not administratively controlled, and because they transformed their culture at their own pace—giving up ethnic values and institutions when it was seen as a desirable exchange for improvements in social position. (1971:396)

Blauner also underscored the importance of control and ownership of the ghetto by European groups. It was usually less than one generation before these white ethnic groups controlled their own buildings, commercial stores, and other enterprises. The Asian groups also have followed this pattern. The black segregated communities, however, have always been controlled from the outside, and political, economic, and administrative decisions have been taken out of their hands. Outsiders come into the ghetto to work, police, and administer. Teachers, social workers, police officers, and politicians represent the establishment, which governs the ghetto as if it were an overseas colony.

One significant effect of this kind of colonialism is to weaken the will of the colonized in resisting oppression. As Blauner said:

> It has been easier to contain and control black ghettos because communal bonds and group solidarity have been weakened through divisions among leadership, failures of organization, and a general disspiritment that accompanies social oppression. (1971:399).

Blauner also stressed that the cultures of overseas colonies were not destroyed nearly to the extent that the African slave cultures were in

America. The language, religion, and family structures of these Africans were almost totally obliterated when they were brought into this country.

The internal colonialism model is derived from an analysis of European external colonialism. As Balandier (1966) noted, the recent history of people of color (often referred to as the Third World) has been their subjugation to and dependency on European and American colonialism.

The withdrawal of colonial rule after World War II has not ended the oppression and dependency of native populations. External colonialism has often been replaced by internal colonialism, since in many African and Asian countries (with the exception of China and Japan), power has been passed on to white colonists and settlers who now "run the show" under local control. The exploitation continues; the system produces economic and other advantages for the dominant group and continues to affect the culture and the learning of the colonized (Feagin, 1978:38).

Hechter (1977) used the internal colonialism model to help understand the conflict between the British and the Irish. He discovered that the model seems to provide a more adequate explanation of the persistence of ethnic identities and loyalties than do other explanations.

CRITICISMS OF THE THEORY

The primary critic of the colonialism perspective is Glazer (1971), who believes that America's racial ethnic groups are not completely trapped and that it is possible for them to move away voluntarily from their pariah status. He cites the increasing number of skilled workers, supervisors, professionals, and white-collar workers from among minorities and sees a strong similarity between their situation and that of the European immigrants.

Glazer admitted that racial minorities face prejudice and discrimination but stated that these barriers are universal and have to be faced by all who are strangers. The level of prejudice and discrimination is determined by what official assistance the minority receives and by the role of the state. Glazer noted that expressed prejudice has steadily declined and that the percentage of minorities has increased on all levels of government employment. Therefore, he believes that the colonial analogy, especially as applied to the American black, is an invalid one.

It is the writer's view that a paternalistic, colonized status has been the experience for most nonwhite immigrant groups to the United States and that racism has delayed or prevented group mobility. The system has permitted a small number of talented ethnics to participate, with some reservations, in the dominant culture.

Model 3:
Acculturation

A. Equal power. One common definition of acculturation is "the process of learning a culture different from the one in which a person was originally raised" (Berelson & Steiner, 1964:646). The term is generally used to specify movement across different cultures, whereas learning in the original culture is usually called socialization.

Acculturation is common to intergroup relations in America. It connotes the coming together of different cultures into a common culture. Hraba writes that acculturation occurs when different racial and ethnic groups become similar in their thinking, feeling, and acting (1979:29).

Figure 3A shows the relationship between two groups with equal power. There is a mutuality so that both groups learn from each other. Equal status acculturation most often occurs when societies are small, informal, and noncompetitive. Equal power acculturation also can be seen in border towns, where individuals from both nations learn about each other and make appropriate adaptations.

FIGURE 3A

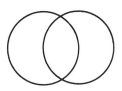

Acculturation:
Equal power groups

B. Unequal power. A more common model of acculturation is shown in Figure 3B, in which people from a less powerful group interact with a more powerful one. This type of acculturation is mainly a one-way process: one group discards its culture in order to become more like the group in power. Acculturation in this model does not necessarily lead to acceptance by the dominant group.

Acculturation is only one of many kinds of assimilation Gordon (1964) posited differences between cultural, behavioral, structural, and other types. Cultural assimilation (or acculturation) is likely to be the first to occur and consists of a change in the cultural patterns of the two interacting groups. It is not necessary for other types of assimilation to occur, and acculturation by itself can go on indefinitely. It also should be noted that a purely one-way flow of acculturation (one group completely overpowering the other) is rare and that some mutual learning

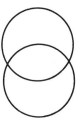

Acculturation between
unequal power groups
Source: Banton (1967:20)

generally occurs. There also may be instances in which persistent contact may lead to hostility and a conscious rejection of the more ''powerful'' culture.

Generally, integration occurs when there are several different racial groups and peoples of mixed descent (Figure 4). As Banton observed:

> Race is then still used as a social sign, though as a sign indicating an individual's background and probably his claims to deference. It is one sign among many others, being irrelevant in some sectors . . . but of some account in status-sensitive situations of social acceptance or rejection. For nearly all purposes, race has much less significance than the individual's occupation and his other status-conferring roles. Thus, in a racially integrated social order, race is a sign of an independent role, signalizing rights and obligations in only a few restricted sets of circumstances. (1967:73)

An integrated order of race relations develops when racial distinctions are disregarded or are given only minor consideration. It means that there is interaction among races on most levels—in housing, in schooling, in employment, in interest groups, and in friendship and social relationships. Rigid definitions and rigid, racially prescribed roles are

**Model 4:
Integration**

Integration
Source: Banton (1967:73)

FIGURE 4

discarded and modified so that there are more degrees of freedom for voluntary choice and movement across racial lines. Integration also occurs on a less than equal basis. An integrated army unit may still be led by white officers or an integrated company may limit the top echelon to white males, even though the labor force may be a mixture of various races. However, integration does not include intimate social relationships, such as marriage between the groups.

Model 5: Assimilation or Amalgamation

By assimilation or amalgamation in race relations, we refer specifically to interracial marriage and its variations, including intimate social interaction and living together. Assimilation can occur without acculturation (for example, war-bride marriages) and is often regarded as an inevitable consequence of integration, which may be one reason why integration is often resisted so vigorously. Once a group can enter freely into the social clubs, cliques, organizations, and institutions of the other group on a peer basis, intermarriage and other levels of assimilation generally will follow (Gordon, 1964).

The fear of racial amalgamation has not been the sole province of the dominant group. The simple question, "Do you want your daughter to marry one?" was an effective device to warn individuals on *both* sides of the racial fence not to stray, although there now appears to be a trend (see Part II, dealing with specific groups) among most minorities toward increasing rates of intermarriage with the majority.

FIGURE 5

Assimilation or Amalgamation
No social and legal barriers
to marriage

Model 6: Pluralism

A. Equal power. In a pluralistic order, racial differences indicate much wider variations in expected behavior than under the model of integration. Equal power pluralism (Figure 6A) is akin to separate nation states, in which groups live side by side with different languages and cultures, and with a minimum of social interaction, integration, or assimilation.

Pluralism
Source: Banton (1967:74)

The cultural pluralist views the necessity of subsocietal separation "to guarantee the continuance of the ethnic cultural tradition and the existence of the group, without at the same time interfering with the carrying out of standard responsibilities to the general American civic life" (Gordon, 1964:158). Wide-scale intermarriage and extensive primary-group relations across ethnic lines pose the gravest threats to a pluralistic society.

Gordon wrote that the American reality is that of structural pluralism rather than cultural pluralism, although some of the latter remains. The major ethnic and religious groups have separate subsocieties that tend to restrict large-scale, primary-group interaction, but most of them are variants of the American culture. The important theoretical problem, then, is "how ethnic prejudice and discrimination can be eliminated or reduced and value conflict kept within workable limits in a society where the existence of separate subsocieties keeps primary-group relations among persons of different ethnic backgrounds at a minimum" (Gordon, 1964:159).

Van den Berghe offered a further perspective on pluralism. Pluralistic societies are segmented into corporate groups and have different cultures or subcultures; their social structure is "compartmentalized into analogous, parallel, noncomplementary, but distinguishable sets of institutions" (1967:34). Additional characteristics frequently associated with pluralism are:

1. Relative absence of value consensus.
2. Relative presence of cultural heterogeneity.
3. Relative presence of conflict between the significant corporate groups.
4. Relative autonomy between parts of the system.
5. Relative importance of coercion and economic interdependence as bases of social integration.
6. Political domination by one of the corporate groups over the others.
7. Primacy of segmental, utilitarian, nonaffective, and functionally specific relationships between corporate groups, and of total, nonutilitarian, affective, diffuse ties within such groups. (Van den Berghe, 1967:35)

Pluralism is a matter of degree. South Africa, which is divided into four major castes and several unrelated cultural traditions, is more pluralistic than the United States, with its two major racial castes; but in both countries whites and nonwhites share the same Western culture and the same language.

There are, however, differences between cultural and structural pluralism. Although in practice they both go together, cultural pluralism refers to the maintenance of ethnic subcultures with their traditions, values, and styles. Structural pluralism refers to the extent that a society is structurally compartmentalized into analogous and duplicatory but culturally alike sets of institutions.

B. Unequal power. When power relationships are unequal, pluralism can be seen as domination (Figure 6B). The same variations of cultural and structural pluralism are relevant.

Domination based on racial criteria is a two category system: all members of one category are subordinated to the other and are responded to, not as individuals, but as representatives of their category. As Banton found, "This kind of subordination is far harsher, and it provides the most clear-cut illustration of race as a role sign. Whatever their personal qualities, individuals are ascribed to one or the other category, and those in the lower are prevented from claiming the privileges of those in the upper category . . . " (1967:71).

Simmel (1965), a German sociologist, felt that all social life was characterized by superordination and subordination. One group or one individual in a social relationship will always dominate, while the other, voluntarily or not, will take the lesser role. Domination is related to power, so that groups with more power become the superordinates of that system. In this model, equality is seldom achieved; rather, groups may be constantly attempting to change their subordinate positions.

The two-category system closely resembles the current stage of race relations in the United States (Daniels & Kitano, 1970). To be white is to belong to the upper half of the system, with its corresponding social-psychological perspectives. Those in power have feelings of superiority, power, and noblesse oblige. They emphasize law and order and gradual-

FIGURE 6B

Domination
Source: Banton (1967:71)

ism in race relations, and place a high value on rational discussion and scientific studies. They feel that if the "others" would only become more like them, the stratification and the boundaries would disappear.

Obviously, those caught in the subordinate positions view the world differently. They may try to escape their subordinate status by changing their names, undergoing facial operations, or using drugs. They may overidentify with the dominant group or vent their frustrations on members of other subordinate groups, including their own. They feel great impatience with the racial status quo and demand immediate action.

In some cases, power, not race alone, determines who plays superordinate and subordinate roles. For example, there are observable differences between West Coast Japanese (subordinated status) and their peers in Hawaii (closer to superordinate status). The less powerful mainland group has acculturated much more rapidly, and is much more respectful and "humble" toward white people than are the Hawaiian Japanese, although this factor is tempered by the retention of many "low posture" Japanese styles on the Islands. Domination will be discussed further in Chapter 4.

Model 7: Bicultural Adaptation

A bicultural adaptation is a variant of both acculturation and pluralism and is based on the observation that exposure to several cultures can be additive, so that a person acquires and is comfortable with both the dominant culture and with his or her own ethnic heritage. A bilingual person is one who has acquired one of the skills important to a bicultural adaptation, although language alone is but one factor. Second-generation (Nisei) children of immigrant parents generally have had a strong opportunity to retain a bicultural heritage; however, many of them have become so American that a true bicultural orientation may have to wait for other generations.

An individual with a bicultural orientation would have friends in several cultures, enjoy various foods, appreciate various languages, and be able to interact with various groups with an appropriate sensitivity to the different cultures. A bicultural perspective would assume the desirability of a variety of cultural styles, but such a response is difficult if one culture is thought to be "superior" or "better" than the other.

FIGURE 7

Bicultural adaptation

MODELS AND STAGES

Banton presented his six orders of race relations with hypothesized sequences. The most familiar is that involving European immigrants: entrance into the American system through peripheral contact, learning the American way and discarding the old (acculturation), participating in the institutional networks of the dominant society (integration), and then into the assimilative stage.

This sequence is often equated with the "American way" or the "melting pot." To study hard, to learn English, to get a good education, and to work diligently, no matter what the job, are common prescriptions. The fact that many individuals have succeeded hides the grim reality that many others, especially those of color, have not attained equal participation in the American dream. Racism has positioned racial minorities in the dominated categories of all of our models; therefore their fate lies more with the actions of the dominant majority rather than with their own efforts. It is also important to note that, even among many European groups who have acculturated and integrated and who are supposedly beyond ethnic concerns, there is evidence of ethnic identity (the "white ethnic"). This topic, the persistence of ethnicity, will be covered in Chapter 6.

The purpose of presenting Banton's orders of race relations as independent models was to introduce the reader to a spectrum of possible outcomes when two groups meet. Although it is interesting to explore the possibility of predictable sequences and a race relations cycle, the lack of data and the unpredictable nature of the many interacting variables may limit the usefulness of such endeavors, except to broad-scale observations.

BIBLIOGRAPHY

BALANDIER, G. (1966). "The Colonial Situation: A Theoretical Approach," in *Social Change,* p. 35, ed. Immanuel Wallerstein. New York: John Wiley.

BANTON, MICHAEL (1967). *Race Relations.* London: Tavistock Publications.

BERELSON, BERNARD and G. STEINER (1964). *Human Behavior.* New York: Harcourt Brace Jovanovich.

BLAUNER, ROBERT (1969). "Internal Colonialism and Ghetto Revolt," *Social Problems,* 16(4):612–17.

BLAUNER, ROBERT (1971). "Colonized and Immigrant Minorities" (Unpublished study; personal correspondence).

BLAUNER, ROBERT (1972). *Racial Oppression in America.* New York: Harper and Row, Pub.

DANIELS, ROGER and HARRY H. L. KITANO (1970). *American Racism: Exploration of the Nature of Prejudice*. Englewood Cliffs, N.J.: Prentice-Hall, Inc.

GLAZER, NATHAN (1971). "Blacks and Ethnic groups: The Difference and the Political Difference It Makes," *Social Problems*, 18, Spring:451.

GORDON, MILTON (1964). *Assimilation in American Life*. New York: Oxford University Press. All excerpts are reprinted by permission of the publisher.

HECHTER, MICHAEL (1975). *Internal Colonialism*. Berkeley and Los Angeles: University of California Press.

HRABA, JOSEPH (1979). *American Ethnicity*. Itasca, Illinois: F. E. Peacock Publishers, Inc.

PARK, ROBERT E. (1950). *Race and Culture*. New York: The Free Press.

SHIBUTANI, TAMOTSU and KIAN M. KWAN (1965). *Ethnic Stratification*. New York: MacMillan.

SIMMEL, GEORG (1955). *Conflict and the Web of Group Affiliations*. New York: The Free Press.

VAN DEN BERGHE, P. (1967). *Race and Racism*. New York: John Wiley & Sons, Inc.

3

GOALS
AND
INEQUALITY

The seven models presented in Chapter 2 will serve as a background for a discussion of intergroup goals in American society. Many of our disagreements appear to be based on different goals; the pluralist sees a different kind of America than the integrationist does, who in turn differs from the biculturalist. This chapter also will focus on the divisions within our society and will analyze the reasons for the unequal positions held by our racial minorities.

DIFFERING GOALS

One example of a conflict involving differing goals is bilingual education programs. From one point of view, the programs are a waste of federal money and effort; from another, they are the best example of federal sensitivity to the needs of certain immigrant populations. It should be recalled that in 1974, the Supreme Court decided in the case of *Lau* v. *Nichols* that a group of Chinese-speaking students in San Francisco were being denied educational opportunity because they did not understand the language of instruction. School systems therefore were mandated to rectify the language deficiency by providing suitable instructional programs in languages other than English.

Bethell (1979) attacked the bilingual program in a magazine article as an educational death wish. He asked how teaching children in the language of their native culture would better equip them for the rigors of contemporary life in the United States. He argued that European immigrants did not need this crutch and were successful, and he castigated the bilingual program as an example of bureaucratic waste and fuzzy thinking. Bethell writes from an acculturative viewpoint (Model 3B) and has a set of assumptions, although not explicitly stated, concerning the desirability of integrating into the American society.

Those who favor bilingual programs also clash over differing goals. One group views the main task as bridging; that is, to aid the child in transferring skills from the familiar native tongue of the parents to the English language used in the schools. Programs following this goal see the instruction as temporary until such time that the child can learn in English. The overall goals of the program are still acculturation (Model 3A) and integration (Model 5), although the means for achieving these goals are different from those of Bethell.

Another group views the bilingual program as more permanent, so that a child is continuously educated and eventually acquires fluency in more than one language. Proponents of this goal view America in bilingual and bicultural terms (Model 7). Mastery of the language of the parental culture is viewed as one part of building ethnic identity, heritage, and pride. It would be difficult to argue for the merits of any of these approaches without a prior discussion of the goals of the system.

It is our observation that there is little consensus as to goals in American race relations. We have posed the question to university classes, groups of teachers, and lay audiences, and the general response is generally a blank stare. Yet these audiences are eager and willing to take active stands on issues such as mandatory busing and the Bakke case, which are related to societal goals. Perhaps it remains for academics, philosophers, and researchers to talk seriously about goals. We shall here present a brief overview of some of the prior goals of the American society.

ANGLO CONFORMITY (MODEL 3A)

Anglo conformity was one of the original goals in the American system. It was an almost inevitable outcome, given the power of the Anglo group and the general desire of immigrant groups to become a part of their culture. Gordon (1964) used the term Anglo conformity to describe the model that was such a strong force in the late nineteenth and early twentieth centuries.

The central assumption behind this model is the desirability of maintaining the English language and its culture as the standard of American life. This is not to deny that many other influences have also shaped America, but as Gordon remarked:

> As the immigrants and their children have become Americans, their contributions as laborers, farmers, doctors, lawyers, scientists, and artists have been by way of cultural patterns that have taken their major impress from the mold of the overwhelmingly English character of the dominant Anglo-Saxon culture or subculture in America, whose domination dates from colonial times and whose *cultural* domination in the United States has never been seriously threatened. (Gordon, 1964:73)

From the point of view of the English colonists, the newcomers were a mixed blessing. On the one hand, they were necessary for the growth and development of the country; on the other hand, they were foreigners with alien ways. Nativist organizations often played upon the fear of strangers, and immigrants to America were subject to much scapegoating and hostility (Higham, 1955).

Restrictions against the open immigration policies began to appear in the late 1800s, and in 1882 the first effective federal legislation controlling immigration was passed. Phrases similar to ''America, Love It or Leave It'' were common, and the immigrants were advised to cast off their old skin, not to look back, to forget the old country, and to adopt the new—and if they did not like it, they could always go back.

''Adopting the new'' clearly meant conforming to Anglo standards; the control of the country was securely in the hands of the descendants of the early English settlers. Madison Grant, in *The Passing of the Great Race* (1916), wrote about inferior breeds in differentiating between the southern Europeans and the Anglo-Teutons. The Anglo-Saxon concepts of righteousness, law, and order were clearly those of a ''superior race''; it was necessary to break up ''inferior'' groups before they could be assimilated.

The height of the Americanization movement occurred during World War I, when the foreigner was stripped of his or her native culture and made into an American as rapidly as possible. Political loyalty, patriotism, the teaching of American history, and Americanization classes reflected the sentiments of the country and culminated in the restrictions of the Immigration Act of 1924. Desirable and undesirable races and nationalities were fully differentiated in this law—no immigration for Asians, low quotas for southern Europeans and other ''less desirable'' races, and high quotas for those of Anglo-Saxon background.

Americanization was successful among certain European groups. By the second generation, vast numbers had discarded their previous culture, learned English, and become patriotic. They had fought and died for the new country (even against their ancestral homelands) and had become the new Americans.

Racial ethnic groups also have gone through the same process, and some have successfully acculturated. They have learned English and the American way; they have fought and died for America and have subscribed to the tenets of patriotism and love of country. But in one dramatic sense they have not become Anglo—their skin color and visibility have not allowed for this critical step. Therefore, the separatist techniques of prejudice, discrimination, and segregation have kept some minority-group Americans at a distance and have raised questions about the validity of Anglo conformity.

Gordon feels that the critical variable in the Anglo-conformity model is not acculturation but structural assimilation. Acculturation often occurs, but structural assimilation does not. Minority-group members have not been allowed to enter into the more intimate circles of the majority:

> The answer lies in the attitudes of both the majority and the minority groups and in the way in which these attitudes have interacted. A folk saying . . . is that "It takes two to tango." To utilize the analogy, there is no good reason to believe that white Protestant America ever extended a firm and cordial invitation to its minorities to dance. Furthermore, the attitudes of the minority-group members themselves on the matter have been divided and ambiguous.
>
> With regard to the immigrant, structural assimilation was out of the question. He did not want it, and he had a positive need for the comfort of his own communal institutions. The native American, moreover, whatever the implications of his public pronouncements, had no intention of opening up his primary-group life to entrance by these hordes of alien newcomers. The situation was a functionally complementary standoff. (Gordon, 1964:111)

It should be emphasized that because of the power of the dominant society, acculturation and cultural assimilation usually have taken place. Minority groups generally have discarded their native cultures and have acquired the ways of the mainstream. But what Gordon called structural assimilation and its variations, such as fusion, amalgamation, and integration, have been much slower to occur.

It is interesting to note that in the 1960s and 1970s there was a reaction by some majority-group children to dominant group norms and values. Dropping out, rebelling, running away, and adopting discontinuous life styles have caused concern among parents of the "privileged groups." There is a certain irony to this, since it occurred at the same time that there was a large number of minority students going to college and attempting to become a part of the mainstream.

A much more idealistic goal for American society lay in the theory of the melting pot. The concept proposed that people from all over the world would come to the United States, meet new people and new races, intermix, and come up with a new breed called "the American." Integration, amalgamation, intermarriage, and fusion would be desirable outcomes from this perspective.

Part of the support for the relatively open immigration policy was based on the underlying faith in the effectiveness of the melting pot. Rather than Anglo conformity and European influence, the uniquely American character could be explained by the intermingling of different people in this new environment. Frederick Jackson Turner (1963), an historian, was especially influential in presenting the thesis that the dominant influence in American institutions was not the nation's European heritage, but rather the experiences created by the ever-changing American frontier. The frontier acted as a solvent for the various nationalities and the separatist tendencies of many groups as they joined in the westward trek. Therefore, the new immigrants would amalgamate and produce a new, composite national stock.

The theme of the melting pot was especially strong during the first third of the twentieth century. In 1908, Israel Zangwill (1909) produced a drama entitled *The Melting Pot,* which brought to popular attention the role of the United States as a haven for the poor and oppressed people of Europe. The major theme of the play was the entrance of a myriad of nationalities and races and how their fusion and mixing produced new individuals.

Studies of intermarriage conducted in the 1940s raised questions about the success of the melting pot. Although there was intermarriage across nationality lines, there was also a strong tendency to restrict marriage within the three major religious denominations: Protestant, Catholic, and Jewish. Therefore, instead of a single melting pot, a variant, the "triple melting pot," was proposed (Kennedy, 1944).

The concept of the melting pot was perhaps a noble one, but in practice it was difficult to form much more than a vague notion of how it would work. Questions as to proportions, power, and the proper blend and mixture could be raised, although the most logical prescription from this model would be intermarriage and the constant intermixing of races, nationalities, and religions. Such a state could have occurred earlier under more natural circumstances, but prejudice, discrimination, and segregation had already created barriers and boundaries to free interaction. People of color especially have been denied entrance into any of the white communities, and even the idea of a "triple melting pot" becomes an exclusivist concept, since it ignores the many individuals who belong to the "other world" that is not Catholic, Protestant, or Jewish.

Perhaps the most successful example of the melting pot has been the American cuisine. Here one can see the contributions of the various cultures and taste their blending and intermixing. An interesting outcome of this process has been the development of certain "foreign" dishes (for example, chop suey) that have actually been invented in America.

The melting pot became very similar to the practices of Anglo conformity. The contributions of minorities were often ignored, and the melting process consisted of discarding the ethnic in favor of the American. Many immigrant groups disappeared completely, without leaving a trace of their own cultures.

> Entrance by the descendants of these immigrants into the social structures of the existing white Protestant society, and the culmination of this process in intermarriage, has not led to the creation of new structures, new institutional forms, and a new sense of identity which draws impartially from all sources, but rather to immersion in a subsocietal network of groups and institutions which was already fixed in essential outline with a general Anglo-Saxon Protestant stamp. The prior existence of Anglo-Saxon institutional forms as the norm, the pervasiveness of the English language, and the numerical dominance of the Anglo-Saxon population made this outcome inevitable. (Gordon, 1964:127)

The basic problem lay in the power differential between the immigrant cultures and the white Anglo society, so that even though the ideal of all groups contributing was an attractive one, the resources of the dominant group made it virtually inevitable that the melting pot would turn out to be another version of Anglo conformity. There remained the problem of the barriers, or as Park (1950) termed it, the doctrine of obstacles, so that cultural assimilation might take place but intimate social interaction would not, except on terms dictated by the majority.

CULTURAL PLURALISM (MODEL 6A)

Both Anglo conformity and the melting pot assumed the absorption and eventual disappearance of the immigrant cultures into an overall "American culture." As it has turned out, this was not the desire of many immigrants themselves, and as early as 1818 there were nationality group petitions soliciting for ethnic communalities. These petitions were denied because of *"the principle that the formal agencies of American government could not be used to establish territorial ethnic enclaves throughout the nation.* Whatever ethnic communality was to be achieved (the special situation of the American Indians excepted) must be achieved by voluntary action within a legal framework which was formally cognizant only of individuals'' (Gordon, 1964:133).

Although ethnic communities could not be legally established, actual ethnic societies developed rapidly. Nationality group settlements were common: the addition of old friends, relatives, neighbors, and countrymen meant that, in a strange new land, ethnic ties in the form of a familiar language and culture flourished.

> And so came into being the ethnic church, conducting services in the native language, the ethnic school for appropriate indoctrination of the young, the newspaper published in the native tongue, the mutual aid societies, the recreational groups, and beneath the formal structure, the informal network of ethnically enclosed cliques and friendship patterns which guaranteed both comfortable socializing and the confinement of marriage within the ancestral group. (Gordon, 1964:134)

Cultural pluralism was therefore a fact in early America, even though its formulation as a plausible theory is of relatively recent origin. The rise of nationalism, patriotism, and Americanism during World War I sorely tested the model of ethnic enclaves and ethnic cultures. Much of what is written about culture conflict, ethnic self-hatred, and identity is a result of these conflicting ideologies.

Social workers, especially those who worked in the settlement houses and ''slums,'' were among the first to recognize the role of an ethnic heritage and its institutions in helping immigrants to adjust to the new society. The effects of rapid Americanization were not always beneficial; there were intergenerational conflicts, with children turning against their immigrant parents, and symptoms of social and family disorganization such as crime, delinquency, and mental illness.

One of the earliest statements of the pluralist viewpoint was by Kallen (1915), who rejected the melting pot as the correct model for American society. Instead, he was impressed by the ability of ethnic groups to adapt to particular regions and to preserve their own language, religion, communal institutions, and ancestral culture. Yet they also learned the English language, communicated with others readily, and participated in the overall economic and political life of the nation. Kallen argued for culture diversity based on a model of a federation or commonwealth of national cultures. He felt that such a model represented the best of democratic ideals because individuals participate in groups, and therefore democracy for the individual must also mean democracy for the group.

Kallen presented several important themes: (1) Since ethnic membership rests on ancestry and family connections, it is involuntary, but it gives the individual a connection that is of special significance to personality satisfactions and development. (2) The pluralistic position harmonizes with American political and social life. The imposition of Anglo-Saxon conformity is a violation of our ideals. Pluralism encourages the right to be different but equal. (3) The nation as a whole benefits from the existence of ethnic cultures. There is a direct ethnic contribution to enrich and broaden the cultural heritage; and the competition, interaction, and creative relationships among the various cultures will continue to stimulate the nation.

The most important of Kallen's themes, from an ethnic perspective, is that of *equality*—an unequal pluralism, based on the "inferiority" of ethnic groups, is not a good model of cultural pluralism. The stratification system in the United States has prevented many ethnic groups from achieving equality, which in turn has affected their perceptions of the desirability of their own cultures.

Another problem in cultural pluralism is the risk of categorically assigning individuals into groups through birth (although ethnic groups are accustomed to this process). Such roles remain frozen throughout a person's life, severely limiting freedom of choice.

The basic problem with the pluralistic model has been that of unequal power. Ethnic groups often were desired in the United States for their labor, but once they outlived their usefulness they were no longer welcome. The idea of ethnics remaining separate and unequal from the mainstream has had a long history. For example, the residual position of ethnics was aptly described in the *San Francisco Chronicle* in 1910:

> Had the Japanese laborer throttled his ambition to progress along the lines of American citizenship and industrial development, he probably would have attracted small attention to the public mind. Japanese ambition is to progress beyond mere servility to the plane of the better class of American workman and to own a home with him. The moment that this position is exercised, the Japanese ceases to be an ideal laborer.

The call for a pluralistic position by America's minorities is difficult to understand if it comes from a dominated position. To be effective in a pluralistic model, the minority subculture must have adequate resources. If large proportions of their population are poor, living in poverty, and dependent on the dominant community for employment and educational opportunities, then pluralism may reinforce already subordinated positions.

There is considerable appeal among groups such as the Asians and the Mexican Americans for a bicultural model. The picture is that of two cultures living side by side and the individual acquiring a familiarity with *both* of them. Accordingly, Japanese Americans would be acquainted with the Japanese language and culture and also would be comfortable with the American language and culture. The same would be true for the Chinese and the Chicanos; they would have friends, acquaintances, and familiarity with both the ethnic and the dominant culture. The model is similar to that of cultural pluralism, with many of the same problems; both must contend with the power and priority of the Anglo system, so that there remains an unequal biculturalism. Nevertheless, the multiple adaptations are not unusual.

For example, Kitano, in writing about the various styles of Japanese Americans noted:

> Therefore, within one individual there are often the many person-alities—the "Uncle Tom" to the white man, deferential and humble; the "good son" to his parents, dutiful and obedient; and the "swinger" to his peers, wise-cracking, loud, and irreverent. (Kitano, 1976:133)

It has generally been the lot of groups with less power to adapt to changing realities. A fuller discussion of these behaviors will be found in Chapter 5.

In summary, the following questions should be kept in mind:

1. What are the goals of American society? Are they Anglo con-formity, the melting pot, cultural pluralism, or what? What are some of the preconditions that must be met before these goals can be realistically assessed by the subordinated minorities?
2. How can we empirically demonstrate and evaluate the effec-tiveness of some of these goals?
3. How do we prevent today's solutions from becoming tomor-row's rigidities and orthodoxies?

STRATIFICATION AND INEQUALITY

No matter what the model or the goal, racial minorities have gen-erally found themselves at the bottom of the hierarchical structures. This phenomenon is defined as social inequality, or "the inequality of social rewards, goods and services, benefits and privileges, honor and esteem, or power and influence available to incumbents of the different social roles and social positions and associated with the different roles and positions" (Matras, 1975:11–12). Social inequality based on racial lines means that whites usually will be assigned the more desirable positions, and that people of color will end up with the leftovers. As Rothman (1978) observed, being a Korean, black, or Mexican may be less desirable than being a Canadian or a Swede. It may result in being excluded from certain clubs, occupations, and neighborhoods.

The methods and procedures used to assign individuals and groups to different roles and positions is called social stratification (Matras, 1975:6). In our society, there is presumably equal access to all positions to individuals with proper qualifications; however our stratification system reveals the absence of racial minorities in the more desirable roles (see Part II).

Is Social Inequality Necessary?

Inequality in all societies is readily recognizable. The question thus arises concerning the necessity of hierarchical stratification. The unequal distribution of rewards (those factors that increase one's control over his or her own destiny, increase material comforts, and make life better), of power (command of resources), of prestige (social honor), of privilege (benefits, opportunities, and exemptions from certain obligations), and of wealth (money and property) is especially evident in complex, urban societies (Burkey, 1978:20). Turner and Starnes (1976:7) found that all societies with an economic surplus have systems of inequality.

Rousseau, the French philosospher, wrote in 1754 that the possession of private property was the basis of social inequality and that it was a negative and destructive practice. Ferguson and Miller from Scotland wrote a few decades later and took on an opposing point of view. They saw the ownership of property and the resulting differences in income and prestige as progressive steps towards a more civilized society (Matras, 1975).

The unequal distribution of rewards has led to the creation of strata or social classes. Social classes "are divisions of whole societies or communities within societies that represent divisions of a combination of rewards" (Burkey, 1978:29).

Burkey discovered that at least three social classes can be identified in almost all complex societies. The greatest amount of rewards, power, prestige, privilege, and wealth is associated with the upper classes; lesser amounts are associated with the middle classes, and the least favored are the lower classes.

According to Karl Marx, the formation of social classes is a result of the forms of ownership, the means of production, and the forms of labor of those who were not owners. Land, industrial wealth, capital, and labor power are the keys to social inequality. An egalitarian, classless society can be achieved only by social ownership of property and the means of production (Matras, 1975:64).

Weber (1946) recognized the role of property as central to social inequality but also pointed to the distribution of honor, prestige, and status as other forms of stratification. He saw differences in the ability of persons or groups to impose their will upon others (power), so that the formation of status and power groups for the purpose of acquiring, maintaining, and exercising social power constituted another form of social inequality.

FUNCTIONAL THEORY OF INEQUALITY

A more systematic way of looking at social inequality is to compare what is known as *functional theory* with *conflict theory* (Matras, 1975:69–75). The functional school is linked with contemporary American sociologists such as Talcott Parsons, Kingsley Davis, and Wilber Moore.

Parsons (1953) viewed inequality as a consequence of value consensus in societies. Achievement and performance are judged on the basis of the needs, priorities, and goals of the system. Therefore as Davis (1948) and Davis and Moore (1945) found, in all societies there are different social positions that are differentially valued but have to be filled. It is incumbent upon the abler members of the society to occupy the important and more difficult positions as well as the other roles to be filled and performed. In order to motivate and to allocate all of the positions with a minimum of friction, differential rewards and gratifications must be given, thus leading to social inequality. The relative size of the rewards is related to the functional importance of the role or social position for society and the relative scarcity of qualified personnel to fill them. The functional perspective emphasizes that inequality is necessary in order to fill the differential occupational and other positions in a society.

Economist Berle (1959), arguing from a functionalist perspective, stated that superior character, high ability, and greater capacity are necessary in any society; people with these attributes should fill the important positions and be rewarded accordingly.

Psychologists too also argued for the virtues of inequality. Herrnstein asserted that unequal material awards are needed to place talented and skillful people in important roles and positions. The notion of intelligent people rising to the top (as measured by IQ scores) and transmitting their mental abilities to their children with the consequent formation of a group of meritocratic elites is central to the positions of Herrnstein and Jensen (Anderson, 1974:82). Jensen further resurrects the view that there is a genetic, racial basis for social and personal inequality.

Functionalist theory was criticized by Matras (1975:70) on the following grounds:

1. It is imprecise. The meaning of the "importance" of positions is unclear, and there is no clarification of the extent and directions of inequality. There is little opportunity for empirical testing.
2. It pays little attention to the dysfunctional aspects of institutionalized inequality.
3. It glosses over variations in patterns of inequality and in patterns of allocating rewards, prestige, and power.
4. The assumption of a congruence between the distribution of talent and the inequality of rewards is conservative and can be interpreted to mean that social inequality is in the best interests of society, an assumption that is empirically doubtful.

Possibly the most effective criticism of functional theory for the lay person is to look at our recent record of leadership and power in places like Washington, D.C. and local city halls and to question the notion that the "cream rises to the top." The blundering, ineptitude, and lack of character and leadership displayed by many in high-salaried positions can lead to the point of view that the semihumorous Peter Principle (the prediction that people are promoted to their highest levels of incompetence) has as much validity as functionalist predictions (Anderson, 1974:82).

Chomsky also observed that wealth and power may not be necessarily reserved for those of noble purpose and character. Instead it may go to the ruthless, the cunning, the avaricious, the self-seeking, and those who are willing to abandon principle for material gain (Anderson, 1974:87).

It is interesting to note that Lenski (1966), Gordon (1978), and Banton (1977), major theorists in the area of race relations, all assume that the basic selfishness of human beings and their overriding desire to maximize their own gains are central to an understanding of human behavior. If their assumptions are correct, the question then might be how to develop a social system that will deter the most selfish and aggressive from taking over, rather than aiding and rewarding those with such qualities.

Conflict theories of inequality are associated with sociologists such as C. Wright Mills and Rolf Dahrendorf. From this perspective, social inequality arises as a result of the struggle within a society "for the goods, amenities, privileges and rewards which are in short supply" (Matras, 1975:71). The theory emphasizes power and coercion in social life, the exploitation by advantaged groups and individuals to get what they want, and their ability to prevent other groups from getting what they want.

Political parties, labor unions, business groups, religious and racial or ethnic groups are examples of conflict groups. The position of conflict theorists is that the dominant values that are supposedly held by a society are, in fact, values imposed on it by individuals and groups that are able to hold or to monopolize strategic power positions. Therefore, it is the distribution of power, rather than the needs or values of shared values in a society, that influences how roles, positions, social rewards, and resources are allocated.

The major criticism of conflict theory is the importance it gives to power and authority. It has been accused of relying on "power determinism" which is difficult to test (Van den Berghe, 1963).

The conflict perspective does not provide the simple role prescriptions and plans of action that are part of the functionalist perspective. The prescriptions of working hard, learning English, and acculturating are not central to this position, although one can argue that these paths are important in order to bring about societal changes. The frustration of finding significant ways to effect broad-scale change from low-power positions can lead to disillusionment, alienation, rhetoric, and cynicism unless there is an ability to organize groups, to achieve an occasional success, and to obtain continued support and reinforcement.

Lenski (1966) found that in every society, those who belong to the dominant social classes have the greatest capacity to explain and to disseminate their view of the existing system of inequality. They are therefore apt to support the social structure and to rationalize their advantage. Thus, functional theory is generally conservative, and inequality is viewed as a natural consequence of value consensus and individual abilities.

The challenging or conflict orientation expresses the voices of discontent in the society. It views inequality as a product of coercion, domination, and power. Lenski noted a historical dialectic between these points of view and found that periods of domination are often followed by challenges to the dominance.

The position between the functionalist and conflict perspectives is called "reformist." The reformer tries to modify inequality by attempting to bring about individual and societal changes.

BIBLIOGRAPHY

ANDERSON, CHARLES (1974). *The Political Economy of Social Class*. Englewood Cliffs, N.J.: Prentice-Hall, Inc.

BANTON, MICHAEL (1977). *Rational Choice: A Theory of Racial and Ethnic Relations*, Working Paper no. 8. Bristol, England: University of Bristol, SSRC Research Unit on Ethnic Relations.

BETHELL, TOM (1979). "Against Bilingual Education," *Harper's*, 258 (1545):30–33.

BERLE, ADOLPH (1959). *Power without Property*. New York: Harcourt, Brace & World.

BURKEY, RICHARD (1978). *Ethnic and Racial Groups*. Menlo Park, Calif.: Cummings Publishing Co.

DAHRENDORF, ROLF (1959). *Class and Conflict in Industrial Society*. Stanford, Calif.: Stanford University Press.

DAHRENDORF, ROLF (1969). "On the Origin of Inequality Among Men," in *Social Inequality*, ed. Andre Beteille. Baltimore: Penguin.

DAVIS, JAMES (1978). *Minority-Dominant Relations*. Arlington Heights, Ill.: AHM Publishing.

DAVIS, KINGSLEY (1948). *Human Society*. New York: Macmillan.

DAVIS, KINGSLEY and W. E. MOORE (1945). "Some Principles of Stratification," *American Sociological Review*, 10:242–49.

EISENSTADT, S. N. (1971). *Social Differentiation and Stratification*. Glenview, Ill.: Scott, Foresman.

GORDON, MILTON (1964). *Assimilation in American Life*. New York: Oxford University Press. All excerpts are reprinted by permission of the publisher.

GORDON, MILTON (1978). *Human Nature, Class and Ethnicity*. New York: Oxford University Press.

GRANT, MADISON (1916). *The Passing of the Great Race*. New York: Scribner and Sons.

HIGHAM, JOHN (1955). *Strangers in the Land*. New Brunswick, N.J.: Rutgers University Press.

KALLEN, HORACE (1915). "Democracy vs. the Melting Pot," *The Nation*, February 18 and 25.

KENNEDY, RUBY JO REEVES (1944). "Single or Triple Melting Pot? Intermarriage Trends in New Haven, 1870–1940," *American Journal of Sociology*, 49 (4):331–39.

KITANO, HARRY H. L. (1976). *Japanese Americans: The Evolution of a Subculture*. Englewood Cliffs, N.J.: Prentice-Hall, Inc.

LENSKI, GERHARD (1966). *Power and Privilege: A Theory of Social Stratification*. New York: McGraw-Hill.

MATRAS, JUDAH (1975). *Social Inequality, Stratification, and Mobility*. Englewood Cliffs, N.J.: Prentice-Hall, Inc.

MILLS, C. WRIGHT (1956). *The Power Elite*. New York: Oxford University Press.

NOEL, DONALD (1968). "A Theory of the Origin of Ethnic Stratification," *Social Problems*, 16:157–72.

PARK, ROBERT E. (1950). *Race and Culture*. New York: Free Press.

PARSONS, TALCOTT (1953). "A Revised Analytic Approach to the Theory of Social Stratification," in *Class Status and Power: A Reader in Social Stratification*, eds. R. Bendix and S. M. Lipset. New York: Free Press.

ROTHMAN, ROBERT (1978). *Inequality and Stratification in the United States.* Englewood Cliffs, N.J.: Prentice-Hall, Inc.

San Francisco Chronicle (1910) (n.d.).

TURNER, FREDERICK (1963). *The Frontier in American History.* New York: Holt, Rinehart & Winston.

TURNER, JONATHAN and CHARLES STARNES (1976). *Inequality: Privilege and Poverty in America.* Santa Monica, Calif.: Goodyear.

VAN DEN BERGHE, PIERRE (1963). "Dialectic and Functionalism: Toward a Theoretic Synthesis," *American Sociological Review,* 28:695–705.

WEBER, MAX (1946). *Class, Status, Party,* in *Max Weber, Essays in Sociology,* ed. and trans. H. H. Gerth and C. Wright Mills. New York: Oxford University Press.

ZANGWILL, ISRAEL (1909). *The Melting Pot.* New York: Macmillan.

48

DOMINATION

In the preceding chapters we discussed a number of outcomes that result when two groups meet, the goals of American society, and some explanations of social inequality. In this chapter we shall analyze the model of domination (Model 6B), since it most closely approximates our view of the current American racial stratification system. Under racial dominance the pattern of rewards, access, status, and power is differentiated, so that one group is "ruling, prevailing, controlling or exercising influence over others" (Burkey, 1978:31).

Racial groups are in the subordinate position: teacher-pupil, adult-child, officers-enlisted persons, supervisor-worker, and master-slave are common examples of dominant-subordinate relationships.

Burkey (1978) stated that a society based on racial dominance exists when one group controls the major positions of the state. The dominance is intensified when the same group occupies positions of authority in nonstate organizations and is able to set the standards for the entire society. It is "their" language and "their" culture that serve as the norms, and it is "their" people who control the positions of power, prestige, and wealth.

BACKGROUND IN EUROPE

The present racial arrangement in the United States did not appear overnight; rather, it developed over centuries and can be traced to European sources. As Banton noted, one dimension for any analysis of race relations is historical ''because beliefs about race and ethnicity have their own history and are explicit in popular consciousness in varying degrees'' (1977:1).

It would be impossible to trace any single source for the appearance of what is currently labeled ''white racism,'' but a short summary will be helpful in placing the superior-inferior dichotomy in historical perspective.

In the early Greek period, Aristotle believed that slavery was a natural state. Slaves, who were clearly ''inferior'' people, could benefit by living under their superior masters. Aristotle's views were influential in justifying the point of view that certain groups should be rulers and that others should be followers.

The European discovery of the new world led to many questions about the newly found people, the native Indians, especially since so many were being slaughtered by the Spanish conquerors. Were they humans? Were they inferiors? How could one justify the barbaric treatment of whole tribes?

The Spanish answer generally was that waging war on the Indians was necessary because, until they were brought under control, they could not be instructed into the religious faith. Barbaric treatment was justified because of the gravity of the Indian sins and also because of their crudeness, which obliged them to serve persons of a more refined nature, such as the Spaniards (Hanke, 1975).

These issues were symptoms of a more fundamental question concerning the origin of the human species. One view held for a single derivation, so that people of all races and colors were really ''brothers and sisters under the skin.'' There were others who felt that humans came from multiple origins, with the inevitable belief of inferiors and superiors.

Bernier, a French physician, proposed a racial taxonomy in 1684. He described various species or races, with the observation that there are enough differences among the races for them to be properly placed in a classification system. The basic criteria for his taxonomy included skin color, hair, and physiognomy.

The Swedish naturalist Carolus Linnaes, in the tenth edition of his *Systema,* published in 1758, recognized four varieties of human species with associated characteristics:

1. *Americanus rufus*: tenacious, free, easily contented (American Indians)
2. *Afer niger*: slow, negligent, cunning, capricious (African)
3. *Asiatic luridus*: haughty, stern, an opinionated fellow (Asian)
4. *Europaeus albus*: lively, creative, considered ''superior'' (European)

He also proposed a fifth class, *monstrosus*, to accomodate supposedly abnormal forms. It would be interesting to discover the classification and descriptions from scholars representing groups other than the European. They would, no doubt, reflect their own brand of ethnocentrism; the early Chinese and Japanese felt that Europeans were "hairy barbarians." The tendency to feel superior to others is obviously not limited to any one group; however, the problem with the European brand of racism was that they had the power and mobility to spread their biases to most countries of the world (Handlin, 1957).

An influential nineteenth-century theory of race relations and the superiority of the whites was that of social Darwinism. Charles Darwin's theory of evolution and the survival of the fittest was used to validate the observable "superiority" of whites over people of color. It should be noted that, in the nineteenth century, the Europeans were in control of most of the world, and it was deemed appropriate that "superior races" would be the "fittest" and naturally would fill the more powerful positions.

The social Darwinists believed that there were younger, less developed races who were lower on the evolutionary scale of development. Africans, Indians, and Chinese were described as members of adolescent races in a stage of incomplete growth. This approach fostered the concepts of lesser breeds, childlike natives, and the white man's burden. Theodore Roosevelt's description of happy-go-lucky black porters, superstitious but good in music ("they all sing"), typified racial thinking of that era.

A psychoanalytic explanation of white racism was advanced by Joel Kovel (1970). There is the notion that light and fair are related to goodness, whereas dark and black represent the polar opposites. Therefore, blackness conjures id impulses, sexual fantasies, identification with death, the devil, dirt, and wickedness. The fear of rape of white women by darker men is another strong fantasy. Thus the hostility of whites towards people of color is related to the unconscious id impulses.

Frantz Fanon (1967), a powerful voice of black consciousness, also emphasized that in Europe, the black man is the symbol of evil: Satan is black; the torturer is the black man. Concretely and symbolically, the black man stands for the bad side of one's character. Kovel stated: "As long as one cannot understand this fact, one is doomed to talk in circles about the 'black problem.' In the Western-dominated world the Negro is the symbol of sin" (Kovel, 1970:188).

Although many of the psychoanalytic propositions are impossible to validate, the history of European oppression of people with darker skins warrants an analysis of the symbolism associated with color. There is also some evidence that lighter skin color is preferred among such diverse groups as the Japanese, the natives of Mexico, and the inhabitants of

Latin America. It is difficult to assess whether these preferences are learned responses, programmed and consciously taught, or are old myths and legends.

THE DOMINATION MODEL:
PREJUDICE, DISCRIMINATION, AND SEGREGATION

In our previous discussions, we indicated that the bottom of the two-category system was the starting point for most immigrant groups in the United States. The majority of immigrants did not know the language; they were often unfamiliar with the culture and all too frequently lacked the necessary capital or resources to succeed. Further, few had the education and competitive skills necessary for rapid mobility. The important point is that some groups achieved a degree of mobility, integration, and assimilation within a short period of time. Other groups, mostly those of non-European background, remained under domination. It is our hypothesis that their mobility and acceptance into the dominant society has been hindered, delayed, and deflected by a number of barriers. These barriers include prejudice, discrimination, and segregation, and in extreme cases have resulted in individuals being confined in concentration camps, expelled from the country, and even exterminated (Daniels & Kitano, 1970:12).

The purpose of this section is to explore the domination model and to see why the experiences in this category are critical to understanding the current position of selected minorities.

Figure 8 shows the domination model and the barriers that have been used to maintain the system. The stratification is effectuated principally through visibility and racism, with the notion that the people in category X are superior to those in category Y. Stratification is strengthened through such active manifestations of race prejudice as discrimination and segregation and is reinforced by stereotypes, laws, and norms that lead to the avoidance, disadvantage, and isolation of target groups. The primary targets for change in the domination model would be the barriers of prejudice, discrimination, and segregation.

FIGURE 8   *BARRIERS*

Domination	Act	Mechanism	Effect
	Prejudice	Stereotypes	Avoidance
	Discrimination	Laws, norms	Disadvantage
	Segregation	Lws, norms	Isolation

There are many definitions of prejudice. It is "a set of attitudes which causes, supports, or justifies discrimination" (Rose, 1951:5); "an emotionally rigid attitude or predisposition to respond to a certain stimulus in a certain way toward a group of people" (Simpson and Yinger, 1965:10); "an antipathy based upon a faulty and inflexible generalization" (Allport, 1958:7). It is generally agreed that race prejudice is a negative attitude toward a racial or ethnic group, and it is maintained through stereotypes: "They smell bad." "They breed like rabbits." "They lower property values." One adverse effect of race prejudice is that individuals of a target group are avoided because of prejudgement and negative stereotypes.

Prejudice is a difficult phenomenon to study because groups and individuals differ in the direction and amount of prejudice, because racial stereotypes may change, and because the objects or targets of these negative attitudes may also change. Further, it is an attitude; thus it is difficult to measure, especially if an admission of racial prejudice is viewed as socially undesirable.

There are many explanations of prejudice. One is its use in exploitation: the dominant group can avoid feelings of sympathy and empathy for the dominated through stereotypes or overexaggerations of negative qualities. One common stereotype in exploitation is to attribute less than human qualities to the subordinates so that they can be compared to and treated like animals.

Ethnocentrism, or the belief that one's own family and society are unique and correct, is another explanation of prejudice. As individuals are socialized to the beliefs and behaviors of their own family and society, they begin to feel that what goes on in their group is "natural," and so begin to judge others from this standpoint. In this sense, ethnocentrism is almost inevitable, since the very standards used to judge others are part of the culture that one has absorbed. Those who deviate are then viewed as "unnatural" and can become the target of prejudice. The family plays an important part in this process. The way one's family conducts itself is "normal." The food, the conversation, and the life style become part of a familiar standard, and other families who differ may be judged strange, foreign, or alien.

Ethnocentrism is a part of the identity of an individual and may be linked to other variables, such as pride, belonging, standards, and the like. In this sense it is normal; and some measure of pride in one's own family and culture is a positive strength. It turns into a negative factor when it becomes overly rigid and the individual becomes intolerant of the behavior of others.

Prejudice also may be a product of structural opposition. Prejudice is a part of the "we-they" phenomenon, and the very formation of one

unity in contrast to another leads to certain conditions. As Daniels and
Kitano stated:

> We prefer . . . an interpretation in which a man is a member of a
> group of a certain kind by virtue of his nonmembership in other
> groups. A person belongs to a tribe or its segment, and membership
> is activated when there is opposition to this tribe. Therefore a man
> sees himself as a member of a group only in opposition to other
> groups, and he sees a member of another group as a member of a
> social unity, however much that unit may be split into opposing
> segments. (1970:19)

In response to stimuli, people choose to associate with certain persons and not with others. A football team is not really an entity until
there is an opponent; once the opposition is present, prejudice between
the "enemies" can be predicted.

Frustration–aggression theories, psychoanalytic perspectives, and
studies of the authoritarian personality view prejudice as transferring
internal, personal problems to external objects. Ready objects for exter-
nalizing one's problems are racial minorities, who can be stereotyped,
blamed, or "scapegoated" for practically any personal failure.

Selective experiences and selective learning also can lead to prejudice. A particularly negative experience with a member of an ethnic
group and the "remember when" phenomenon can dredge up negative
feelings that might appear on the surface to be irrational. The psychiatric
term *transference* is appropriate to this context—the feelings toward
people and experiences in the past are transferred to people and situations
in the present.

The personal element in any analysis of prejudice should not be
underestimated. In discussing the topic with individuals in such diverse
areas as Scotland, England, Brazil, Hawaii, the mainland United States,
and Japan, we have noticed that the answer to the question, "Is there
racial prejudice?" is most often answered by a personal reference. Even
though there may be rather blatant instances of racism in all of these
areas, the individual answer may be "no" if the victims are the "others"
and the individual has been spared. Conversely, a negative experience
may lead to an indictment of the whole society.

There is also the "earned reputation" approach in which the justification for prejudice is shifted to the target group (Rose, 1951). It is
presumed that prejudice would disappear if the objects of the attitude
would mend their ways.

The stereotype. In our model of domination, there is an interrelationship among prejudice, stereotyping, and avoidance. The negative attitude
(prejudice) is reinforced and maintained by racial stereotypes, which is

defined as "an overgeneralization associated with a racial or ethnic category that goes beyond existing evidence" (Feagin, 1978:12). The combination of hostile feeling and faulty overgeneralization can lead to avoidance ("They all smell bad."); to discrimination ("They lower property values; we can't let them in."); to segregation ("Keep them on the reservations."); and to even more severe actions, such as concentration camps ("They're treacherous and can't be trusted; put them behind barbed wire."); extermination ("They're animals and the only way to handle them is to get rid of all of them."); and to genocide ("The whole race and tribe should be eliminated."). The sequence is an obvious oversimplification of a complex process but is presented here as a sober reminder that these terrible statements have been used in the past and will no doubt continue to be used in the future to control and to eliminate unwanted groups.

Reducing prejudice. Since the hypothesized causes of prejudice vary so widely, there is no simple program that can reduce the phenomenon. There is some agreement that prejudice can be lessened under the following conditions: equal status contact under a spirit of cooperation, shared goals, people working on a common problem and faced with an external enemy, appropriate education activities, and that the contact is sanctioned by law and by the political authorities (Allport, 1958).

The mass media. The effect of television and the movies is important since their portrayal of racial and ethnic groups may be a person's principal source of information. Therefore, if the media deal primarily in stereotypes and the viewer has little opportunity for personal contact with members of that minority, the probability of the stereotype becoming the reality to the viewer is high.

Engelhardt (1975) believes that Hollywood movies have thoroughly dehumanized the nonwhite world. The whites, who are the exploiters, consistently show up as the "good guys"—as the bearers of civilization and all that is just and humane. Their superiority is taken as the natural order of things, and their "justified" extermination of the nonwhites provides a "happy" ending. Hollywood stereotypes have made it almost impossible to explain rationally that the colonized people also are human and that their resistance to invasion, colonization, exploitation, and mass slaughter can be understood.

Margulies, reporting in the *Los Angeles Times* (1979), assessed the state of minorities in television. The report focused on 1977 network newscasts and employment figures. Television drama continued in its failure to reflect the gender and racial/ethnic composition of American life. White males, for example, who comprised 39.9 percent of the population, made up 62.7 percent of the characters. Minorities other than blacks continued to appear only rarely in TV drama. The writer also deplored the fact that of the minorities who did get TV roles, about 50 percent appeared in the same handful of shows. These shows often placed minorities in ridiculous roles, so that if "television serves as a creator or reinforcer of beliefs," it plays a negative role in regard to minorities and women. The report concludes that white males continued in their dominance in official and managerial positions.

In closing we should note the multiple functions of prejudice. It promotes group unity and identification, supplies cues and scapegoats, serves ethnocentric purposes, and provides needed symbols. In fact, a not so facetious statement might be that if we did not have prejudice, we would have to invent it. The goal of eradicating prejudice (even if we had the necessary technology) thus may not be the highest priority, although any diminution of negative racial feelings would be welcome. Rather, the task may be to prevent the attitude (prejudice) from being acted out (discrimination). As MacIver stated: "Whenever the direct attack is feasible—that is, the attack on discrimination itself—it is more promising than the indirect attack—that is, the attack on prejudice itself. It is more effective to challenge conditions than to challenge attitudes and feelings" (1948:64).

Discrimination

The second variable in maintaining the dominance of one group over the other is discrimination. Traditional analysis has linked prejudice to discrimination in a causal sequence, so that both our example of prejudice as a step leading to extermination and genocide and our quotation from MacIver are in keeping with this tradition. Allport (1954) saw discrimination as the acting out of prejudice. Myrdal (1944) in his study, *An American Dilemma*, linked valuations and beliefs as being behind discriminatory behavior against blacks. Kinloch (1974) used the term "applied prejudice" in discussing discrimination in which one stream of thought links prejudice (an "intent to harm") and discrimination in a causal fashion.

Another perspective ignored the "intent to harm" motive and instead saw discrimination as motivated primarily by a desire to maintain one's own privileges or territory (Feagin, 1978). There is a difference between gain-motivated discrimination and prejudice-motivated discrimination (Antonovsky, 1960). Discrimination from this perspective is a result of the struggle over resources. The dominant group practices discrimination to protect its advantage.

Another related type of discrimination that may not necessarily include prejudice is "institutional discrimination," a term linked to "institutional racism," first introduced by Hamilton and Carmichael (1967). Their book *Black Power* pointed out the effects of social and governmental practices in perpetuating inequalities against blacks.

Yetman and Steele (1975) cited two analytically distinct types of institutional discrimination that may not be related to prejudice. Structural discrimination is the result of the normal operation of social structures, so that a business moving out to the suburbs may effectively discriminate against inner-city blacks by becoming inaccessible. Cultural discrimination refers to the ability of the group in power to set standards and criteria that may effectively screen out people with other cultural backgrounds.

Bullock and Harrell (1976), in writing about institutional discrimination, offered a threefold typology. The first step is the establishment of prerequisites or preconditions that are drawn at a point at which a disproportionate number of blacks cannot qualify. The second step is labeled *freezing,* in which after a period of leniency during which many whites have qualified, all new applicants are placed under newer, more stringent standards and requirements. Finally there is a strategy called *mapping,* which consists of drawing geographic lines so as to minimize competition from racial minorities.

Our definition of discrimination is that drawn from Feagin. Discrimination is the "actions or practices carried out by members of dominant groups, or their representatives, which have a differential and harmful impact on members of subordinate groups" (Feagin, 1978:14–15). Therefore, discrimination involves actions with the actors discriminating and the victims on the receiving end. The actions may be overt or hidden, direct or indirect, intentional or unintentional. Actors may include individuals, groups, or organizations; victims may be individuals, groups, or organizations.

Feagin (1978:15) suggested four types of discriminatory practices:

Type A: Isolate discrimination
Type B: Small group discrimination
Type C: Direct institutionalized discrimination
Type D: Indirect institutionalized discrimination

Type A: Isolate discrimination. Isolate discrimination refers to harmful actions intentionally taken by a member of the dominant group against members of the minority. It may still be the most widespread and common type, even though the discriminator is taking the action without the immediate support of norms or standards of conduct in a large group or organizational context. For example, a waitress may serve the minority member last; the salesperson may be rude or indifferent; a police officer may handle the minority suspect much more roughly. Although relatively minor in terms of societal impact, this type of discrimination may prove to be the most irritating to the minority individual because it is so common and is a daily reminder of his or her inferior status.

Type B: Small group discrimination. This category refers to harmful actions taken intentionally by a small number of dominant-group individuals acting in concert against members of subordinate groups. Church bombings, floggings, vigilante groups, and the Ku Klux Klan type of activities are examples of small group discriminatory behavior.

Type C: Direct, institutionalized discrimination. Type C discrimination refers to organizationally prescribed or community prescribed actions that are intentional and have been in practice continuously so that they have become institutionalized. Country clubs, social groups, and exclusive schools with restricted membership lists are examples of direct, institutionalized discrimination.

Type D: Indirect institutionalized discrimination. Type D refers to discrimination by organizations that is not directly motivated by prejudice or intent to harm. Regulations on seniority (last hired, first fired), requisites of education, training, and graduation from ''good'' schools are examples of institutional practices that may not be directly linked to prejudice but are effective in limiting the mobility and access of subordinated members. It should be noted that only this category of discrimination is not directly linked to prejudice.

Various combinations of the categories may coexist. From a broader perspective, the picture of the dominant group and their interlocking political, economic, and social organizations, their intentional and unintentional practices, and a mixture of prejudice and racism, is what Feagin labeled systematic discrimination. The cumulative effects of systematic discrimination delineate the oppression that is a part of a subordinate status.

Reverse discrimination. One current charge that comes mainly from white males is that of ''reverse discrimination.'' The implication is that heretofore advantaged dominant group individuals are now being deliberately excluded or passed over for positions by ''less qualified'' females and minorities. The issue is not a simple one because it involves definitions of qualifications, standards, and measurement within a political context of shrinking resources and great emotion. Our definition of racism (from the powerful to the powerless) raises the question of how dominated members can become the discriminators, unless one assumes that current legal decisions are now reflecting minority rather than majority perspectives.

Kahng (1978) took the issue of reverse discrimination further, asking rhetorically, can minorities and women do what white males have done to them? For if reverse discrimination were actually to occur, white males would have to be brutalized, degraded, and dehumanized to the same extent that racial minorities and women have, which is not likely to occur.

It is important to understand the intimate relationship between discrimination and power. Without power, discrimination is ineffective; with power, discrimination maintains the dominance of one group over the other.

According to Schermerhorn (1970), power is related to numbers, cohesion, and resources (Table 4.1). The majority group is characterized by numerical superiority (+) and high cohesion (+), is in control of resources (+), and therefore is a group with power (+). The elite group may lack the size (−) but is characterized as cohesive (+), in control of resources (+), and is therefore another group with power (+). The masses may have large numbers (+) but often are disorganized (−), lack resources, and are therefore a group with low power (−). The minority group will be deficient in size (−), in cohesion (−), and in resources (−), so it remains a powerless group.

Resources include money, prestige, property, natural and supernatural powers, and such factors as knowledge, competence, deceit, fraud, secrecy, physical strength, voting rights, the ability to bear arms, and membership in organizations. Power is a multiplicative function of total resources and the degree to which these resources are mobilized (Bierstedt, 1950).

The groups in power are those which can effectively discriminate. They can pass the laws and the rules that help to define who belongs and who remains on the outside.

Sources of power. French and Raven (1959) classified the sources of power into five types:

1. reward power
2. coercive, or punishment power
3. legitimate power
4. referent power
5. expert power

Discrimination and Power

POWER AND MINORITY GROUPS

Table 4.1

		Size, Number	Cohesion	Resources	Power
Dominant Groups	Majority	+	+	+	+
	Elite	−	+	+	+
Subordinate Groups	Masses	+	−	−	−
	Minority	−	−	−	−

SOURCE: Adapted from R. A. Schermerhorn, *Comparative Ethnic Relations* (Chicago: University of Chicago Press, 1978), p. 13. Reprinted by permission.

The first two types of power depend on the possession of resources that permit the holder either to reward or punish. Legitimate power relates to authority, often based on contracts, promises, commitments, elections, or made by one individual to another. Referent power relates to the notion of charisma in which one individual identifies with and likes another and desires to do as the other requests; love and sexuality may be variants of this. Expert power is based on special knowledge.

To this list we would add morality, which may control some of the more naked uses of power by arousing feelings of guilt. Discriminatory behavior, however, can be justified by appealing to moral superiority. Invoking the name of God for one's side has often led to some of the highest levels of discrimination.

Many hypotheses are suggested by the French and Raven list. Referent power is one of the historical facts of race relations—certain charismatic majority (as well as ethnic) group leaders have been regarded as people to trust and to follow, while others, who may be advocating the same programs, are regarded with hostility and suspicion. Legitimate power based on treaties and promises continues to "explain" our treatment of the American Indian. Appropriately enough, the Indians also are analyzing past treaties in order to exert pressure for more equitable treatment. A more permanent means of maintaining power is for the powerless group to internalize the differential roles. Once internalization occurs, the observable source of power (old treaties) can disappear but the powerless behavior will continue.

Causes of Discriminatory Behavior

There are a number of variables suggested by Schermerhorn (1978) and Blalock (1967) that are hypothesized as causes of discrimination. They include group size, social distance, competition, power threat, and status consciousness. All of these variables can be linked to prejudice.

Group size. Perhaps the simplest explanation for discriminatory behavior among dominant group members is the fear of being overwhelmed by the sheer number of the subordinated "masses."

The threat and power of numbers may be actual or imagined—the effects are similar. For example, in California, elaborate geometric charts were devised showing the state being overrun by "yellow hordes." (In reality these hordes almost never exceeded 1 to 2 percent of the population.) One reaction was that of V. S. McClatchy, the publisher of a major California newspaper chain, who believed that "Careful tables of increase of the Japanese population in the United States . . . place the total in the United States . . . in 1923 at 318,000; in 1933 at 542,000; in 1943 at 870,000; in 1963 at 2,000,000; in 2003 at 10,000,000; and in 2063 at 100,000,000" (Daniels & Kitano, 1970:52).

It is interesting to note that the estimated Japanese population in the United States in 1978 was about 600,000, a figure well below McCatchy's projected 2,000,000. Nevertheless, the specter of hordes of Japanese was one important factor leading to discriminatory legislation against them and other Asians. Racial groups who are perceived to "breed like rabbits" have always been targets for some form of control.

Generally, the smaller the ethnic minority group, the less threatening it is. The one nonwhite family in an all-white community is accepted with friendliness (although it invariably has a low status), and these communities generally congratulate themselves for their racial openness. During the evacuation of World War II, many Japanese Americans experienced much less discrimination in the East Coast and Midwest because their groups were small and scattered. The overall belief is that discrimination arises only if larger numbers of the minority begin to enter the "paradise."

Numbers by themselves are not reliable predictors of discriminatory behavior under most circumstances and may be relevant only when there are actually only one or two visible ethnic minorities in a town or city of some size.

Social distance. The attempt to retain a social distance between the dominant and subordinate categories is another cause of discriminatory behavior. Attempts to remain at a distance in terms of schools, jobs, housing, and personal relationships have long characterized our past.

Numerous empirical examples are available. Early studies by Bogardus (1930) used the concept of social distance to assess the degrees of social intimacy in relation to specific minorities. The degrees of social intimacy ranged over marriage, club membership, friendships, neighbors, employment, citizenship, and exclusion. Overall there was a predictable pattern: nonwhite groups were kept at a social distance. The one group that appeared consistently at the bottom was the Turks; even among American blacks, Turks were ranked at the bottom. As we can infer, discrimination against them had little to do with the threat of numbers.

Social distance is maintained through attitudes of liking and disliking. In many instances the object of dislike is unknown or heavily stereotyped. For example, Katz and Braly (1933) asked students to list all the traits they thought typical of a number of ethnic groups. Blacks were regarded to be superstitious, lazy, happy-go-lucky, ignorant, and musical. Jews were seen to be shrewd, mercenary, industrious, grasping, intelligent, and ambitious. A more recent study using the Bogardus scale (1968) indicated that there has been no significant change in the ranking of groups.

The important point in this study of stereotypes was how this "fantasy" about other groups, whether phrased positively or not, becomes the "reality" of intergroup relations. People feel that they can avoid or discriminate against their fellow citizens through perceived imaginary traits.

Competition. Competition arises from a simple premise—that when two or more individuals are striving for the same scarce resources, the success of one implies relative failure for the other. Discriminatory behavior, therefore, can limit competition. The intensity of the competition is related to several factors, such as the strength of the goals, the number of satisfactory alternatives, and the number and power of the competitors.

The area of economic competition provides examples of how this belief can be translated into a motive for discrimination. For example, many Californians felt that the Chinese laborers of the early twentieth century were unfair competitors. They worked long hours for low wages, used their family and friends for cheap labor, seldom took holidays, and were therefore a threat to the American standard of living. It was felt that white workers would be the main victims. Their loss of jobs and income lowered their ability to buy goods, which in turn hurt others. Chinese laborers and their unfair competition were among the presumed causes for the high unemployment during the economic depression of the 1870s.

Professional sports provides an interesting example of a competitive situation in which feedback is generally quick and objective (batting averages, pennants won, touchdowns scored), so that racial discrimination may be less likely to occur. It was not always thus; Jackie Robinson entered professional baseball only after World War II. Curiously enough, the field of competitive athletics may be one of the arenas in which functional theory is most likely to be valid, since there is a high probability that those with the talent and motivation are likely to rise to the top.

Blalock (1967) proposed a number of correlations between athletic teams (and by implication, other similar groups) and discrimination. If discriminatory barriers are maintained, an individual, and therefore the team, will not be able to perform to its maximum capabilities. Under these conditions discriminatory barriers will be greatly lowered. This is especially true in professional sports, particularly basketball and baseball. It was not too long ago that both of these sports were all-white. Now there is a preponderance of black athletes on all-star teams.

Power threat. Perceived minority-group power is related to discrimination; power threat is related to numbers, average resources, and mobilization. The admission of Hawaii to the United States was fought vigorously by those who perceived a threat to white power by a state with a highly visible Asian population. The denial of voting rights to Southern blacks for many years was in part motivated by the fear of their potential voting power.

Status plays an important part in the lives of most Americans, and the role of minority group is strongly influenced by this consideration. As Blalock observed, "One of the most pervasive and subtle forms of minority discrimination is that of avoidance, particularly in situations implying social equality or involving potential intimacy" (1967:51).

Minority groups occupy a generally low status in American society. Therefore, status-conscious whites avoid lower-status individuals, especially those of color, and thus strengthen prejudicial perceptions. Even professions are stigmatized if they involve working with low-status groups, the prestige of professions often being related to their client group. For example, professions who work with the poor are generally of lower status; even within a profession, the Beverly Hills doctor has a higher status than his or her colleague who works with the poor.

Although not all avoidance behavior is motivated by status considerations (for example, there may be differences based on values, interests, personalities, or styles of life), much of the avoidance of minorities is. The mixture of ethnicity and status is often difficult to unravel; the junior executive avoids all close contact with the janitor, both because the janitor is of low status and because he is black.

Equal-status contact between dominant- and subordinate-group members can be threatening to and uncomfortable for both sides. The white individual may be irritated at the familiarity of the "uppity" minority-group member, and the ethnic individual may be sensitive to any sign of condescension from his or her white peer. Therefore, ritualistic, or "gaming," behaviors are often used to mask the conflict.

Status in the past often resulted in predictable reciprocal behavior. Whereas dominant-group styles encouraged the avoidance of lower-status ethnic groups, lower-status groups prided themselves on their friendships with dominant-group members. Ethnic groups could gauge their rise in status by the number of whites who could be expected to attend a social gathering. The things that make up status and "fashionability," the styles and the people associated with them, however, can shift dramatically, as they have in the past. If interracial gatherings become fashionable, status-oriented individuals may go out of their way to attend them.

Ethnicity, social position, and status are interesting topics for research. For example, for a white person, does associating with an Asian, a Chicano, or a black provide more status? What if the Asian were a gardener, the Chicano a lawyer, and the black a doctor?

Segregation

The third variable in maintaining the dominant-subordinate stratification system is racial segregation. By segregation, we refer to the act of separating and isolating members of a racial group from the main body.

Van den Berghe (1971) discussed three different kinds of segregation, each designed by dominant group members for different situations. The first is *micro-segregation,* referring to separation in washrooms, waiting rooms, the post office, and other public facilities. The Jim Crow laws are examples of this category; their purpose was to segregate as much as possible racial groups in frequent contact situations. The second level is *meso-segregation,* such as in urban housing, in which racial categories are assigned to ghettos. The final level is *macro-segregation,* in which there is a complete geographical separation, such as in reservations and concentration camps.

Housing. Housing is one of the most important areas for racial segregation.

Although there are laws to prohibit segregation and discrimination in housing, many methods have been employed to skirt these laws. The method cited by the United States Commission on Civil Rights as the most effective and widely used is simply the refusal to sell. Another method is the racial restrictive covenant made between two parties stipulating that the purchaser of the property will not sell or rent the property to members of specific minority or religious groups. This method is no longer legal. Housing provides one example of the conflict between the "right" of the individual to sell to whom he or she pleases and societal "rights" in specifying nondiscriminatory clauses in the sale.

A more current issue is that of "red lining," or the practice of mortgage-lending institutions imposing artifical restrictions on housing loans for particular areas in which minorities have started to buy (Vitarello, 1975). However, Vitarello reported that political pressure has proved to be successful in discouraging this practice. For example, in Chicago, all banks and savings and loan associations bidding for deposits of city funds must sign anti-red-lining pledges.

The cost of discrimination in housing has been great. Members of minority groups are not free to obtain housing according to their financial means, and they pay higher prices for lower quality housing than whites would pay. The effects on morale, ambition, and expectation are destructive. The blight of slum areas spreads, urban renewal lags, and racial tension increases.

Segregation intensifies the visibility of the minority group and demarcates its boundaries, producing problems of conflict and social control. Ethnic riots often occur along the boundaries, and social-control problems within segregated areas are usually quite serious; police officers, fire fighters, and other representatives of the larger community are regarded as intruders and often are treated with hostility.

There may be a voluntary element in segregation. The minority-group members may feel more comfortable among his or her own "kind"—food, services, language, and customs are more attuned to ethnic needs. In the ghetto, one can limit contact with the dominant group, and life can continue with old friends who have also chosen to live within the segregated enclave.

One effect of segregated housing was reflected in a report by Greenwood (*Los Angeles Times,* 1972). The flight of the whites to the suburbs is dramatically illustrated by 1970 census data showing that the nonwhite population of the nation's central cities climbed by 4 million since 1960, while the white population dropped 600,000 for the same period. Cities such as Detroit, St. Louis, and Baltimore are approaching a 50-percent level of nonwhites.

A more recent article by William Trombley in the same newspaper (1979) reported on white flight as a result of school busing in Los Angeles. In the fall of 1978, white pupil enrollment had dropped 15 percent (from 194,800 to 165,400), although the total drop could not be attributed only to busing.

The rise of ethnic populations in the cities per se is not a problem, but the general neglect that follows the white exodus is. Jobs, services, and other necessities of city living generally drop as nonwhites take over, and there is often a rise in crime and delinquency, as well as increased welfare roles. As Sol Linowitz, former ambassador to the Organization of American States stated: "[Tax revenues] and better housing are following the migration of affluent whites to the suburbs and leaving the cities in worse shape than before the riots of the mid-1960s" (*Los Angeles Times,* 1972:6).

Role of Law

In our model of domination, the primary mechanism for the support of discrimination and segregation is the law. Le Melle, in the foreword to Burkey's book (1971) saw law mostly as an instrument of the dominant group and a reflection of their desires, values, and interests. It thus becomes the force of the strong against the weak. The ultimate sanction of the law is power, since without the sanction of force, law becomes legal fiction. The task of eliminating racial discrimination and segregation is made extremely difficult because the primary responsibility for change lies with the perpetrators.

In summary, this chapter analyzed the model of domination and the role of prejudice, discrimination, segregation, stereotyping, and the law in maintaining the racial stratification system. The racially dominated, already at a position of disadvantage, are further suppressed because they are isolated and avoided by the group in power.

BIBLIOGRAPHY

ADORNO, T. W., ELSE FRENKEL-BRUNSWIK, D. J. LEVINSON, and R. N. SANFORD (1950). *The Authoritarian Personality.* New York: Harper & Row, Pub.

ALLPORT, GORDON (1954). *The Nature of Prejudice,* pp. 51–52, 100. Boston: Beacon Press.

ANTONOVSKY, AARON (1960). "The Social Meaning of Discrimination," *Phylon,* 21:81.

BANTON, MICHAEL (1977). *Rational Choice: A Theory of Racial and Ethnic Relations,* Working paper no. 8. Bristol, England: University of Bristol, SSRC Unit on Ethnic Relations.

BANTON, MICHAEL (1967). *Race Relations.* London: Tavistock Publications.

BIERSTEDT, ROBERT (1950). "An Analysis of Social Power," *American Sociological Review,* 15:730–38.

BLALOCK, HUBERT M. (1967). *Toward a Theory of Minority Group Relations.* New York: John Wiley.

BOGARDUS, EMORY (1968). "Comparing Racial Distance in Ethiopia, South Africa and the United States," *Sociology and Social Research,* 52:149–56.

BOGARDUS, EMORY (1933). "A Social Distance Scale," *Sociology and Social Research,* 17:265–71.

BULLOCK, CHARLES and RODGERS HARRELL, JR. (1976). "Institutional Racism: Prerequisites, Freezing and Mapping," *Phylon,* 37:212–23.

BURKEY, RICHARD (1978). *Ethnic and Racial Groups.* Menlo Park, Calif.: Cummings Publishing Co.

DANIELS, ROGER and HARRY H. L. KITANO (1970). *American Racism.* Englewood Cliffs, N.J.: Prentice-Hall, Inc.

DOLLARD, JOHN, LEONARD DOOB, NEAL MILLER, and OTHERS (1939). *Frustration and Aggression.* New Haven: Yale University Press.

FANON, FRANTZ (1967). *Black Skin, White Masks.* New York: Grove Press.

FEAGIN, JOE (1978). *Racial and Ethnic Relations.* Englewood Cliffs, N.J.: Prentice-Hall, Inc.

FRENCH, JOHN R. and BERTRAM RAVEN (1959). "The Bases of Social Power," in *Studies in Social Power,* 9, ed. Darwin Cartwright. Ann Arbor: University of Michigan Press.

FRIEDMAN, ROBERT (1975). "Institutional Racism: How to Discriminate without Really Trying," in *Racial Discrimination in the United States,* pp. 384–401, ed. Thomas F. Pettigrew. New York: Harper & Row, Pub.

GREENWOOD, NOEL (1972). "School Desegregation—Successes, Failures, Surprises," *Los Angeles Times,* May 2, 1972, section C, p. 1.

HAMILTON, CHARLES and STOKELY CARMICHAEL (1967). *Black Power.* New York: Random House.

HANKE, LEWIS (1959). *Aristotle and the American Indian.* Bloomington: University of Indiana Press.

HANDLIN, OSCAR (1957). *Race and Nationality in American Life.* Boston: Little, Brown.

KAHNG, ANTHONY (1978). "EEO in America," *Equal Opportunity Forum,* 5 (10):23.

KAIN, JOHN, ED. (1969). *Race and Poverty.* Englewood Cliffs, N.J.: Prentice-Hall, Inc.

KATZ, DANIEL and KENNETH W. BRALY (1958). "Verbal Stereotypes and Racial Prejudice," in *Readings in Social Psychology,* pp. 40–46, eds. Eleanor Maccoby, Theodore Newcomb, and Eugene Hartley. New York: Holt, Rinehart & Winston.

KATZ, D. and K. BRALY (1933). "Racial Stereotypes in One Hundred College Students," *Journal of Abnormal Social Psychology,* 28:280–90.

KINLOCH, GRAHAM (1974). *The Dynamics of Race Relations.* New York: McGraw-Hill.

KOVEL, JOEL (1970). *White Racism.* New York: Vintage Books.

Los Angeles Times (1972). "Starting Flight of Whites to Suburbs Noted," June 1, part I-B, pp. 6–7.

Los Angeles Times (1976). "Home Hunting Blacks Still Face Bias, Survey Finds," April 17, part I, p. 6.

MACIVER, ROBERT M. (1948). *The More Perfect Union.* New York: Macmillan.

MARDEN, CHARLES and GLADYS MEYER (1968). *Minorities in American Society.* New York: Harper & Row, Pub.

MARGULIES, LEE (1979). "Bleak Picture for Minorities, Women in TV," *Los Angeles Times,* January 16, part IV, p. 1.

MYRDAL, GUNNAR (1944). *An American Dilemma.* New York: Harper & Row, Pub.

PETTIGREW, THOMAS T. (1973). "Racism and Mental Health of White Americans: A Social Psychological View," in *Racism in Mental Health,* eds. Charles V. Willie, Bernard M. Kramer, and Bertram S. Brown. Pittsburgh: University of Pittsburgh Press.

PETTIGREW, THOMAS (1971). *Racially Separate or Together.* New York: McGraw-Hill.

ROSE, ARNOLD (1951). *The Roots of Prejudice.* Paris: UNESCO, Pub. 85.

SCHERMERHORN, R. A. (1978). *Comparative Ethnic Relations.* Chicago: University of Chicago Press.

SIMPSON, GEORGE E. and J. M. YINGER (1965). *Racial and Cultural Minorities.* New York: Harper & Row, Pub.

TROMBLEY, WILLIAM (1979). "Some 'White Flight' Reported by Expert," *Los Angeles Times,* January 18, part II, p. 1.

VAN DEN BERGHE, PIERRE (1971). "Racial Separation in South Africa: Degrees and Funds," in *South Africa: Sociological Perspectives,* ed. Herbert Adams. London: Oxford University Press.

VITARELLO, JAMES (1975). "The Red Lining Route to Urban Decay," *Focus,* 3 (10):4–5.

YETMAN, NORMAN and C. HOY STEELE (1975). *Majority and Minority* (2nd ed.). Boston: Allyn & Bacon.

68

5

MINORITY ADAPTATIONS
TO
DOMINATED STATUS

The area of race relations that elicits the most value judgments is the adaptation of minority groups to their dominated status. Terms such as good, healthy, model minority, and dysfunctional are common. But what is functional, good, and desirable from positions of dominance may be viewed differently among the dominated. Wilson (1973) discussed three possibilities in a dominant-subordinate system: the dominant group acceding to all of the demands made by the minority group, meeting some of the demands through some concessions, or rejecting all demands—often through repressive tactics. In general, the weaker the group, the more safely the dominant group can ignore or reject their proposals.

PAST ACCOMMODATION

One of the more dramatic examples of the adaptability of human beings to given conditions and situations has been the past accommodation of many subordinate groups to their less-than-equal status with minimal signs of overt conflict. Racially oppressed groups, whether in the United States or in other parts of the world, have seldom challenged the inequities. As Berry and Tischler stated:

69

> It is an amazing fact . . . that some human beings have an infinite
> capacity to endure injustice without retaliation, and apparently
> without resentment against their oppressors. Instances . . . are nu-
> merous, and they come from every part of the world where one
> group dominates another. Militant leaders of protest movements
> have been driven to despair by the apathy. . . . Members of domi-
> nant groups have often commented on the cheerfulness and loy-
> alty . . . among those who would seem to have no reason for such
> sentiments. (1978:387)

The ability of the oppressed to mask their resentment and hostility,
and the inability of the majority to perceive beyond their stereotypes
have combined to prolong some of the more common sayings of the past,
such as "Our Negroes are always happy," "The Japanese are content
behind barbed wire," "Indians enjoy reservation life," and "The Chinese
like it in Chinatown."

Even under terrible conditions, humans have adjusted with relative
docility, so that the death ovens at Buchenwald and the World War II
concentration camps for Japanese Americans were characterized by the
lack of overt resistance on the part of the majority. Perhaps it is the
idealism of the oppressed that both sustains and destroys.

This chapter will review some of the consequences of our racial
stratification system and will focus on the adaptation of the minorities to
their subordinate position in society.

Conflict

One important question of intergroup relations concerns conflict.
Does conflict always follow the meeting of diverse groups? There does
appear to be some type of conflict in almost all interethnic contacts, as
Berry and Tischler found:

> . . . even before the dawn of history, primitive bands were moving
> over the face of the earth, encountering strange peoples, and tres-
> passing upon their lands. Archaeologists suspect that these prehis-
> toric contacts resulted in wars and bloodshed, and in the destruction
> and displacement of one group by another. Historic evidence sup-
> ports such guesses, and indicates that conflict of some sort is a
> common occurrence when unlike peoples meet. (1978:117)

But as we indicated in Chapter 2, there are a variety of outcomes
when different people meet. A "conflict-free" adaptation seems to be
difficult to achieve, although not always, as the following example shows.

The Tungus and the Cossacks. Lindgren (1938) published a report in
1932 about two racially and culturally different groups, the Tungus and
the Cossacks, who resided as neighbors without any apparent conflict.

The Tungus were Mongolian nomads who lived off the reindeer and hunted for their sustenance. The Cossacks were Caucasoid descendants of the Russians who invaded Asia at an earlier time. They were Christian village-dwellers who relied primarily on agriculture and stock-raising for their livelihood. Hypothesized reasons for the lack of apparent conflict between these groups included the following:

1. The numbers of both groups were small (less than 1,000) and of approximately equal size.
2. There was little competition for land and resources. There was ample room for both groups to practice their own different ways of making a living.
3. The outside influences were of a nature that drew the groups together. For example, in 1908, the Chinese government imposed taxes upon the fur trade of the Cossacks, which affected the Tungus too. Therefore, both groups viewed themselves as being oppressed by an outside force.
4. The two cultures established a supplementary and complementary relationship, rather than one based on antagonism and competition.
5. Neither group thought itself racially superior. They respected each other's attitudes, values, and cultural practices such as marriage, use of land, and property.

If these factors are the key to peaceful intergroup neighborliness, this kind of harmony would be difficult to duplicate in today's world. Size has become virtually uncontrollable, and numerical equality is almost never a reality. Perhaps even more important, power relationships between groups are usually unbalanced. Technology, specialization, and urbanization have created increased competition for space, housing, employment, and shrinking resources; and our economic system values competition over cooperation. Race and color are divisive symbols, and the feeling of white superiority and the development of a stratification system built upon color has limited any dreams of racial equality and harmony.

There is a great need for systematic research to explore those variables that affect race relationships. For example, is it possible to predict the consequences of change by using the Tungus and Cossacks as a model? What would be the effect of competition on scarcer resources? How would urbanization and a change in the economic system affect race relations? Would a change in numbers or the balance lead to increased conflict? What would happen if one group began to feel superior? Because social scientists cannot bring large groups into a laboratory to test their hypotheses, they must rely on field studies and sophisticated observations for information.

Any analysis of intergroup relations can be misleading if the research

covers only a narrow period of time. Even the most conflicting relationships, whether in marriage, international relations, or interracial contacts,
will have periods of relative tranquility. Therefore, the assumption that
the Tungus and Cossacks are a "conflict-free" example may be erro-
neous. Finally, some forms of conflict are difficult to assess because they
are not obvious. Groups may internalize conflict and give only intangible
evidence of it.

Conflict as a value question. The idea of a conflict-free adaptation
reflects a value orientation and goes back to our discussion of the functional and conflict perspectives. Horton (1971) referred to the biases
based on one or the other position and asserted that many social scientists
are apparently unaware of their own values. For example, Freudian
terminology arises from an upper bourgeois patriarchal group with a
strong sexual and individualistic orientation; American sociologists' anal-
yses of social problems before 1940 reflect a small, rural town bias; and
much current contemporary analysis reflects the researchers' experiences
under bureaucratic and administrative organizations.

Horton contrasted the two approaches to social problems. Conflict
theory focuses on the failure of the system to meet the needs of the
individual, whereas the functionalist sees the individual as not adjusted
to the system.

Explanations of ethnic problems invariably include the writer's values, ideology, and perspectives. "Terms like 'moral dilemma,' 'pluralism,' 'assimilation,' and 'integration' describe motives for desirable action: they are definitions placed on human action, not the action
independent of social values" (Horton, 1971:31). The error is not that
the scientist thinks in these terms, but that he or she *is not aware of it.*
The comfort of "objectivity" is an untenable myth. The idea of a "conflict-free" adaptation between ethnic groups may in reality reflect only
the values of the researcher, rather than any "outside" phenomenon.

Since there are at least two viewpoints from which to assess conflict,
it is interesting to note which position is chosen. Those who choose the
majority perspective often see minority groups as deviant, disorganized,
in great conflict, and as examples of social problem behavior. Others,
writing from a minority perspective, see the conflict as noble, militant,
and having high moral justification.

Means-ends dilemma. Merton (1957) suggested a relationship between societal structures and individual responses. Merton's theory was
designed to discover how some "social structures exert a definite pressure upon certain persons in the society to engage in nonconforming
rather than conforming conduct" (Merton, 1957:132). Merton's theory
consists of several elements, including culturally defined goals, acceptable modes of reaching those goals, anomie, and types of adaptation. It

attempts to demonstrate the importance of sociological variables in creating deviant behavior.

For example, success (the goal) in American terms may mean acquiring material wealth. If the pressures towards this goal are exceptionally strong, then considerations of how to attain the goal (the means) may become less important. When the technically most effective procedure takes precedence over culturally approved values or institutionally prescribed conduct, the society becomes unstable, or to use Durkheim's term, it is in a state of "anomie" or normlessness.

There are numerous examples. In competitive athletics the strain towards winning might include deliberate attempts to injure a "star" opponent or to subsidize and recruit athletes by bending rules and redefining the game so that winning, no matter what the costs, becomes more important than participation. Those athletes who show faint twinges of conscience and protest their innocence when caught in illegal acts demonstrate that they are familiar with the institutional rules of the game but have deliberately ignored them in order to win.

Merton's model may be appropriate to ethnic groups. Minorities strive for the same success goals as other groups in American society do, but the barriers of racism limit their access by legitimate means. The resultant strain may lead to high levels of anomic behavior, including retreatism, rebellion, and overconformity.

Class and ethnic stratification systems from this perspective are not the critical factors in creating strain; rather, strain results more from the defeat and disappointment of heightened expectations. Presumably, under slavery, in which an individual did not expect to become "successful" in general societal terms, there was less stress than under the current conditions, which creates an obvious incongruence.

In this chapter we shall discuss minority-group responses to prejudice, discrimination, and segregation. These adaptations are the dependent variables to dominant group actions. The three hypothesized responses are (1) acceptance of their dominated status; (2) aggression, fighting back, and attempts to change the system; and (3) avoidance (Simpson & Yinger, 1965).

ACCEPTANCE

Perhaps the most common adaptive pattern of ethnic minorities has been their seeming acceptance of subordinate status. The power relationships may leave them almost no alternative; and even if many minorities may not really believe in the superiority of the white person, most often they act as if they do.

It is necessary to hypothesize several motivations to explain this pattern. Perhaps the most important is the desire to be like the majority group; conformity to dominant-group role prescriptions is a primary goal. Another important factor is that most minorities prefer the "means" of the American system—law and order, conformity, conflict-free adaptation, and a "don't rock the boat" attitude. No matter what the provocation, an ethnic individual's response is primarily acceptance. It would be considered poor form to do otherwise.

Finally, the reality for many has been adaptation and socialization to vertical structures (the family), so that lower positions on a stratification system are reasonably congruent with existing and expected realities. The unfairness of a racial stratification system in which color determines one's position (and is quite permanent) remains the chief irritant.

Certain subcultural values that lead to acceptance are another factor. The "fate orientation," expressed by the Japanese as *shikataganai* ("it can't be helped") or by Latin Americans as *que será, será* ("what will be, will be"), encourages this type of adjustment. There is also the belief in some cultures that hardship and suffering are important ingredients of character building, and the stoic, accepting response is a test of one's nature.

Forms of acceptance vary: ritualistic behavior, superpatriotism, and the internalization of stress are three of them.

Ritualistic Adaptation

Ritualistic adaptation is scaling down or abandoning high cultural goals and retaining the moralistic prescriptions of the society. Therefore, persons in this situation lower their level of aspiration: "He is playing safe," "She's not sticking her neck out," and "He's not shooting for the stars." They will conform to the mandates of the larger society and will socialize their children accordingly. Merton hypothesized that ritualism may be most appropriate to the lower-middle class; the person who always goes by the rules and the bureaucratic mind are examples of ritualistic adaptation. It also appears as one of the dominant adaptations for ethnic minorities.

By ritualism, minority groups retain a faith that some of the means and norms in the system will guarantee their acceptability. For example, many ethnics vote faithfully with the expectation that their participation in this procedure is significant. Voting, however, does not basically change the system, unless the minority has achieved power through political and organizational maneuvers. Then, of course, it is no longer a minority, in a political sense.

The ballot has been used by the majority group as a tool for discrimination. Californians of previous eras voted for restrictions on the immigration of Chinese and for alien land laws to deny the ownership of land to the Japanese. Current referendums, often deceptively worded, attempt to foster racist practices through the ballot. The problem of the popular ballot is that it is a two-edged sword, and if one group has numerical superiority, its power can be used to strengthen its position at the expense of the minority.

Superpatriotism

Another means of adapting to the problems of isolation from a system is to overidentify with it. The rituals of belonging—learning the anthems and slogans, copying the slang, adopting the dress and the styles—are an important part of the acculturation of nonwhite groups.

The dynamics of ritualism often include incongruous actions. For example, many Japanese who were placed in the wartime "relocation" centers maintained a strict loyalty to the United States. The Pledge of Allegiance, "The Star-Spangled Banner," and the American flag became extremely important to them, and many purchased war bonds and donated quantities of blood. Others even volunteered for the army and eventually gave their lives for "democracy" while their parents, brothers, and sisters were still behind barbed wire. They practiced these rituals believing that these actions would prove to the larger world that they too were Americans.

Internalization of Stress

Another form of acceptance is the internalization of stress. To grit one's teeth and accept reality is considered to be mature in some cultures. From a psychoanalytic perspective, the internalization and repression may have dysfunctional effects upon the individual. For example, in the Japanese population, there is a high incidence of such internal disorders as stomach ulcers and bowel problems. (My father used to relate how when walking in San Francisco, he would be deliberately shoved off the sidewalk by white bullies. Rather than venting his anger, he would internalize his feelings by gritting his teeth and using the Japanese concept of *ga-man*—accepting whatever one is dealt. It was considered more mature to draw in one's breath and not cry, complain, or strike back.) Stress is a killer among blacks.

The major decisions on acceptance are made by the majority. They can prescribe the conditions by which ethnic members live and react, and they can make those stringent and arbitrary conditions that strain the level of acceptance to the breaking point. History shows how difficult it is for groups in command to understand that their intelligent use of power is the most important factor in the survival of their system. The old adage tying power and corruption remains a true one.

The basic dynamic of internalization is the lack of overt cues exhibiting discomfort and hurt. Insensitive dominant-group members often misinterpret this "quietness" as a reason for maintaining a racial status quo, and even heretofore "nonproblem" minorities (for instance, some Asian groups) are beginning to perceive that the "squeaky-wheel" model will gain more attention.

AGGRESSION

Aggression generally includes some kind of retaliation. Aggression takes many forms: it may be a direct retaliation to the dominant group; it may mean striking out at more vulnerable groups; or it may be so masked as to be barely detectable.

At an earlier time, the lack of overt aggression was often taken as a sign of contentment, especially among slaves. More recent interpretations of slave adjustment have revealed the indirect and hidden ways in which less powerful groups often show their hostility to and resentment of their plight. For example, Powdermaker (1943) coined the term "aggressive meekness" to illustrate a style of adapation that masks the true thoughts and feelings of slaves in their overtly meek and submissive public role.

Aggression can be classified into four kinds: direct, indirect, displaced, and a change of goals.

Direct Aggression

Direct aggression grows out of acute despair. The power arrangements are such that most ethnics see little hope of gaining much through this approach. The resources of the dominant group are truly impressive, especially when compared to those of the minorities. Money, numbers, firepower, legal justification, and institutional resources are so clearly under the control of the majority that only under unusual circumstances will minorities direct their aggression at the dominators.

Insurrections. An insurrection uses armed force against the established order. The main differences among insurrections, rebellions, and revolutions are those of purpose, size, and scope.

Racial insurrections have been frequent in the history of the United States. Contrary to some interpretations of American history that emphasize the contentment of the slaves, there were constant plots, though never seriously threatening the institution of slavery, that caused much concern to the white population (Aptheker, 1943; Carroll, 1938; Franklin, 1948).

Denmark Vesey purchased his freedom in 1800. He established himself as a carpenter in Charleston, South Carolina, and for twenty years lived as a respectable "free Negro" and enjoyed a relatively comfortable existence. He was, however, a sensitive person, and he was unhappy over his own freedom and success while others of his race were in slavery. He therefore set about to plot a revolt. His plans were carefully laid, and his associates were chosen with utmost scrutiny. Over a period of years they collected their weapons—daggers, bayonets, and pike heads. The second Sunday in July, 1822, was set as the date for the revolt. The whites, however, were informed, and Vesey hastily moved the date ahead one month.

His assistants, scattered as they were for miles around Charleston, did not all get the word, and the insurrection was readily quashed. Estimates of the number of blacks involved in the plot ran as high as 9,000. About 139 were arrested, 47 of whom were condemned. Four white men were imprisoned and fined for implication in the plot and for encouraging the blacks. (Berry, 1978:133)

Nat Turner was a slave who belonged to a Virginia planter, Joseph Travis. He was a mystic who felt a divine call to free his people. The solar eclipse of February, 1831, convinced him that the time had come for him to deliver the slaves from bondage. The date was to be the Fourth of July; but Turner became ill, and he postponed the date until he should see another divine sign. On August 13, 1831, it seemed to him that the sun turned "a peculiar greenish blue," and he therefore chose August 21 as the date for the revolt. He and his followers began by killing their master and his family, and then roamed the countryside destroying other whites. Within twenty-four hours a total of sixty whites had been killed. State and federal troops were called, and the slaves were speedily overwhelmed. More than a hundered slaves were killed in the encounter, and thirteen slaves and three free blacks were immediately hanged. Turner himself was captured two months later and was promptly executed. (Berry, 1978:134)

Novelist William Styron's fictionalized account of Nat Turner's rebellion was an immediate success; it was reviewed in major publications and was a Book of the Month Club selection. However, a most dramatic adverse reaction came from members of the black intellectual community; most felt that Styron's Nat Turner bore little resemblance to the real man and instead saw a racist caricature of a black slave, motivated by lust for white women.

Hamilton declared:

We will not permit Styron's "meditation" to leave unchallenged an image of Nat Turner as a fanatical black man who dreams of going to bed with white women, who holds nothing but contempt for his fellow blacks, and who understands, somewhat, the basic human desire to be free but still believes in the basic humanity of some slaveholders.

We will not permit Styron to picture unchallenged Nat Turner as a leader who did not understand that the military defeat should not be confused with the ideological victory: i.e., a blow for freedom. The rebellion of 1831, led by Nat Turner, is important today for blacks to understand and for whites to accept precisely because its lesson is that there will be leaders who *will* rise up—against all odds—to strike blows for freedom against an oppressive, inhumane system. And there can be no refuge in the thought that Turner felt himself divinely inspired or waited for signs from heaven, etc. The important thing is that the desire for human freedom resides in the

black breast as well as in any other. No amount of explicating about
the harshness of slavery or the gentleness of slavery, about the
docility of the masses of slaves, etc. can keep that desire from
exploding. Man—black or white or yellow or red—moves to maximize his freedom: That is the lesson of Nat Turner that Styron did
not deal with. (Hamilton, 1968:74)

Race riots. Rioting is as old as history. It is a temporary outbreak,
mostly spontaneous, of mass disorder. Racial antagonisms are not necessarily the sole occasions for riots. Rioting, often involving more than
one side, is more of an urban phenomenon and is different from insurrections, rebellions, or revolutions in that there is no overt intention of
overthrowing the existing political order.

The history of the United States is dotted with race riots. In 1837,
over 15,000 Bostonians participated in an Irish riot; black-white riots
were constant from three decades before the Civil War to the present.
Longres, Roberts, and Shinn (1966) analyzed race riots in the twentieth
century and included some of the more prominent: Springfield, Illinois,
1908; East St. Louis, 1917; Washington, D.C., 1919; Chicago, 1919; Los
Angeles, 1943; Detroit, 1943; Harlem, 1943; New York, 1964; Rochester,
1964; and Los Angeles, 1965. One interesting pattern emerged—the earlier riots were generally characterized by the whites being the aggressors
with a reversal of roles over time. Most of the injured and arrested were
black.

The Watts riots of August 11–17, 1965, probably marked a watershed
in recent race relations. As Daniels and Kitano found:

> Watts was not the first riot—there had been serious disturbances in
> seven Eastern cities the summer before—but it was the first that
> appeared to have the character of a rebellion. Perhaps the most
> surprising thing about it was that it happened in Los Angeles, which,
> only the year previous, had been ranked by the National Urban
> League as most favorable to Negroes of sixty-eight American cities
> examined. Although the riots have been widely studied, there is no
> consensus among its students, but the basic facts are reasonably
> clear.
>
> On the evening of August 11, 1965, the Negro ghetto of Los
> Angeles erupted into a flurry of outbreaks of mob violence, at first
> centered near (but not in) a small area known as Watts; it soon
> spread over much of the vast ghetto. It was set off by a seemingly
> routine arrest of a drunken driver; it produced 144 hours of anarchic
> looting, arson, assault, and homicide. This happened in an area that
> supposedly had exemplary race relations. More than half the Negro
> population of the state lived in Los Angeles County (461,000 as
> enumerated by the 1960 Census), most of them in the overcrowded
> South Los Angeles ghetto that sprawled over some fifty square
> miles. The housing there was (and remains) substandard. It consists

of one- and two-story single and multifamily structures, most of which have at least the hint of a lawn. About half were built before World War II, which is very old for Los Angeles housing. Many of these units, however, are sound and well maintained. These atypical ghetto conditions made it possible for civic leaders (including some Negro leaders) to insist that the city had no real race-relations problem, a kind of dream state peculiarly appropriate to a region that boasts Hollywood and Disneyland. Similar wishful thinking prevailed in the same quarters during much of the Great Depression, when local leaders tried to maintain that Los Angeles was the economic "white spot" of the nation. Reality finally punctured both illusions; both however, like most illusions, had some basis in reality. As bad as conditions were for the white emigrés of the 1930s—think of Steinbeck's Joads—and are for the Negro newcomers now, they are distinctly better than the conditions they left behind. But in all too many instances these conditions have not lived up to the expectations of the new arrivals, and it is these partially thwarted expectations that have made California, and other Northern and Western "promised lands," sociological and political powder kegs, with a markedly lower flash point than the objective conditions within them might suggest.

If the Watts riots seem similar to earlier ethnic violence, that similarity is largely superficial. The most obvious difference is that the earlier violence had been that of a majority directed against a particular minority. The Watts riots (and similar events in other cities) saw a minority—really a small minority within a minority—lash out blindly against the society which, it seemed to them, was oppressing them intolerably. (Historically it would probably be more accurate to suggest that society was not easing its restrictions as fast as expectations were rising.) Another difference is that these riots were largely directed against property, and quite often Negro-owned and occupied property. The aggressors were almost all Negroes, and so, ironically, were most of the victims.

The ingredients for the Watts and other riots—apart from mimesis after Watts—were simple: an alienated group squeezed into a small ghetto. Within that group there are growing numbers (almost all the estimates are too small) of undereducated, underskilled, and therefore unemployed youths in a nation with the greatest educational system in the world. In Los Angeles the ghetto is not an area of abject poverty—about 60 percent of the population get some kind of welfare, and California standards are relatively high—but of apathy, resentment, and hopelessness. These ingredients were detonated, in Los Angeles, by a casual incident which resulted in an opportunity for some to lash back at society in general and the police in particular, and gave many, many more a chance for vicarious pleasure in watching them do it.

That this widespread alienation exists so noticeably at a time when Negroes seem to be making such great strides, has puzzled and perplexed many, but it should be quite clear that although the social revolution that John Kenneth Galbraith has dubbed "affluence" has affected the American Negro, North and South, not nearly enough of it has trickled down. But within the same society that sees many Negroes achieving upward social mobility and a few grasping political and economic power, there are within most Negro communities large numbers of socially alienated young men and women, children of the welfare state at its worst, who have neither known extreme economic deprivation nor ever experience a "normal" family life. They have not even been able to indulge in the humblest aspect of the American Dream, *the reasonable expectation that their children would have a chance to better themselves.* It was these people who made and enjoyed the Los Angeles riots, and the many similar incidents that have followed. (Daniels & Kitano, 1970:82–84)

Strikes and boycotts. Strikes and boycotts are more often associated with economic conflict and labor disputes than with racial interaction. Nevertheless, these forms have also been used and vary in their effectiveness.

One of the most effective boycotts in recent history was that involving Martin Luther King and the Montgomery, Alabama, bus system. The incident started on December 1, 1965, when a black seamstress, Mrs. Rosa Parks, refused to give up her seat and move to the back of the bus when ordered to do so by the bus driver. By the time the blacks called off the boycott approximately one year later, black patronage of the bus lines had dropped as much as 90 percent; Dr. King was found guilty of an illegal boycott and was fined and sentenced to jail. The case was referred to the Supreme Court; on November 13, 1966, the United States Supreme Court declared that the Alabama law requiring the segregation of buses was unconstitutional.

Boycotts and strikes have been used on both sides and in a variety of different ways. Early Californians were urged to boycott "Jap" businesses; often Chinese and Japanese laborers were used as strike breakers, and the Japanese often banded together to boycott certain white establishments known to be antioriental.

Air highjacking. A newer form of aggression has been the threat to blow up or to kidnap airplanes in order to effect change. It is based on the old principle of ransom and blackmail, in which one group attempts to extract concessions from another group by holding something of value.

The motivations for highjacking vary—personal profit, the release of political prisoners, the dramatization of the plight of a pariah group, or a change in a dominant group's policy. The tactics are usually a desperate attempt by a powerless group to equalize the power differential, if only temporarily, and its effectiveness to bring about long-term change is open to question. The precautions instituted by air lines as a response to the threat of bombing and highjacking indicate the vulnerability of more powerful groups to such acts.

Other recently revived forms of showing dissatisfaction include kidnappings, ransom notes, death threats, bomb threats, reprisals, and human sacrifice. As with most desperate acts, the lasting effects for bringing about change using these strategies remain questionable.

A more typical method of handling aggressive feelings is through indirect actions. Much indirect aggression must be inferred and therefore suffers the limitations of interpretation. Nevertheless, it is an important adaptation, since it may invite less retaliation than a direct act would.

Indirect Aggression

Fine arts and literature. Writers, poets, painters, musicians, and actors often deal with oppression and interracial relationships in their own fashion. Black writers such as Richard Wright, LeRoi Jones, and James Baldwin were able to convey their message of conflict and suffering to much larger audiences. Utilizing the fine arts as weapons of protest is not limited to the American black. Perhaps all oppressed peoples do so, even the preliterate peoples.

Ethnic humor. Ethnic humor is another important way of dealing with conflict. The "put on," the "bad mouth," and ethnic jokes are all attempts to find a more socially acceptable way of handling conflict and aggression. The number and continued popularity of jokes about the Jews, Negroes, Italians, Irish, Chinese, Japanese, Poles, and Mexicans can be viewed as symptomatic of the use of humor to handle aggression.

There is a hypothesized pattern of ethnic humor that is related to the cohesion, identity, and perceived acceptance of a group. The pattern takes two different forms.

The first form is humor directed against the oppressor. The first stage is so disguised that only in-group members perceive the butt of the jokes. As the group feels more comfortable, the humor becomes much more overt—the disguise is replaced by euphemisms, then eventually by direct references. The final stage occurs when the humor is not limited to ethnic-group audiences but is shared with the oppressor.

The second form is humor by the ethnic group about itself. The first stage is private and confined to the membership; this is followed by a more public display, but still within a localized group. As the group gains acceptance, a fellow ethnic member may feel comfortable enough to carry the humor outside the group. The final stage in this pattern occurs when the ethnic group is able to tolerate a nonethnic member telling ethnic jokes.

This proposed series may help to explain the sensitivities of various ethnic groups to jokes and stereotypes; not all groups are at the same stage, and what is considered appropriate for one group may be offensive to another.

Passive resistance. Another means of forestalling overt conflict is passive resistance. The origins of passive resistance are probably as old as humans themselves, and phrases such as "turn the other cheek" or Martin Luther King's exhortation to his followers, "Face violence if necessary, but refuse to return violence" indicate its philosophical underpinnings.

The name most intimately linked to passive resistance is Mohandas K. Gandhi, and more recent followers such as Reverend King acknowledged Gandhi's influence. There is a strong oriental aura in passive resistance as well as elements of stoicism and internalization.

Job slowdowns, turnover, inefficiency, tardiness. Simpson and Yinger (1965) mentioned several variations of aggression that are forms of passive resistance. One is the job slowdown, in which ethnic members may work extremely slowly; another is "carelessness," in which objects are accidentally dropped and broken. Irresponsibility, shoddy work, and inefficiency also are ways in which minorities react against the dominant system. Dominant group reactions provide an interesting commentary on the dominant group's perceptions. Instead of linking some of these actions to aggression, there is a tendency to characterize and stereotype the minority culture as careless, sloppy, or accident prone. Some even advance a genetic inferiority explanation.

Other techniques of indirect aggression include high labor turnover, tardiness, and unreliability. Suddenly walking off a job or coming in late and then leaving early fall into this category. A practice that makes producers and coordinators of programs uncontrollably angry is when ethnics agree to participate in a program, then cancel at the last minute, or do not show up at all; if they do show up, they may make a number of outrageous demands as the price of their participation.

Role changes. Another indirect means of handling aggression is either to withdraw or to change the forms of racial roles. For example, ethnic individuals may suddenly change their deferential pattern in a social situation and ask to be served first, or they may publically challenge the opinions of majority-group members at unusual times, or they may exaggerate their ethnic role in a manner calculated to embarrass a majority-group member. Cohen (1958) gave an example of how a form of military etiquette, the hand salute, can mask aggressive feelings. By overconforming one can strain the system; ten enlisted men saluting separately can force ten response salutes from a single passing officer.

Behavioral patterns at variance with expected roles can also be a means of indirect aggression. The stereotype of the welfare mother with a Cadillac and a color TV (if there are such people) is an example of an aggressive response through behavior not normally expected of individuals in this category. The outraged reactions of society to this stereotype indicates the reciprocal feelings held by many against those who do not follow prescribed norms for "poor" people.

Some ethnic groups handle aggression through high achievement and competitive excellence. Instead of carelessness, indifference, and inefficiency, they may handle their aggression by sublimating their drives and outperforming members of the dominant group.

Displaced aggression. The displacement of aggression is similar to scapegoating. Displacement may occur within a group, making fellow ethnic members targets for much hostility and aggression. Often without realizing that discrimination, segregation, and prejudice are the major problems, minorities consider each other to be the cause of their frustrations. Other minorities can also be targets of displaced aggression, such as in squabbles over the funding of poverty programs.

Change of goals. Perhaps the most revolutionary and rebellious action of the ethnic minorities has been to change their goals. The narrow goal of "being white" and its variations, including integration, no longer have the almost universal support that they once had. The unrealistic goal of becoming white, with its subsequent strains and anomie, has been replaced by newer goals. Many of these goals are still not clearly articulated, but major variations include pluralism and separatism.

Much of the action has come in the form of organized protests. There has developed a wide variety of social movements—from highly emotional, religious, and nationalistic movements to those that use sophisticated legal, political, and economic weapons. In the black group alone are such diverse groups as the NAACP, the Urban League, CORE, the Black Panthers, and the Black Muslims. Some movements are dedicated to changing the goals, and others strive to open the American system to include more people of color; most have reacted to the stresses caused by the barriers that limit the participation of ethnics in American democracy.

AVOIDANCE

Because of the difficulty in abolishing racial barriers, as well as the penalties of active aggression, many ethnics adapt by avoiding the problem altogether. Avoidance covers two broad types of adaptation: (1) withdrawing from most forms of interracial contact and (2) assimilating, denying, or retreating from the intolerable situation.

For example, ethnics may avoid situations in which they may face prejudice in housing by not applying in certain areas; they may walk across the street rather than face even the simplest communication with someone from the majority group. They may use certain lotions or cosmetics that enable them to "pass"; or they may resort to drugs or withdraw into mental illness.

According to Simpson and Yinger (1965:159), the most complete form of avoidance is withdrawing entirely from the minority group. "Passing," however, is quite difficult for most ethnics because of the color line. By changing their names and accents and by altering their physiological features, some ethnics hope to pass into the larger community. Although there is always the fear of discovery, this is perhaps the most decisive way to avoid the penalties of ethnic status.

Some groups try to "seal off" contact. Sealing off can occur on different levels: the upper class of an ethnic group might voluntarily seclude itself from both lower-class members of its own ethnic group and members of the dominant group; other ethnic classes might form purposely segregated communities to limit contact with the majority. This type of adaptation is often insufficient because members remain dependent on the majority community for economic and other needs. Finally, some try to insulate themselves by remaining constantly mobile. Mobility may help limit interaction in some ways, but in the long run, it leads to greater exposure and higher intergroup contact.

The method of denial or repression means that an ethnic avoids racial problems by behaving as if he or she is no longer there. Instances of prejudice and discrimination are repressed; the individual instead focuses on the positives, so that racial realities are glossed over. Like most adaptive mechanisms, the degree of reality distortion remains important to the mental health of the perceiver.

Retreatism and withdrawal. Retreatism is the rejection of cultural goals and institutional means. People who retreat have dropped out; they may be in the society but are not part of it. They adapt to the problem through defeatism and resignation. Mental patients, pariahs, outcasts, vagabonds, tramps, chronic alcoholics, drug addicts, and hippies are examples of individuals and groups who have adopted a retreatist posture, because of their continued failure to reach a goal by legitimate means or by illegitimate means, caused by internalized and societal prohibitions. It is most often a private, rather than a group adaptation.

A large percentage of school drop-outs, mental patients, and drug addicts are ethnic children. Taking drugs is one of the oldest ways to escape from reality and to avoid conflict. But the ultimate retreat is mental illness—the flight into a world of dreams and fantasy. Schizophrenia and suicide are the most extreme examples of avoidance.

Not all forms of adaptation and aggression discussed in this chapter are direct results of prejudice, discrimination, and segregation. Hostility, aggressiveness, and conflict are present wherever there is human inter-action; even without racism, these behaviors would continue to exist. The range of coping behaviors used by individuals and groups is very wide; racism exacts a greater toll in ruined lives and potentials than is realized by those who consider it only morally unjustified or economically expensive.

BIBLIOGRAPHY

APTHEKER, HERBERT (1943). *American Negro Slave Revolts*. New York: Columbia University Press.

ATKINSON, J. W. (1964). *An Introduction to Motivation*. New York: Van Nostrand Reinhold.

BARTH, ERNEST and DONALD NOEL (1975). "Conceptual Frameworks for the Analysis of Race Relations: An Evaluation," in *Majority and Minority*, pp. 15–31, eds. Norman Yetmen and C. Hoy Steele. Boston: Allyn & Bacon.

BERRY, BREWTON AND HENRY TISCHLER. *Race and Ethnic Relations*, 4th ed. Boston: Houghton Mifflin. © 1978. All excerpts are reprinted by permission of the publisher.

CARROLL, JOSEPH C. (1938). *Slave Insurrections in the United States, 1800–1860*. Boston: Chapman and Grimes.

COHEN, JEHUDI (1958). "Some Aspects of Ritualized Behavior in Interpersonal Situations," *Human Relations*, 2:195–215.

DANIELS, ROGER and HARRY H. L. KITANO (1970). *American Racism: Exploration of the Nature of Prejudice*. © 1970. Englewood Cliffs, N.J.: Prentice-Hall, Inc. All excerpts are reprinted by permission of the publisher.

FRANKLIN, JOHN HOPE (1948). *From Slavery to Freedom*. New York: Knopf.

HAMILTON, CHARLES (1968). "Our Nat Turner and William Styron's Creation," in *William Styron's Nat Turner: Ten Black Writers Respond*, pp. 73–78, ed. John H. Clarke. Boston: Beacon Press.

HORTON, JOHN (1971). "Order and Conflict Theories of Social Problems as Competing Ideologies," in *Majority and Minority*, pp. 15–31, eds. Norman Yetman and C. Hoy Steele. Boston: Allyn & Bacon.

LINDGREN, ETHEL JOHN (1938). "An Example of Culture Contact without Conflict," *American Anthropologist*, 40(4):605–21.

LONGRES, JOHN, CAROL ROBERTS, and KENNETH SHINN (1966). "Some Similarities and Differences in Northern-Urban Race Riots Involving Negroes during the 20th Century" (unpublished master's thesis, University of California, Los Angeles).

MARDEN, CHARLES and GLADYS MEYER (1978). *Minorities in American Society* (5th ed.). New York: D. Van Nostrand.

MERTON, ROBERT (1957). *Social Theory and Social Structure* (rev. ed.), pp. 131–94. New York: Free Press.

POWDERMAKER, HORTENSE (1943). "The Channeling of Negro Aggression by the Cultural Process," *American Journal of Sociology*, 5(48):750–58.

SIMPSON, GEORGE EATON and J. MILTON YINGER (1965). *Racial and Cultural Minorities: An Analysis of Prejudice and Discrimination*. New York: Harper & Row, Pub.

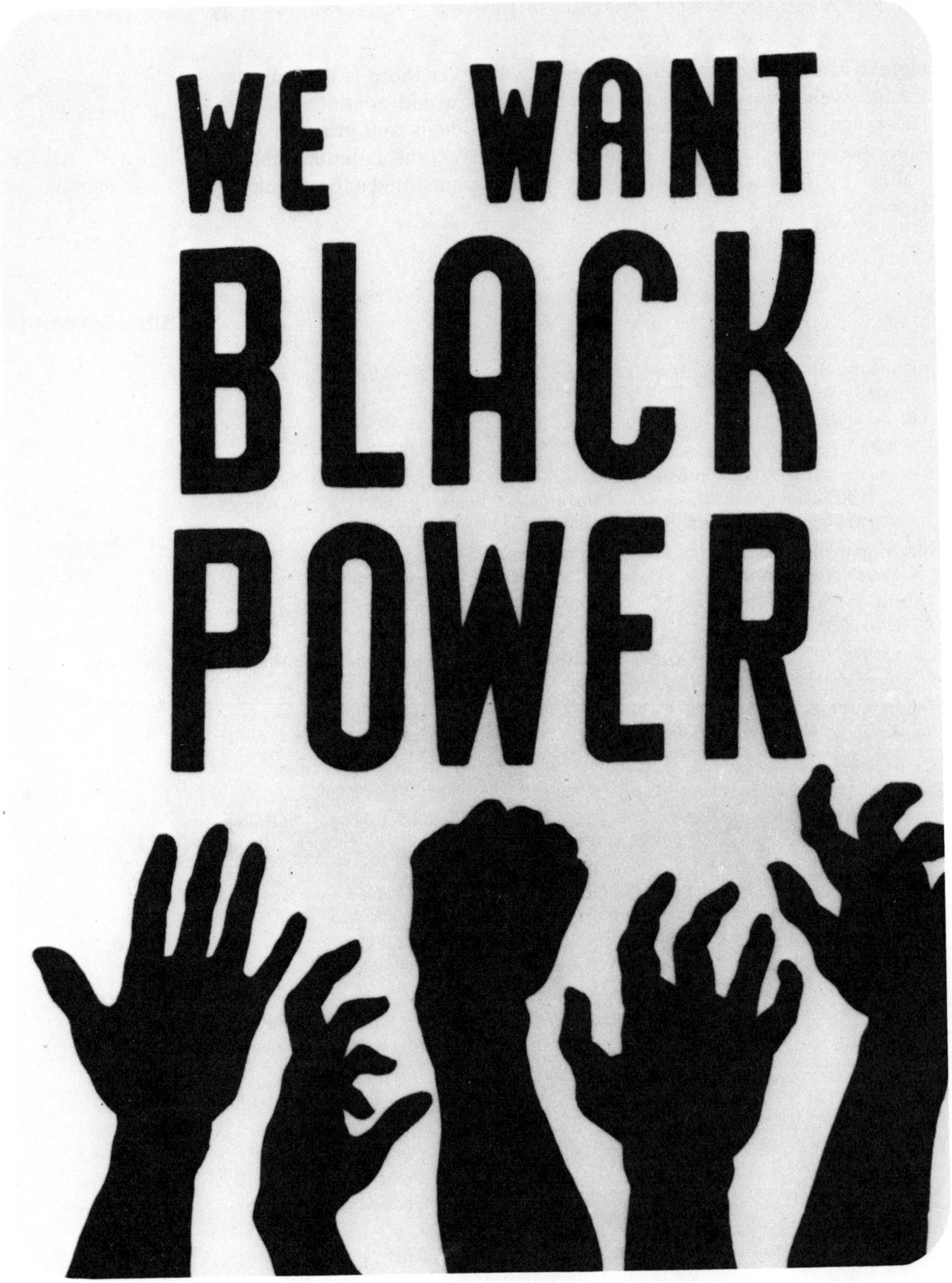
WE WANT
BLACK
POWER

IDENTITY

How an individual perceives and feels about self remains one of the most important consequences of racial stratification. It is individual identity that serves as the end result of a process of socialization that includes the family, the community, the ethnic group, and the society.

If discrimination, prejudice, segregation, and racism had no effect on the development of groups and individuals, whether of the minority or the majority, there would be little point in discussing them. It can be demonstrated, however, that racism raises formidable barriers to personal fulfillment and maturity. A newspaper article appearing in the *Washington Star* (1972) offered a relatively common story of interracial contact.

> *Lagos, Nigeria* (AP). Thirteen years in Britain, with education at Eton College, has left a Nigerian youth facing a cruel dilemma that many African blacks suffer when they go abroad. It is the problem of lost identity. "Who do I really belong to?" the youth asked in an article he wrote for a Nigerian newspaper. "I am virtually ashamed of my race and color. I have no desire to be white; but my mind is a hundred percent white. As a result, my parents and I do not speak the same language. I cannot picture the day when I will, if ever, return home to settle. . . . When people have amicably asked my name, I have no name. I have often actually replied: My friend, I have no name. My fellow blacks call me Uncle Tom. In

America they call me nigger, and in England they call me immigrant. . . ."

Although drawn from a different setting, this situation is similar to that of ethnic groups in the United States. The concept of an ethnic identity—the "who am I?"—is compounded by the essentially negative connotations saddled upon the questioner if he or she happens to have identifiable racial features at variance with what is considered "desirable" in the United States.

The problem of an overall identity, not just ethnic identity, is critical in modern society. The problem of identity is minor in more traditional cultures in which populations have remained relatively homogeneous and stable, and family names, villages, and neighborhoods have continued unchanged. But immigrants to the United States have been required to discard their ancestral and national identities and to adopt newer ones based on the image of the self-made individual. In addition, the highly mobile social system with heterogeneous populations and ever-changing life styles has made the problem of establishing one's identity very difficult in America. Some of the hypothesized correlates of the lack of identity include rootlessness, alienation, anomie, and confused self-concept.

Psychoanalyst Erik Erikson (1950) saw identity as the product of the interaction between self and the social environment. The internal organization of the self provides the framework from which the individual views the world; the environment provides the surrounding, the stimulus, and the input. The self goes through a number of developmental stages (oral, anal, genital) and the successful integration of each stage is important in achieving maturity.

Dai (1961) provided a perspective similar to Erikson's. The parents' love and security form the base from which the individual is socialized into the culture through an ever-widening perspective. Diverse group membership during adolescence offers exposure to various roles and role conflict; later stages include intimate sexual relationships and a sense of productivity through occupational accomplishment. The full personality is a result of the successful integration of the various stages.

The sociologist Gordon (1964) also was concerned with problems of identity. Figure 9 illustrates the various "layers" that comprise the core of an American identity. American identity includes race, religion, and national origin. The term *ethnic group* is used as the key to social psychological identity, and the individual's ability to come to grips with his or her race, religion, and nationality provides the tools for dealing with this identity.

Isaacs (1975) made one of the most comprehensive models of identity. He included: (1) body (physical characteristics, genetic structure,

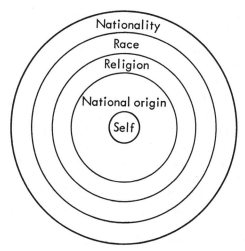

FIGURE 9

Identity of an American
Source: Gordon (1964:24)

skin color, hair texture, facial features), (2) name, (3) language (there are over 4,000 languages, each playing a particular role in the lives of people who speak it), (4) history and origins, and (5) religion and nationality. The search for a basic group identity has led to discarding larger unities.

Newman (1973) analyzed the role strain on members of minority groups when majority-group definitions are unfavorable. Strain occurs when the minority individual perceives the discrepancy between majority-group definitions and his or her own community's definitions of self.

ETHNIC AND RACIAL IDENTITIES

Racial identity is linked to skin color, physical identifiability, and a social definition of race. Because non-Europeans look different, they cannot participate fully in the American mainstream, and many attempt to formulate an identity that addresses the problem. One response is the hyphenated identity—the Chinese-American or the Japanese-American—which acknowledges that the racial attributes can not be readily discarded or erased. Because of their inescapable features, many understood that developing racial and cultural pride were important and tried to understand their own history and culture.

Ethnic identity, a broader term that includes the racial aspect, is a relatively new term. Glazer (1975) commented that the word ethnicity was not in the Oxford Dictionary of 1933. Patterson (1975) defined ethnicity as a condition in a society in which certain members choose and emphasize a cultural, racial, or national tie as their primary intrafamilial identity. An ethnic group exists only when members consider themselves to belong to such a group.

Greeley (1974) used the term *ethnogenesis,* which means the persistence of an ethnic-group identity among whites. Bell (1975) explained the resurgence of ethnicity among whites as a product of the new problems and new alignments induced by advanced industrial societies. With the onset of a postindustrial society, there develops a professional and technical stratum based on credentials and certification. The mechanisms for occupational advancement become increasingly difficult because of formalization and specialization; the political route becomes one of the few alternatives for individuals and groups without the requisite technical skills for mobility. In this sense, ethnic identification becomes a political unit for purposes of power and for obtaining a larger slice of the American pie.

Bell gave three reasons for the upsurge of ethnic identification: (1) the greater intermingling of people and the rise and growth of bureacracy; 2) the breakup of traditional structures and units, such as the nation and social class; and 3) the politicization of decisions. These changes have led people to look for smaller, more relevant units and organizations. Ethnic identity in this explanation is a strategic choice, rather than a primordial phenomenon deeply rooted in a group or individual, and its salience may fade in and out, depending on the circumstances.

Patterson (1975) observed that an ethnic identity can be understood only in terms of a dynamic and contextual view of group allegiances. A static descriptive ethnicity that attempts to isolate a set of characteristics or traits, including endless descriptive items of the culture, its festivals, and events, becomes an absurdity; ethnicity must be seen dynamically. Explaining some of the holidays and festivals held by Puerto Ricans is less relevant than their conscious use of different ethnic identities to serve their own best interests: ethnicity and blackness may be emphasized in an affirmative action setting, the Spanish language and culture in another, and a lighter skin color in another. Patterson's view is that people seldom make decisions on the basis of ethnic allegiance, but rather on economic and general class interests.

Pavlak (1976) found that among Mexican, Irish, Polish, Lithuanian, and Slovak samples in Chicago, there remained a strong ethnic identification into the second and third generations. The ethnicity persisted in political party affiliation and voting preference, and in attitudes and stereotypes toward blacks. The respondents held many stereotypical beliefs about the blacks ("They want something for nothing." "They should work and help themselves."), but they also showed sympathy for the black struggle if it did not come at the expense of their own gains.

Stein and Hill (1978) saw the new ethnicity of groups such as the Slovaks and Poles as a reversal of many of the assumptions of the

American dream. The parents and grandparents fled from older European patterns of authority, hierarchical structure, and group loyalty, but the new ethnic appears to want to return to more stringent cultural and religious settings. There seems to be a preference for stability and security over liberation and autonomy.

The quest for an identity among the new ethnics, which provides close bonds and ties, appears to be local and regional in orientation. It is different from the nonwhites' in that it is less self-conscious, less ideological, and less universal. The white ethnic movement of the late 1970s appears to be more a counterculture response to problems of the American dream than a return to contemplating one's ancestral roots.

It is interesting to compare the new white ethnics with the older nonwhite ethnics, since many of the reasons for turning to an ethnic identity appear similar. One difference has been the timing; most nonwhites perceived their inability to become a part of the American dream quite early and are therefore much further developed in the rationale and the rhetoric that accompanies a search for identity. But the basic difference is that of physical identifiability and the body, as mentioned by Isaacs, which includes skin color, facial features, and hair texture. The easy identification of the ethnic leads to an instant categorization that shapes much of the initial interactions in a color-conscious society. The unsuccessful integration of this variable can lead to repression, denial, avoidance, and gross distortions of identity. Shame of one's self and one's own background are detriments when dealing with the larger society. Attempts to alter one's image through operations (eye or hair straightening) are desperate attempts to alter the negative view of self.

Other variables making up an ethnic identity, such as cultural styles,

Stages in an Ethnic Identity for Racial Groups

FIGURE 10

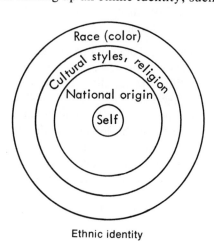

Ethnic identity

national origin, and religion, have been discussed in previous chapters and, although important, are not nearly as critical as race. Figure 10 illustrates the components that make up ethnic identity.

BARRIERS TO DEVELOPING ETHNIC IDENTITY

The major differences between the development of an identity between whites and nonwhites are in the background conditions that provide the ambiance for individual and group development. We label them as barriers and have identified five such background factors; we have also hypothesized seven steps in the development of a negative ethnic identity.

Barrier 1

Ideas about white superiority and racism arise from diverse sources. They include all the causes of prejudice and discrimination discussed in previous chapters. Removing all these causes will not necessarily have an immediate effect on race relations because of the racial attitudes that have become a part of our culture. The search for a cause or causes is not the most important step because of the impossibility of ever isolating such phenomena. But it is important to understand the background of American racism. This background affects the ethnic individual and ethnic group because it provides the context of racial categorization, classification, and role assignment.

Barrier 2

Relative to the number of overt and professed racists in the United States, the number of unverbalized and therefore "unknown" racists is extremely high. Kovel (1970) discussed three "ideal" types of racists and illustrated how historical changes have affected their styles:

The overt racist. This type openly professes his or her racism and is active in keeping nonwhites down. Kovel used the term "dominative racist," and the descriptions are familiar. The studies in *The Authoritarian Personality* (1950) described the "little man," whose life begins to revolve around external power and his hate relationship to people of color. He is apt to come from the lower middle class and both envies and hates those whites who are above him.[1]

When blacks were slaves, overt racists were better able to act out their dominative strategy, but they find it much more difficult in modern

---

[1] The popular TV show "All in the Family" depicts Archie Bunker as a prototype of the overt racist. See also: Theodor Adorno and others, *The Authoritarian Personality* (New York: Harper & Row, Publishers, Inc., 1950).

conditions. The prototype of the overt racist was Dennis Kearney (see Chapter 9); today he might be a member of the Ku Klux Klan or the American Nazi Party. But times have changed, and the actual number of overt, professed racists is probably not too large. There is little to gain from directly dominating another group, even if that were possible; the aversive racist is a true representative of today's problem.

The aversive racist. The aversive racist is much more responsive to the demands of the modern culture than the overt bigot is. Aversive racists may behave in exceedingly constructive and principled ways; they may give money and support civil rights causes, and will more often than not be on the "right" side of racial issues. But aversive racists always maintain a distance between themselves and people of color. Whereas dominative types desire personal ties with their victims, aversive types turn away and isolate themselves.

Kovel mentioned the early Quakers as one historical example of this type. Although they were among the first to attack slavery and to attend to the welfare of the blacks, they also retained their sense of aversion. Their cemeteries had separate sections for blacks, and no significant number of blacks participated in the society.

President Woodrow Wilson was another example. As Kovel pointed out:

> Wilson stated in 1912 that he wished to see "justice . . . to the colored people." Yet [he] equated white virtue with power. He did not hesitate to apply that power . . . despite [his previous] fine ideals. Wilson put the coup de grace to the misfortunes of black Americans by issuing an executive order which racially segregated the eating and toilet facilities of federal civil workers. (1970:31)

Wilson also gave Southern officials the right to discharge black employees on any ground they saw fit, and he unhesitatingly dismissed black criticism of his position.

Aversive racists often are highly educated—they may be persons of intelligence, style, and class. But when minority members get too close, they are apt to flee to the suburbs and worry excessively that "their daughter might marry one"; under extreme stress, they may regress into open bigotry.

Kovel feels that most Americans are either dominative or aversive racists, although there is an obviously broad overlap. There are racists who wish to oppress minorities either directly through domination or indirectly through avoidance. One is "hot," and generally comes from the South, the other is "cool" and comes from the North. When the "hot" one is provoked, he or she may resort to violence; when the "cool" one is faced with a problem, he or she tends to turn away or hide

behind a wall of restrictions and laws. Aversive racists may even fear
ethnic groups they have never met or ever will meet, and their behavior
will almost always ensure it. The number of Americans who fall into this
category must be very high.

The institutional racist. Some of the previous forms of racism have
become obsolete. Racism, which began as the direct domination of one
person over another, has evolved into a much more complex phenomenon. The terms *institutional racism* or *metaracism* (Kovel, 1970), reflect
this more subtle problem. The individuals who participate in it may not
be particularly racist themselves, but they reinforce and strengthen the
problem through their acquiescence in the racism of the larger cultural
order.

Because of its subtlety, it is one of the more difficult types of racism
to identify or combat. The prototype of metaracism, according to Kovel,
is the modern United States Army. This immensely powerful system has
incorporated and elevated many minorities, but its top echelons remain
almost all white. This racism takes a much more subtle form than leadership structure. It is the irony of the plight of the minority in this equal-
opportunity setting:

> Isn't [the Army] simply the mechanized—indeed the robotized—
> reduction of humanity to selfless tools of the will of culture, the
> grinding of both black and white into gray? Nowhere in our culture
> is there less freedom, less autonomy, less originality, joy and affir-
> mation; nowhere is there more cold calculation, more mindless
> regimentation, more dullness, more banality—and *more racial
> equality*. (Kovel, 1970:217)

Institutional racism exists in large corporations, unions, and bureaucracies. The need for token numbers of minorities often results in decent
employment for a few; there is little direct oppression, and certain real
gains can be observed. But in the long run, the metaracist structures may
be the most frightening. The state, bureaucracy, or corporation that
functions with computerized efficiency makes demands that in themselves are destructive. For in our culture, the worship of output and
production leads to some degree of equal treatment for minorities, but
the great bureaucracies and corporations need deadened and abstracted
beings in order to operate and therefore must police and control their
own populations.

A pamphlet entitled *Fact Sheets on Institutional Racism* (1975) demonstrated the high degree of white control and the insignificant number
of minorities in power positions in our major societal institutions. For
example, minority participation in business and farm equities, in the
stock exchange, in big business, in banks, in the control of major unions,
in the building trades, and in national corporations remains insignificant.

Similarly, minorities are left out of power positions in institutions of higher learning, in government, in the health and the legal professions, and in the mass media. Housing, education, and income remain as areas needing further work, and the ethnic individual seldom sees or expects the kind of visibility that will provide identifiable, realistic role models.

Most racist actions and thoughts are either denied or are transistory, and therefore they may not be an integral part of the personality of the average American. This is a corollary of Barrier 2. Many Americans make bigoted remarks, and racial slurs are a common part of our social system, but they may not necessarily be that deeply ingrained in the mind of the speaker. The notion that racial prejudice is ''bad'' and something to be denied indicates that the ''norms towards conformity'' may be working to the benefit of race relations. But one should also be aware that racism is taking on more modern and subtler forms.

    Barrier 3

Several other factors may serve to reduce racial divisions. There are alternate classification systems that dilute pure racial hostility, such as religion and social class. There is also the change of American goals to include variations of pluralism that may prove more tolerant of differences. Multiple minority groups can also serve to deflect attacks. Nevertheless, it will be rare for a minority-group member not to hear remarks about his or her inferiority and race undesirability. Rather than being taken for an American, the minority-group member suffers from stereotyping. The Asian American, whether of the second, third, or fourth generation, is asked how he or she likes it here in the United States; the Latino is stopped on the streets and asked for his or her ''papers''; and the legends about black sexuality have taken on heroic proportions.

Racist thoughts and actions are sufficiently widespread to maintain discriminatory restrictions. Aversive and institutional racism reflect the current barriers. The quest for equality by minority groups is blocked mainly by institutions and organizations. Pressure has come from the federal government through its equal opportunity and affirmative action programs, but there are constant counterpressures. The passage of Jarvis-Gann in California in 1978 and the Bakke decision, also in the same year, are reminders that significant segments of the population are not overly sympathetic to minority group aspirations and problems.

    Barrier 4

Formal and legal restrictions are one portion of the barrier; the informal network of social and fraternal organizations that reinforce racism are another, almost impregnable barrier. Issues such as local and

    Barrier 5

community control, public and private facilities, and school busing often have strong racial overtones. Social and fraternal organizations will be difficult to change under the present environment. For example, Bradshaw (1972) conducted a survey of private social clubs for the *Los Angeles Times*. Membership in these exclusive clubs has many benefits, such as a second home, a sense of status, a wide range of athletic activities, and important business, social, and political contacts. One of the overriding characteristics of these clubs was the racism that systematically excluded blacks, Chicanos, Asians, and Jews. The Los Angeles Country Club, located on one of the most valuable pieces of undeveloped real estate in the United States, was composed principally of elderly Anglo-Saxon whites who paid up to $25,000 to join. One member suggested that show-business people were excluded because if actors were to join, then their bosses, the Jewish studio heads, might also gain a foothold. The possibility of any nonwhite minorities becoming members remained very remote and unlikely.

The five barriers are the major input from the majority. The message comes through to the minority-group member from the mass media, the educational system, the political, legal, judicial, and economic systems, and even from members of his or her own group. Even though there are strong minority voices standing up for the integrity of the self and a positive identity for the ethnic individual, these voices are often drowned out by those who repeat, "You are inferior; you are less than a whole American."

DEVELOPMENT OF NEGATIVE IDENTITY

The five barriers represent the climate of racism; the following steps hypothesize how the process "takes," so that the actors on both sides of the stratification system begin to behave in accordance with some of the prescriptions. Relatively stable racial roles begin to develop through the power of the majority and the deference of the minority. The individual's identity is built upon continuity of experiences, expectations, performance in social interaction, and ability to read the cues for interaction. Entry into the role is complete when the role becomes a part of the individual's expectations, and these expectations are reaffirmed and validated in social interaction.

Step 1

Stereotyped minority-group behavior is learned in early childhood. The ability to differentiate between white people (and power) and one's own ethnic people is constantly learned and relearned. Conversely, white people learn about their "superiority" and fulfill the role of validating the "inferiority" of the ethnic. These roles are constantly reinforced by social and organizational interaction.

The ethnic child learns much from urban areas and types of residence; the less desirable areas and shabbier houses are linked to ethnics, while the dominant group lives in the better sections. Mass media, the school system, cultural heroes, and other models reinforce the image of a superior and desirable group distinct from the rest.

If these surroundings were not sufficient, childhood socialization in ethnic families is also geared towards the "realities of life." Richard Wright (1937) described how his mother taught him to live under Jim Crow, after he had been severely beaten by some white boys.

> When night fell my mother came from the white folks' kitchen. I raced down the street to meet her. I could just feel in my bones that she would understand. I knew she would tell me exactly what to do next time. I grabbed her hand and babbled out the whole story. She examined my wound, then slapped me.
>
> "How come yuh didn't hide?" she asked me. "How come yuh always fightin'?"
>
> I was outraged, and bawled. Between sobs I told her that I didn't have any trees or hedges to hide behind. There wasn't a thing I could have used as a trench. And you couldn't throw very far when you were behind the brick pillars of a house. She grabbed a barrel stave, dragged me home, whipped me naked, and beat me till I had a fever of one hundred and two. She would smack my rump with the stave and, while the skin was still smarting, impart to me gems of Jim Crow wisdom. I was never to throw cinders any more. I was never to fight any more wars. I was never, never, under any conditions, to fight white folks again. And they were absolutely right in clouting me with the broken milk bottle. Didn't I know she was working hard every day in the hot kitchens of the white folks to make money to take care of me? When was I ever going to learn to be a good boy? She couldn't be bothered with my fights. She finished by telling me that I ought to be thankful to God as long as I lived that they didn't kill me. (Wright, 1937:10)

The realization that the warm, loving parent perceives ethnics and "white folks" differently is often difficult for the ethnic child to handle. But the realities of the power differential are such that most ethnic parents socialize their children to recognize the color and the power differences. In most instances, such a pattern is deemed necessary for survival.

It may be easier to learn the realities of race from early childhood. The jolt of finding out that one is different and therefore less acceptable is always difficult, and this realization at a later age without previous preparation can be a severe trauma. For example, we have met many

Asians who had grown up on the East Coast "with little overt prejudice and discrimination" until they reached the age of serious dating and marriage. They then discovered that they were undesirable, and many of them have moved to areas in which there are more ethnics, such as Los Angeles, and have thoroughly immersed themselves in the ethnic community, isolating themselves from the white world.

Step 2

The stereotype of one's ethnic group is continually reaffirmed, especially in schools and on the job. As was pointed out earlier, the stereotypes often become the reality. Concepts such as the self-fulfilling prophecy, Skinner's operant conditioning, and other precepts of learning theory all are applicable—what minorities do and do not do in school, on the job, in their homes, and in their social interaction is shaped by the expectations and reinforcements of the more powerful group.

The mass media play an extremely important part in the process. Labeling and stereotyping are reinforced by discriminatory laws, prejudices, habits and customs; individuals and institutions shape the behavior of both the minority and majority according to the stereotype.

Step 3

Minority-group socialization has another dimension—socialization into one's own ethnic group. Very little research evidence is available in this area, but the duality of the socialization—behaving in one way in white society, and in another way with one's own group—is a part of growing up for all minorities. Perhaps, the freer, more exploratory type of self that develops with one's peers becomes part of the buffer that enables many minority-group individuals to grow up with an adequate view of self. Most members of the majority group never see this side of the minority group.

For example, the stereotype of the quiet, conforming, hard-working, highly motivated Japanese-American student is quite widespread. If one limits one's observations to the public schools, the observation appears valid. However, the behavior of many Japanese-American students in ethnic language schools cancels this image. The Japanese-language school that the author attended after the regular school day was often pure chaos. Shouting, profanity, book-throwing, cheating, rowdiness, and disorder were all widespread. The students often bragged about how many Japanese teachers they had been able to drive out of the profession. Interviews with current Japanese-American students indicate that some of this behavior still persists in ethnic schools. Kingston (1976) made a similar observation concerning Chinese-American students attending Chinese schools.

Ethnics are forced to employ multiple identities and roles. Not only do they have to adjust to the normal societal roles in their families and in their jobs, but they also have to come to terms with their subordinate ethnic status. Ethnics must be careful about going to certain places, filling certain positions, performing out of the generally prescribed roles; they must remain wary in social situations. For example, a cross-country automobile journey may call for much more careful planning by ethnics in order to avoid embarassing situations. Ethnics often choose "first class" hotels and restaurants (despite the additional expense) to forestall possible stressful incidents.

Conversely, majority-group members are more able to develop a single, universal identity. Dominant-group members do not have to be as careful since their position allows them to perform in a consistent manner. Others generally have to adapt to them. They define the situation and are in control of the interaction. They therefore can travel throughout the world secure in their status and can interact with others on a fairly predictable basis. The picture of domineering, aggressive Americans ("ugly Americans") who "come on strong" no matter where they are, is an example of individuals who generally are used to having their way.

Clues to feelings about ethnicity, self, and the treatment accorded to majority-group members can be deduced from the following interview with an articulate Japanese woman:

> The way my family treats my white husband as something special really stands out. The rest of my sisters are married to Nisei [Japanese] men; they are all good citizens and nobody makes a fuss. But the special niche given to the white man—bowing, scraping, deferring, and the attempts to please him—should give you some idea of the role differences, even today.

The final stage of the ethnic identity is confirmed when the individual begins to accept the roles prescribed by the majority society. Roles become stabilized under the following hypothesized conditions.

The labeled minority is rewarded for playing the stereotyped role.   **Step 4**

The labeled minority is punished if it attempts to play a less conventional role. This applies to the great majority of ethnics. There are individual exceptions—the talented few—but it is more comfortable for most to play the role. Some of the roles may even be well paid and include a rise in status. Nevertheless, they are stereotypes, and the irony is that selected ethnics often are used to demonstrate the openness of the system. Once a person is placed in such a status, he or she is rewarded for conformity and is punished for deviant behavior.   **Step 5**

Overt punishment is not the only barrier. There are few opportunities to play other roles (for example, ethnics are restricted to a few roles in movies and television); thus the range of choices is narrowed, and the ethnic stereotype is reinforced.

Step 6

In times of crisis for the minority group, options are greatly reduced, and the stereotyped role may be the only feasible alternative. Ethnic-group individuals are constantly reminded of their vulnerability. During World War II, the Japanese American survived by playing the role of a patriot. During race riots in Watts, the normal activities of those ethnics not even remotely involved were also restricted; black respondents reported that many white colleagues were constantly suspicious ("Are you one of them?").

Step 7

The final stage of the ethnic identity is achieved when ethnic individuals internalize the stereotyped roles preferred by the majority. They may even believe that their role is the best of all possible roles and that those who wish to change the ethnic stratification system are crackpots, "commies," or worse. They may even believe that they are not ethnics at all and overidentify with the majority group.

The process of achieving a healthy identity for those who do not have the requisite or desired physiological attributes or for those who are in subordinate positions has generally been ignored. We hear terms such as "losers," "second best," and the like, with the implication that working hard and becoming more desirable are the solutions. Yet these powerless positions are the reality for many. Can individuals and groups assigned to subordinated positions on the basis of race ever achieve a positive self-image?

There is no easy answer to this question, but one of the interesting developments among racial minorities is that of an instant ethnic identity. There is a reversal of previous negative color prescriptions so that "black is beautiful," and "yellow is mellow." The turnabout has reversed the "white is right" mentality and is accompanied by a new vocabulary of metaphors such as oreo, banana, coconut, and apple—each used as pejorative terms for ethnics who are, respectively, black, yellow, brown, and red on the outside, but white on the inside.

The pride in blackness, yellowness, redness, and brownness has served a useful function. It has made possible an alternative and perhaps a healthier self-identity, since becoming white seldom could be achieved or only at a high cost (repression, alterations) to the nonwhite individual.

Ethnic identity also raises questions about child development and personality theories that emphasize "normal" stages of development.

Most people of dominated status are seldom afforded such normal stages; they are constantly reminded of their secondary positions in the society. Yet a generalization concerning their deficiencies and lack of normality is inappropriate since most function well, with positive self-identities. It appears that we have just barely scratched the surface on how self and identity develop.

BIBLIOGRAPHY

ADORNO, THEODOR et al. (1950). *The Authoritarian Personality*. New York: Harper & Row, Pub.

BELL, DANIEL (1975). "Ethnicity and Social Change," in *Ethnicity*, pp. 141–74, eds. Nathan Glazer and Daniel Moynihan. Cambridge, Mass.: Harvard University Press.

BRADSHAW, JON (1972). "Any Number Can't Play," *Los Angeles Times*, pp. 7, 9, 10, 12.

DAI, MASUOKA JITSUICHI and PRESTON VALIEN (1961). *Race Relations: Problems and Theory*. Chapel Hill: University of North Carolina Press.

ERIKSON, ERIK (1950). *Childhood and Society*. New York: W. W. Norton & Co.

Fact Sheets on Institutional Racism (1975). New York: Foundation for Change.

GLAZER, NATHAN (1975). "Introduction," in *Ethnicity*. Cambridge, Mass.: Harvard University Press.

GORDON, MILTON (1964). *Assimilation in American Life*. New York: Oxford University Press.

GREELEY, ANDREW (1974). *Ethnicity in the United States*. New York: John Wiley.

ISAACS, HAROLD (1975). *Idols of the Tribe*. New York: Harper & Row, Pub.

KINGSTON, MAXINE HONG (1976). *The Woman Warrior*. New York: Vintage Books.

KOVEL, JOEL (1970). *White Racism*. New York: Pantheon Books.

NEWMAN, WILLIAM (1976). "Multiple Realities: The Effects of Social Pluralism on Identity," in *Ethnic Identity in Society*, pp. 39–47, ed. Arnold Dashefsky. Chicago: Rand McNally.

PATTERSON, ORLANDO (1975). "Context and Choice in Ethnic Allegiance," in *Ethnicity*, pp. 305–45, eds. Nathan Glazer and Daniel Moynihan. Cambridge, Mass.: Harvard University Press.

PAVLAK, THOMAS (1976). *Ethnic Identification and Political Behavior*. San Francisco: R and E Research Associates.

SCHEFF, THOMAS (1968). "The Role of the Mentally Ill and the Dynamics of Mental Disorder," in *The Mental Patient*, pp. 8–22, eds. Spitzer and Denzin. New York: McGraw-Hill.

STEIN, HOWARD and ROBERT HILL (1978). *The Ethnic Imperative: Examining the New White Ethnic Movement*. University Park, Pa.: Pennsylvania State University Press.

Washington Evening Star (1972). January 12, B-11.

WRIGHT, RICHARD (1937). "The Ethics of Living under Jim Crow," *Uncle Tom's Children*. New York: Harper & Row, Pubs.

THE MINORITY GROUPS

We have seen in Part I that the question of the desired interracial goals of the United States can best be understood by analyzing the variety of outcomes that result when different groups meet. These outcomes, presented as models, include peripheral contact, institutionalized contact, acculturation, integration, assimilation, pluralism, domination, and biculturalism.

The current racial stratification system approximates that of domination, in which the dominant group is able to maintain its superiority through such actions as prejudice, discrimination, and segregation, which lead to the continued avoidance, disadvantage, and isolation of the racial minorities. The question of the reasons behind racial inequality has produced conservative, reformist, and radical positions, with one extreme indicating that inequality is inevitable as a product of natural and social forces (the cream rising to the top), and with the contrasting analysis that inequality is a product of a dominant group structuring a society for its own benefit and prescribing inferior positions for others.

Although on the surface it appears that groups assigned to a pariah status have adapted to their circumstances quietly, closer analysis indicates that the apparent docility may be deceptive. There have been racial revolts and riots, strikes, boycotts, ethnic humor, job slowdowns, role changes, changes in goals, avoidance, and retreat. Even those who have seemingly accepted their lot may mask their resentment through indirect aggression.

One of the most serious consequences of racism is its possible effect on an individual's identity. An ethnic identity may include lower self-perceptions, lower feelings of worth, lower expectations, and the internalization of the role of a second-class citizen. However, such developments may be avoidable with the current redefinitions of positive ethnic identities and greater self-awareness.

Part II examines how selected minority groups have adapted to life in the United States. Although we could analyze each ethnic group as if it lived in a vacuum, we cannot ignore the most important factor—its *interaction* with the majority culture.

Minorities have often been forced into positions where sheer survival has been a primary task. Subordinated groups have little power to impose their culture on others, in contrast to dominant groups. Yet much writing ignores this critical factor in the relationship between dominant and subordinated groups. Minority groups have been viewed as isolated entities, and their adaptations have been given various labels by the majority group. The general implication is that minorities have created their own problems by maintaining their cultural traditions, and that they would become more acceptable and successful if only they could get rid of them.

Much scholarly writing in the past has been racist. Even "scientific" writing reeks of paternalism at best and outright racism at worst. The one universal standard has been white Anglo-Saxon Protestantism, and "success" and "failure" have had to be evaluated from this norm. Groups closest to WASP norms in values, life styles, family patterns and culture have been deemed the most successful.

Kinloch (1979:196) saw minority groups as products of power elites on the basis "of perceived physical, cultural, economic, and behavioral characteristics." The three major factors in their creation included: (1) the migration of the minority group; (2) their roles, institutions and sub-cultures as a result of discrimination, segregation, exploitation, and majority control; and (3) the effects of these roles on personal identities and patterns of socialization.

Kinloch (1979:7) further differentiated minority groups into (1) physiological types (nonwhites, women, young people, and the aged), (2) cultural types (non-Anglo Europeans, such as Italians and Greeks), (3) economic types (the poor, the lower classes without power), and (4) behavioral types (the legal and social deviants, including criminals and the mentally ill). Our major emphasis will be on the physiological, nonwhite minorities, although there may be a correlation between various minority types.

Ethnic groups from more distant cultures have been considered deviant, and the implication has been that they must be changed, isolated, or destroyed. In a power sense, the interpretations may be correct: dominant groups do what they think is right, and they develop and maintain organizations that reinforce their system. Those groups that do not adjust are considered deviant and become primary targets for "assistance."

We expect the reader to view the interaction between ethnic groups and the white majority in a nonmoralistic way—that is, to avoid the use of labels such as "good" or "bad" when looking at the phenomena. We shall examine the following groups: Afro-Americans, American Indians, Asian Americans (including Chinese, Japanese, Koreans, Samoans, and Pilipinos), Mexican Americans, and Puerto Ricans.

Before turning to the ethnic groups, we shall first present a chapter that provides an overall comparative picture of some of America's minorities, which includes women.

7

THE CURRENT STATUS
OF
MINORITY GROUPS

In Part I we examined the subordinated status of America's racial minorities. This chapter will provide data from the United States Census for the years 1960, 1970, and 1976 (where available) to ascertain the current status of selected minority groups.

Dahl (1961) posited a three-stage process through which ethnic groups must pass on their way to social and political assimilation. Stage 1 is the level on which the socioeconomic life of the group is homogeneous, proletarian, and on which the group is low in status, income, and influence. The group will tend to be politically homogeneous, sharing political attitudes and voting preferences. Stage 2 sees the beginning of socioeconomic and political heterogeneity. Many have achieved middle class status, and if the group is sizeable they may even run their own ethnic candidate. Ethnic ties are strong, but there are also strong class interests, so that the ethnic candidate must avoid divisive socioeconomic issues. The third stage is the one at which the group is heterogeneous, and political attitudes and loyalties are more a function of socioeconomic characteristics than of ethnic ties. According to Dahl, the Germans, Irish, Russian Jews, and Italians of New Haven, Connecticut have passed into this third stage. Dahl's framework is useful as one method of assessing the status of our ethnic groups.

DOMINANCE

Dominance in a society occurs when one group controls the major power positions of the state in both the public and private sectors, and when its members control the positions of power, prestige, and wealth. Therefore, our analysis of the current state of our ethnic minorities will include the following measures of dominance: (a) social indicators, (b) top decision makers, and (c) social status.

SOCIAL INDICATORS OF INEQUALITY

In a special report of the the United States Commission on Civil Rights entitled *Social Indicators of Equality for Minorities and Women* (1978), United States Census data for 1960, 1970, and 1976 compared the following groups: Indians, blacks, Mexican Americans, Japanese Americans, Chinese Americans, Pilipino Americans and Puerto Ricans, both males and females.

All of these groups are compared to the white male. The data are quite useful, and dominant-subordinate relationships can be assessed. The social indicators of inequality include: (1) education, (2) employment, (3) income, and (4) housing. All tables and data in this section are drawn from the United States Commission on Civil Rights Report (1978).

Educational Indices

Under education, the variables are (a) delayed education, (b) high school nonattendance, (c) high school completion, and (d) college completion.

Delayed Education. Delayed education is correlated with early school dropouts. The delay in schooling creates many difficulties for the child; he or she may be labeled a slow learner and will be older than others in the same grade or class level.

The patterns in delayed education have not changed significantly over time. In 1976, American Indians, blacks, Mexican Americans, and Puerto Ricans, both males and females, were significantly delayed more than white males in education.[1] Japanese Americans and Pilipino Americans did slightly better (but the differences are not statistically significant) than white males, while the sample of Chinese Americans was too small to be included in the analysis.

High School Nonattendance. Not attending high school is pivotal for minorities, since it affects their employment opportunities and earning potentials throughout their lifetimes. Very few have the luxury of rich

[1] Statistical significance in this and all of the following tables in this chapter is at the 0.10 level.

DELAYED EDUCATION

TABLE 7.1

	1960	1970	1976
Males			
Amer. Ind./Alask. Nat.	2.50	2.92	3.20*
Blacks	2.00	2.17	2.30
Mexican Americans	2.28	2.17	2.80
Japanese Americans	.28	.33	.80
Chinese Americans	.72	.83	NA†
Pilipino Americans	.78	1.08	.70
Puerto Ricans	2.44	2.17	3.90
Majority	1.00	1.00	1.00
Females			
Amer. Ind./Alask. Nat.	2.28	1.92	2.60
Blacks	1.39	1.42	1.50
Mexican Americans	1.83	1.92	2.40
Japanese Americans	.44	.08	.10
Chinese Americans	.33	.75	NA
Pilipino Americans	.17	.58	.30
Puerto Ricans	1.61	2.00	2.70
Majority	.56	.50	.70

SOURCE: U.S. Commission on Civil Rights, August 1978, p. 9.

* This can be interpreted as follows: In 1976 the delayed education rate for American Indian and Alaskan Native males was 3.2 times greater than the rate of majority males.
† NA = Data not reported because of insufficient sample size.

HIGH SCHOOL NONATTENDANCE

TABLE 7.2

	1960	1970	1976
Males			
Amer. Ind./Alask. Nat.	1.61	1.67	2.80*
Blacks	1.17	1.78	1.40
Mexican Americans	1.44	1.44	2.20
Japanese Americans	.11	.67	.40
Chinese Americans	.50	.67	NA
Pilipino Americans	.67	.89	1.20
Puerto Ricans	1.39	2.89	1.00
Majority	1.00	1.00	1.00
Females			
Amer. Ind./Alask. Nat.	1.33	1.78	3.00
Blacks	1.28	1.67	1.20
Mexican Americans	1.72	1.89	2.80
Japanese Americans	.17	.67	.20
Chinese Americans	.78	1.00	NA
Pilipino Americans	.39	1.00	2.00
Puerto Ricans	1.67	2.89	3.20
Majority	.67	.89	1.20

SOURCE: U.S. Commission on Civil Rights, August 1978, p. 10.

* This can be interpreted as follows: In 1976 the high school nonattendance rate for American Indian and Alaskan Native males was 2.80 times greater than the rate for majority males.

parents or of inheriting desirable jobs without the educational credentials, so attending school remains one of the main paths of upward mobility.

In 1976, the male American Indian and Mexican American were significantly higher in high school nonattendance than the white male. The Blacks and Pilipinos also were higher but on a nonsignificant level; Puerto Ricans were identical (an interesting reversal of their 1970 figure), while the Japanese were below the Anglo rato.

Similar patterns are seen in the female samples, with the exception of significantly higher rates of nonattendance for Puerto Rican females and lower rates for Japanese females.

High School Completion. Acquisition of a high school diploma is a necessary step toward higher education. In 1976 American Indians, blacks, Mexican Americans, and Puerto Ricans, both males and females, were significantly below white males in high school completion. Chinese Americans, both males and females, and Pilipino males were similar to white males while Pilipino females were significantly below. Japanese American males and females were significantly higher than white males in high school completion.

College Completion. College completion is another important step in achieving higher occupational and economic status. American Indians, blacks, Mexican Americans and Puerto Ricans, both males and females, were significantly below white males in college completion. Male Pilipinos and female Japanese Americans were similar to majority-group males, while male Japanese Americans, male and female Chinese, and female Pilipinos were significantly higher in college completion.

Occupational Indices

Under occupational indices we include (a) unemployment, (b) teenage unemployment, (c) occupational prestige, (d) occupational mobility, and (e) occupational segregation.

Unemployment. In 1976 American Indians, blacks, Mexican Americans, and Puerto Ricans, both males and females, had significantly higher rates of unemployment than white males. Chinese Americans, both males and females, and white females were also higher, but not significantly so, while Japanese Americans were significantly below white males in unemployment.

Teenage Unemployment. All groups had significantly higher levels of teenage unemployment in comparison to white males (with the exception of Japanese-American females, who were higher but not statistically significant). The most alarming figures are for teenage blacks, who were over eight times, and male Puerto Ricans, who were over nine times the rate for white males.

HIGH SCHOOL COMPLETION

TABLE 7.3

	1960	1970	1976
Males			
Amer. Ind./Alask. Nat.	.48	.70	.80*
Blacks	.59	.71	.85
Mexican Americans	.49	.66	.74
Japanese Americans	1.29	1.13	1.13
Chinese Americans	1.22	1.08	1.01
Pilipino Americans	1.17	.93	.93
Puerto Ricans	.35	.53	.78
Majority	1.00	1.00	1.00
Females			
Amer. Ind./Alask. Nat.	.42	.67	.67
Blacks	.61	.75	.85
Mexican Americans	.51	.61	.67
Japanese Americans	1.22	1.13	1.14
Chinese Americans	1.19	1.06	1.03
Pilipino Americans	1.10	1.01	.90
Puerto Ricans	.35	.51	.69
Majority	1.01	.99	.99

SOURCE: U.S. Commission on Civil Rights, August 1978, p. 12.

* This can be interpreted as follows: In 1976 the high school completion rate for American Indian and Alaskan Native males was 80 percent of (or 20 percent below) the completion rate for majority males.

COLLEGE COMPLETION

TABLE 7.4

	1960	1970	1976
Males			
Amer. Ind./Alask. Nat.	.15	.36	.24*
Blacks	.20	.27	.32
Mexican Americans	.20	.23	.32
Japanese Americans	1.75	1.77	1.56
Chinese Americans	2.45	2.64	1.76
Pilipino Americans	.95	1.27	1.00
Puerto Ricans	.20	.18	.18
Majority	1.00	1.00	1.00
Females			
Amer. Ind./Alask. Nat.	.10	.23	.12
Blacks	.30	.36	.32
Mexican Americans	.10	.14	.15
Japanese Americans	.65	1.41	1.03
Chinese Americans	1.30	1.91	1.29
Pilipino Americans	.80	2.27	1.50
Puerto Ricans	.05	.14	.12
Majority	.45	.64	.65

SOURCE: U.S. Commission on Civil Rights, August 1978, p. 14.

* This can be interpreted as follows: In 1976 the college completion rate for American Indian and Alaskan Native male was 24 percent of (or 76 percent below) the rate for majority males.

TABLE 7.5

UNEMPLOYMENT

	1960	1970	1976
Males			
Amer. Ind./Alask. Nat.	3.49	3.03	2.07*
Blacks	1.83	1.97	2.69
Mexican Americans	1.72	1.78	1.88
Japanese Americans	.51	.50	.49
Chinese Americans	.77	1.03	1.22
Pilipino Americans	1.04	1.50	.95
Puerto Ricans	1.87	1.75	2.76
Majority	1.00	1.00	1.00
Females			
Amer. Ind./Alask. Nat.	2.53	3.03	2.64
Blacks	1.91	2.33	3.20
Mexican Americans	2.04	2.53	2.52
Japanese Americans	.68	.89	.64
Chinese Americans	.72	1.11	1.12
Pilipino Americans	3.98	1.42	1.02
Puerto Ricans	2.36	2.58	3.78
Majority	1.00	1.39	1.47

SOURCE: U S. Commission on Civil Rights, August 1978, p. 30.

* This can be interpreted as follows: In 1976 the American Indian and Alaskan Native male unemployment rate was 2.07 times as high as the rate of majority males.

TABLE 7.6

TEENAGE UNEMPLOYMENT

	1960	1970	1976
Males			
Amer. Ind./Alask. Nat.	3.60	5.11	5.92*
Blacks	2.57	5.70	8.10
Mexican Americans	3.06	4.11	4.12
Japanese Americans	1.49	2.25	2.32
Chinese Americans	N.A.	2.39	N.A.
Pilipino Americans	N.A.	5.06	3.75
Puerto Ricans	3.15	4.97	9.36
Majority (teenage)	2.09	2.94	2.54
Majority Total	1.00	1.00	1.00
Females			
Amer. Ind./Alask. Nat.	4.45	4.94	6.10
Blacks	4.00	6.83	8.69
Mexican Americans	2.66	4.64	4.59
Japanese Americans	1.83	2.28	1.68
Chinese Americans	N.A.	1.56	N.A.
Pilipino Americans	N.A.	1.58	4.12
Puerto Ricans	2.34	4.67	6.47
Majority (teenage)	.62	3.03	3.25

SOURCE: U.S. Commission on Civil Rights, August, 1978, p. 32.

* This can be interpreted as follows: In 1976 the American Indian and Alaskan Native male teenage unemployment rate was 5.92 times the majority male unemployment rate.

Occupational Prestige. According to the report of the Commission on Civil Rights, occupational prestige reflects the honor or social esteem generally accorded to those working in an occupation. For example, prestige scores ranged from 88 for physicians to a low of 1.5 for bootblacks.

All groups, with the exception of Japanese and Chinese males, Pilipino females (who ranked above), and Japanese and Chinese females (who ranked below but not significantly) ranked significantly below American males in occupational prestige.

Occupational mobility. Occupational mobility refers to an average change of prestige scores among those who have changed occupations in the past five years. The change can be made to an occupation with a similar prestige score.

The measures are for the period between 1965 and 1970. Most male groups advanced, although only for Mexican Americans was change statistically significant. Conversely, all female groups lagged in occupational mobility, with the lag for Mexican, Chinese, and Pilipino females being statistically significant.

OCCUPATIONAL PRESTIGE

TABLE 7.7

	1960	1970	1976
Males			
Amer. Ind./Alask. Nat.	.69	.79	.86*
Blacks	.70	.76	.77
Mexican Americans	.71	.77	.77
Japanese Americans	.98	1.02	1.03
Chinese Americans	1.06	1.07	1.11
Pilipino Americans	.74	.87	.94
Puerto Ricans	.78	.80	.81
Majority	1.00	1.00	1.00
Females			
Amer. Ind./Alask. Nat.	.75	.83	.85
Blacks	.69	.76	.81
Mexican Americans	.78	.77	.76
Japanese Americans	.93	.96	.91
Chinese Americans	1.01	1.01	.97
Pilipino Americans	.93	1.02	1.02
Puerto Ricans	.84	.87	.83
Majority	1.02	1.00	.98

SOURCE: U.S. Commission on Civil Rights, August 1978, p. 36.

This can be interpreted as follows: In 1976, on the average, the prestige values of American Indian and Alaskan Native males' occupations were 86 percent of the average prestige values for majority males.

TABLE 7.8   *OCCUPATIONAL MOBILITY (1965—1970)*

Males

Amer. Ind./Alask. Nat.	.96*
Blacks	1.25
Mexican Americans	1.42
Japanese Americans	1.43
Chinese Americans	.37
Pilipino Americans	−.07
Puerto Ricans	1.10
Majority	1.00

Females

Amer. Ind./Alask. Nat.	.46
Blacks	.98
Mexican Americans	.29
Japanese Americans	.17
Chinese Americans	−1.80
Pilipino Americans	−1.97
Puerto Ricans	.41
Majority	.71

SOURCE: U.S. Commission on Civil Rights, August 1978, p. 40.

This can be interpreted as follows: In 1970 the American Indian and Alaskan Native males who had different occupations in 1965 had, on the average, increased their occupational prestige 96 percent of the majority male average increase.

TABLE 7.9   *OCCUPATIONAL SEGREGATION*

	Compared with majority males			Compared with majority females		
	1960	1970	1976	1960	1970	1976
Males						
Amer. Ind./Alask. Nat.	44.1	38.2	35.7*			
Blacks	44.7	44.3	37.9			
Mexican Americans	36.7	36.6	38.2			
Japanese Americans	28.9	31.3	41.5			
Chinese Americans	50.6	52.2	61.4			
Pilipino Americans	50.7	46.0	59.7			
Puerto Ricans	49.2	44.1	50.4			
Females						
Amer. Ind./Alask. Nat.	69.1	70.7	69.4	47.1	31.5	33.8†
Blacks	72.4	71.1	69.3	52.4	40.4	35.8
Mexican Americans	63.5	68.3	75.1	31.0	27.5	36.9
Japanese Americans	63.8	68.9	72.1	26.6	22.5	32.6
Chinese Americans	71.8	70.9	79.7	36.4	34.1	52.9
Pilipino Americans	69.0	73.0	79.2	40.9	42.2	48.3
Puerto Ricans	71.6	70.9	78.9	53.9	37.7	48.3
Majority	62.4	65.8	66.1	—	—	—

SOURCE: U.S. Commission on Civil Rights, August 1978, p. 42.

This can be interpreted as follows: In 1976, at least 35.7 percent of American Indian and Alaskan Native males would have had to change occupations in order to have an occupational distribution identical to the majority males.
† This can be interpreted as follows: In 1976, at least 33.8 percent of American Indian and Alaskan Native females would have had to change occupations in order to have an occupational distribution identical to the majority females.

114

Occupational Segregation. Occupational segregation was measured by an index of dissimilarity. The index represents "the percentage of a group who would have to change occupations in order for the group to have the identical occupational distribution of the comparison (white male) group."

All groups, both males and females, were segregated to such an extent that large proportions (from 35.7 percent of American Indians to 61.4 percent of Chinese-American males, and from 32.6 percent of Japanese-American females to 52.9 percent of Chinese-American females) would have to change their occupations in order to approximate white male distribution.

Under income, the variables are (a) earnings differentials for college-educated persons, (b) median household income, (c) adjusted mean earnings, (d) earnings mobility, and (e) poverty rates.

Income Indices

Earnings Differentials for College-Educated Persons. All groups, both males and females, who were college graduates earned less than white college male graduates did. The figure on earnings does not lend itself to tests of statistical significance.

EARNINGS DIFFERENTIAL   *TABLE 7.10*
FOR COLLEGE-EDUCATED PERSONS

	1959	1969	1975
Males			
Amer. Ind./Alask. Nat.	.66	.68	.77*
Blacks	.66	.73	.81
Mexican Americans	.79	.74	.71
Japanese Americans	.77	.94	.94
Chinese Americans	.82	.85	.84
Pilipino Americans	.54	.73	.86
Puerto Ricans	.60	.80	N.A.
Majority	1.00	1.00	1.00
Females			
Amer. Ind./Alask. Nat.	N.A.	.29	.68
Blacks	.40	.55	.65
Mexican Americans	.20	.25	.46
Japanese Americans	.29	.20	.55
Chinese Americans	.07	.18	.42
Pilipino Americans	.24	.36	.60
Puerto Ricans	.07	.21	N.A.
Majority	.25	.18	.53

SOURCE: U.S. Commission on Civil Rights, August 1978, p. 24.

* This can be interpreted as follows: In 1975 American Indian and Alaskan Native males with 4 or more years of college earned 77 percent of the average for majority males with the same educational attainment.

TABLE 7.11

MEDIAN HOUSEHOLD PER CAPITA INCOME

	Raw measure†			Social indicator values (Ratios of raw measures to the majority population)		
	1959	1969	1975	1959	1969	1975
For All Households				.32	.43	.57*
Amer. Ind./Alask. Nat.	$ 467	$1122	$2453			
Blacks	680	1303	2263	.46	.50	.52
Mexican Americans	742	1334	2130	.50	.51	.49
Japanese Americans	1680	3184	6105	1.14	1.22	1.41
Chinese Americans	1416	2449	3867	.96	.94	.89
Pilipino Americans	1145	2208	3897	.78	.85	.90
Puerto Ricans	869	1362	2153	.59	.52	.50
Majority	1472	2601	4333	1.00	1.00	1.00
For Female-Headed Households						
Amer. Ind./Alask. Nat.	378	711	1310	.26	.27	.30
Blacks	399	783	1310	.27	.30	.30
Mexican Americans	428	808	1228	.29	.31	.28
Japanese Americans	1168	2051	2341	.79	.79	.54
Chinese Americans	1309	2163	1778	.89	.83	.41
Pilipino Americans	569	999	2333	.39	.38	.54
Puerto Ricans	716	759	1252	.49	.29	.29
Majority	1099	1658	2563	.75	.64	.59

SOURCE: U.S. Commission on Civil Rights, August 1978, p. 50.

† The median household per capita income is based on the income distribution of the total personal income for persons not living in a family situation and each family member's equal share of their family income. Because this indicator is based on medians, standard techniques for estimating sampling error do not apply.
* This can be interpreted as follows: In 1975 members of American Indian and Alaskan Native headed households had a median household per capita income that was 57 percent as much as the median for members of majority-headed households.

Median Household Income. All groups, with the exception of Japanese-American males, are below white males in median income. Overall female income figures are especially depressed, although the Puerto Rican, Mexican-American, black and Indian male figures are also very low.

Adjusted Mean Earnings. All groups, with the exception of Pilipino males, had adjusted mean earnings below those of white males. Female income figures are consistently low. It should be emphasized that this table refers only to those individuals who are employed with earnings.

Earnings Mobility. Earnings mobility is especially critical to racial minorities, for without it the impoverished conditions would continue on indefinitely. All males from 1959 to 1975 showed some earnings mobility

ADJUSTED MEAN EARNINGS FOR THOSE WITH EARNINGS

TABLE 7.12

	Original means			Original ratios (group/majority males)			Adjusted† means			Earnings ratios for adjusted means (group/majority males)		
	1959	1969	1975	1959	1969	1975	1959	1969	1975	1959	1969	1975
Males												
Amer. Ind./Alask. Nat.	$2878	$5623	$ 8302	.54	.62	.73*	$3926	$7097	$10575	.73	.78	.92**
Blacks	2808	5434	7470	.52	.59	.65	3793	6885	9741	.71	.75	.85
Mexican Americans	3412	5852	7456	.64	.64	.65	4527	7219	9414	.84	.79	.82
Japanese Americans	5142	9159	12615	.96	1.00	1.10	4490	8363	9999	.84	.91	.88
Chinese Americans	4771	8001	10339	.89	.87	.90	4465	7430	8817	.83	.81	.77
Pilipino Americans	3603	6852	11366	.67	.75	.99	3707	7550	11874	.69	.82	1.04
Puerto Ricans	3200	5839	8269	.60	.64	.72	4654	7776	11233	.87	.85	.98
Majority	5369	9150	11427	1.00	1.00	1.00	5369	9150	11427	1.00	1.00	1.00
Females												
Amer. Ind./Alask. Nat.	$1924	$3378	$ 3958	.36	.37	.35	$2824	$4683	$ 6136	.53	.51	.54
Blacks	1566	3383	4918	.29	.37	.43	2502	4707	6973	.47	.51	.61
Mexican Americans	1790	3030	3527	.33	.33	.31	2572	4298	5525	.48	.47	.48
Japanese Americans	2550	4617	5881	.48	.50	.51	2911	5303	6670	.54	.58	.58
Chinese Americans	2639	4366	6759	.49	.48	.59	3163	5348	7960	.59	.58	.58
Pilipino Americans	2268	4499	6784	.42	.49	.59	2862	4996	6712	.53	.55	.70
Puerto Ricans	2244	4071	4714	.42	.44	.41	2958	5060	6468	.55	.55	.57
Majority	2686	4072	5122	.50	.44	.45	3039	4958	6568	.57	.54	.57

SOURCE: U.S. Commission on Civil Rights, August 1978, p. 54.

† The adjusted technique substitutes the majority male mean values in a regression equation for the following variables: occupational prestige, age, education, weeks worked, hours worked last week, and the average income in the state of residence.

* This can be interpreted as follows: In 1975, American Indian and Alaskan Native males earned, on the average, 73 percent of the majority male average earnings.

** This can be interpreted as follows: In 1975, American Indian and Alaskan Native males with the same characteristics as majority males (in terms of occupational prestige, age, education, weeks worked, hours worked last week, and state of residence) could be expected to earn 92 percent of the amount that majority males earned.

TABLE 7.13

EARNINGS MOBILITY

	Raw measure†			Social indicator values (Ratios of raw measures to the majority male population)		
	1959	1969	1975	1959	1969	1975
Males						
Amer. Ind./Alask. Nat.	$ 74.40	$145.60	$320.15	.58	.60	.85*
Blacks	60.00	108.90	185.30	.46	.45	.49
Mexican Americans	84.20	136.00	147.40	.65	.56	.39
Japanese Americans	157.50	272.20	536.85	1.22	1.12	1.43
Chinese Americans	156.50	306.50	459.45	1.21	1.26	1.22
Pilipino Americans	69.00	251.80	283.30	.53	1.03	.75
Puerto Ricans	41.20	83.80	97.95	.32	.34	.26
Majority	129.20	243.80	375.75	1.00	1.00	1.00
Females						
Amer. Ind./Alask. Nat.	−19.10	0.20	81.30	−.15	.00	.22
Blacks	4.30	4.80	29.95	.03	.02	.08
Mexican Americans	9.80	10.10	5.55	.08	.04	.02
Japanese Americans	−39.00	79.40	−11.00	−.30	.33	−.03
Chinese Americans	−20.20	40.20	41.70	−.16	.16	.11
Pilipino Americans	−10.00	−6.30	8.35	−.08	−.03	.02
Puerto Ricans	− 9.20	−6.60	−20.00	−.07	−.03	−.05
Majority	18.00	22.20	57.55	.14	.09	.15

SOURCE: U.S. Commission on Civil Rights, August 1978, p. 58.

† The average annual increment in earnings by single years of age for full-time workers ages 20 to 44. The indicator is based on medians, and therefore standard techniques for estimating sampling error do not apply.
* This can be interpreted as follows: In 1975 American Indian and Alaskan Native males' average earnings increment by age was 85 percent as much as the earnings increment for majority males.

(see raw measure in Table 7.13), but with the exception of the Japanese and Chinese, all were below that of white males. The female figures provide a contrast; both Japanese and Puerto Rican females registered a decrease in earnings, and the general mobility of all females was minimal.

Poverty Rates. Poverty is measured by a poverty index that "is an attempt to specify in dollar terms a minimum level of income adequacy for families of different types in keeping with American consumption patterns."

All groups, with the exception of Japanese and Pilipino families, had higher rates of poverty than majority families did. All the groups with female heads had higher rates of poverty than those of the comparison group.

TABLE 7.14

	1969	1975
Families and Unrelated Individuals		
Amer. Ind./Alask. Nat.	2.73	2.89*
Blacks	2.50	3.11
Mexican Americans	2.12	2.67
Japanese Americans	0.91	0.78
Chinese Americans	1.21	1.89
Pilipino Americans	1.44	0.67
Puerto Ricans	2.12	3.56
Majority	1.00	1.00
Female-Headed Families and Female Unrelated Individuals		
Amer. Ind./Alask. Nat.	4.09	5.44**
Blacks	4.01	5.11
Mexican Americans	4.02	5.11
Japanese Americans	2.42	2.44
Chinese Americans	2.20	2.11
Pilipino Americans	2.95	2.22
Puerto Ricans	3.94	5.44
Majority	2.12	2.44

SOURCE: U.S. Commission on Civil Rights, August 1978, p. 62.

* *This can be interpreted as follows: In 1975 American Indian and Alaskan Native-headed families were 2.89 times as likely to be living in poverty as majority-headed families.*

** *This can be interpreted as follows: In 1975 American Indian and Alaskan Native female-headed families were 5.44 times as likely to be living in poverty as all majority-headed families.*

Under housing, the variables are (a) complete household facilities, (b) households that are owner occupied, and (c) overcrowding.

Housing Indices

Complete Household Facilities. Complete household facilities means units with ''a flush toilet, hot water, complete kitchen, bathtub or shower, central heat and direct access from the outside or through a common or public hall.'' All groups lacked complete housing facilities compared to those of white males.

In general, minorities are unequal in education, occupation, income, and housing. Some groups, especially American Indians, blacks, Mexican Americans, and Puerto Ricans, are consistently disadvantaged on all levels, whereas Asian-American groups fare somewhat better. Females in all groups also show a consistent inequality in comparison to white male norms.

TABLE 7.15

COMPLETE HOUSEHOLD FACILITIES

	1960	1970
All Households		
Amer. Ind./Alask. Nat.	.62	.88*
Blacks	.79	.92
Mexican Americans	.79	.91
Japanese Americans	.95	.98
Chinese Americans	.85	.94
Pilipino Americans	.89	.98
Puerto Ricans	.90	.97
Majority	1.00	1.00
Female-Headed Households		
Amer. Ind./Alask. Nat.	.63	.87
Blacks	.76	.90
Mexican Americans	.73	.88
Japanese Americans	.96	.95
Chinese Americans	.85	.89
Pilipino Americans	NA	.95
Puerto Ricans	.89	.98
Majority	.97	.98

SOURCE: U.S. Commission on Civil Rights, August 1978, p. 80.

* This can be interpreted as follows: In 1970 American Indian and Alaskan Native-headed households were 88 percent as likely to have complete housing facilities as majority-headed households.

TABLE 7.16

HOUSEHOLDS THAT ARE OWNER OCCUPIED

	1960	1970	1976
All Households			
Amer. Ind./Alask. Nat.	.68	.68	.70*
Blacks	.58	.63	.64
Mexican Americans	.87	.84	.77
Japanese Americans	.58	.66	.56
Chinese Americans	.64	.64	.61
Pilipino Americans	.62	.54	.64
Puerto Ricans	.37	.51	.50
Majority	1.00	1.00	1.00
Female-Headed Households			
Amer. Ind./Alask. Nat.	.78	.57	.37
Blacks	.46	.45	.43
Mexican Americans	.71	.61	.41
Japanese Americans	.44	.45	.30
Chinese Americans	.55	.47	.24
Pilipino Americans	NA	.19	.31
Puerto Ricans	.21	.26	.16
Majority	.79	.78	.68

SOURCE: U.S. Commission on Civil Rights, August 1978, p. 72.

* This can be interpreted as follows: In 1976 American Indian and Alaskan Native-headed households were 70 percent as likely to be owner-occupied as majority-headed households.

Households That Are Owner Occupied. Home ownership is generally viewed as desirable for many reasons. There are a number of financial advantages (tax purposes, inflation, appreciation of real estate values), as well as social-psychological benefits. Home ownership is often regarded as one of the cornerstones of becoming an American. All groups were well below white males in owner-occupied housing.

Overcrowding. All groups, with the exception of Japanese and majority females, were in overcrowded rental units. All groups, with the exception of Japanese males and females, and Chinese and majority-group females, were in owner-occupied, overcrowded housing.

OVERCROWDING   TABLE 7.17

	Renter Occupied		Owner Occupied	
	Social indicator values (Ratios of standardized measures to the majority population)		Social indicator values (Ratios of standardized measures to the majority population)	
	1960	1970	1960	1970
All Households				
Amer. Ind./Alask. Nat.	3.51	2.88*	4.17	2.89**
Blacks	2.21	2.33	2.13	2.31
Mexican Americans	2.70	5.88	3.28	5.07
Japanese Americans	1.44	1.36	.95	.84
Chinese Americans	1.57	2.88	2.33	2.87
Pilipino Americans	1.68	3.80	4.51	2.74
Puerto Ricans	3.16	3.24	3.75	3.23
Majority	1.00	1.00	1.00	1.00
Female-Headed Households				
Amer. Ind./Alask. Nat.	2.32	2.74	3.64	3.22
Blacks	1.66	2.14	1.10	1.54
Mexican Americans	1.86	4.10	2.00	2.96
Japanese Americans	.22	.40	1.32	.04
Chinese Americans	NA	1.43	NA	.76
Pilipino Americans	NA	2.17	NA	2.63
Puerto Ricans	2.40	2.78	NA	1.94
Majority	.47	.42	.28	.29

SOURCE: U.S. Commission on Civil Rights, August 1978, p. 76.

*This can be interpreted as follows: In 1970 American Indian and Alaskan Native-headed rental households were 2.88 times as likely to be overcrowed as majority-headed rental households.

**This can be interpreted as follows: In 1970 American Indian and Alaskan Native-headed owner-occupied households were 2.89 times as likely to be overcrowded as majority-headed owner-occupied households.

TOP DECISION MAKERS IN AMERICA

Another measure of inequality is the absence of racial minorities in top decision-making positions. Rhetorical questions such as: "Who controls the political machinery? The press? The major unions? The newspapers? Television? The movies? The universities? The Army? The Navy? The Air Force? Congress? The Supreme Court? The corporations? The wealth? can be answered by "Well, not any of the ethnic minorities."

Dye (1976), in a book with the intriguing title *Who's Running America?* identified 4,000 people considered to be top decision makers in the corporate government and public interest sectors. People in these elite positions were generally affluent, white, Anglo-Protestant, and male. There were two blacks and no Chicanos, native Americans, or Asian Americans in his list. There were also very few recognizably Irish, Italian, or Jewish names in this list. Therefore according to Dye, power in the United States is generally controlled by a tiny handful of men whose social origins and "ethnic" makeup is remarkably similar.

SOCIAL STATUS

Another measure of dominance is social status. Indicators of social status are subjective and are often subject to change. But social leaders—the jet set, the beautiful people, the people who are on the covers of *Time* and *Newsweek,* who achieve celebrity and star status, who appear on the society pages, and who set the pace—are dominant-group people, with rare exceptions.

Social-distance scales, discussed previously, also provide an assessment of the social status of a group. In Bogardus's measure of social distance (1968), there was very little difference over time in the ranking of minority groups. Native Americans, Japanese, Chinese, Koreans, Mexicans, blacks and Indians from India clustered on the bottom end of the scale in the 1930s and still held their socially undesirable positions four decades later. We gave a similar scale to classes of students and the results were similar. One interesting finding is that racial minorities, aside from giving their own group a high ranking, generally ranked other minorities on the lower end of the scale.

In summary, the current picture supports the model of ethnic and sexual stratification on a dominant-subordinate basis. But it is not as clearly demarcated as it might have been several decades ago, and the generalization varies by ethnic group. The following chapters focus on selected ethnic groups and analyze their experiences, expectations, and adaptations to the dominant culture.

BOGARDUS, EMORY (1968). "Comparing Racial Distance in Ethiopia, South Africa and the United States," *Sociology and Social Research,* 52:149–56.

DAHL, ROBERT A. (1961). *Who Governs? Democracy and Power in an American City.* New Haven: Yale University Press.

DYE, THOMAS R. (1976). *Who's Running America?* Englewood Cliffs, N.J.: Prentice Hall, Inc.

KINLOCH, GRAHAM (1979). *The Sociology of Minority Group Relations.* Englewood Cliffs, N.J.: Prentice-Hall, Inc.

Social Indicators of Equality for Minorities and Women 1978. A Report of the U.S. Commission on Civil Rights. Washington, D.C.

8

AFRO-AMERICANS

Afro-Americans have been the principal victims of racism in the United States, so that, appropriately enough, they have been the leaders in the movement for change in America's race relations. Several factors have interacted to place blacks at the forefront of social change. Most important, they have become American, including an identity and expectations that are a part of the system. In the process, blacks have raised the fundamental question, "Can people of color truly share in the American dream?" Some immigrant groups have not had to face the question as directly as the blacks have, because of a nationality or religious identity that could serve as a substitute.

The process of incorporating American ideals and the high expectations that go with them has created what Festinger (1957) labeled a *cognitive discrepancy* that appears to have been resolved through a push for social change. (The discrepancy refers to a gap between what is expected and what can be realistically achieved.) Finally, Afro-Americans, or blacks, have suffered the longest and the most severely under our present system.

Even though blacks have been in the United States from its very beginnings, they still do not possess the economic, educational, or political resources to exert the necessary leverage for an independent existence. Rather, the dependency relationship with the dominant group and the position at the bottom of the racial stratification system have continued. Their power lies in their numbers, although for a long period these masses could not be translated into action such as voting because of discriminatory and other barriers.

One of the most divisive issues for blacks, ever since their forced arrival, has been the question of whether to establish a separatist existence or to integrate into the dominant culture. This question, which has been constantly debated, has created bitter enmities and divisions, and has strained efforts toward a workable coalition.

The most eloquent spokespersons for these positions, who have always been at the forefront of black consciousness, were Malcolm X (1925-1965) and Martin Luther King (1929-1968). Both were known as leaders, heroes, traitors, or fools—depending on one's point of view— and both died prematurely at the hands of assassins.

Malcolm challenged a Harlem audience in 1963 by asking whether they wanted to integrate into the wicked white society or to separate themselves from the group that had enslaved them. He understood that whites considered themselves far superior to blacks and that integration was meant only for blacks who thought like whites, and on their terms. Therefore, the only intelligent and lasting solution was for blacks to separate themselves completely from that world (Blair, 1977:34).

Malcolm X articulated nine essential components of a black nationalist movement (Blair, 1977:58-59):

1. Unity among all blacks throughout the world.
2. Black self-determination: the right to control their own lives, their history, and their future.
3. Community control: strong, all-black communities and organizations to fight injustice (high rents, high prices, lack of jobs).
4. Education: black-led institutions raising people to levels of excellence and self-respect.
5. Economic security: black control of the economy for the benefit of blacks.
6. Armed self-defense: the ability to fight back when unlawfully attacked.
7. Social and moral uplift: the community to get rid of the effects of years of exploitation, neglect and apathy, and to fight against police brutality, organized crime, and drug addiction.
8. Rediscovery of the African heritage: opening up communications with Africa; a study of African history, culture, philosophy.
9. Internationalization of the black struggle.

Malcolm X summarized many of the dreams and expectations voiced by black leaders of the past and charted a course for future action. He rejected the model of black working people being led by the black middle class that, in turn, was allied with and dominated by the white power structure. Instead, he placed the interests of all blacks against all whites and later the interests of all revolutionary forces, whether black or white, against all regressive forces—black or white.

Martin Luther King saw a different goal for blacks. He saw the breakdown of barriers, the fight for civil rights, and the achievement of equality as the highest priorities. In his famous "I have a dream" speech, he spoke of the time when "little black boys and black girls will be able to join hands with little white boys and white girls as sisters and brothers." He envisaged the day when "we will be able to work together, pray together, to struggle together . . . and all of God's children, black men and white men, Jews and Gentiles, Protestants and Catholics will be able to join hands and sing . . . " (Schulke, 1976:218).

The two leaders defined the goals of the American system, with Malcolm X advocating pluralism (Model 6) and Rev. King, integration (Model 4). Both men were also in agreement about the current dominated state (Model 6B) of the black community.

EARLY HISTORY

The first African arrivals in the United States were twenty slaves sold to Virginia settlers in 1619, one year before the *Mayflower* arrived. Studies by Donnan (1935) and Herskovits (1941) indicate that many of the slaves imported to the American colonies came from an area not more than two hundred miles inland from the coast of West Africa. The black migrants represented many different African cultures, ranging from sophisticated empires to isolated groups; but once in America, they all were mistreated alike. Slaves were sold and dispersed throughout the country, and systematic efforts were made to stamp out their native cultures. Although some of the African culture has survived in language, folk tales, and music, it was generally impossible for slaves to maintain their old ways. Therefore, although there were many slaves, they were powerless. They were scattered, family units were destroyed, their cultures were dismantled, and they were permanently assigned to the lowest rung of the stratification system.

Several conditions were responsible for this state. First, slaves were generally young. Upon arrival, they were thrown in with Africans from all different groups; then finally, their socialization was geared toward the slave system. The two categories—white/nonwhite, superior/inferior—were beginning to form.

Initially, the status of the black was not clearly defined; in the seventeenth century, he or she was an indentured servant with rights to freedom after fulfilling contractual obligations. Because of color and ease of identification, a racial caste system evolved; white indentured servants, on the other hand, were not faced with the prospect of being permanent pariahs.

The transformation from laborer to slave was a complicated process, and it can never be accurately traced, according to Jordan (1968). It must have been made partly in accordance with the English view of the black person's blackness, religion, different style of life, animality, and sexuality. Further, slaves became social and economic necessities because conditions in America required a permanent, subservient, and controllable labor force.

The need for laborers was one major reason for the constant search for new groups to migrate to the United States. But not just any group would do; they first had to be good workers with a replenishable supply; perhaps most important, they had to be satisfied with their low position, so that they would not expect to want the same things other Americans did. It is a tribute to the American system and to its immigrants that the "ideal" laborer, that is, those groups content to remain at the bottom, could never be found, although the current search may be more successful because it seeks to replace the human being with machines. But until this new technology can take over, we will continue to import laborers, mostly nonwhite, to fill jobs deemed undesirable by the native born.

The greatest problem in race relations has been the variable of color as an almost impenetrable barrier, so that there has been a clustering of nonwhites at the bottom half of the stratification system. For example, there are currently no white indentured servants identified as such; they were absorbed and integrated into the mainstream centuries ago, and, no doubt, many of their descendants refer proudly to their early pioneer stock. But the blacks, who arrived at the same time, could not advance nor be absorbed, and many of their descendants remain as residuals of the American system.

There were "free" blacks. But "free" is a comparative term. On one hand, they were freer than slaves, but on the other hand, they were surrounded by restrictions created by white society. The boundary restrictions of the two-category system were already in effect—occupations were closed; voting was difficult; and property rights were limited. Laws, customs, and power were lined up against the free blacks; and if the regular means of maintaining social control seemed insufficient, race riots, burnings, and killings kept the blacks in their place. Finally, they were under the constant threat of being returned to slave status.

SLAVERY

The single most important experience for the black person in the United States has been living under the conditions of slavery. It has stamped both slave and slave-owner with an indelible mark that has been difficult to erase, even though the Emancipation Proclamation is well over 100 years old, and today no one can claim to have lived under slavery. Yet, the system that classifies people into human/subhuman, master/servant, adult/child, owner/owned, and the techniques for maintaining this disparity have survived in both overt and subtle forms.

As with most institutions, slavery evolved in various styles, depending on the locale. Different owners took different tacks, and there were instances of humane treatment. The picture of the contented, loyal black slave beside his or her kind white master sometimes was quite real. Nevertheless, slavery always meant the degradation of a human being to the status of property.

The notion that slaves were property was central to their treatment. Since they were defined as subhuman they could be completely dominated by their master and used in whatever way he or she chose. They were bought, sold, given away, or eliminated. The master, for his or her part, provided room and board, medical care, and any other treatment he or she saw fit.

The Notion of Property

Because they were regarded as property, slave women were used sexually or for breeding purposes. The great disadvantage from the owner's perspective was the constant problem of socialization and social control. Discipline was important; the slave had to be trained for a subservient but productive role. Submission and loyalty were inculcated by making slaves fearful and dependent.

The slave "culture" could not be maintained by a single family or community alone; a host of supporting organizations served its needs. Because they were property, slaves did not enjoy a legally based family life, nor could they enter into contractually binding relationships such as marriage. Since husbands, wives, and children could be separated at any time, a tradition of a stable family system was nonexistent. The father was not the head of the family; parents had little say or power in running their family; and the child's status was determined to a great extent by his or her relationship with the mother (Stampp, 1956). Slavery was also a permanent state; once a slave, always a slave. There was no reasonable hope of passing on higher expectations to a new generation.

The adverse conditions of slavery included high morbidity and mortality rates, illness, filth, disorder, and disruptive life conditions. Equal social interaction with whites was nonexistent, and education and other means of self-advancement and upward mobility were restricted.

A more benign and much criticized view of life under slavery was presented by Fogel and Engerman (1974). They wrote that the system was a functional one and that the excesses found in individual cases were neither very widespread nor very common.

The numerically inferior whites were able to maintain their domination over the more numerous blacks in the South through superior technology, better organization, control of resources (power), an ideology of superiority, and their ability to break up the cohesion and culture of the slave population.

Indians as Slaves?

The same logic that led to the use of Africans as slaves could have been applied to the American Indians. As Jordan (1968) indicated, Indians also were different from the English people in complexion, religion, nationality, "savagery," and "bestiality." In short, they were closer to blacks than to whites. They were treated similarly, yet they were not considered to be as desirable slaves as the blacks were.

Jordan mentioned certain factors that contributed to the difference. First, in the initial confrontation, English people were more interested in "converting" and "civilizing" the Indians than they were the blacks. Second, the "culture" of the Indians made them less enslavable. They were not used to settled agriculture, and their life styles (although there were so many different Indian life styles that some of them might have fit readily into the pattern of slavery) generally were not suited to slavery.

But the most important single difference was power. The Indians had land and resources that the white people wanted, and Indians were able to retaliate and to mount reprisals in a way that the blacks never could. Therefore the Indians were handled through diplomacy, which meant a degree of equal-status conduct. There were also "friendly" Indian tribes and nations—not all were placed into a negative category.

Finally, Indians had to be treated as nations, and this created social distance, detachment, and even respect, since English people admired independent, fighting nations, even if they were antagonists. Conversely, the blacks did not represent a nation, and since their labor was so necessary, intimate daily contact was established under less than equal conditions.

As Jordan indicated, the Indian, rather than the black, became symbolic of America—the profile of the Indian and the buffalo, not the black, graces the famous five-cent piece.

The Civil War

The problem of slavery was one of the critical factors leading to the Civil War. Neither side really conceived of the black as an equal. For example, the Northern armies rejected early black enlistees for a variety of reasons, most of them overtly racist and pertaining to black inferiority and cowardice.

As the war developed . . . army commanders were permitted to use their own discretion about utilizing Negroes. Some commanders insisted on returning runaway slaves to their owner, and others permitted them to fight. . . . When they were finally permitted to enlist . . . Negroes did so enthusiastically. By the end of the Civil War, approximately 186,000 black troops had been enrolled. These troops took part in 198 battles and suffered 68,000 casualties. (Pinkney, 1975:19).

Even more took part in the overall war effort as servants, laborers, and spies; but a familiar racist pattern was in evidence—blacks served in segregated units under white officers.

The Confederate armies were less successful in enlisting black soldiers. The South was limited by one basic fear—that armed blacks might turn against their former masters. Late in the war, the Confederates drafted a conscription bill, but most blacks fled rather than be drafted into the Southern army.

The Emancipation Proclamation, signed on January 1, 1863 while the war was still in progress, brought a formal end to the institution of slavery. In retrospect, although the bill was a dramatic political gesture, it created many problems for most slaves. There had been very little planning for active black citizen participation, a necessary step since blacks had lived under the bonds of slavery, illiteracy, and dependence for so many years. The President also made it clear that the primary purpose of the Proclamation was to preserve the Union, rather than to abolish slavery.

The Postwar Period

The South was a defeated and devasted country at the end of the Civil War. Reconstruction of the area seemed far more important than the civil rights and living conditions of the newly emancipated. Moreover, the defeated Southerners still maintained their feelings about the inferiority of their former slaves, and violence, both legal and illegal, was a common solution to racial problems.

For example, DuBois (1935) found that Southerners tried to reinstitute slavery through a series of legalisms that would recreate the institution in everything but name. The Black Codes specified conditions of work, property rights, rights to public assembly, ownership of firearms, and other aspects of black life. Blacks could be arrested by any white man—suggesting apartheid: "Every Negro freedman who shall be found on the streets . . . after ten o'clock at night without a written pass or permit . . . shall be imprisoned . . . or pay a fine" (DuBois, 1935:177). Although the Black Codes were suspended by the Freedman's Bureau before they became fully effective, most Southerners actively opposed granting equality to their former slaves. Rather, a return to the two-category system, whether called slavery or another name, was their choice.

Reconstruction   For a short time after the Civil War, blacks actively participated in the political arenas in the South. A series of reconstruction acts and the passage of the Fifteenth Amendment (1870) guaranteed blacks the right to vote. The Civil Rights Act of 1866 gave blacks the rights of American citizenship, and the Fourteenth Amendment prohibited states from depriving any person of life, liberty, or property without due process of law and also guaranteed equal protection. According to Pinkney:

> During the period of Radical Reconstruction black people participated in politics to a greater extent than in any other period in American history. . . . They often held important offices, but there was never a Negro governor. There were two lieutenant-governors, and several Negroes represented their states in the United States Congress. (1975:25)

However, violence against blacks was a constant problem. The disputed election of Republican President Rutherford Hayes, which resulted in the Compromise of 1877, was a turning point for the freed slaves. Rather than advancing toward equality, they were moved back to the pre-Civil War era. Federal troops were withdrawn from the South, and the old Southern leadership rapidly returned.

The years from 1877 to World War I were difficult for blacks in the United States. The Civil War had been fought and won; the Emancipation Proclamation had abolished formal slavery; the opportunity for a new relationship existed, but the clock did not move forward.

In 1896 the Supreme Court decision on the *Plessy* v. *Ferguson* case strengthened the Jim Crow laws, and separate but equal (which in reality was separate but unequal, or the model of domination) became the law of the land. One critical factor affecting the power position of the blacks in the South during this era (and lasting much beyond this time) was their inability to purchase the land on which they lived. Many were in debt and found that putting in long hours, working hard, and following "American" values were not translated into upward mobility and economic independence. For example, throughout the nineteenth century, blacks were the majority of the labor force in the rural South, yet they never owned more than 6 percent of the land, and these were typically small operations on marginal land. The situation in the Southern cities was similar. Black labor was at the mercy of the dominant group, which was content to retain a racial caste system (Hraba, 1978:275).

The conditions under which blacks were forced to live belied any free status. The boundaries of the two-category stratification system—prejudice, discrimination, and segregation—became stronger than ever. Blacks were, for all intents and purposes, relegated to a caste position based on color, and no black person could expect equal treatment. Informal, "spontaneous" methods of maintaining the boundaries and keeping the blacks in their place were frequently used. Lynchings were one of the most popular.

Lynching has long been a part of interracial history. Although the origin of the lynch law is somewhat clouded, there is an association with Charles Lynch, a Virginia Quaker who was born near the present city of Lynchburg, Virginia in 1736 (Shay, 1938). Although Lynch was sympathetic to the colonies during the revolution, he did not actively participate in the rebellion. But when the existing laws and courts of justice were unable to cope with some Tories who were stealing horses for the British armies, Lynch and several companions decided to take the law into their own hands. They caught the thieves, held court, brought witnesses, then meted out punishment to those who they felt were guilty. The first "lynchings" were whippings and lashings, not hangings.

Lynchings

Lynching was one means of handling conflict, usually with only a semblance of a trial, with individuals who were suspected, accused, or convicted of a violation of laws, customs, or mores. At this early stage, blacks were seldom the victims; instead, the victims were horse thieves, wife beaters, gamblers, and murderers. Execution was an added "refinement."

Blacks became the primary targets in the decades preceding the Civil War, and increasingly so after the war. According to Berry:

> Finally, the period of the Civil War and the Reconstruction saw the pattern of lynching firmly established: courts of law, though in full operation are circumvented; no effort is made to determine the guilt of the accused; punishment is invariably death, often accompanied by torture; and the victim is usually a Negro. (1951:125)

As with much "official data" in the social sciences, secondary sources must be used to ascertain the number of lynchings, and they often offer unreliable statistics. One source estimates the number of lynchings since 1882 to have been more than 5,000 (Shay, 1938:7). Lynching declined in popularity over time. It reached its height in 1892, when there were 235 recorded lynchings; by the 1920s the average number had dropped to 31.2 per year, and since the 1920s, there have been only scattered reports.

Although lynching served mainly as a symbolic device to keep the blacks "in their place," it was symptomatic of the racial barriers. Any form of behavior that threatened the ego of the white Southerner could be punished violently.

As could be expected under these negative conditions, there was an exodus of blacks from the South to the northern urban areas. There was the promise of more jobs and better social opportunities. But, the blacks discovered that racism was not confined to the South and that northern white behavior was less than "Christian." A number of laws, customs, standards, and rationalizations brought barriers and created segregated areas often as stringent as those in the South. A newer feature, mob violence in the form of race riots, was added to the already impressive list of techniques to maintain white superiority.

THE TWENTIETH CENTURY

Booker T. Washington (1856–1915), W. E. DuBois (1868–1963), and Marcus Garvey (1880–1940) were prominent names during the early part of the century. Washington advocated a drive toward self-sufficiency and self-determination through training in vocational pursuits and business. He felt that proficiency in specific skills was far superior to liberal arts training and that investing dollars for profit made more sense than to "spend a dollar for an opera" (Hall, 1977). Washington's model was that of acculturation and adaptation to existing realities.

DuBois, whose name is linked with Pan-Africanism, the Niagara movement, and the National Association for the Advancement of Colored People (NAACP), opposed Washington's programs. He criticized Washington for abandoning the fight for political and civil rights, although he agreed on the need for racial pride and improved economic conditions.

DuBois (1935) perceived the basis of southern white power as a combination of high social prestige, ownership of property, and ability to disenfranchise the blacks. The gentleman Southerner was able to use power and prestige in the context of economic interests and gain to establish and maintain the two-category system. Henderson (1976) wrote that DuBois was one of the first blacks to show the relationships among the Southern economic structure, racial discrimination, segregation, brutality, and the exploitation of black labor.

Garvey, originally from Jamaica, established the Universal Negro Improvement Association (UNIA) in Harlem around 1919 (Hall, 1977:6). Garvey saw Africa as the national homeland and envisaged blacks from all over the world marching to the continent and taking it back from its colonial oppressors.

All of these approaches had their adherents, but they all failed because of the lack of power in the local community. There was never the combination of unity, cohesion, numbers, and resources necessary to put these plans into operation. Nevertheless, the dream of black liberation and escape from white domination, which was the common motivating factor behind these plans, continues as the main theme for black leaders to the present day.

Hall (1977) saw the 1930s, the depression years, and the New Deal as changing the emphasis of black movements. Most of the black organizations could not deliver viable economic programs, whereas the New Deal sponsored by the federal government could, and people opted for "meat to eat" plans rather than "pie in the sky" programs. Therefore, in the mid-1930s, there was increased concern among blacks for getting a piece of the pie, no matter how small, rather than concentrating on separatist, ideological movements. Possibly the most important document in this era was the publication of Myrdal's *American Dilemma* in 1944, which concluded that it was to the advantage of American blacks to work toward assimilation into the white, dominant system. But it also pointed out that a resolution of the black-white dilemma was critical to America's future.

The 1940s brought World War II, and the main black activity was focused on the NAACP and its legal battles for obtaining fair and equal employment. President Franklin D. Roosevelt issued an executive order banning discrimination in industries with federal contracts. But Garfinkel (1959) questioned the effectiveness of that order.

The year 1955 saw the beginning of a changed social movement among blacks (Geschwender, 1971:3). Previously there had been revolts, insurrections, runaways, the Niagara movement, and Marcus Garvey's "Back-to-Africa" drive that signaled the desire for social change among many blacks. But generally, these acts were isolated, uncoordinated, and lacked continuity, although the last two were more ambitious. There had also been organizations—the underground railroad, the abolitionist movement, the NAACP, and the Urban League—that aimed at amelioration and change, but they all were under white control.

The Black Revolt

Several important factors underlie the historical development of these social movements. World Wars I and II provided a major impetus for social change: (1) they opened up job opportunities previously unavailable to many blacks; (2) they provided new experiences and new exposure, especially to those who were sent overseas; and (3) they raised the level of black expectations and standards of living so that during the postwar readjustment period, many blacks were unwilling to settle for less.

Blacks began to feel acutely deprived and dissatisfied when they compared their situation to the rapid progress of the whites. Whites had made impressive gains in jobs, income, and education but blacks lagged far behind. Even so, between 1940 and 1960, blacks began to enter the universities at an accelerated rate. Rather than feeling alienated from their background, these educated blacks felt a responsibility toward their communities and reestablished ties with them. Thus arose a collective sense of deprivation, an awareness of common grievances, a view of the white as the maintainer of the barriers, and the beginning of black solidarity.

The civil rights movement in the early 1950s was dominated by middle-class blacks and college students. As late as 1962, the middle-class black was at the forefront (Orbell, 1967), but by 1964 differences in class background began to diminish (Orum & Orum, 1968). As the movement shifted from black middle-class domination, its tactics also became more militant. Leaders also changed rapidly as the moods and responses of the movement evolved and strategies shifted. Newer organizations came into being—a wider spectrum of tactics replaced the accommodationist strategies of the previous era. Terms such as ''direct action,'' ''confrontation,'' and ''nonnegotiable demands'' reflected this newer response.

Supreme Court Decision of 1954

The 1954 Supreme Court decision prohibiting racial segregation in public education was another important milestone in race relations. But, as with most landmarks, it was not an isolated, accidental occurrence. Rather, the decision itself was both the culmination and the beginning of a series of actions affecting the two most important features of boundary maintenance—legal discrimination and legal segregation.

There was a corresponding change in the Afro-Americans. Many no longer accepted the status quo of the two-category stratification system; the past had given way to a new series of strategies. Whiteness and white role prescriptions were no longer the desired norms; blackness in the form of black militancy, black power, black identity, and black autonomy had come to the fore. Similar movements in former colonized African areas added an impetus and led some whites to suspect a worldwide conspiracy. Other members of the dominant majority were now aware that their ideas of democracy and the melting pot were based on ethnocentric and racist assumptions. They recognized that adaptation, adjustment, and acculturation had been a one-way flow, from people of color to people of one color—white.

But the stresses created by newer goals, strategies, and techniques led to conflict, often of a tragic nature. Violence had been used to maintain the boundaries, and violence was used to change them. The rhetoric flowed as newer leaders replaced new leaders.

One of the results of the changes in tactics and strategies has been the increase in violent interaction. The period from 1964 to 1968 was characterized by urban riots and slogans such as "Burn, baby, burn," and "Kill the pigs." Expectations had risen through a series of advances in civil rights. For example, the Civil Rights Acts of 1964 and 1965 desegregated public facilities, ensured voting rights, and addressed the problem of job discrimination. But the effect of these changes on black lives was very slow; there were numerous instances of white intransigence and violence—bombings, intimidation, and the ever-present charges of police brutality (Lieberson & Silverman, 1965). It did not help when most of these charges went unheeded.

Increasing Violence and Urban Riots

Only small percentages of the total black population actually participated in outbursts in any given city; most of the urban riots were spontaneous (Meir & Rudwick, 1969) and loosely organized, if at all (Downes, 1968) The participants tended to be younger blacks between the ages of fifteen and twenty-four, better educated, and with incomes comparable to nonparticipants, although the blacks had a slightly higher rate of unemployment. They were motivated by a sense of relative deprivation, which gave the groups a feeling of solidarity. White-owned property was the primary target of violence (Downes, 1968; Meier & Rudwick, 1969).

Government and industry responded to the outbursts with jobs and promises of better conditions. But as the riots of 1967 continued into 1968, many blacks began to question the cost in black lives in cities such as Newark and Detroit. The riots were seen to be counterproductive, and potentially violent outbursts were defused. Ghetto riots diminished and virtually disappeared in the early 1970s but were replaced by a series of shoot-outs between black militants and police (Knopf, 1969).

The Black Power slogan emerged during a nonviolent march through Mississippi led by William Meredith in 1966. A shot fired by a white hit Meredith and turned a relatively small demonstration into a major one. Stokely Carmichael became the chief advocate of Black Power, defining it as "the ability of black people to politically get together and organize themselves so that they can speak from a position of strength rather than a position of weakness" (Ladner, 1967:202). Since that time there have

Black Power

been so many definitions and applications of this phrase that its original meaning has been misunderstood (Franklin, 1969)

Generally, the Black Power movement has sought to redistribute the power in society by any means possible. The Black Power ideology is mainly socialistic and sees capitalism as the major problem because it is exploitative. The overthrow of capitalism would eradicate the exploitation; black autonomy, community control of the ghettos, and economic self-sufficiency are viewed as means by which power can be established to oppose all forms of capitalism.

Another branch of its ideology sees power in the hands of a few whites. Blacks, as well as poor whites, are exploited by this select few. Black Power contains the possibility of an alliance between blacks and exploited whites.

One goal of black separatism is to create an independent black nation. This may be a temporary goal in order to integrate the blacks and to build a power base from which they can attain full equality. Though the advocates of Black Power and black separatism may differ in rhetoric and tactics, their goals are essentially the same (Gerschwender, 1971).

The two major variations within the black separatist movement are *tactical separatism* and *ultimate separatism* (Gerschwender, 1971:434). Tactical separatism views separation as a means of gaining control over one's own destiny and achieving self-determination by driving out the white colonists who own or control the ghetto industries and schools. Ultimate separatism sees separation as an end in itself, rather than as a means to gain power, and desires a strictly black state.

Among the first avowedly separatist movements after World War II was the Nation of Islam (Black Muslims) which espoused ultimate separatism (Howard, 1966). It preached that white people were devils created by a black scientist named Yakub. The whites were considered mentally, physically, and morally inferior to the blacks, who were the first to populate the earth. Yakub's work was met with anger by Allah, who ordained that the white race shall rule for a fixed amount of time over the blacks. In the process the blacks will suffer, but they will gain a greater appreciation of their spiritual worth by comparing themselves to the whites. The Black Muslims desired to free blacks from all white influence and secure land for themselves within the continental United States. Further, their goal was to make black people aware of their special role and future destiny and to educate them in their past history.

Though the Black Muslim movement has split since its inception and its actual membership has never been fully ascertained, it proved to be a threat to the white establishment. The Muslims became the targets of police harassment and negative publicity.

All these changes in strategies threatened white domination. Predictably, in some instances whites mounted a counterreaction out of fear and hostility (Franklin & Starr, 1967), which in turn triggered the formation of black protective and defense organizations.

In 1966, Huey Newton and Bobby Seale founded the Black Panther Party which became one of the leading revolutionary black nationalist groups in the country. Originally organized as a self-defense group, it soon developed a radical ideology, which included goals of overthrowing capitalism (Foner, 1970). The program appealed to large numbers of unemployed, poor blacks. Because of the Panthers' policy of maintaining arms for self-defense and their radical ideology, they soon became targets of police throughout the country. Between 1968 and 1970, dozens of Panthers were killed; thousands of others were arrested, and the group was constantly under police surveillance and harassment. By 1971 the party was divided internally, and Eldridge Cleaver went to Algiers to head the international section, in opposition to Newton and the national organization. In 1972, the national organization redirected its efforts toward providing services for the black community. Although the history of the Black Panthers is brief, it was a powerful influence on other racially oppressed groups in the United States, such as the Chinese Americans, Chicanos, and Puerto Ricans (Pinkney, 1975:216).

Black Panthers

Fueled by nationalist movements, civil rights struggles, and radical ideology the momentum of the 1960s cooled down in the early 1970s. The halt came about partly because of the politics of President Richard Nixon, who impounded congressional funds to aid the poor, appointed racial conservatives to the Supreme Court, and endorsed a policy of "benign neglect" for blacks. Nixon was able to consolidate white support for his policies so that in the 1972 election "two-thirds of white America voted for him while at least 87 percent of blacks voted against him" (Pinkney, 1975:219).

The 1970s

The affirmative action program, aimed at increasing employment and education opportunities for minorities and women, began in the mid-1970s. The program was a recognition by the federal government that employers (including the federal government) could play a more active role in searching for qualified minorities in hiring. Affirmative action is essentially a process-centered approach to discrimination in that it emphasizes an open competition for positions, while discouraging the "old boy'' network of friends and acquaintances as the mechanism for filling slots. Affirmative action programs are built on a functionalist model of society; fully qualified minorities and women constitute the pool for upward mobility. The main problem of the program is institutional discrimination built on past racist policies, so that definitions of who can qualify and who possesses the relevant credentials result in intense competition and in very slow overall progress in changing the basic ethnic makeup of the institutions.

Ethnic studies and black studies programs also began in this era. By 1978 questions concerning both affirmative action and black studies were raised by Middleton (1978). Despite progress, evidence of a white backlash, ''ghettoization,'' and isolation were felt by black professors and students. Some professors indicated that they were not real members of ''the club'' and instead found that they formed friendships with black faculty members in other universities. Declining student interest in black studies was another problem. A recent interview with a black chairman of a sociology department at a major midwestern university revealed that the current crop of students and faculty is faced with feeling that they were there only because of affirmative action and a ''lowering'' of standards.

Black athletes have been able to rise to the level of their ability without overt discriminatory barriers. Medoff (1975) compared the salaries of white and black baseball players for the 1967–1968 season and saw no differences. Mogull (1975), studying the 1971 baseball season, also saw no salary discrimination.

Opinions vary concerning the current status of blacks. Much depends on the color of the respondent, although even whites working in the field appear pessimistic because of the lack of any fundamental change in socioeconomic structures. For example, O'Gorman (1978), a white teacher in Harlem, sees the forces of evil continuing to destroy ''his'' children through lack of proper food, proper rest, medical attention, generally filthy conditions, and the intolerable situation which continues to cry for curative psychiatric, spiritual, and parental care. He looks with disfavor on some black intellectuals who romanticize the plight of a deteriorating Harlem. James Baldwin, the novelist (1974), painted a bleak picture in which institutional racism is even more powerful today and in which blacks have been left alone in their struggle. Yette (1971) maintained that blacks have been allowed to become obsolete, so that the very survival of a residual population is now at stake. He cited the nation's priorities to illustrate his thesis. For example, when the Southern Christian Leadership Council asked for one billion dollars to feed the country's poor, they were turned down; on the other hand, over $30 billion were spent to destroy Vietnam.

The sheer number of blacks presents a threat to white domination. In 1965, they numbered over 21 million, or 10.8 percent of the population; by 1970 they numbered 22,580,289, or 11.1 percent.

Pinkney stated (1975) that at the time of the first U.S. Census in 1720, blacks represented an even higher percentage, constituting 19.3 percent (750,000) of that early population.

In 1960, 73 percent of all blacks lived in the urban areas; in the North and West, they were almost exclusively (95 percent) urbanites.

The Urban Community

In 1970, four out of every ten Negroes in the United States were living in the 30 cities with the largest Negro population. This percent

THE BLACK POPULATION OF THE UNITED STATES, 1790–1970   *TABLE 8.1*

Year	Total U.S. population	Total Black population	Percent Black
1970	203,211,926	22,580,289	11.1
1965	193,818,000	20,944,000	10.8
1960	179,323,175	18,874,831	10.5
1950	150,697,361	15,042,286	10.0
1940	131,669,275	12,865,518	9.8
1930	122,775,046	11,891,143	9.7
1920	105,710,620	10,463,131	9.9
1910	91,972,266	9,797,763	10.7
1900	75,944,575	8,833,994	11.6
1890	62,974,714	7,488,676	11.9
1880	50,155,783	6,580,973	13.1
1870	39,818,449	5,392,172	13.5
1860	31,443,321	4,441,830	14.1
1850	23,191,876	3,638,808	15.7
1840	17,069,453	2,873,648	16.8
1830	12,866,020	2,328,642	18.1
1820	9,638,453	1,771,656	18.4
1810	7,239,881	1,377,808	19.0
1800	5,308,483	1,002,037	18.9
1790	3,929,214	757,208	19.3

SOURCE: Computed from data from the following U.S. Bureau of the Census publications: *Historical Statistics of the United States, Colonial Times to 1957,* Series A 59–70, p. 9, and Series A 17–21, p. 8; *1960 Census of Population, Characteristics of Population,* Table 9, p. 11. The 1965 data represent estimates published in *Current Population Reports,* Series P-20, No. 155, "Negro Population: March, 1965," p. 1. The data on the Negro population for 1870 have been adjusted by the Bureau of the Census to account for underenumeration in Southern states.

TABLE 8.2

BLACK POPULATION, 1970, 1960, AND 1950, FOR 30 CITIES WITH THE LARGEST BLACK POPULATION (RANK ACCORDING TO 1970 BLACK POPULATION; NUMBERS IN THOUSANDS)

| Rank | | | 1970 | | 1960 | | 1950 | |
Total popu-lation	Black popu-lation	City and State	Number	Percent Black	Number	Percent Black	Number	Percent Black
1	1	New York, N.Y.	1,667	21	1,088	14	749	10
2	2	Chicago, Ill.	1,103	33	813	23	493	14
5	3	Detroit, Mich.	660	44	482	29	299	16
4	4	Philadelphia, Pa.	654	34	529	26	376	18
9	5	Washington, D.C.	538	71	412	54	280	35
3	6	Los Angeles, Calif.	504	18	335	14	171	9
7	7	Baltimore, Md.	420	46	326	35	224	24
6	8	Houston, Tex.	317	26	215	23	125	21
10	9	Cleveland, Ohio	288	38	251	29	148	16
19	10	New Orleans, La.	267	45	234	37	181	32
27	11	Atlanta, Ga.	255	51	186	38	121	37
18	12	St. Louis, Mo.	254	41	214	29	153	18
17	13	Memphis, Tenn.	243	39	184	37	147	37
8	14	Dallas, Tex.	210	25	129	19	58	13
36	15	Newark, N.J.	207	54	138	34	75	17
11	16	Indianapolis, Ind.	134	18	98	21	64	15
48	17	Birmingham, Ala.	126	42	135	40	130	40
29	18	Cincinnati, Ohio	125	28	109	22	78	16
38	19	Oakland, Calif.	125	35	84	23	48	12
23	20	Jacksonville, Fla.	118	22	106*	23*	82*	27*
26	21	Kansas City, Mo.	112	22	83	18	56	12
12	22	Milwaukee, Wis.	105	15	62	8	22	3
24	23	Pittsburgh, Pa.	105	20	101	17	82	12
57	24	Richmond, Va.	105	42	92	42	73	32
16	25	Boston, Mass.	105	16	63	9	40	5
21	26	Columbus, Ohio	100	19	77	16	45	12
13	27	San Francisco, Calif.	96	13	74	10	43	6
28	28	Buffalo, N.Y.	94	20	71	13	37	6
75	29	Gary, Ind.	93	53	69	39	39	29
30	30	Nashville-Davidson, Tenn.	88	20	76*	19*	64*	20*
		United States, total	22,578	11	18,872	11	15,042	10
		30 selected cities, total	9,217	29	6,837	22	4,501	15
		Percent of U.S.	41	(X)†	36	(X)†	30	(X)†

SOURCE: U.S. Department of Commerce, Bureau of the Census, 1970: 17.

† Indicates not applicable.
* 1960 and 1950 populations revised in accordance with 1970 boundaries.

of the total Negro population of the United States residing in the 30
selected cities has shown a steady increase since 1950.

Among these 30 cities, New York and Chicago have maintained
their first and second rank, respectively, over the last three decades.
Detroit, in 1970, has displaced Philadelphia as the third ranking
place and Washington, D.C. has remained fifth. (U.S. Department
of Commerce, 1970:17)

Numbers are most readily translated into political power. The rise
of blacks to elected positions is one indication of their rise in political
power. The number of blacks in government, from county officials and
mayors to members of Congress, is increasing steadily: "Their numbers
leaped from 100 in 1965 to 1,185 in 1969, and had nearly tripled by 1975,
when there were 3,503 black elected officials in forty-five states and the
District of Columbia" (Blair, 1977:192). The major gains were in the
South, which accounted for 55 percent of all black elected officials.

The increased concentration of blacks in urban areas means that the
probability of electing blacks as mayors and other elective officials will
remain high, given any kind of organizational unity. But it would not be
too difficult to predict that the divisions inherent in most groups will
surface, so that the internal struggles for power may at times be decisive
in allowing other, more organized groups to gain power, even where
there may be a high population of blacks.

Most of the status distinctions within the ethnic community parallel **Stratification**
those of the white community. Variables such as income, occupation,
education, and family background are common measures of status in
most cultures. Other indications of social status include property ownership, organizational affiliation, leadership ability, charisma, and life
style. Life style is an especially interesting variable and will be discussed
more fully later.

Certain distinctions in social status such as white ancestry, skin
color, speech accent, and cultural similarities to the whites used to be
important to the black subculture. The growth of black identity and
changed views of color and white ancestry have led to a reevaluation of
these variables.

The Upper Classes. A relatively visible class structure has appeared
in the black community. Drake and Cayton (1945) described a small
upper class made up of persons with the most money, education, political
power, and the "best" family backgrounds. Most of them were doctors,
lawyers, newspaper editors, civic leaders, and politicians. More stress

was placed on education, professional status, and life style than on income.

Billingsley (1968) commented on the differences between the old and new upper classes. The group described by Drake and Cayton was primarily the old upper class. They were men and women whose parents belonged to the upper or middle classes. Their privileged status extended back to the slave days, when they were given inheritances and more education. Many have done remarkably well—men such as former Senator Edward Brooke and Justice Thurgood Marshall are exceptional by any standard. But Billingsley added that it would be an error to think that these men pulled themselves up by the bootstraps. They came from families who had already given them a head start, and they were able to build upon the many opportunities available to upper-class people.

The most common characteristic of the new upper class is that their mobility has been achieved in one generation. The principal attributes have been talent and luck. Many have gained wealth and prestige by becoming athletic and show business celebrities. Another small group receives an upper-class income by means of the "shadier" occupations—gambling, racketeering, and hustling; through their own abilities they are able to wield a considerable amount of influence in the black community (Billingsley, 1968). There is a small group of newly elected government officials such as mayors (ex-mayors Stokes of Cleveland, Hatcher of Gary) who have risen from humble origins to become attorneys and then to gain high political office.

Freeman, in writing about the black elite (1976), attributed the "success" of the new group to education and the emergence of black professionals. Comer (1972), a black psychiatrist at Yale, described his personal experiences on the way to professional status. The stereotyping of blacks by white colleagues and their overall insensitivity were common aggravations.

The black upper class as a group generally supports civil rights activities through the NAACP or the Urban League; they are usually Protestants and are active in social clubs such as fraternities and sororities (Pinkney, 1975). They usually entertain at home, and their guests are of equal status. The "black elite" in the Los Angeles community has changed. An upper class has not been established, and there appears to be a rapprochement between the social classes on the issue of black identity. Leadership positions have not gone automatically to the financially successful.

Tate (1976) studied 350 traditional black elites and 350 new elites in Oakland, California. He found few ideological differences between the groups and discovered that both were evenly divided as to the concept of internal colonization of their community. All respondents saw an increasing stratification by economic class in the black community.

The Middle Classes. There is a growing black middle class. The occupational categories cover a wide range—professionals, independent business persons, clerical and service workers, and laborers. There are many civil service workers, public school teachers, ministers, and social workers.

Like the white middle class, black middle-class families are small, stable, and planned; they want to own their own homes and are concerned about the quality of public schools. They usually belong to a number of organizations and social clubs and have perceptions and values similar to those of their white counterparts.

But there are several important differences. Billingsley referred to the precarious economic situation of most blacks; they do not enjoy the same measure of financial security as do whites. They tend to make up for this insecurity by highly visible spending and consumption patterns—the familiar stereotypes of Cadillacs, sharp clothes, and traveling first class that have nothing to do with income. Life style becomes extremely important.

Frazier (1957) used the term "black bourgeoisie" for members of the middle class. He saw many living in a fantasy world and emulating white values and culture. The world of fraternities and sororities is a way of escaping the stigma of color and traditional black culture; the establishment of an American life style without the corresponding economic basis is at the root of the fantasy. They are concerned about respectability and want to maintain certain standards of living, often without adequate economic means, and this creates great stress.

The Lower Classes. The lower-class blacks are at the bottom of the community class structure. Most blacks fall into this category—Pinkney (1975) estimated that as many as two-thirds of the urban blacks belong to the lower class. But they do not belong to the simple, stereotyped group of welfare recipients. According to Billingsley:

> Most Negro families are composed of ordinary people. They do not get their names in the paper as outstanding representatives of the Negro race, and they do not show up on the welfare rolls or in the crime statistics. They are headed by men and women who work and support their families, manage to keep their families together and out of trouble most of the time. They are now what might be generally conceived of as "achieving families." They are likely to be overlooked when the white community goes looking for a Negro to sit on an interracial committee, or take a job where Negroes have not been hired before. For they have not gone to college and they are not part of that middle- and upper-class group most likely to come into intimate, daily contact with the white world. At the same time, they are likely to be overlooked by the poverty program and

other efforts to uplift the poor and disadvantaged. They often do not qualify to take part in these programs because they are not on welfare. They are, in a word, just folks. . . . And yet, these ordinary Negro families are often the backbone of the Negro community. They are virtually unknown to white people, particularly white people who depend on books and other mass media for their knowledge of life in the most important ethnic subsociety in America today. (1968:137)

Billingsley divided the lower class into three distinct groupings: the working nonpoor, the working poor, and the nonworking poor. The working nonpoor are semiskilled but often well-paid men in industrial jobs: truck drivers, construction workers, and auto mechanics; if it were not for the color of their skins, they would comprise a majority of some labor unions and possess modest homes in the suburbs. But only a relatively small elite constitutes the hard-hat lower class among the blacks.

The working poor are the majority of poor blacks. They live "in nuclear families headed by men who work hard every day, and are still unable to earn enough to pull their families out of poverty" (Billingsley, 1968:139). These families are self-supporting and include the unskilled laborers, service workers, domestics, janitors, and porters. Many of the values that are associated with working-class people—hard work, frugality, a college education, and wanting a better life for their children—are part of their culture. But this group remains invisible and is likely to be ignored when individuals representing the black community are selected.

The bottom rung of the lower-class ladder holds the nonworking poor, sometimes referred to as the "underclass." Pinkney (1975) estimated that as many as two-thirds of the urban blacks fall into this category. They include the chronically unemployed, the welfare recipient, and the newcomer from the South. Family disorganization is great and is brought to the attention of the larger public only through violent acts or political slogans. These individuals become the stereotype of the urban, disorganized black; they are readily available scapegoats for absorbing some of the frustrations of the taxpayer. Their interaction with the larger society consists mostly of being "clients" to social workers, teachers, and other professionals, or of being "problems" to the police. Needless to say they are "nothings" to the majority who ignores and forgets their existence.

The overriding characteristic of lower-class blacks is alienation. They are powerless; they have very little hope for a better future; and they lack the education and organization to help alleviate their despair and suffering. Many tend to belong to fundamentalist churches and are rejected by blacks of higher status. One of the more damaging factors affecting the status of all blacks is that the lower-class black man serves as the stereotype for those who want to maintain the boundaries between races.

The Family

It is impossible to talk about the black family without discussing the influence of the surrounding communities, both black and white. It is shortsighted to assume that the family exists in isolation and is therefore the independent variable that causes problems. From this perspective "family disorganization" becomes the "cause," and social problems such as crime, delinquency, and mental illness become the "effects" of the family pattern. But the family itself can be thought of as a response or adaptation to the pressures of survival, and its structure and function is a reflection of a host of other variables.

The distortions are even more pronounced when the white family is used as the standard of excellence. For many members of ethnic groups, there is nothing magical about the white family structure, with its ever-increasing rates of separation and divorce. But a report by Moynihan, then assistant secretary of labor, entitled *The Negro Family: The Case for National Action* (1965), saw the deterioration of the black family as the fundamental source of weakness in the black community. The author cited the number of dissolved marriages (one-quarter), illegitimate births (one-quarter), female-headed households (one-quarter), and the startling increase in welfare dependency (no figures given).

Black writers like Billingsley have questioned the Moynihan report's emphasis—"nearly one-quarter"—which leaves over three-quarters of black families with a normal structure. Bernard observed:

> Many readers . . . will be surprised to learn that the "typical" (in the sense of commonest) type of family among Negroes is one in which both husband and wife are living together in their first marriage. (1966: preface)

Berger and Simon (1974) found no significant differences between black and white families, while the MacDonalds (1978), in criticizing the Moynihan report, emphasized that it is both unrealistic and ethnocentric to exaggerate black family structure as an explanation of social problems brought about by racism, unemployment, low wages, menial occupations, poor housing, and poor schools.

Disorganization in many black communities extends far beyond the family itself. Racism, boundary-maintenance mechanisms, and pariah-group status are but a few of the variables that have created pressures on all black institutions, including the family. For example, adequate

TABLE 8.3

BLACK FAMILY STRUCTURE

Type of family	Household head		Other household members		
	Husband and wife	Single parent	Children	Other relatives	Non-relatives
Nuclear Families					
Incipient nuclear family	X				
Simple nuclear family	X		X		
Attenuated nuclear family			X		
Extended Families					
Incipient extended family	X			X	
Simple extended family	X		X	X	
Attenuated extended family		X	X	X	
Augmented Families					
Incipient augmented family	X				X
Incipient extended augmented family	X			X	X
Nuclear augmented family	X		X		X
Nuclear extended augmented family	X		X	X	X
Attenuated augmented family		X	X		X
Attenuated extended augmented family		X	X	X	X

SOURCE: Andrew Billingsley, *Black Families in White America* (Englewood Cliffs, N.J.: Prentice-Hall, Inc.) © 1968, p. 17.

income alone would help greatly in making black families independent. The lack of income forces an interdependence with the surrounding community. If jobs are scarce and the black father is unemployed, the nuclear family will break down (as would any family), especially when the presence of a male in the home makes the family ineligible for public welfare. Conversely, as job security and income are assured, stable, middle-class family patterns will no doubt emerge.[1]

Family Structures. There is a wide range of black families, and they have many variations. Billingsley (1968) presented the various structures (Table 8.3).

Each structure represents a different constellation of members and is a response to certain needs and circumstances; each fulfills certain functions. Given such complex structures, it would be quite false to say

[1] Billingsley (1968) showed that the black family in Africa was strong and central to African civilization. Generally, it was male-dominated and had various patterns of marriage, lineage, kinship ties, rights, and obligations. Slavery broke up these patterns and did not permit black families to assimilate American culture.

that the black family is a "tangle of pathology"; rather, the families are legitimate subsystems of the larger society and represent groups adapting to the needs of their membership.

Since 1950, there has been a gradual decline in the number of black (and other nonwhite) husband-wife type families (a decrease of 77.7 percent to 67.4 percent), and a corresponding rise in the female-headed household (Table 8.4). It is difficult to pinpoint any one reason for this change.

Other Problems. The stereotype of the black family—many children fathered by separate males, desertion, dependence on welfare, and matriarchal structure—more accurately describes the underclass. The lower the income, the fewer goods, services, and opportunities there are. The stress of living for the poor is therefore extremely high; and when the duration and intensity of poverty is taken into consideration, the high rate of problem behavior comes as no surprise.

Statistics indicate that the rate of illegitimacy for black Americans is eight times the rate for whites and that a disproportionately high percentage of black children grow up in broken homes (Pinkney, 1975:96). Crime, delinquency, mental illness, drug addiction, and other signs of a troubled population all are present. Official data on social problems are difficult to interpret because they are subject to a large number of biases.

PERCENT DISTRIBUTION OF FAMILIES BY TYPE: 1950, 1955, 1960, AND 1966 TO 1971*　　　　　　　　　　　　*TABLE 8.4*

Year	Husband-wife		Other male head		Female head†	
	Negro and other races	White	Negro and other races	White	Negro and other races	White
1950	77.7	88.0	4.7	3.5	17.6	8.5
1955	75.3	87.9	4.0	3.0	20.7	9.0
1960	73.6	88.7	4.0	2.6	22.4	8.7
1966	72.7	88.8	3.7	2.3	23.7	8.9
1967	72.6	88.7	3.9	2.1	23.6	9.1
1968	69.1	88.9	4.5	2.2	26.4	8.9
1869	68.7	88.8	3.9	2.3	27.3	8.9
1970	69.7	88.7	3.5	2.3	26.8	9.1
1971	67.4	88.3	3.7	2.3	28.9	9.4

SOURCE: U.S. Department of Commerce, Bureau of the Census, 1970: 107.

* *Most of the tables in this section show data on families for the year 1970. Figures on families from the March 1971 Current Population Survey, which recently became available, have been included only in this table in this section.*

† *Female heads of families include widowed and single women, women whose husbands are in the armed services or otherwise away from home involuntarily, as well as those separated from their husbands through divorce or marital discord.*

Nevertheless, these high rates continue because of tremendously negative environmental conditions, rigid boundary maintenance mechanisms that "keep them in their place," overall lack of opportunities, and the racist attitudes of most Americans.

In other areas, statistics[2] show that 17 percent of blacks (including other nonwhite races) are on welfare, as opposed to 4 percent of whites. (It is interesting to note, however, that the total number of whites receiving public assistance is several million higher than the total nonwhite group.) Likewise, the unemployment rate for blacks remains disproportionately high. In 1970, it was almost two times the white unemployment rate. This has been relatively constant over the years. School dropouts also show a disproportionate number of black youths. At age nineteen, 44 percent of black males were not completing high school as compared to 12.9 percent of white males.

Black Churches

The best known and the earliest community organization in the black community has been the church. There are a number of reasons for its importance. First, religious gatherings were the first forms of association permitted under slavery, so that it reaches far back into black history in the United States (Simpson & Yinger, 1965). Second, the strong interest in religion and its ritualistic practices reflects ancient African traditions, so that the church builds on a cultural continuity (Herskovits, 1941). Finally, the church satisfies a wide variety of needs, in addition to its religious function.

For example, the church made life bearable for the masses and gave meaning to a harsh and often cruel life. It allowed self-expression, provided entertainment and recreation, helped individuals adjust to life crises, and met economic and welfare needs. It offered opportunities for developing leadership skills and helped individuals achieve recognition and status. It served as a community center and was especially helpful in aiding rural inhabitants adapt to urban life. It is no surprise that black leaders such as Martin Luther King and Ralph Abernathy came from ministerial backgrounds.

However the very large number of black churches with their different leaders, ideologies, forms of worship, and congregations may be an indication of the divisions in the community. Some church goals include an acceptance of the status quo, no matter how dreadful, but others provide models for social change.

[2] For complete statistics see the U.S. Department of Commerce, Bureau of the Census, 1970:42, 48, 77.

The two models that most closely approximate the black position in the society are domination and paternalism (also called domestic colonialism and neocolonialism). Data on social indicators of inequality (Chapter 7) demonstrate black inequality in comparison to white male norms on all levels, including education, occupation, income, housing, power, and status.

The lack of power was aptly demonstrated by Pinkney:

> Chief among the characteristics of the urban black community are its powerlessness and its dependence on the frequently hostile white community which surrounds it. These enclaves are kept powerless by powerful individuals and institutions in the white community. The dwellings of the urban black community are usually owned by absentee white landlords and institutions, and no attempt is made to maintaining the buildings or to provide the customary services to their inhabitants. Residential buildings, for which the occupants are charged high rents, frequently do not provide safe and adequate shelter. Often they are owned by wealthy and politically prominent suburban residents. (Pinkney, 1975:62)

The analogy to a colonial possession seems appropriate. Blacks are there to serve the larger community with a supply of cheap labor. Major decisions are made for them from the outside. During periods of disorder the ethnic ghetto can be sealed off, and specially trained police and military forces can be rushed in to meet the "enemy." Ghetto residents themselves often see the police, social workers, and teachers as the enemy or as representatives of an alien force.

Both models of domination emphasize the role of prejudice, discrimination, and segregation in maintaining the inequality. Recent evidence from public opinion polls indicates a diminution of prejudice against blacks. For example, Pavlak (1976) showed that a majority of whites do not mind eating at the same table or working with blacks, although there still is a considerable sentiment against interracial marriage. A poll conducted for the National Conference of Christians and Jews and reported in *Newsweek* magazine (1979) supported the claim of diminishing white prejudice (Table 8.5).

For example, to questions that concerned black stereotypes, the number of whites in agreement shows a steady drop from 1963 to 1978 (with the exception of 1967). The question asked pertained to black ambition, living on handouts, being more violent, being less intelligent, caring less for family, and being inferior to whites.

But prejudice is a minor variable in bringing about basic structural

151

TABLE 8.5

WHAT WHITES THINK OF BLACKS

	(Percent agreeing)					
	1963	1966	1967	1971	1976	1978
Blacks tend to have less ambition than whites	66	65	70	52	50	49
Blacks want to live off the handout	41	43	52	39	37	36
Blacks are more violent than whites	—	—	42	36	35	34
Blacks breed crime	35	33	32	27	31	29
Blacks have less native intelligence than whites	39	36	46	37	28	25
Blacks care less for the family than whites	31	33	34	26	22	18
Blacks are inferior to white people	31	26	29	22	15	15

SOURCE: Fenga & Freyer Inc., as reported in *Newsweek*, February 26, 1979, pp. 48–53.

changes. According to McConahy and Hough (1976), old-fashioned racism is no longer popular and symbolic issues have taken the place of direct prejudice. They observed that code words for racism currently include welfare, busing, school desegregation, affirmative action, and fair housing, and that behavior in these areas may be closer to the true sentiments of dominant-group members.

The *Newsweek* poll also demonstrated the importance of position to the perception of the diminution of prejudice. White leaders saw little rise in prejudice (19 percent), as compared to black leaders (64 percent). Conversely, whites saw a reduction of prejudice (40 percent), whereas black leaders did not (8 percent).

Pinkney emphasized that racism in the United States has been institutionalized, and a mere reduction in prejudice is insufficient to bring about significant changes (1975:220). Discrimination remains, although national norms (federal government and affirmative action) now oppose the negative use of race. But there has been a backlash. A Supreme Court decision in 1978 supported Allan Bakke, a white applicant for admission into medical school, in his claim that he was the victim of discrimination. The issues of preferential admissions and hiring, of the use of overt and implied racial quotas, of due process, and of racial justice remain topics of heated discussion. Generally sides are drawn on the basis of identification with either the dominated or the subordinated sectors of the stratification system.

Segregation, especially in housing, still is an issue. Rabinovitz (1975), in studying the Los Angeles experience, remarked that blacks are not residing in the suburbs as much as expected, and the prospect of achieving stable, racially mixed communities is not hopeful. Tauber (1975) regarded living in the suburbs as a means of achieving social and economic heterogeneity for whites, but found that the black population remains highly segregated. The principal barrier remains discrimination in the sale and renting of homes. A study by the National Committee against Discrimination in Housing reported in the *Los Angeles Times* (April 17, 1978) found that black buyers still face much discrimination in buying or renting in the Midwest. A study in New Haven, Connecticut indicated that a year after a black family had moved in, they were not yet assimilated into their suburban neighborhood.

FUNCTIONAL MODEL

Colonization and domination have not been complete—there are exceptions in which talent and ability have made a breakthrough.

Perhaps the most obvious exception to a totally colonized model is the growing number of blacks who have become successful. Perhaps it is inevitable that in an individualistic, capitalist system, mobility and achievement occur on a one-by-one basis. The two most prominent fields for the breakthrough have been athletics and the entertainment industry. Willie Mays, Henry Aaron, Kareem Abdul-Jabbar, and Muhammad Ali have become household names, heroes, and idols to thousands of youngsters of all ethnic backgrounds; entertainers such as Bill Cosby, Flip Wilson, Sidney Poitier, Nancy Wilson, Mahalia Jackson, Louis Armstrong, and Duke Ellington have won universal acclaim. Recognition has come relatively late for many—the breaking down of the color barrier in baseball by Jackie Robinson seems ages ago, but measured in historical terms, it occurred only yesterday.

The acceptance and success of individual stars does little to alter the status of the great majority of blacks. The colonial system, although not a completely closed one, is still impenetrable to most. Some have referred to it as a net or a sieve, in which the majority is trapped by certain boundaries and cannot get any farther, but a few do manage to slip through.

Mobility for blacks appears qualitatively different from that of most other groups. First, they are in a much lower position in the stratification system and have been there longer than most other groups have. Second, they have never been an integral part of the society because of discrimination and other exclusionary policies. As Pinkney observed, "They have maintained a detachment from society which is difficult for those who have been accepted by society and who identify with it to understand" (1975:223). As outsiders, few have any vested interest in maintaining the status quo and are more apt to advocate social changes. Third, according to Pinkney, blacks have never developed one concrete theory or strategy of liberation or goals around which the various segments of the black community can rally. Often the theories they do espouse have come from revolutionary movements outside the United States, such as the Soviet Union, China, Cuba, or those African countries that have developed successful anticolonial systems. Many of these approaches are difficult to transfer to the United States, and "short of a complete transformation of the social structure of the country, it is unlikely that Afro-Americans will achieve liberation from oppression . . . " (Pinkney, 1975:219). Fourth, there is a deceptive quality about black mobility. A few individuals have achieved stardom and are visible examples of success. The number of poor blacks is also declining (Kilson, 1975), but there also appears to be a widening gap between the "able and prepared" and the "less able" and the "less prepared" (Cameron, 1977). Billingsley called this group the underclass. What may develop within the black community is a dominant/subordinate subsystem, with a numerically small but more powerful group of "have" blacks and a numerically large, subordinated group of "have not" blacks. Federal programs such as affirmative action, job retraining, and financing small minority businesses have a greater influence on the dominant, rather than on the subordinated black groups in the structure and may help to accentuate the stratification. As Wilson stated (1978), race relations for the blacks has moved from racial oppression to a form of class subordination.

In closing it would be useful to ponder the difficulties of most groups in most countries to achieve a peaceful and stress-free transition from models of domination and paternalism. Perhaps the residual effects of these models, especially under extreme racist conditions (for example, Rhodesia and South Africa) are such that the expectation of sensible change with a minimum of disruption and violence may be an unrealistic one.

BIBLIOGRAPHY

BALDWIN, JAMES (1974). *If Beale Street Could Talk*. New York: Dial Press.

BALDWIN, JAMES (1962). *The Fire Next Time*. New York: Dell Pub. Co., Inc.

BERGER, ALAN and WILLIAM SIMON (1974). "Black Families and the Moynihan Report: A Research Evaluation," *Social Problems*, 22(2):145–61.

BERNARD, JESSIE (1966). *Marriage and Family among Negroes*. Englewood Cliffs, N.J.: Prentice-Hall, Inc.

BERRY, BREWTON (1951). *Race Relations*. Cambridge, Mass.: Riverside Press.

BILLINGSLEY, ANDREW (1968). *Black Families in White America*. Englewood Cliffs, N.J.: Prentice-Hall, Inc.

BLAIR, THOMAS (1977). *Retreat to the Ghetto*. New York: Hall.

CAMERON, JUAN (1977). "Black America: Still Waiting Full Membership," in *Uncertain Americans,* pp. 289–96, eds. Leonard Dinnerstern and Frederic Jaher. New York: Oxford University Press.

CLARK, KENNETH B. (1965). *Dark Ghetto.* New York: Harper & Row, Pub.

COMER, JAMES (1972). *Beyond Black and White.* New York: Quadrangle/The N.Y. Times.

DOHRENWEND, BARBARA S. and BRUCE DOHRENWEND (1970). "Class and Race as Status-related Sources of Stress," in *Social Stress,* pp. 111–40, eds. Sol Levine and Norman Scotch. Chicago: Aldine.

DONNAN, E. (1935). *Documents Illustrative of the History of the Slave Trade to America.* Carnegie Institute Publications, 4(409).

DOWNES, BRYAN T. (1968). "Social and Political Characteristics of Riot Cities: A Comparative Study," *Social Science Quarterly,* 49:504–20.

DRAKE, ST. CLAIR and HORACE CAYTON (1945). *Black Metropolis.* New York: Harcourt Brace Jovanovich.

DuBOIS, W. E. B. (1935). *Black Reconstruction.* New York: Harcourt, Brace Jovanovich.

FESTINGER, LEON (1957). *A Theory of Cognitive Dissonance.* New York: Harper & Row, Pub.

FOGEL, ROBERT and STANLEY ENGERMAN (1974). *Time on the Cross.* Boston: Little, Brown.

FONER, PHILIP, ED. (1970). *The Black Panthers Speak.* Philadelphia: Lippincott.

FRANKLIN, RAYMOND S. (1969). "The Political Economy of Black Power," *Social Problems,* 16:286–301.

FRANKLIN, JOHN HOPE and ISIDORE STARR, eds. (1967). *The Negro in 20th Century America,* pp. 185–258. New York: Random House.

FRAZIER, E. FRANKLIN (1957). *Black Bourgeoisie.* New York: Free Press.

FREEMAN, RICHARD B. (1976). *Black Elite.* New York: McGraw-Hill.

GARFINKEL, HERBERT (1959). *When Negroes March: The March on Washington Movement in the Organizational Politics for FEPC.* New York: Free Press.

GARFINKEL, HERBERT (1957). *The Negro in the United States.* New York: Macmillan.

GENOVESE, EUGENE (1974). *Roll, Jordan, Roll.* New York: Pantheon.

GERSCHWENDER, JAMES A., ed. (1971). *The Black Revolt.* Englewood Cliffs, N.J.: Prentice-Hall, Inc.

HALL, RAYMOND L. (1977). *Black Separatism and Social Reality: Rhetoric and Reason.* Elmsford, N.Y.: Pergamon Press.

HAMILTON, CHARLES (1973). *The Black Experience in American Politics.* New York: Putnam's.

HARPER, ROBERT (1975). "Black Administrators and Administrative Law," *Journal of Afro-American Issues,* 3(2):197–206.

HENDERSON, VIVIAN (1976). "Race, Economics and Public Policy with Reflections on W. E. B. DuBois," *Phylon,* 37:1–11.

HERSKOVITS, M. J. (1941). *The Myth of the Negro Past.* New York: Harper & Row, Pub.

HOWARD, JOHN R. (1966). "The Making of a Black Muslim," *Trans-Action,* 4:15–21.

HRABA, JOSEPH (1979). *American Ethnicity.* Itasca, Ill.: F. E. Peacock.

JENSEN, ARTHUR R. (1969). "How Much Can We Boost IQ and Scholastic Achievement?" *Harvard Educational Review,* 4(39):1–123.

JORDAN, WINTHROP D. (1968). *White over Black*. Baltimore: Penguin.

KILLIAN, LEWIS M. and CHARLES U. SMITH (1960). "Negro Protest Leaders in a Southern Community," *Social Forces*, 38:253–57.

KILSON, MARTIN (1975). "Blacks and Neo-Ethnicity in American Political Life," in *Ethnicity*, pp. 236–66, eds. N. Glazer and D. Moynihan. Cambridge, Mass.: Harvard University Press.

KNOPF, TERRY ANN (1969). "Sniping—A New Pattern of Violence?" *Trans-Action*, 47:22–29.

KOCH, SHARON FAY (1972). "Changing Attitudes of Los Angeles' Black Elite," *Los Angeles Times*, April 16, section I, p. 1.

LADNER, JOYCE (1967). "What 'Black Power' Means to Negroes in Mississippi," *Trans-Action*, 5:7–15.

LIEBERSON, STANLEY and ARNOLD R. SILVERMAN (1965). "The Precipitants and Underlying Conditions of Race Riots," *American Sociological Review*, 30:887–98.

Los Angeles Times, April 17, 1978, part I, p. 6.

McCONAHAY, J. B. and J. C. HOUGH, JR. (1976). "Symbolic Racism," *Journal of Social Issues*, 32:23–45.

MacDONALD, JOHN and BEATRICE MacDONALD (1978). "The Black Family in the Americas: A Review of the Literature," *Sage Race Relations Abstracts*, 3(1)1–42.

MEDOFF, MARSHALL (1975). "A Reappraisal of Racial Discrimination against Blacks in Professional Baseball," *Review of Black Political Economy*, 5(3):259–68.

MEIER, AUGUST and ELLIOTT RUDWICK (1970). *From Plantation to Ghetto* (rev. ed.). New York: Hill & Wang.

MEIER, AUGUST and ELLIOTT RUDWICK (1969). "Black Violence in the 20th Century: A Study in Rhetoric and Retaliation," in *Violence in America: Historical and Comparative Perspectives*, eds. Hugh Graham and Ted Gurr. A Report to the National Commission on the Causes and Prevention of Violence.

MIDDLETON, LORENZO (1978). "Black Professors on White Campuses," *The Chronicle of Higher Education*, Oct. 2.

MOGULL, ROBERT (1975). "Salary Discrimination in Major League Baseball," *Review of Black Political Economy*, 5(3)269–79.

MOYNIHAN, DANIEL (1965). *The Negro Family: The Case for National Action*. Washington, D.C.: U.S. Department of Labor: Government Printing Office.

MYRDAL, GUNNAR (1964). *An American Dilemma*. New York: McGraw-Hill.

Newsweek, "A New Racial Poll," February 26, 1979, pp. 48–53.

O'GORMAN, NED (1978). *The Children Are Dying*. New York: Signet Classics.

ORBELL, JOHN M. (1967). "Protest Participation among Southern Negro College Students," *The American Political Science Review*, 61:446–56.

ORUM, ANTHONY M. and AMY M. ORUM (1968). "The Class and Status Bases of Negro Student Protest," *Social Science Quarterly*, 49:521–33.

PAVLAK, THOMAS (1976). *Ethnic Identification and Political Behavior*. San Francisco: R and E Research Associates.

PINKNEY, ALPHONSO (1975). *Black Americans*. Englewood Cliffs, N.J.: Prentice-Hall, Inc.

RABINOVITZ, FRANCINE (1975). *Minorities in Suburbs: The Los Angeles Experience*. Cambridge, Mass.: Joint Center for Urban Studies of the Massachusetts Institute of Technology and Harvard University, Working Paper no. 31.

SCHULKE, FLIP (1976). *Martin Luther King, Jr.* New York: W.W. Norton & Co., Inc.

SEARS, DAVID O. and T. M. TOMLINSON (1968). "Riot Ideology in Los Angeles: A Study of Negro Attitudes," *Social Science Quarterly,* 49:485–503.

SELIGMAN, LEE and ALBERT KARNIG (1976). "Black Representation in the American States: A Comparison of Bureacracies and Legislatures," *American Politics Quarterly,* 4(2):237–45.

SHAY, FRANK (1938). *Judge Lynch: His First Hundred Years.* New York: Ives Washburn.

SIMPSON, GEORGE and J. MILTON YINGER (1965). *Racial and Cultural Minorities* (3rd ed.). New York: Harper & Row, Pub.

The Socioeconomic Newsletter (1978). 3(5).

STAMPP, KENNETH (1956). *The Peculiar Institution.* New York: Knopf.

STAPLES, ROBERT (1976). "The Black American Family," in *Ethnic Families in America: Patterns and Variations,* eds. Charles Mindel and Robert Habenstein. New York: Elsevier.

TATE, WILL D. (1976). *The New Black Urban Elites.* Palo Alto, Calif.: R and E Research Associates.

TAUBER, KARL (1975). "Racial Segregation: The Persisting Dilemma," *Annals of the American Academy of Political and Social Science,* 422:87–96.

UNITED STATES DEPARTMENT OF COMMERCE, BUREAU OF THE CENSUS (1970). *Special Studies: The Social and Economic Status of Negroes in the United States.* Washington, D.C.: Bureau of Labor Statistics Report, U. S. Government Printing Office.

UNITED STATES DEPARTMENT OF COMMERCE, BUREAU OF THE CENSUS (1979). *Perspectives on American Husbands and Wives.* Washington, D.C.: U.S. Government Printing Office.

UNITED STATES DEPARTMENT OF LABOR, BUREAU OF LABOR STATISTICS (1966). *The Negroes in the United States: Their Economic and Social Situation,* p. 141. Washington, D.C.: U.S. Government Printing Office.

WILSON, WILLIAM (1973). *Power, Racism and Privilege.* New York: Macmillan.

WILSON, WILLIAM (1978). *The Declining Significance of Race.* Chicago: University of Chicago Press.

WOODWARD, C. VANN (1951). *Reunion and Reaction.* Boston: Little, Brown.

YETTE, SAMUEL (1971). *The Choice: The Issue of Black Survival in America.* New York: Putnam's.

158

9

AMERICAN INDIANS

The word "Indian" elicits images of tom-toms, war whoops, horses, loincloths, and scalps. Decades of Hollywood epics depicting the Indian as a savage have established the stereotype as the Indian reality. Perhaps at one time the image might have been laid mercifully to rest, but the late night reruns and the simplicity of the Westerns with their built-in good and evil characterizations will no doubt continue to haunt the Indian.

The popular mind conceives of an American Indian who talks in monosyllables ("Ugh"), who runs around almost totally naked (except for a few feathers), who is stoic and expressionless (the cigar-store Indian), and who can follow a trail over granite mountains.

There is also the popular dichotomy between the "good" Indian—faithful, loyal, but inferior to the white person (Tonto)—and the "bad" one—tricky, treacherous, sly, and resistant to the white person's ways (Geronimo). As with most stereotypes, these perceptions contain elements of truth, but the error in them is the error of all caricatures—the Indian does not emerge as a human being with qualities that elicit empathy, understanding, and identification.

Even more damaging to the Indian are some of the beliefs held by the more sophisticated, who blame the Indians' culture for their plight: high rates of alcoholism, early school dropouts, and poverty. Simplified deductions are then drawn. The Indian culture should be destroyed and the Indians acculturated to American ways, even if many die in the process. If acculturation does not work, then isolation in reservations is a partial solution, with the requirement that "we" teach "them" how to live, survive, and raise their children.

But as we have indicated, it is not the fault of the Indians' culture that they are not successful in American terms, any more than the cultures of the blacks, Chicanos, Asians, and Puerto Ricans are the main causes of their problems. We instead are observing the *interaction* between cultures and ethnic groups—what happens when one culture encounters another. The problem is intensified when one group (the whites) has been able to establish dominance over the other and through its power has been able to sustain a dominant-subordinate relationship resulting in social inequality. The question faced by all subordinated groups is how to adapt to these unequal positions.

BACKGROUND AND HISTORY

The European view of the Indians is perhaps best exemplified by the name "Indian," which was given to the natives of North and South America by explorers such as Columbus who were actually seeking a direct route to the East Indies and Southeast Asia. The epithet "Indian," which has stuck up to the present day, covers a widely disparate group of peoples with different languages, cultures, political divisions, and levels of civilization and organization. Rather than indicating differences, the term conceals them and automatically demotes all Indians to the lower level of the ethnic stratification system. The most important ignored fact about the Indians is their diversity. There was, and still is, no one kind of Indian, nor one tribe, nor one nation. Rather, the American Indians represent as much variety as the peoples living on the Eurasian land mass. Their linguistic resources include at least a dozen distinct stocks, and within each stock are languages as disparate as English and Russian.

Indian technology and culture also reflect this diversity. The Mayas, Aztecs, and Incas developed complex social organizations and a sophisticated technology, while tribes such as the Paiute had a much simpler social system.

One explanation for the origin of the Indians is that they emigrated over the Alaskan land bridge from Asia over 20,000 years ago. By the time Columbus arrived in 1492—their "official discoverer"—they numbered several million, but because they were militarily weaker than the Europeans, they soon lost their land and have had to struggle ever since to retain their culture and their way of life.

At the time of the European invasion, the numerous native American societies could be divided into seven major geographical areas, each linked to cultural adaptations based on local conditions. These seven areas were: (1) the Eastern tribes, who hunted, farmed, and fished and whose first encounters were with the English; (2) the Great Plains hunters and agriculturists, whose first encounters were with the Spanish; (3) the fishing societies of the Pacific Northwest; (4) the seed gatherers of the California area; (5) the shepherds and Pueblo farmers in the Arizona and New Mexico area; (6) the desert societies of southern Arizona and New Mexico; and (7) the Alaskan groups, including the Eskimo (Feagin, 1978:191).

There were a wide variety of views of the native American, some even friendly, during the early stages of European contact. But as accomodation changed into conflict and a fight for Indian land, stereotypes and prejudices came to share one common denominator—that the Indians did not deserve to own their own land (Hraba, 1979:210).

For a period of time, from the sixteenth to the late eighteenth century, Indian tribes were viewed as "nations," and they often held the balance of power as the Americans, British, Dutch, French, and Spanish struggled for control of North America. The European powers generally accomodated Indian rights, were concerned with protecting Indian lands, and some tribes were even sought as allies. But most of the tribes allied themselves with losing European factions, so when the Americans eventually established dominance, the native Americans found themselves in a vulnerable position.

Nevertheless, during the early years the British colonies promised good-faith treatment of the Indians. The 1787 Northwest Ordinance emphasized respect for property rights, due process, and justice (Deloria, 1972). Written policy could be interpreted as sincere, although the empirical facts showed recurrent land thefts, with or without the sanction of federal officials (Feagin, 1978:195).

The principal conflict was over land, and a process began that took several forms. One pattern that did not necessarily involve violence was the encroachment of white settlers on Indian land, bringing diseases that often decimated Indian populations. The settlers also drove away the game that hunting tribes neeeded, so that very soon the Indians would have to move to new lands, leaving the territory to the encroachers. But then the Indians might stage retaliatory raids against the white settlers; the colonists would call for the protection of federal troops; they would fight, and the conflict would end in a signed treaty. The result was the same—the Indians were moved out and lost their land. The pattern might then be repeated with the encroachment of white settlers on the new Indian land.

The election of Andrew Jackson to the presidency instituted a much more overt policy of taking away Indian lands. Congress passed the Indian Removal Act in 1830, and within a decade many of the Eastern tribes migrated to lands west of the Mississippi River, voluntarily or at gunpoint. The most infamous was the "Trail of Tears" of the Cherokees, a forced march that resulted in 4,000 deaths and terrible suffering (Cunningham, 1930). Vogel (1972) compared the forced move of Indians to Oklahoma to a move to concentration camps, citing the fact that Indians from as far away as New York and California were "concentrated" into a territory that already had five large tribes.

Indian resettlement in Oklahoma and the Great Plains states was only a temporary respite, since the westward expansion of the American settlers continued. Plains tribes such as the Sioux and the Comanches fought with the white people. These struggles have been popularized in Hollywood Westerns.

The most effective Army strategy was to destroy the tribes' food supply and possessions, leaving them helpless and unable to fight back. The actual war on the Plains resulted in men, women, and children dying from cold, disease, and starvation in less than epic circumstances. Although the Plains Indians had long participated in limited-scale intertribal warfare, they had never experienced the "genocidal actions of federal troop and settlers . . . " (Feagin, 1978:196).

Another factor leading to the destruction of tribal life was through the life style of the white settlers, which included the slaughter of the buffalo, the clearing of the forests, and the commercial use of rivers and streams. By drastically altering the economic and cultural bases of tribal survival, the whites were able to destroy Indian groups such as the Comanches (Fehrenbach, 1974).

The Plains Indians did not passively accept the encroachment into their territory. Their war parties attacked white settlers and used guerilla tactics extensively, with much cruelty and savagery on both sides. As Andrist (1964) indicated, the white-Indian struggle on the Plains was a gruesome and bloody one.

A particularly bloody incident occurred in 1864 when Colonel John Chivington, a minister, and a band of Colorado volunteers massacred nearly 200 peace-seeking Indians in Sand Creek, described by Meyer (1971) as one of the most brutal incidents in Western history. "Both male and female genitals were later exhibited by the victors as they marched into Denver" (p. 32).

Perhaps the symbolic end to overt Indian resistance was the massacre at Wounded Knee, South Dakota, in 1890. The "battle" was the culmination of the army's attempt to disarm and herd the Indians under Chief Big Foot into a cavalry camp. By the end of the massacre, an estimated 300 (out of 350) Indian men, women, and children had been gunned down (Brown, 1970).

The army had been aroused to panic by a Pan-Indian movement centered on the Ghost Dance. In 1890 Kicking Bear related that a voice had commanded him to go forth and meet the ghosts of Indians who were to return and inhabit the earth. He had had visions of a messiah, a crucifixion, and the return of great herds of buffalo and wild horses. The Indians who danced the Ghost Dance would be suspended in the air to await the coming of a new earth, inhabited only by Indians. The Ghost Dance spread rapidly, and white agents were empowered to stop it (Brown, 1970: 434–35). The Ghost Dance caused rumors of potential Indian unity and was one factor leading to the massacre at Wounded Knee. From this time on, the Indians became a part of the various bureaucracies, created to "help" them. Wax concluded:

> Wounded Knee was not the only massacre by whites of defenseless Indians, nor was Custer's Last Stand the only defeat by Indians of an Army unit; however, both involved flamboyant and heroic people, and so have been remembered by Americans and added to their folklore. Both events were also to be the last of their kind, not only for the Sioux, but for the Plains Indians; thereafter, the history of the peoples becomes a matter of reservation life under the aegis of the Indian service. (1971:21–22)

Because of their status as an independent nation, the main legal process in dealing with the Indians was the treaty. "The treaties, which became part of United States law, were often masterpieces of chicanery and fraud; consent was often gained by deception, coercion or threat" (Feagin, 1978:197). Between 1790 and the Civil War, up to 400 treaties had been signed, the great majority pertaining to land issues. Burkey observed that scarcely one has remained unbroken (1978:176).

Treaties

Treaty violations often led to conflict. The federal bureacracy moved slowly, even in those early days; appropriations from Congress were granted annually; corruption and inefficiency caused many delays in living up to the treaties that promised financial assistance and supplies to the Indians. The treaty approach to the native Americans was abandoned by 1871.

By the 1860s Indians were no longer viewed as quasi-nations, to be dealt with through treaties, but as "wards" of the government. Administrative regulations were set up by federal bureaus which exercised tremendous control over the lives of the Indians in a manner analogous to a parent or guardian over a child (Burkey, 1978:234).

The Reservations

For the next several decades, the reservations became the accepted administrative and political solution to the question of what to do with the Indians. Although the ostensible purpose of the system was to assimilate the Indians, Hraba (1979:224) noted that the reservation became an evolutionary cul-de-sac. The Indians were without capital or technology and had little access to industrial work or to educational institutions, so that reservation life left most of the residents totally unprepared to understand and to cope with the vast industrial changes taking place in the American economy and in the "outside world."

The government attempted to Christianize the Indians, to teach them the English language, and to practice American agricultural methods and mechanical arts. In the early 1880s off-reservation schools were established to hasten the acculturation of the Indian children, with generally unfavorable results (Burkey, 1978:235).

By the end of the 1880s, those interested in Indian welfare became convinced that the reservation system, with its attendant paternalism and corruption, would not accomplish its mission of assimilating the Indian into the American mainstream. One result of this new thinking was the Dawes Act, or the General Allotment Act of 1887, which visualized the Indian as an independent landowner (Burkey, 1978:235).

Under the act, which served as official government policy for the next forty years, reservation Indians were supposed to act like white settlers by becoming farmers and tillers of the soil. European conceptions of the meaning of property and the management and use of farm lands, both unfamiliar practices to the Indians, meant that soon thereafter much of the better farm lands ended up in the control of the whites. Instead of aiding in the assimilation of the Indians into the mainstream, the act instead deprived them of whatever base they had had on the reservations.

By the 1930s, the government was ready to shift to another Indian strategy. John Collier, who later became Commissioner of Indian Affairs, and other influential whites helped draft the Indian Reorganization Act of 1934, designed to improve the reservation system and to encourage cultural and structural pluralism. Its provisions included a return to tribal management of reservation land, replacement of the Indian boarding schools, and respect for tribal practices, including native religions (Hraba, 1979:230).

Burkey (1978:275) found that many Indians were against the Reorganization Act for a variety of different reasons. Some were assimilationists and did not support the return to pluralism. Others with private land holdings resulting from the Dawes Act opposed a provision that called for a return of family-owned land to the reservation. Some were antitribal, and many opposed the act on the basis that anything the United States government supported was bound to be detrimental to the Indians. The vote of the Navahos illustrates the divisive nature of the issue: 8,197 opposed the act while 7,679 voted for it. According to Burkey (1978:275), instead of strengthening tribal governments, the unintended consequence of the Reorganization Act was to increase federal control and Indian dependency.

The spirit of protest can be seen in Indian activity over the past several decades. Feagin (1978:209) reported that between 1961 and 1970 there were 194 instances of protest. The largest number were legal suits and formal complaints.

Protest activities included tribes in the state of Washington fishing with nets outside the boundaries of their reservations and a sit-in by some Passamaquoddy Indians in Maine against a logging company. The most publicized event was the occupation of Alcatraz Island from late in 1969 to 1971, which helped to dramatize the plight of the American Indian.

Other Indians also used occupation tactics. Armed Menominees occupied the Alexian Brothers' novitiate building in 1975, while members of the American Indian Movement (AIM) were instrumental in the occupation and siege of Wounded Knee in 1973.

The Alaskan Native Claims Settlement Act of 1971 (Havighurst, 1977) restored forty million acres of land to the natives. The program included $962.5 million as compensation for land taken over by the state and federal governments and the development of regional corporations to invest in productive enterprises such as hotels, supermarkets, mineral exploration, reindeer herds, and fish canneries.

TRIBAL HISTORIES

An analysis of the interaction between the Europeans and specific Indian tribes will be presented here to demonstrate the different types of experiences and adaptations. The Yaquis represent a pluralistic experience; the California Indian, a case of genocide; the Iroquois, a tribe fleeing to Canada; and the Dakota Horse Nomads, a group going through almost every phase, ending up in reservations and now beginning to move into American cities.

The earliest European contact with the Yaquis took place in 1553 along the coast of the Gulf of California. Early Spaniards quickly found the Yaquis to be brave and dangerous fighters; they were stubborn, independent, and extremely courageous in their willingness to fight for their own way of life. They were also highly curious about the culture of the Europeans. Wax wrote:

> The Jesuits found the Yaqui a highly receptive people. Their population of about 30,000 had been dispersed in some 80 rancherias; it was now baptized and concentrated in eight new towns. Agricultural cultivation was improved and intensified, and soon the fertile

river bottoms were producing sufficiently for a considerable surplus
to be exported. However, in time, the area of Spanish settlement
crept close to the Yaqui border, and civil authorities began pressing
to divide the Yaqui lands (which were held in common), to require
payment of tribute and taxation, and to open the area for settlement.
In 1740 the Yaqui "revolted" and killed or chased away all Spaniards other than "their" Jesuits. When, in 1767, the Jesuits were
expelled from New Spain, leadership devolved upon the Yaquis
themselves, and although they had continually to defend themselves
against Spanish and Mexican attempts at conquest and absorption,
they remained fundamentally autonomous communities for over
another century. (Wax, 1971:11)

The Yaquis learned much from the Spaniards. They developed agricultural patterns and worked in the mining and fishing industries. However, the most interesting development was in their religion. The Yaquis
developed their own cult of the Virgin and were guided by the belief that
Jesus had been born in one of their eight towns, Belém (Bethlehem). The
Yaqui belief included a story that Jesus had traveled in their own country,
curing the sick and fighting evil.

Integration. In 1828, after Mexico became an independent nation,
three idealistic laws were passed designed to integrate the Indians into
the new state. It was felt that the Spanish distinctions of race and birth
had perpetuated a caste system that had led to the divisive Indian struggles. By declaring that *all* people would be Mexican citizens entitled to
land and titles, the new government hoped that a truly integrated Mexico
would emerge.

The Yaquis and their neighbors had visualized an independent Indian
nation, rather than integration into the new Mexican republic. The stage
was set for continuous conflict and battles, and massacres and cruelty
were common. The capture and execution of the Yaqui leader Cajeme in
1887 signaled the end of organized resistance; but guerrilla warfare continued, and as late as 1926, Mexican military campaigns were mounted
against the Yaquis.

The Yaquis' resistance was based on a number of factors. Probably
the most important was their communal orientation, which meant that
such progressive programs as the redistribution of lands and integration
would destroy their own economic and spiritual communal base.

Their effectiveness in resisting the government was aided by their
cohesion and organization. They had developed an autonomous system,
including a military arm that was closely tied to their spiritual existence.
Yaqui pluralism was not narrow and parochial, but instead included many
who were fluent in Spanish and had participated in the wider world.

After the collapse of organized resistance in the late nineteenth
century, the Mexican government instituted a dispersal policy that forced
the Yaquis to move away from their homes, while inducing outsiders to

colonize Yaqui land. The Yaquis soon spread throughout Mexico and the southwestern United States, although many tried to return to their own lands when possible. In 1939 the less fertile bank of the Yaqui River was reserved exclusively for the Yaquis, and they were able to resettle where three of their original towns had been. Yaqui communities have also been established recently in the United States. In the 1920s several thousand Yaquis were residing on the outskirts of Tucson.

The War on Poverty of the Johnson administration (Bee, 1969) is an example of the difficulties faced by tribal leaders in administering a well-intentioned government program. The subjugation of the Yaquis resulted in the politics of the powerless, which includes constant intratribal conflict, fights with the Bureau of Indian Affairs (BIA), and arguments among their own leaders. As a result, Yaqui leaders had problems in using poverty program funds to benefit their tribe because they were caught between the expectations of their own people and those of the government and were hampered by their own lack of administrative skills, all of which were necessary to deal with the War on Poverty bureaucracy.

The California Indians met two major invaders—the immigrants who came north from Mexico and west from the states. According to Daniels and Kitano:

The California Indian: The Yahi

> Each group brought with it a common contempt for the native Indian, but a contempt shaped by the quite different values of Ibero- and Anglo-America. Each group subjugated and suppressed the Indian in the quite different ways suggested by its own culture and its own experience in white-Indian relations. Each ran roughshod over the natives and neither considered, in any way, their wishes. Each group regarded the Indian as subhuman; neither accorded him any real say about his own destiny, except perhaps, giving him a choice of how he wanted to die—in hopeless battle or in an even more hopeless existence. California racism, then, dates back to the eighteenth century, back to the earliest settlement by Europeans and their descendents. (1970:29)

One California Indian is known, and his story, as written by Theodora Kroeber, will have to stand as proxy for an otherwise unknown people. Whether Ishi, as he was called, was representative, is, of course, a question that cannot be answered. There is no doubt about the quality of his story; it is one of almost unsurpassed horror. By a historical accident, he was perhaps the last "wild" Indian—the sole survivor, by a few years, of the Yahi tribe.

The Yahi were a tiny "tribelet" of perhaps 2,000 souls occupying a few dozen square miles of territory north of Sacramento. In the space of one bloody year, 1864, when Ishi was a small boy, all but a few dozen of his people were hunted down and destroyed by organized and legally sanctioned parties of armed whites. The survivors of this bloody year, perhaps fifty in all, were further harassed and hunted and killed for the next few years. Then, the surviving handful, a remnant of a remnant, went into what Mrs. Kroeber called "the long concealment," which lasted about four decades. When, on August 29, 1911, an exhausted, middleaged male Yahi Indian was captured near Oroville, California, the "tribelet" was down to a lone survivor, Ishi. He lived four and half more years in the friendly "custody" of anthropologists at the University of California. When he died of natural causes on March 25, 1916, a minor variety of *homo sapiens* ceased to exist; the Yahi had become, in the words of our pioneer ancestors, "good Indians."

The fate of the Yahi, symbolically at least, stands for the majority of California's Indians and is an extreme example of the way whites have treated nonwhites. But thousands of Indians did survive; some merged into the general population; the majority of ethnically identifiable Indians continue to exist on the fringes of American life, technically within our society, but actually almost wholly apart from it. Those surviving, less dramatic casualties of what one writer called the "transit of civilization" from the Old World to the New, also represent a kind of extreme example of white-nonwhite relations in America: physical and legal separation—what we would call apartheid in another land.

The Iroquois

Whereas the Spanish had sought precious metals and had been zealous missionaries, the English, French, and Dutch had been primarily interested in furs. The exchange of animal pelts for guns, ammunition, and other manufactured goods established a trade relationship between the Europeans and the Indians of the Northeast.

The name of *Iroquois* was given to the League of Five Nations, consisting of the Seneca, Onondaga, Cayuga, Oneida, and Mohawk. Later a sixth tribe, the Tuscaroras from North Carolina, was added. According to Wax:

> Its peoples had been living in settled villages near streambeds where the women could plant their gardens of maize, beans and squash. In addition to serving as warriors, the men contributed fish and game to the diet. The machinery of their League was primarily an arrangement for maintaining peace and harmony among the member tribes, and except for issues of conflict among tribes, affairs were largely in the hands of the separate tribes and villages. (1971:13–14)

By the middle of the seventeenth century, the Iroquois had exhausted the furs (especially beaver) in their own territory. They began to look for new lands and became an expansionist nation. They eventually came into conflict with tribes of the northern confederacy such as the Huron, who were active in the French trade. By forming a much more aggressive military and commercial alliance, the league was able to achieve large-scale military victories and to expand its hegemony. It appeared for a time that the Iroquois would extend their power over the entire eastern seaboard, but the Creek confederacies in the South were too powerful, and the Canadian tribes remained more closely allied to the French.

The league fought with the British in the French and Indian Wars, and by the 1700s:

> The Iroquois were becoming both powerful and acculturated: eleven Indian nations were living with the Seneca, numerous whites were intermarrying and a distinctive blend of cultures was emerging. . . . (Wax, 1971:14–15)

Many white colonists were not pleased by the success of the Iroquois. Nevertheless, the British Crown perceived the Indians as powerful allies against the French: the Royal Order of 1763 sealed off the western lands from white settlers and recognized Indian ownership. Wax stated:

> Th Order was not received well among the colonists, and was one of the grievances that was to lead to the Revolutionary War. During the conflict, the League, following its successful system of neutrality in the wars of the whites, tried at first to hold itself aloof. (1971:15)

The peace treaty that followed the end of the Revolutionary War made no provision for the Indian allies of the British. Settlers and land speculators seized the opportunity to invade Indian lands. Maltreatment and conflict led to the decimation of the Iroquois. The national government preferred the friendship of the Indian allies, but they could not control the actions of the settlers and speculators, who often threatened to organize new border states and to secede. Eventually the Iroquois were forced to flee to their English friends in Canada.

The Dakota Horse Nomads

Wax gives the name "horse nomads" to those Indian tribes who developed elegant skills on horseback and who adopted a nomadic existence of following the buffalo. These tribes developed skin tepees and other features of light travel that enabled them to carry on their nomadic activities. In the process, they developed competitive and aggressive warriors who could travel long distances swiftly and quietly, constantly in search of horses, buffalo, scalps, loot, and fame.

Among the tribes who took up this style of existence, after the early Spanish colonists had brought the horses to the Rio Grande Valley in 1598, were the Blackfoot, Arapaho, Cheyenne, Comanche, and the Crow. The Tetons, one of the tribes making up the Sioux, were among the earliest to take to the Plains. Said Wax:

> The Teton became the scourge of the northern Plains, acquiring a reputation for irascibility, impetuosity and stealthy ferocity. The settled agriculturalist tribes, which had built a rich ceremonial existence and complex societal organization, could not cope with the Dakota raids, even though they themselves acquired the horse and some of the traits of the horse nomads. The Teton harassed the traders who attempted to utilize the Missouri River; later they continued the sport with the wagon trains crossing the Plains. Peaceable contact with the whites was mainly via French traders who established their posts along the riverine routes and took Indian women to wife. (1971:18–19)

The development of the rapid-fire revolver and the introduction of cattle ranches spelled the end of the horse nomad. With the advent of barbed wire, the Homestead Act, cattle ranches, and the railroad, the Plains Indians came to be seen as a menace to law and order. Although pitched battles were generally won by the whites, the most effective means of gaining control over the Indians was by paper and pencil—the treaty. These documents, of which there were many, provided certain conditions that both sides promised to live up to in order to guarantee a more peaceful coexistence.

Relationships under various treaties were periodically strained. In 1874, the discovery of gold in the Black Hills brought a flood of new white settlers. Many of them complained about harassment from the Sioux and demanded that they return to their reservation; this conflict ended with the defeat and annihilation of General Custer at Little Big Horn in 1876. But the Indian victory was only temporary, and in the long run, they were the losers. Reservation life, dependency on congressional appropriations, white opportunism, and swindling left most Indians half-starved and diseased.

The history of the Indian is one of maltreatment. There was forced acculturation, extermination and genocide, and isolation on the reservations. Of all the ethnic groups, the Indian is in the best position to question "law and order," "justice," and the credibility of the whites. Deloria (1973) traced the logic of white people in their quest for Indian lands and territory. Although much of the land was conquered by simple armed force, the more powerful weapon was the concept of the Doctrine of Discovery. This doctrine had been used by Christian nations and the Church to establish hegemony over large portions of the earth by simply declaring them "discovered." By a few simple statements ("I plant this flag in the name of my King"), aboriginal lands came under Christian mandate.

The Indian has been an extremely successful "integrator," and there is a problem of identifying just who is an Indian. In the past, white soldiers, vagabonds, trappers, hunters, and traders—primarily adult, single men—invaded Indian lands and mated with Indian women. Of course, there were strong taboos against half-breed offspring, but the number of Americans with some percentage of Indian blood must run in the millions.

At the time of European settlement, the number of Indians in the United States had been estimated as low as one million and as high as ten million. By 1800 the native population was about 600,000, and by 1850 it had shrunk to about 250,000; malnutrition and disease (with extermination and genocide thrown in) were the primary causes. The 1960 Census showed a total of 523,591 Indians; the 1970 figures were 792,730.[1]

The question of who is to be counted as an Indian is extremely complex. The U.S. Census Bureau procedures allow much leeway to the census-taker and the self-report. Since there have been social, psychological, and political disabilities connected with being classified as an Indian, many Indians with an incentive to pass have become non-Indians. But it may soon be in vogue to be Indian again, and the census statistics may rise.

The Bureau of Indian Affairs regards any person who qualifies as an heir to reservation land an Indian, and the definition arises from his or her legal responsibilities. When awards and benefits are given to Indian tribes as plaintiffs, individuals who are marginal in terms of Indian social life, traits, and identification may become Indian. Finally, there are many who have adopted an Indian life style, some permanently, others on weekends or on festive occasions, and yet may not have a drop of Indian blood. Depending on the criteria, they all may qualify as "Indians."

INDIAN PROBLEMS AND SURVIVAL

The Family and the Band

The ethnocentric ideal of white America is the nuclear family—husband, wife, and two children. One of the targets for many reformers was the Indian "band," composed of kinspeople "who recognized obligations to each other, including the sharing of certain kinds of property, and the joint organization of rituals and festivals" (Wax, 1971:75). Bands were most common to reservation life; decisions and actions emerged from group discussion and concensus, rather than from a leader.

[1] The major areas of Indian settlement include Oklahoma with 98,468; followed by Arizona with 95,812; California with 91,108; and New Mexico with 72,788.

Bands were quite egalitarian and served as mutual assistance societies. There was much sharing, and there might be a massive redistribution of property when someone died. Therefore, there was little opportunity for one man or one family to accumulate and maintain vast amounts of property for any length of time. Band organization limited the opportunities for individual Indians to become wealthy, but it also prevented others from being ignored or left to starve.

Another characteristic of the band was its particularistic pattern. Members of one band network were not obligated to share with those outside their own network. This "ignoring" of outsiders has caused much white misunderstanding.

There is no single Indian nation per se. There are instead many local units, such as bands of kith and kin. But white administrators are used to dealing with such units as countries and nations or with smaller units, such as the family. They frown upon band interdependence, especially when there appears to be much freeloading. There is no incentive to gather, hoard, and save, because those Indians who have accumulated some food or cash are visited by their band members until the surplus is exhausted. This band culture conflicts with the American values of individual achievement, accumulation of wealth, saving for the future, and individual industry.

Although recognizing some of the problems caused by the band, Wax feels that it is the strength of the band organization—its vitality, tenacity, and flexibility—that has enabled Indian communities to survive at all. The patterns of sharing, voluntary cooperation, equality, and solidarity have sustained the Indian under the most severe conditions of hardship, whereas other forms of organization (such as the individual family) probably would have led to the total destruction of the group.

Money

Acculturated and urbanized Indians use money in the same manner as the majority culture does. However, money takes on a different value for those on reservations, where there is little opportunity for agricultural or industrial employment and low cash incomes.

The Indian is able to survive on little money because of the band organization, with its mutual assistance, sharing, and pooling. This unit goes far beyond the nuclear family and the extended family, and includes a complex of families living close together. There are also many free services: surplus foods and health care are provided; wood and water are available; and while they are not grand, there are cabins. Since everyone lives under similar circumstances, the competitive strains of the American social system (having a bigger house, keeping up with the Joneses) are absent.

Under these circumstances, the Indians use money for specialties and luxuries. Cash is paid out for sweets, clothes, and trips to relatives, which appalls the "sensible" welfare workers, who have nuclear families and live on fixed, scheduled incomes. They accuse the Indian of being irresponsible, haphazard, and ignorant of the value of money; they try to deprive the Indians of their cash and provide instead the goods and services they think are necessary.

A similar situation exists in some colleges and universities that are granted large amounts of money to teach and train Indians. According to Wax:

> In a sense, the universities have inherited the social role played in the nineteenth century by missionary groups who came to control the reservations because the federal operations could not be kept free of the taint of political corruption. But, just as the missionaries, the universities are insulated from the influence of local Indian communities, and organize their programs according to ideologies, professional codes, and bureaucratic procedures that exclude any control by the relatively uneducated Indians. As the universities build staffs and operate programs, they become increasingly dependent upon these monies, and constitute a vested interest of some potency in maintaining reservations in a subordinated state. (1971:82)

Education

Immigrant groups have always believed education to be the major route to "success"; they think education will allow them to be assimilated into the American way of life. Many of them give up their ethnic ways, only to find their entrance into the American system blocked. This leaves them in the category of part-white ethnics, with its subsequent problems of identity, alienation, and marginality. The Indian child who does extremely well in school may be regarded as marginal or deviant if the majority of his or her peers adopts other norms.

The interaction between Indians and white society's schools is often painful. There is a gulf between the parents and the school system, especially on the reservations. The cultural separateness of the children and their teachers is another barrier. The outsider (the teacher) vainly tries to impose unfamiliar and even dysfunctional styles on the lives of the insiders (the Indian children). There may be much confusion, inattention, and little actual learning, even though by the middle grades there may be a semblance of order and quietness. Predictably, scholastic achievement test scores reveal a steady decline with advancement in grade. Wax feels that the failure of educators to recognize and integrate the Indian peer society in educational tasks is at the root of the difficulty. Other explanations include the alienation of the children from both schools and parents, the inadequate curriculum of the schools (English as a second language), the simple lack of linguistic facility, and the questions of motivation, identification, and confidence. One could also question the meaning of an American education for the Indian.

Wax cited some typical conflicts that occur in the schools when teachers are unaware of the peer society. Indian pupils hesitate to perform individually before the class, not only because they do not want to be exposed as inadequate, but also because they do not want to demonstrate their individual superiority and thereby the inferiority of their peers. If competition is based on a peer-group basis (such as on athletic teams), however, they can become excellent participants.

The Cherokees have an ethnic of harmony. Gulick (1960) emphasized that the self-assertive, aggressive individual destroys this harmony, and yet many teachers promote "self," aggressiveness, and assertiveness as student ideals. For the tribal Cherokee, this individuated emphasis is morally very troublesome. Individual victory, achievement, and exposure—desirable norms in the larger society—are met with uncomfortable and passive resistance by the minority. Wax claimed that a blindfolded person could discern the sharp differences between the Oklahomans of white and Cherokee background. The timbre and loudness of the voices and the frantic attempts to get the attention of the teacher clearly differentiate the whites from the Indians.

The error of many teachers is their desire to disrupt the peer society for individual reward and effort. It is the peer society that provides the Indian with a sense of identity and self; destruction of this tie deprives the individual of one of his or her most important sources of security and worth.

Educational reforms have proved to be as difficult to carry out as reforms in any other area of Indian-white relationships. More and more Indians are moving into urban areas, and federal monies set aside for their special education are probably absorbed into the general fund. The BIA schools continue to have their problems and tend to reflect the interests of the local pressure groups. There are few Indians in colleges and universities; education has not been the "ladder to success" for most Indians.

Alcoholism

The vulnerability of the Indian to alcohol has become a legend. The Indian style of drinking does not consist of demure cocktails before dinner or "holding one's liquor like a gentleman." Rather it is what Wax called "binge drinking." This drinking takes place in peer groups, usually of young males, and is often associated with driving at high speeds and encounters with the police, with the promise of danger and possible disaster.

Some have argued that the relative newness of liquor in Indian life has led to some of the current problems, and that the Indian has not yet had time to work out a culturally acceptable way of drinking (at least according to majority norms). The problem is compounded by the fact that many Indians value states of trance and euphoria and that the all-important warrior rituals are recreated under the influence of alcohol. The conflict between being an Indian warrior or a "failure" in Western terms can be partially forgotten when one is inebriated.

Dozier (1966) provided a sociocultural explanation for the Indians and alcohol. Wars, contemptuous settlers, cultural invasion, military subordination, loss of property, and invasion of their hunting and fishing grounds are historical factors that have led to sociocultural deprivation and consequent drinking among present-day Indians.

Whatever the reason, liquor has often gotten Indians into trouble with law-enforcement agencies. The rate of Indian arrests for crimes related to alcohol is many times the national average, and drunkenness seems to rise as the Indian migrates to urban areas.

Statistics also show a high proportion of Indians in penal institutions. For example, in South Dakota, where the Indians represent about 5 percent of the total state population, they constitute over 33 percent of the prison population. As with most official statistics, the reasons behind the incarceration may be questioned; nevertheless, it is one indication of a continuing social problem.

THE INDIAN MODEL

The Indians' adaptation to their conquerors covers the entire range of intergroup interaction. On the one hand, there are individuals and tribes who have acculturated and integrated to such an extent that a measure of their "Indianness" may be "a drop of Indian blood" from a distant ancestor; there have been other tribes that have been completely annihilated; and there are those Indians who have retained a strong tribal affiliation and are deeply committed to a pluralistic perspective.

The native Americans are probably the closest example of the paternal or colonial model (Model 2B) among all of our ethnic groups. As Jorgensen asserted: " . . . the metropolis-satellite capitalist economy has harnessed the military and the BIA to conquer and control North American Indians, and it is this political economy that has maintained Indian deprivation" (1977:190).

There are no doubt facets of the Indian economy and culture that have contributed to the problem, but the greatest burden lies on the dominant group. It expropriated and exploited the resources of the Indians; it put the Indians on reservations and ran their lives, and it established political, economic, and welfare systems that have rendered most Indians powerless and alienated. It attempted to destroy the Indians' culture and life. It is a credit to the tenacity of some Indians that any part of that cultural integrity still survives.

Thomas (1975), in writing about the internal colony system, emphasized that many of the intentions of the federal programs were benevolent but that their effects were negative (institutional racism). No matter how well intentioned, the administration and leadership still come from outside the group. The structure impedes Indian advancement. For example, in Pine Ridge, South Dakota, the Sioux cannot get loans from private banks because the land is held in trust. Their few, small industries are accountable to the BIA, not to the tribe. Their main resource, the land, is leased out to white ranchers, so that the majority of the Sioux end up as migrant workers, recipients of social welfare, unskilled workers in low-paying government jobs, or in tribally subsidized industries. The structure helps keep the Sioux people away from the mainstream economy, exploits the land resources for the benefit of others, and keeps the majority of the tribe as a reservoir of unskilled migrant workers for the surrounding area. If they complain too loudly, there is fear that Congress may dismantle the costly BIA, the bureau that has trapped the tribes in a dependency relationship.

Dependency

The United States' treatment of the Indian has encouraged dependency and irresponsibility, especially in relation to inheritance laws. Instead of considering rights, duties, privileges, and responsibilities in the complex net of Indian social relationships, the United States views the membership of each person as a case of heirship to a piece of property (Wax, 1971). This encourages the individual to think solely in terms of rights, privileges, and rewards, and not in terms of duties, responsibilities, and obligations. For example, anyone who can prove having Indian blood may be eligible for various federal benefits (in health, education, employment), regardless of whether he or she participates in an Indian community or contributes to its existence. Similar Anglo-Saxon inheritance logic is applied to voting on tribal matters, the sale of property, and other proceedings, with the result that the functioning Indian tribal society is constantly disrupted by those whose only bond with the group is that of blood.

Dependence continues to be encouraged by a decision-making apparatus that has historically been under the control of outsiders. Indian "experts" continue to make decisions on what is good for the Indians, ignoring the needs and desires of the population.

Another important structural factor that maintains the dominant/subordinated separation has been the BIA community and the tribes that it serves. A BIA complex in Barrow, Alaska was studied by Hennigh (1975), who found that highly competent federal officials maintained negative stereotypes of the Eskimo. The source of the stereotype was the aloofness and autonomy of the BIA community as it viewed the more "primitive" Eskimo community and the vast discrepancy in creature comforts and life styles.

General Nguyen Cao Ky, a former prime minister of Vietnam, also discussed the impact of American culture on less developed, poor nations. He talked about the hidden price of United States aid and warned that it was the American technician who took the first step in destroying the culture. The highly paid American technician living in luxury apartments and freely spending money creates a conflict between the foreign and the native way of life, and reminds the citizenry of just how far they must go to reach a comparable standard of living (Wood, 1979).

There has been a rise of Indian employment in the BIA. A study by Seligman and Canter (1976) showed that 52.1 percent of the employees are now Indians (from a population base of one-half of 1 percent). But most are concentrated in the lower and nonexecutive positions.

The rise in the number of Indians in the BIA may be a progression from external to internal colonialism. Nkrumah (1965) observed that under neocolonialism, power may still be under outside control, but that a neocolonialist government (made up mainly of the natives) may be instituted. Frustration and anger over unchanged conditions may then be directed at the ethnics who appear to be in control, but who in reality are not.

The Immigration

It seems impossible to think of the original inhabitants of the country as immigrants; yet in one of the ironies of the interaction between groups, this appears to be the case for the native American.

In 1952 the BIA established a national program of relocation assistance, which encouraged the employment of Indians outside the reservation. In 1956 vocational planning programs were added for Indian youths, and in 1962 a program of employment assistance at seven urban centers was started (Miller and others, 1975). One result of these programs has been the rise in the number of Indians in urban areas. In 1910 only 10 percent of the Indians lived in urban areas; by 1970 the number of urban-dwelling Indians was estimated at over 50 percent.

A study by Miller, herself an Indian, and a group of native American researchers analyzed the adaptation of 120 Indian families to urban life (1975). These are the urban Indians, or the "new immigrants"—made up of many tribes, attempting to succeed in the city by speaking English, going to school, working for wages, and behaving as most working-class Americans are supposed to. But very few have become "Americanized," and Miller's group developed three hypotheses for this resistance to acculturation.

1. The land still belongs to the Indians. They did not come here

from another place; they are the original inhabitants. Who has to adapt to whom?

2. Indians do not see the white way as superior to or more desirable than their own cultural ways.

3. The majority society does not wish Indians to be partners and has created legal and structural barriers to deny them full and equal access.

Steele (1975) questions the assumptions behind the acculturation-assimilation model for the new Indian immigrant. They are based on a small number of Indian migrants and the assumed contrast between urban and reservation life. More relevant questions include discrimination, realistic possibilities for decent employment in the cities, and constructive assistance available to low-income migrants in large cities. The other major question is not concerned with the "superiority" of the white culture to Indian culture but with the political and economic power of the white society, which can almost totally change Indian life.

Denton (1975), in a Canadian study, showed that in the move from rural to urban areas, Indians found themselves stigmatized. They adapted to this negative situation by concealing their Indian identity or by admitting that they were Indians but acting in such a way so as not to be discredited by this identity.

Price (1975) argued that in order for Indian migration to be successful, tribal identities must be fostered. The urbanization process that has decimated the tribes and is leading to a Pan-Indian identity in a white racial society is seen as trivializing and confusing. Miller's study (1975) found that those Indians following a bicultural model and achieving a degree of comfort with both the Indian and white world exhibited a greater ability to survive and to adapt to the city than those families who were comfortable with only the Indian world.

Another important factor remains the accessibility of the homeland, or reservation. Very few of the other immigrant groups had available such an easy option, and there is some evidence that many are taking advantage of returning "home." A study of a group of Spokane Indians (Chadwick & White, 1973) focused on reasons why some decided to stay in the cities and others chose to return to the reservation. Contrary to expectations of the importance of economic factors, the most significant variable was the Indians' feeling of acceptance by the white community.

There have been attempts to help keep the Indians on the reservations. Stoffle (1975), in describing an electronics factory on a Zuni reservation, emphasized the necessity of understanding both the functional requisites of the industry and the culture of the tribe. Conflicts were satisfactorily resolved when cultural and subcultural differences were accommodated by all parties.

A major handicap for the Indian has been the lack of a cohesive, **Lack of Cohesion**
united front. Because they were the original inhabitants, they already
had developed tribal loyalties that included centuries-old enmities, feuds,
and differences. Thus the Indians fought the whites as separate tribes,
often while continuing to fight one another (Josephy, 1969). The threat
of the white conqueror did not serve as a unifying element for the tribes;
in fact, it may have even exacerbated the differences. On the other hand,
the loosely organized white settlers from vastly different backgrounds
who were almost total strangers to each other found the Indian threat a
unifying and organizing influence. They submerged their differences and
achieved cohesion under the threat of the "Indian menace."

The major problem in the reservation is not the Indian culture or its **Poverty**
distinctiveness, but rather, economic exploitation and poverty. The same
is true wherever the Indians live in America, for they, like the blacks,
are considered unequal to white male norms on all measures of inequality
(Chapter 7).

To a considerable extent, poverty is responsible for the lack of
education, especially at the college level, the unemployment, and the
lack of skills. Poverty is also related to powerlessness. As Deloria (1970)
indicated, Indian children were "kidnapped" and taken away to government boarding schools, often thousands of miles away. They were
whipped if they used their native language. Indian ceremonies were
banned, even on their own reservations. "People thought that by banning
everything Indian, they could bring the individual Indians from the Stone
Age to the Electric Age in one generation" (Deloria, 1970:109).

The tragedy of the Indians' plight is, in a sense, the irony of America.
In their rage for progress, white people have not only threatened the
Indians with extinction, they also have plundered the land, decimated its
natural resources, produced overcrowding and pollution, and destroyed

INDIAN POPULATION OF THE UNITED STATES FOR SPECIFIED   *TABLE 9.1*
*YEARS**

1890	248,253
1920	244,437
1940	333,369
1950	357,499
1960	523,591
1970	792,730

SOURCE: U.S. Department of Commerce, Bureau of the Census, 1970.

* *Many students of Indian affairs feel that the Census reports are underestimated.*

much of the natural richness of the country. One national magazine put it this way:

> From its Indian citizens, the United States may yet learn some lessons about restoring the balance between man and his surroundings. The Indian has always been a partner of nature, not a destroyer of it. In the legends he wrote about mountains, trees, lakes and canyons, in his understanding of the spiritual force of nature, he has maintained a vision of coherence and beauty: the land and the men upon it must exist in harmony. (*Life*, 1971:38)

BIBLIOGRAPHY

ANDRIST, RALPH (1964). *The Long Death*. London: Collier-Macmillan.

BAHR, HOWARD (1972). "An End to Indian Invisibility," in *Native Americans Today*, eds. Howard Bahr, Bruce Chadwick, and Robert Day. New York: Harper & Row, Pub.

BONACICH, EDNA (1973). "A Theory of Middleman Minorities," *American Sociological Review*, 380, 583–94.

BROWN, DEE (1970). *Bury My Heart at Wounded Knee*. New York: Holt, Rinehart & Winston.

BURKEY, RICHARD (1978). *Ethnic and Racial Groups*. Menlo Park, Calif.: Cummings Publishing.

CAHN, EDGAR, ED. (1969). *Our Brother's Keeper: The Indian in White America*. New York: New Community Press.

CHADWICK, BRUCE A. and WHITE, LYNN C. (1973). "Correlates of Length of Urban Residence among the Spokane Indians," *Human Organization*, 32(1):9–16.

CUNNINGHAM, HUGH T. (1930). "A History of the Cherokee Indians," *Chronicles of Oklahoma*, 8(3):291–314; 8(4):407–40.

DANIELS, ROGER and HARRY KITANO (1970). *American Racism*. Englewood Cliffs, N.J.: Prentice-Hall, Inc.

DELORIA, VINE (1970). *We Talk, You Listen*. New York: Macmillan.

DELORIA, VINE (1972a). *Of Utmost Good Faith*. New York: Bantam.

DELORIA, VINE (1972b). "An Indian's Plea to the Churches," *Los Angeles Times*, February 6, section G, pp. 1–2.

DELORIA, VINE (1973). "Bury our Hopes at Wounded Knee," *Los Angeles Times*, April 1, p. 1

DENTON, TREVOR (1975). "Canadian Indian Migrants and Impression Management of Ethnic Stigma," *Canadian Review of Sociology and Anthropology*, 12:65–71.

DOZIER, EDWARD P. (1966). "Problem Drinking among American Indians: The Role of Socio-Cultural Deprivation," *Quarterly Journal of Studies on Alcohol*, 27(1):72–87.

EVANS, JAMES L. (1967). "The Indian Savage, the Mexican Bandit, the Chinese Heathen . . . Three Popular Stereotypes" (unpublished doctoral dissertation, University of Texas, Austin).

FEAGIN, JOE (1978). *Racial and Ethnic Relations*. Englewood Cliffs, N.J.: Prentice-Hall, Inc.

FEHRENBACK, T. R. (1974). *Comanches: The Destruction of a People*. New York: Knopf.

GULICK, JOHN (1960). *Cherokees at the Crossroads*. Chapel Hill: University of North Carolina, Institute for Research in Social Science.

HAVIGHURST, ROBERT (1977). "Indian Education since 1960" (paper presented at the meeting of the American Sociological Association, Chicago, September 5).

HENNIGH, LAWRENCE (1975). "Negative Stereotyping: Structural Contributions in a BIA Community," *Human Organization,* 34(3):263–68.

HRABA, JOSEPH (1979). *American Ethnicity*. Itasca, Ill.: F.E. Peacock.

JORGENSEN, JOSEPH (1977). "Poverty and Work among American Indians," in *American Minorities and Economic Opportunity,* pp. 170–97, ed. H. Roy Kaplan. Itasca, Ill.: F.E. Peacock.

JOSEPHY, ALVIN JR. (1977). "What the Indians Want," in *Uncertain Americans,* pp. 277–88, eds. Leonard Dinnerstein and Frederic Jaber. New York: Oxford University Press.

KROEBER, THEODORA (1964). *Ishi*. Berkeley, Calif.: Parnassus Press.

LIFE, July 2, 1971, vol. 71, no. 1, pp. 38–59.

McFEE, MALCOLM (1972). "Modern Blackfeet Montanans on a Reservation," in *Native American Cultures: Four Cases,* eds. George and Louis Spindler. New York: Holt, Rinehart & Winston.

McSWAIN, ROMOLA MAE (1965). "The Role of Wives in the Urban Adjustment of Navaho Migrant Families to Denver, Colorado" (unpublished master's thesis, University of Hawaii).

MEYER, WILLIAM (1971). *Native Americans*. New York: International Publishers.

MILLER, DOROTHY and others (1975). *Native American Families in the City*. San Francisco: Scientific Analysis.

NASH, GARY (1970). "Red, White and Black: The Origins of Racism in Colonial America," in *The Great Fear,* pp. 1–26, eds. Gary Nash and Richard Weiss. New York: Holt, Rinehart & Winston.

NKRUMAH, KWAME (1965). *Neo-Colonialism*. New York: International Publishers.

PRICE, JOHN (1975). "U.S. and Canadian Indian Urban Ethnic Institutions," *Urban Anthropology,* 4(1):35–52.

SELIGMAN, LEE and ROBERT CANTER (1976). "American Indians in the Political Kingdom," *Administration and Society,* 8(3):343–54.

STEELE, C. HOY (1975). "The Acculturation-Assimilation Model in Urban Indian Studies: A Critique," in *Majority and Minority,* (2nd ed.), pp. 305–14, eds. Norman Yetman and C. Hoy Steele. Boston: Allyn Bacon.

STOFFLE, RICHARD (1975). "Reservation-Based Industry: A Case from Zuni, New Mexico," *Human Organization,* 34(3):217–25.

THOMAS, ROBERT K. (1975). "Powerless Politics," in *Majority and Minority* (2nd ed.), pp. 394–401, eds. Norman Yetman and C. Hoy Steele. Boston: Allyn Bacon.

VOGEL, VIRGIL (1972). *This Country Was Ours*. New York: Harper Row, Pub.

WISE, JENNINGS C. S. and VINE DELORIA (1971). *The Red Man in the New World Drama: A Politico-Legal Study with a Pageantry of American Indian History*. New York: Macmillan.

WOOD, TRAY (1979). "Ky Reflects on Hidden Price Tag of U.S. Aid," *Los Angeles Times,* January 20, section 1, p. 18.

WAX, MURRAY (1971). *Indian Americans*. Englewood Cliffs, N.J.:Prentice-Hall, Inc. All excerpts are reprinted by permission of the publisher.

10

MEXICAN AMERICANS

The Mexican Americans are a most diverse ethnic group. On one hand, they are an indigenous people who were overpowered by white settlers and are therefore similar to the native Americans. On the other hand, their continuing immigration from Mexico to the United States also makes them one of the newest and largest immigrant groups. Their immigration has included the temporary worker, or *bracero,* the legal immigrant, and an unknown number of illegals, or the undocumented. Some have a European complexion and can pass as white, while others are of pure Indian descent and are darker. Some are fully integrated and assimilated into the United States and have a high rate of intermarriage, and some live almost exclusively within their ethnic enclaves. Some are aristocrats and millionaires, but most are desperately poor. Some retain strong ties to Mexico and return there frequently, while others prefer a more acculturated posture and remain in the United States. There are also those who partially integrate without assimilating, but whose lives do not center exclusively on the ethnic enclave.

There also are differences in the area of settlement. The California experience is different from that of New Mexico and Texas, which in turn is different from that of the Midwest. Developing one model to explain this diversity is clearly an impossible task.

The Mexican Americans are a large and complex ethnic group; yet in the minds of the majority, there remains a simple stereotype of a lazy, stoic peasant, or its opposite, a ruthless, cruel *bandito.*

183

EARLY HISTORY

The interaction of Mexican natives with the Europeans started with the Spanish invasion of Mexico during the sixteenth century. The translated chronicles of Diaz (1963) illustrate several factors that are relevant not only for an understanding of Mexico but also for an insight into race relations. First, the Mexicans were extremely active in defending their lands, and the natives would probably not have been overwhelmed so easily, except for the in-fighting among themselves. The use of dissident tribes as allies was a critical factor in the Spanish success. Second, the natives thought that Cortés was a god, with his white face and those strange creatures he brought with him—horses. The superiority of European technology and weaponry proved decisive in combat. Finally, the Spanish were strongly motivated by their religious and imperialistic zeal.

The United States became involved with Mexico several centuries later. The Battle of San Jacinto and the fall of the Alamo occurred in 1836. The Gadsden Purchase enabled the United States to acquire Texas, New Mexico, and parts of Colorado, Arizona, Utah, Nevada, and California in 1853. The actual number of Mexicans in these new territories was relatively small, and they were quickly engulfed by the more restless and ambitious white settlers. All Mexicans, whether they were "pure" Spanish and landed or "half-breed" laborers, were perceived by the whites as inferior. By 1900 they were already a subordinated population, having lost title to their land because they could not supply proof of ownership. The white settler made no distinction between the original Mexican inhabitants—the "old-timers"—and the immigrant newcomers; they all were consigned to the same low status. Only in New Mexico, where the Mexicans retained numerical superiority, did they retain any degree of political power.

The basic conflict was over land, and the story is now a familiar one—the more powerful Anglo settlers coming into contact with the established but weaker Hispanic community and eventually acquiring the land. Hraba (1979:237) indicated that up to the time of losing their lands, the fate of the Mexicans and Indians was similar, but instead of being herded into reservations, the Mexicans were incorporated into the economy of the Southwest.

There were many reasons why the Mexicans were included in the southwestern economy, albeit at the lower part of the structure, whereas the Indians were not. The Mexicans were experienced in farming, ranching, and mining; most Indian tribes were not. The Mexicans lived near the fertile river valleys in sufficient numbers to constitute a readily available labor pool, while the Indians were scattered and less accessible. Mexican labor was also easier to organize into work gangs because of their *padrone-peon* (master-servant) system; thus the Anglo employer had an efficient way of dealing with the labor force. It should also be noted that the Mexicans had few competitors; black laborers did not move into the Southwest in significant numbers, Asian field workers remained in the Pacific area, and European laborers generally secured better employment positions (Hraba, 1979:244–45).

Large-scale Mexican migration took place in the 1900s. Factors leading to the move (the pushes) included a revolution and the unsettled economic conditions in Mexico. The attraction (pulls) was the rapid expansion of the southwestern economy through a number of actions occurring at that time. One was the National Reclamation Act of 1902, which ensured an adequate water supply for the arid region; another was the acquisition of large private and public holdings of land by business interests with the assistance of the United States government. There also was a need for labor, especially in cotton farming and other forms of agriculture, and in labor gangs on the railroads (McWilliams, 1968).

This pattern of employment meant that most Mexicans were kept isolated and segregated. They were hired in groups, primarily in rural and migratory jobs, and were kept apart from workers of other backgrounds. During the 1920s and 1930s there were attempts to unionize the Mexican laborers, but hopes for recognition and a more equitable share of the American pie were constantly frustrated by repression and discrimination (Meier & Rivera, 1972:184). As a consequence, the pre-World War II era saw the Mexicans as shunted aside from the American mainstream—not as isolated as the Indians, but also not participating in the dominant society as easily as immigrants of European background did.

It was not until the 1940s and World War II that the mechanisms for keeping the Mexican laborer on the periphery of the American economy began to change. The increasing mechanization of agriculture and the need for urban labor to meet the wartime economy began to break down the old pattern of Mexican employment. Thus, " the Mexican American entered America's urban economy a generation later than even the most recent of European immigrants" (Hraba, 1979:245). This delay meant that other groups had gained a head start in establishing occupational niches in the cities, where they had organized and become a part of the unions, where they had taken advantage of urban schools, and where they had oriented themselves to compete in the American economic system.

Discrimination remained a major problem for Mexicans during World War II. For example, in Texas there was a pattern of discrimination in employment, management, and the labor unions; continuing exploitation in agriculture, including competition from illegal aliens; refusal of service in some public and private places; denial of access to real estate and housing, exclusion from jury duty; and terrorism by police officers (Marden & Meyer, 1978:248). The following two incidents are dramatic case histories of the treatment of Mexicans in California.

Sleepy Lagoon   Although Mexicans generally shared in the increased opportunities of the World War II years, there were several incidents in California that revealed the extent of white prejudice. The antagonism can be seen in two discrete incidents in Los Angeles in 1942 and 1943: the "Sleepy Lagoon" murder case and the "Zoot-suit" riots.

The Sleepy Lagoon murder (the press invented the romantic title—the scene of the crime was actually an abandoned gravel pit) took place on the night of August 1-2, 1942 (Daniels & Kitano, 1970:74). The victim was a young Mexican American, José Diaz, apparently slain as the result of intraethnic gang rivalry. Throughout that summer, an artificial crime wave had been fabricated by the press and local police and attributed to Mexican Americans. When the press made a sensation of Diaz's murder (ordinarily not considered newsworthy), the police followed suit with a mass roundup of suspects. Some twenty-four youths were arrested for the murder, and seventeen of them were actually indicted. There was no tangible evidence against any of them, but nevertheless the local authorities embarked on the largest mass trial for murder ever held in the United States. The defendants were beaten by police, were forced to appear in court with unkempt appearances (for a time they were not even allowed to have their hair cut), and eventually, after a long trial, nine were convicted of second-degree murder, and the other eight found guilty of lesser crimes. More than two years after the crime, which remains unsolved, the California District Court of Appeals unanimously overturned all of the convictions.

What made this homicide significant was the illegal behavior of local law-enforcement officers, the reaction of the Mexican community to this incident, and the overt message of prejudice directed at the Mexican community.

The hostility of the local police to the Mexican-American population is hard to overstate and was of long duration. Innumerable instances of prejudice could be cited, but perhaps most illuminating are the following excerpts from a report given to the Los Angeles County Grand Jury by the sheriff's "expert" on Mexican-American behavior, Captain E. Duran Ayres. After presenting rather fanciful statistics on ethnicity and crime—the official taxonomy was black, yellow, and red for Negro, Oriental, and Mexican respectively—Captain Ayres embarked on a historio-sociological account of the Mexican in California. "Mexicans," he reported accurately enough,

are restricted in the main only to certain kinds of labor, and that
being the lowest paid. It must be admitted that they are discriminated against and have been heretofore practically barred from
learning trades. . . . This has been very much in evidence in our
defense plants, in spite of President Roosevelt's instructions to the
contrary. . . . Discrimination and segregation . . . in certain restaurants, public swimming plunges, public parks, theaters, and even
in schools, cause resentment among the Mexican people. . . . There
are certain parks in the state in which a Mexican may not appear,
or else only on a certain day of the week. There are certain plunges
where they are not allowed to swim, or else only on one day of the
week [and that invariably just prior to cleaning and draining], and
it is made evident by signs reading . . . "Tuesdays reserved for
Negroes and Mexicans." . . . All of this [and much more] applies
to both the foreign and American-born Mexicans. (Daniels & Kitano, 1970:75)

Ayres followed this narrative with a blatantly racist explanation for
Mexican-American crime and delinquency, an explanation apparently
accepted by the grand jury, most of the press, and probably most of the
population.

The Caucasian [and] especially the Anglo-Saxon, when engaged in
fighting . . . resort[s] to fisticuffs . . .; but this Mexican element
considers [good sportsmanship] to be a sign of weakness, and all he
knows and feels is a desire to use a knife or some other lethal
weapon. In other words, his desire is to kill, or at least let blood.
That is why it is difficult for the Anglo-Saxon to understand the
psychology of the Indian or even the Latin, and it is just as difficult
for the Indian or Latin to understand the psychology of the Anglo-
Saxon or those from northern Europe. When there is added to this
inborn characteristic that has come down through the ages, the use
of liquor, then we certainly have crimes of violence. (Daniels &
Kitano, 1970:75)

**The Zoot-suit
Riots**[1]

These riots, in the late spring of 1943, have been largely ignored by
historians, but when they are discussed, it is usually made to appear that
the young Mexican Americans were the aggressors (Daniels & Kitano,
1970:76). For instance, A. A. Hoehling, in *Home Front, U.S.A.* (1966)
wrote:

[1] A play entitled "Zoot Suit," based on this incident, became a hit in Los Angeles in 1978
and played in New York in 1979.

> . . . the zoot-suiters of Los Angeles . . . were predominantly Mexican youths with some Negro disciples, between the ages of sixteen and twenty. They wore absurdly long coats with padded shoulders, porkpie hats completed by a feather in the back, watch chains so long they almost touched the ground, and peg-top trousers tapering to narrow cuffs. . . . At best, as one pundit observed, they were "not characterized primarily by intellect." They formed themselves into bands with flamboyant names: the "Mateo Bombers," "Main Street Zooters," "The Califa," "Sleepy Lagooners," "The Black Legion," and many more. Their targets for physical harm were members of the armed forces, with a special predilection for sailors. The latter fought back with devastating effect. The situation quickly deteriorated to the point that the Navy declared Los Angeles out of bounds. The city council outlawed the wearing of zoot suits for the duration and the city simmered down. (Daniels & Kitano, 1970:76)

This account, more fantasy than fact, faithfully summarizes what Hoehling read in the newspapers. The facts are that after certain clashes between sailors on pass or leave (not generally the most decorous group in the population) and civilian teenagers, the sailors, with the tacit approval of both the naval authorities and the police, made organized assaults not just on zoot suiters, who were a tiny fraction of Mexican-American youth, but on any Mexican they could catch. Carey McWilliams, in *North from Mexico* (1968), described one organized foray in which "about two hundred sailors" hired "a fleet of twenty taxicabs" and cruised around town beating up Mexicans in ones and twos. After receiving accolades from the press—"Sailor Task Force Hits L.A. Zooters"—the "heroic" servicemen came in even greater force the next night. The police, although forewarned, did little if anything to inhibit the violence against Mexicans, although they did arrest twenty-seven Mexican youths. For several nights the streets of Los Angeles were turned over to informal posses of servicemen who proceeded to beat, strip, and otherwise humiliate every Mexican American (and some blacks) they could find. Bars were wrecked and movie theaters invaded, all with the same kind of impunity once granted to vigilantes in San Francisco. Throughout it all, the press made it appear that the Mexican American youths were the aggressors rather than the victims, with headlines like:

44 Zooters Jailed in Attacks on Sailors

Zoot Suit Chiefs Girding for War on Navy

Zoot Suiters Learn Lesson in Fight with Servicemen

An exception to this biased coverage was a small community paper, *The Eastside Journal,* which published eyewitness accounts by reporter

Al Waxman. He described coming upon

> a band of servicemen making a systematic tour of East First Street
> [in the heart of the main Mexican quarter]. They had just come out
> of a cocktail bar where four men were nursing bruises. Three autos
> loaded with Los Angeles policemen were on the scene but the
> soldiers were not molested. Farther down the street the men
> stopped a streetcar, forcing the motorman to open the door and
> proceeded to inspect the clothing of the male passengers. . . . (Dan-
> iels & Kitano, 1970:77)

When Waxman pleaded with local police to put a stop to these activities,
they answered that it was a matter for the military police. But the local
police themselves contributed positively to the disorder. Waxman continued:

> Four boys came out of a pool hall. They were wearing the zoot
> suits that have become the symbol of a fighting flag. Police ordered
> them into arrest cars. One refused. He asked, ''Why am I being
> arrested?'' The police officer answered with three swift blows of
> the night-stick across the boy's head and he went down. As he
> sprawled, he was kicked in the face. . . . At the next corner, a
> Mexican mother cried out, ''Don't take my boy, he did nothing.
> He's only fifteen years old. Don't take him.'' She was struck across
> the jaw and almost dropped [her] baby. (Daniels & Kitano, 1970:77)

If they had not already known, Sleepy Lagoon and the Zoot-suit
riots made it clear to California's Mexican population just how second
class their citizenship was. At the same time that the community's older
sons were dying on foreign battlefields, some of the younger ones were
casualties in their own neighborhoods. Before these wartime incidents,
a paternalistic myth had somewhat obscured the real relationships between the Mexicans and their Anglo neighbors; from that time until the
present day, that relationship has been more and more resented. Both
the Sleepy Lagoon murder case and the Zoot-suit riots were important
realities to be faced by the Mexicans. Perhaps the most dramatic was the
realization that racism could turn into violence toward any nonwhite
group. Furthermore, ''officialdom,'' in the form of consuls and Mexican
establishment leaders, was not as influential as had been previously
supposed. Finally, the riots were aided by the racist attitudes of many
officials, such as the police and those in city hall, who were supposed to
protect, rather than to persecute the victims.

World War II exposed many Mexicans to a broader world. A large
number went into military service and were transported to different parts
of the globe. New ideas, new perceptions, and new styles were being

tried, and as with most people who benefited from these new exposures, things were never the same again.

The Present

Before World War II, kinship and friendship patterns were common among the Mexicans, but political organizations were not. With the return of the veterans, the GI Bill, and chances for breaking out of the *barrio*, came the development of more politically oriented organizations. The League of United Latin American Citizens (LULAC), one of the earliest organizations, began in the 1950s and 1960s to press for reforms and to bring grievances before state and federal officials (Marden & Meyer, 1978:252). The GI Forum, composed of World War II veterans, was active in the 1950s; the Mexican American Political Organization (MAPO) and the Political Association of Spanish-speaking Organizations (PASO) were concerned with equal employment, voter registration, and the election of Mexican-American politicians.

The level of consciousness of the mainstream American to Mexican-American issues has been raised by several individuals. Rodolfo "Corky" Gonzales, author of a poem entitled "Yo Soy Joaquin" (1972), was active in the "Viva Kennedy" movement in the early 1960s and in the antipoverty programs in the Denver area. Reis Tijerina, sometimes compared to Don Quixote, wished to establish a separate Hispanic state and claimed millions of acres of land that were lost to the Mexicans through the American conquest and the Treaty of Guadalupe Midalgo. His movement was built on a return to traditional pastoral life and its accompanying values of justice, faith, and salvation (Marden & Meyer, 1978:260).

The best known leader is Cesar Chavez, who began his career as a community organizer in the 1950s. In 1962 Chavez was able to organize Mexican and Pilipino farm workers, and by 1968 his United Farm workers were successful in negotiating contracts with nearly all of the name-brand wine distillers. The Chavez group spearheaded the lettuce boycott of 1972, which achieved nationwide publicity when Senator Edward Kennedy opened his nomination speech for Senator George McGovern at the Democratic National Convention with the words, "Fellow lettuce boycotters" (Marden & Meyer, 1978:254–55).

THE CHICANO

There are a number of explanations concerning the derivation of the term *Chicano,* such as a short form of Mexicano or an obsolete pronunciation of *x* as *ch* (Marden & Meyer, 1978:255), but the social definition is more important. Aguirre (1973:122) defined the Chicano as a Mexican American with a non-Anglo definition of self, which ties in with the process of self-definition other racial minorities are also experiencing.

The Chicanos began as young urban militants who felt that they represented the poorer stratum of Mexican Americans who emphasized their Indian heritage (Marden & Meyer 1978:254). Today the terms *Chicano* and *Chicanismo* reflect an ecletic ideology that sees Mexican Americans as a conquered and dominated people who have lost their land, history, and culture to the Anglos. Central to their ideology is rejection of materialistic standards and individual self-achievement for collective orientations and group advancement (Moore, 1976:152).

This period of increasing political awareness, activist leadership, and the emergence of a Chicano identity was also characterized by protest activities. Morales (1971) revealed that from the late 1960s to the early 1970s there were thirty-four Mexican-American riots in the urban areas of the Southwest. One of the most publicized riots occurred after a Los Angeles policeman shot and killed Ruben Salazar, a *Los Angeles Times* correspondent, in August 1970. Tension between law enforcement officials and Chicanos remains high to this day.

IMMIGRATION

Several factors make the relationship between the United States and Mexico unique. Most of them are related to the proximity of the countries and the disparity of wealth and power between them. Given this disparity, it would be logical to predict the direction of migration and flow, for in the United States even low-level jobs are often better paying than high-level jobs in Mexico. Therefore, the attractiveness of the United States as a place to work provides a tremendous incentive that is a constant stress between the countries. One attempt to handle this problem is the *bracero*.

The Bracero

The slaves, the Chinese, the Japanese, and the Pilipinos all were sought for their ability to work at hard and tedious jobs that most white Americans did not want. They became problems when they desired things that were reserved primarily for white Americans—marriage, a family, civil rights, decent housing, a good education, equal opportunities, and ultimate peer status as Americans. The *bracero* provided an "ideal" solution. They were brought across the border for a specific purpose and could be returned when their services were no longer required. After the harvest, they did not have to go on welfare, nor did their children have to be educated at the American taxpayers' expense. As one grower said, "We used to own slaves but now we rent them from the government." (Dinnerstein & Reimers, 1975:101). However, by 1964 minimum wage laws, increased mechanization, and pressure from a coalition of Mexican Americans enabled the Kennedy administration to bring the importation of laborers to a halt.

Illegal or Undocumented Aliens ("Wetbacks")

A group that has had a pronounced impact on the Mexican-American community is the illegal alien, or "wetback," an epithet invented by the Anglo community. A more recent term is the "undocumented," and the recession of the late 1970s has brought renewed attention to this group. No one can provide exact figures on the current number of undocumented Mexicans in the United States, but estimated figures range anywhere from one to ten million and above.

It is reasonable to assume that the undocumented worker has very little power and can be the victim of abuse and exploitation. A study by Salcido (1977) described the experiences of such a group and its ability to survive through the development of its own network of health and welfare services. Although most are employed in jobs that the native born shun, they are constantly accused of taking jobs away from Americans. It is interesting to note that Mexican laborers were also scapegoats in an earlier depression; Betten and Mohl (1975) pointed out that in the 1930s Mexican-born immigrants, numbering over 9,000 in Gary, Indiana and East Chicago, were partially blamed for the depression and were repatriated, rather than being put on welfare.

The ease of crossing a border that has no differential markings was emphasized by McWilliams (1968). Rather than taking a ship and crossing an ocean, the Mexican immigrant moves north into an environment that is geographically, culturally, and historically familiar. Mexicans emigrating to the Southwest have had a feeling of being close to their ancestral roots, and it would not be far-fetched to say that no Mexican is really an immigrant or alien in this territory.

This situation has led to complicated legal entanglements governing immigration, citizenship rights, and deportation between the two countries. It also has generated great animosity between the Mexicans and the law-enforcement agencies. Since there is no immediate way of differentiating between citizens and aliens, anyone who looks like a Mexican is halted, seached, identified, and sometimes arrested by immigration and naturalization officers at the border. United States citizens of Mexican origin have often been deported because they could not immediately produce the proper documents.

Halt of Unrestricted Immigration

Up until 1965 there was unrestricted immigration between the United States and Mexico. There was no official quota limiting the entrance of Mexicans, but in 1965 Congress imposed a ceiling of 120,000 immigrants from all Western Hemisphere countries, which took effect in 1968. Although there has been no formal evaluation of the effects of this legislation, it is expected that the imposition of quotas will simply increase the traffic on the illegal immigration routes.

The history of Mexican immigration can be summarized by the following statements (Moore, 1976:38–40):

1. Mexican immigration has never been regulated by formal quotas; therefore, records of early immigration are useless.
2. Immigration has been continuous, but the greatest numbers have migrated in recent times.
3. The various types of immigration have resulted in complicated legal definitions. There are permanently legal and permanently illegal immigrants. There are those who contract on a seasonal basis; others commute daily across the border. Then there is the two-way flow of businessmen, tourists, and students to add to the complexity and confusion.
4. It is still easy for Mexicans to enter the United States by rail, car, and bus.
5. No other minority has ever been deported in such large numbers as the Mexicans. Massive roundups of illegal aliens such as "Operation Wetback" have been regular procedures; Moore reports that in five years Operation Wetback had rounded up the astonishing total of 3.8 million illegal Mexican immigrants. Most of them were simply expelled without formal proceedings.
6. As long as the discrepancy of wealth and opportunities remain between the two countries, there will continue to be problems of immigration.

At present the issue of the undocumented Mexican remains unresolved. President Jimmy Carter talked about amnesty in 1978 by granting citizenship to those undocumented aliens who could prove five years of residence in the United States. There have been proposals to erect a "Berlin wall," to increase the border patrol, and to penalize employers of the undocumented. Other proposals favor the improvement of economic conditions in Mexico (a type of Marshall Plan) so that the incentives for emigration will be reduced. The discovery of large reserves of gas and oil in Mexico is an unknown factor in a possible resolution of the problem, but it certainly is ironic in view of the United States' current, desperate need of these resources.

The Current Immigrant

Most recent Mexican immigrants come from the central area of Mexico, where there is great poverty. Most of them are young unskilled males with little education (Moore, 1976). They face a difficult time in the United States. Earlier, the United States could have absorbed them into its economy, but current opportunities, especially in the less industrialized Southwest, are limited. The additional barrier of the racist stereotype—that Mexicans are lazy, slow, uneducable, and ignorant—will continue to block their mobility for a long time to come.

THE MEXICAN AMERICAN TODAY

Population

The Mexican population in the United States in 1970 was estimated to be just over five million. Because of their high concentration in several states—Texas, California, Arizona, and New Mexico—they are a significant minority.

In the cities, Mexican Americans are usually found in *barrios* (akin to ghettos). Barrios have been formed from an original Mexican population; these people did not necessarily move there from somewhere else. It is a young population: the overall median age is 20.2 years, and the median age of the third generation is only 15.8 years. The typical family size is 4.5 persons, in comparison with the 3.6 persons among Southwestern Anglo groups (Moore, 1976:59-60). The large number of young children implies rapid population growth, at a time when growth curves for many other groups have declined. The increased pressure of a young, growing population confronting a relatively rigid, racially restrictive opportunity structure may lead to great conflict unless there are significant changes in race relations.

However, the number of Chicanos is deceptive. There is a large undocumented population who have no rights of citizenship, and many Mexican immigrants have not become United States citizens. Part of the problem stems from the confusion resulting from dual citizenship. Children born to contract laborers or illegal immigrants in the United States are presumably citizens, but many Mexicans are not aware of the duality. Some Mexicans have lost their United States citizenship by participating in Mexican elections or serving in the Mexican Army.

Moore hypothesized that the low rate of citizenship is consistent with the social isolation of the group. Other reasons for the low rate include distrust of United States authorities, expectation of returning to Mexico, bad socioeconomic conditions, a high rate of illiteracy, and the language barrier. There are the additional difficulties with the written examination on United States history that prospective citizens must pass and the anxiety raised by the excessive paperwork and bureaucracy of the citizenship procedures. Grebler (1966) showed that between 1959 and 1966 less than 5 percent of eligible Mexicans became citizens, whereas other immigrant groups were becoming naturalized at rates of over 25 percent.

As a consequence, there are very few elected Chicano political officials. Los Angeles, with a very large number of Mexican American residents, had no members on the County Board of Supervisors on the City Council in 1978, and only one elected member to the Congress, Edward Roybal. Continued immigration coupled with white flight should lead to a high concentration of blacks and Chicanos in the core cities. Any effective coalition between these two groups could lead to impressive political power, although the probability of a close black-Chicano alliance, even on a temporary basis, appears slim.

194

Moore (1976) wrote that, except for the relatively small Indian group, no population in the Southwest is as economically impoverished as the Mexican. The Chicano head of family must make his lower income support a large household, and his chances of earning a livable income are relatively low and are improving only slowly.

In our chapter on inequality (Chapter 7), we saw that the Chicano was significantly below the white Anglo male on all indices, from education, to income, to occupation and housing. Most Mexican males are no longer underrepresented in skilled blue-collar operations, but they are still overrepresented in the operative category and among farm workers. But the majority of Mexican-American workers are no longer farm laborers (Golden & Tausky, 1977). Although there have been improvements over time, the average Mexican American remains marginal in the job market. Mexicans hold the low-paying, less desirable jobs in most occupations. Those in the managerial category are usually self-employed in marginal occupations. They are excluded, except in token numbers, from civil service jobs such as those in fire and police departments, and are not found in large numbers in higher paying, unionized jobs (Moore, 1976). Other discriminatory trends indicate that even in similar kinds of work Mexicans are paid less than whites. Unrealistic standards (for example, the high school diploma requirement for unskilled jobs) keep the unemployment figures high.

Poverty

As can be inferred from the occupational picture, the most pressing problem for Mexican families is poverty. They are consistently at the bottom of the economic ladder, and as a population they remain greatly overrepresented in the lowest income categories (Mittelbach, 1966).

The relationship between poverty and other variables is well documented. Generally, the poor receive the worst in health care, housing, and education; they are regarded with disfavor by the police, teachers, and other representatives of the dominant culture; and there is a high correlation between poverty and crime, delinquency, drug usage, and mental illness. For Mexicans, as well as for most ethnic minorities, poverty compounds the prejudice and discrimination already present because of race and nationality.

Education

Up to now, education has not provided Mexican Americans with a ladder to success. Segregation, isolation, inappropriate curricula, and poor teaching are all partially responsible for this state of affairs. The incidence of functional illiteracy (0 to 4 years of elementary school) is seven times that of the Anglo population and nearly twice that of nonwhites (Moore, 1976:66–67).

High dropout rates and low achievement are the principal problems. Educators have blamed bilingualism, implying that the Spanish language is a major handicap and therefore should be abolished. Others blame their lack of motivation, apathy, and noncompetitive outlook.

The ethnic community blames the irrelevance of the school curriculum and Anglo teachers' prejudiced, stereotyped responses to Mexican children. For example, community members feel that Mexican students are often arbitrarily advised to take nonacademic courses; sometimes they are placed in classes for the mentally retarded (the language handicap may be an important factor in this placement). Whatever the reason, the American educational system is not meeting the Mexicans' needs. For example, a 1971 report by the U.S. Civil Rights Commission showed the consistent lag in the reading level of Mexican-American children. The results support the claim that Mexican Americans are receiving an inferior education (see Table 10.1).

The Church

The Roman Catholic Church has been presumed to have a strong influence on Mexican Americans ever since the days of the Spanish conquistadors, who arrived with a sword in one hand and a cross in the other. But it is difficult to assess the influence of the Church on modern Mexican-American life. Generalizations differ by area. There certainly is an overall lessening of religious influence on most facets of American life, and it is occurring within this ethnic group as well. There also is some indication that at an earlier time the Catholic Church lost its place as a relevant instrument of social change. Rather than serving as a vehicle for understanding the unique problems faced by a disadvantaged ethnic community and providing leadership in effecting social change, the Church, dominated by white leadership, instead adopted a much more conservative, static position. But there have been changes: pastoral concerns have been modified in the past to answer the needs of "Americanization," and current appeals for social justice may accelerate the process of making the Church more responsive (Moore, 1976:90–91).

Grebler (1970:449) stated that two factors conditioned the relationship between the Church and Mexican Americans. One was the clergy's

TABLE 10.1   *PERCENTAGE OF MEXICAN-AMERICAN STUDENTS BELOW AVERAGE READING LEVEL IN VARIOUS LOCALITIES BY SELECTED GRADE*

	4th grade	8th grade	12th grade
Los Angeles	57	60	75
California	52	57	62
Texas	52	73	64
Arizona	43	65	75
New Mexico	48	58	53
Colorado	56	55	59

SOURCE: U.S. Civil Rights Commission, 1971.

point of view that Mexicans were uninstructed in their faith and deficient in their adherence to the norms of church practice. Therefore, much of the clergy's time and energy was spent in ministering to the religious needs of the group, rather than providing a place where the immigrants could find support and comfort in a new and strange land. The other factor was the general poverty of the Catholic Church in the Southwest. The constant shortage of funds and priests has made it difficult to plan and expand programs beyond narrow ministerial functions.

McNamara (1973) indicated that the Catholic Church has made assimilation and patriotism its priorities. The Church's goals were to aid Mexican Americans to become loyal, trustworthy, law-abiding citizens; to protect them from the social evils of the day, such as Protestantism, Bolshevism, Communism, delinquency, and relativism in doctrine and morality; to equip them with the means to move upward in the socioeconomic system; and to accomplish their goals without resorting to violence and social disturbance.

The Church has had some influence. Values, rules of conduct, and other standards have been an integral part of its programs. Parochial schools have been important to the education of many Mexican Americans. But the Church, with a few exceptions, has not provided the leadership in addressing the primary problems facing the Mexican American—discrimination, poor education, lack of economic opportunities, and poverty.

Law Enforcement. There has been a strain between the Chicano community and representatives of the American legal system from the very beginning. For example, the well-publicized Texas Rangers were founded in 1835 to deal with the Mexican "problem." The Western tradition of vigilante law enforcement aided Arizona mine owners, Texas ranchers, and California fruit growers in dealing with the Mexican American under the sanction of dominant-group definitions of law and order. Chicanos feel that they have been the victims of much unnecessary brutality and overzealous law enforcement.

Other Institutional Contacts

Social Welfare and Other Public Agencies. Poverty has forced many Mexican Americans to depend on the public welfare system. The problem of public welfare is a recurring one that goes far beyond its implications to one ethnic minority. Upward economic and social mobility is extremely difficult for any ethnic group that finds significant proportions of its members on public welfare, especially when occupational opportunities are limited.

Relations between Mexicans and the American social welfare establishment were especially difficult during the Great Depression. The need for Mexican labor quickly vanished as jobs became scarce; there was a great push to deport both citizens and aliens by a variety of strategies.

Voluntary repatriation was encouraged, and subsistence money was cut off. A bureau was set up for Mexicans applying for relief; it served as a deporting agency and waived questions of constitutionality, justice, and morality in order to save the taxpayers' dollars. It was cheaper simply to transport large groups of Mexicans back to Mexico.

At present, Mexican Americans are very reluctant to use the larger community services available to them. The number of Mexican clientele at health, psychiatric, and counseling clinics is so low that they are often referred to as the "hard to reach." They tend to visit hospitals, child-guidance clinics, family service agencies, and psychiatric facilities only as a last resort. There are very few Mexican Americans in California mental institutions, and hospitalization records indicate that their official mental illness rates are the lowest of any ethnic group (Kitano, 1969). Cultural misunderstanding is the major reason for this state of affairs; modern medicine, with its appointments, impersonal attitudes, and treatment by complete strangers does not appeal to them as a way of handling stress and sickness. So some Mexicans prefer to use local healers (*curandera*) who know their language and the customs. There also are the factors of distance and cost (most professional facilities in a city like Los Angeles are virtually inaccessible except by private car). This is a very serious situation; many Mexican Americans arrive at a hospital near death, when they could have been helped by earlier treatment.

The Family and Community

The significant aspects of the Mexican family cannot be covered by any easy generalization, but some broad statements on social class and the urban-rural factor can be made.

For example, the low-class rural family generally has an extended family structure. Relatives on both sides provide emotional and economic support, as well as a reference group for accomplishment. Male and female roles tend to be clearly proscribed; masculinity (*machismo*) is of great importance, even outside marriage. The family remains the most important unit; close relationships outside the family are mostly with age peers. Godparents (*compadrazgo*) provide another linkage.

The family patterns in the city are varied. Increasing numbers are moving out of the barrios—some to the periphery and others to the suburbs. Generally, there are differences in life style between those families remaining in the barrio and those surrounded by white neighbors. The rates of assimilation, integration, and change are closely related to the housing patterns. The traditional family is arranged hierarchically: the father occupies the top and is followed by the sons; together they shelter and protect the wife and daughters. The women are expected to cook, raise the children, and serve the needs of the men.

The middle-class family patterns are generally similar, but their more adequate income gives them more freedom of choice. For example, middle-class Mexicans may go to a physician rather than a *curandera*, an attorney rather than a priest; and their children may go to college. Nevertheless, most Mexican families remain quite isolated from the Anglo world, since they prefer to associate with their own relatives and the ethnic community.

In urban areas, poverty has shifted the burden of family financial responsibility to the public services and public welfare agencies. It offers an option to many who previously had no recourse but to depend on relatives; now they may choose to be more independent of the kinship system. Such a breaking away will have both positive and negative consequences, although the underlying factors of poverty and dependence remain untouched.

Urbanization and acculturation are changing family roles, especially that of the Mexican male. He now helps care for the children and shares family decisions with his wife. The input of the mass media showing models at variance with the traditional roles is important, especially in cities like Los Angeles. The extended family system is also being modified. But much is hidden from majority eyes because of the highly segregated living conditions and the constant flow of new immigrants.

In the early days there was the *patron* system. The patron was a large landowner who lived on or near his property surrounded by his peasants. There was a personal dependence on the patron by the workers and a reciprocal obligation by the owner. The unit was highly self-sufficient and paternalistic; the patron served as legislator, judge, and jury as well as protector, provider, and employer (Taylor & West, 1975).

The vertical structure is similar to some of the family and economic structures in Asia, and significantly, these structures seem to discourage horizontal organizations. At present, the Mexican American does not have a nationwide organization similar to the NAACP for blacks or the JACL for Japanese Americans.

Social Class

Most Mexican-American families are very poor, though other groups "above" them are constantly changing and evolving away from the older traditions (Moore, 1976).

Before the American annexation, the upper class was reserved for the Spanish, and when the United States acquired the territories, most retained this status, the "half-breeds" (*mestizos*) and the native Indians filling the lower positions. The upwardly mobile wanted to be identified as Spanish—the purer the better—and traces of this point of view remain.

The mobility pattern for Mexican Americans has several forms. As income and other related circumstances rise, individuals may begin to lead more comfortable lives within the ethnic community. But their contacts and interactions are confined to their ethnic group. Although there may be strong resemblances to the Anglo middle-class, middle-class Mexicans and Anglos are generally ignorant of each other, especially since the Anglo stereotype usually does not include a middle-class Mexican.

Another type of mobility leads away from the ethnic community. Education, income, and other marks of status result in increased majority-group contacts and perhaps a conscious decision to leave the barrio. The success of this pattern depends on the accessibility of the Anglo world; if it is perceived as open, there may be a permanent move into the larger community. Individuals choosing this path take serious risks. Even if they have tried to think and behave like Anglos, they may find their new world inhospitable and may alienate their old friends in the ethnic community.

The third type is bilingual and bicultural, most often a college student, who partially integrates without assimilating. He or she learns the Anglo system very well but retains many ethnic contacts; his or her life does not center exclusively either on the ethnic enclaves or on the academic world. As their numbers grow, they may develop a subcommunity of ethnic intellectuals.

College students, especially those recruited from the barrios, are often subject to serious conflicts. Much of the initial impetus for going to school came from community members who wanted to be proud of the fact that some of their own could enter a university. Ethnic students' interests change, however, and their former friendships in the barrio become strained. Some college students report being called "sell-outs" by those who have remained in the community.

In the larger society, Chicanos seldom achieve positions of power. For example, in the occupational hierarchy of "Border City," located some 250 miles south of San Antonio, Texas, the top level, which includes growers, packers, canners, businesspersons, and professionals, is overwhelmingly Anglo. In the white-collar occupations, Mexicans are prominent only where bilingual abilities have made them useful, such as clerks and salespersons. The bottom of the hierarchy, such as farm laborers, shed and cannery workers, and domestics is overwhelmingly Mexican (Simmons, 1972).

Goals, Norms, Values

In spite of discrimination, poor treatment, and poverty, Wright and others (1973) indicate that the long-range goal of most Mexicans is eventual assimilation into the broader society. There are modifications of this goal, which include a retention of ethnic identity and a degree of cultural pluralism, but there seems to be no strong movement toward separatism, a separate state, or a mass return to the homeland.

Mexican middle-class norms—the dominant ideal for most Mexicans—are congruent with Anglo prescriptions. There is an emphasis on respect and deference to elders, on getting along with people, and getting ahead in the world. Mexican-American leaders state that as they prepare for their first school experience, most Mexican-American children are willing to learn and to respect, obey, and please the teacher.

Many consider the Mexicans' values to be the cause of their problems. The literature of the social sciences abounds with comparisons of Mexican and American values and cultural explanations for the low collective achievements of the Mexican. Perhaps the most widely disseminated study was that of Kluckhohn and Strodtbeck (1961) which reinforced the impression that Mexican Americans were distinct from Anglos. Subsequent interpretations and generalizations from their study ignored two major points that they had made: (1) that the Mexican-American sample was from a remote village in New Mexico, and (2) that basic changes were predicted even in this isolated village. Therefore the "scientific" generalization that the Mexicans were "fate-oriented" and focused on the present rather than on the future, became rather widely accepted in social science circles.

Current information indicates that the range of responses of urban Mexican residents is "generally within the range of American cultural values in such critical arenas of life as family, neighbors, and social class" (Grebler and others, 1970:423). Most Mexicans are no different from most Americans. The stereotyped Mexican peasant could not survive in an urban environment without some change. Most Mexican Americans, like other Americans, want to get ahead in their work; they want job satisfaction, security, and a higher income. They direct their young toward the professions and on the whole, "Mexican Americans are not notably more passive, nor do they value integration with relatives more than most populations on which data are available" (Grebler and others, 1970:439).

The most distinct feature of Mexican-American culture is the Spanish language. Yet the great majority of Americans is prone to rely more on the stereotypes and their own interpretations of what constitutes Mexican "culture"—the fate orientation, the *mañana* attitude, the passivity, the lack of individualism, and the "Jose Jimenez" image.

Those Anglos who do have some interaction with Mexicans often select information that supports their prejudices. For example, interethnic contact between middle-class Anglos and Mexicans most often takes place under institutionalized auspices; professionals such as social workers, nurses, teachers, probation and other law enforcement officers generally see only the Mexicans who are in trouble. Their contacts are generally limited to those Mexicans exhibiting social problems, and their observations become the inferred norm for all Mexicans.

The predictable outcome of these perceptions, therefore, has been the tendency to blame the Mexican culture for the lack of progress. As we have and will continue to emphasize, ethnic groups do not live in a vacuum; the problem lies in the *interaction* between the majority and the minority, not in the culture of the minority.

It is also our impression that the Mexican American belongs to the ethnic group with the widest spread of political views and ideologies. It is not unusual to see spokespersons advocating both extremely liberal and extremely conservative points of view, whereas it is often difficult to find many right-wing spokespersons in the other ethnic groups.

Visibility   Mexican Americans exhibit a wide range of skin colors—from light Caucasian to dark Indian, and all shades in between. Color was an important stratification variable within the group even before contact with the United States.

Spanish surnames provide another index for identification, although they are not infallible guides. Latin Americans, Puerto Ricans, Cubans, and Pilipinos share many of the same surnames. Dress, food, and music reflect other highly visible cultural styles. But because most Mexicans remain isolated, such visibility is confined to typical tourist havens, such as Olvera Street in Los Angeles.

One conspicuous Mexican-American style in the urban areas is the gang. The gang phenomenon, especially as an adolescent socialization force (which may continue through adulthood), is especially intriguing. One common stereotype, even before the Zoot-suit riots, was that Mexican-American youngsters generally belonged to gangs and that there was continuous fighting among them. It is an area that has been much observed but underresearched.

THE CHICANO PATTERN

It is difficult to envisage any one model for handling the diversity within the group. The Californios (Pitt, 1966) are different from the undocumenteds, who are different from the legal immigrants, who are in turn different from the braceros. Their motivations, the local conditions, and resources all are different.

One model for understanding the group is the colonial one. As Acuna pointed out (1972), the land of the original inhabitants was invaded and occupied by military force, and the native Mexicans became involuntary subjects. The conquerors imposed an alien culture and an alien form of government on the vanquished. They were denied access to the structures of the dominant group through discrimination and racism, and were relegated to a subordinated status. The conquerors attempted to dismantle the ethnic institutions and the ethnic culture, and were able to gain control over the political, economic, and educational lives of the conquered. The distinguishing characteristics of this model are invasion, subjugation, cultural genocide, imposition of an alien culture, and political and economic disenfranchisement.

Several other variables are suggested by Benitez (1977) to provide a fuller picture of the current stage of Chicano interaction with the dominant culture. One factor is the core of what Benitez called the Mexican-American heritage and the meaning of work. Chicanos come from a background in which physical stamina and an ability and willingness to withstand physical deprivation and punishment are valued. Courage (*macho*) is necessary to survive in a harsh environment, but this type of orientation minimizes the need for much education or cultural sophistication. Life in the desert and the plains called for people who could ride, shoot, rope, brand, and cook.

There also is the previously discussed patron system, which included protection from hostile Indians, bandits, and white nesters, and which encouraged the concept of familism. The colonial stratification system reinforced the subordinated status of the Mexican. One basic model was the Anglo commercial farmer with the hard-working Mexican wage laborer. Texans often viewed Mexicans as being there just to work and as being childlike and emotional. Benitez found that certain Mexican qualities, such as their ability to endure hardships and to be helpful, have contributed to the maintenance of the dominant-subordinate system.

Moore (1979:44) raised questions about the appropriateness of the internal colony model in analyzing residents of the urban minority ghetto. The territorial boundaries in the barrio are ambiguous (in contrast to Indian reservations, where the boundaries are clear); the definition of the intermediary elite or bourgeois stratum as the vehicles of exploitation is ambiguous; and just what is meant by exploitation also is ambiguous.

An alternative analysis of Mexican-American subgroups, including the uncounted number of undocumented, is that of the dual economy society (Moore, 1979:45). The current racial minorities in the barrios (and ghettos) face a different situation from that of European immigrants. Large-scale corporate enterprise no longer values a large labor pool in order to depress wages and to inhibit unionization; rather, the incentive is to hire, train, retain, and promote stable workers. It is assumed that anyone with the talent, motivation, skills, education, and training can enter into these core economic institutions. But another set of industries on the periphery (the dual market) plays an important role in the economy; labor in the restaurant and hotel industry and in garment factories are examples of employment opportunities that often rely on unmotivated and unqualified workers, illegals, and minors (the sweatshops and child-labor shops of a bygone area). Urban minority barrio and ghetto residents probably contribute a disproportionate share to this secondary labor market and provide the principal pool of workers.

The role of welfare is another issue when discussing poverty, the barrio, and the Chicano. The internal colony model views welfare as a mechanism for control of the barrios and ghettos (Piven & Cloward, 1971), but an unanswered question is the cost to the dominant society for maintaining an extensive welfare structure.

In summary, although the evidence of social inequality and the dominant-subordinate model for the Mexican American is strong, the theoretical explanations of the stratification are rather weak. There are probably many explanations for different Chicano groups, depending on time, place, situation, visibility, and power. The internal colony model and the dual labor society model are possible explanations. The traditional models for European immigrant groups do not fit the Chicano.

BIBLIOGRAPHY

AGUIRRE, LYDIA (1973). "The Meaning of the Chicano Movement," in *We Are Chicanos*, ed. Phillip Ortega. New York: Pocket Books.

BENITEZ, JOSEPH S. (1977). "Dimensions for the Study of Work-Related Values in Mexican-American Culture: An Exploratory Essay," in *American Minorities and Economic Opportunity*, pp. 109–49. Itasca, Ill.: F.E. Peacock.

BETTEN, NEIL and RAYMOND MOHL (1975). "From Discrimination to Repatriation: Mexican Life in Gary, Indiana during the Great Depression," in *The Chicano*, pp. 124–42, ed. Norris Hundley, Jr. Santa Barbara, Calif.: ABC-Clio.

BULLOCK, PAUL (1973). *Aspiration vs Opportunity: Careers in the Inner City*. Ann Arbor, Mich.: Institute of Labor and Industrial Relations.

BURKEY, RICHARD (1978). *Ethnic and Racial Groups*. Menlo Park, Calif.: Cummings Publishing.

DANIELS, ROGER and HARRY H. L. KITANO (1970). *American Racism*. Englewood Cliffs, N.J.: Prentice-Hall, Inc.

DE LA GARZA, RUDOLPH O., Z. ANTHONY KRUSZEWSKI, and TOMAS ARCINIEGA (1973). *Chicanos and Native Americans*. Englewood Cliffs, N.J.: Prentice-Hall, Inc.

DIAZ, BERNAL (1963). *The Conquest of New Spain*, trans. J. M. Cohen. Baltimore: Penguin.

DINNERSTEIN, LEONARD and DAVID REIMERS (1975). *Ethnic Americans*. New York: Dodd, Mead.

GOLDEN, HILDA and CURT TAUSKY (1977). "Minority Groups in the World of Work," in *American Minorities and Economic Opportunity*. Itasca, Ill.: F. E. Peacock.

GONZALES, RODOLFO (1972). *Yo Soy Joaquin (I Am Joaquin)*. New York: Bantam.

GREBLER, LEO (1966). "The Naturalization of Mexican Immigrants in the United States," *International Migration Review*, 1:17–32.

GREBLER, LEO, JOAN MOORE, and RALPH GUZMAN (1970). *The Mexican American People*. New York: Free Press.

HERNANDEZ, DELUVINA (1970). "La Raza Satellite System," *Aztlan*, 1(1):13–34. Los Angeles: University of California, Chicano Cultural Center.

HERRING, NORMA P. (1972). "Reies Lopez Tijerina: Don Quixote in New Mexico," in *Pain and Promise: The Chicano Today*, pp. 286–95, ed. Edward Simmons. New York: New American Library.

KAGAN, S. and M. C. MADSEN (1971). "Mexican American and Anglo American Children of Two Different Ages Under Four Instructional Sets," *Developmental Psychology*, 5(1):32–39.

KITANO, HARRY H. L. (1969). "Japanese American Mental Illness," in *Changing Perspectives of Mental Illness*, eds. Plog and Edgerton. New York: Holt, Rinehart & Winston.

KLUCKHOHN, FLORENCE and FRED L. STRODTBECK (1961). *Variations in Value Orientations*. Evanston, Ill.: Row, Peterson and Co.

LANAR, HOWARD (1966). *The Far Southwest, 1946–1919*. New Haven, Conn.: Yale University Press.

LIGHT, IVAN (1977). "Ethnic Succession," (unpublished paper, University of California, Los Angeles).

McNAMARA, PATRICK (1973). "Catholicism, Assimilation, and the Chicano Movement: Los Angeles as a Case Study," in *Chicanos and Native Americans*, pp. 124–30, eds. Rudolph De La Garza and others. Englewood Cliffs, N.J.: Prentice-Hall, Inc.

McWILLIAMS, CAREY (1968). *North from Mexico*. New York: Greenwood Press.

MARDEN, CHARLES and GLADYS MEYER (1978). *Minorities in American Society* (5th ed.). New York: D. Van Nostrand.

MEIER, MATT and FELICIANO RIVERA (1972). *The Chicano: A History of Mexican Americans*. New York: Hill & Wang.

MITTLEBACK, FRANK G. and GRACE MARSHALL (1966). *The Burden of Poverty, Advance Report 5*. Los Angeles: University of California, Mexican American Study Project.

MOORE, JOAN (1979). "American Minorities and 'New Nation' Perspectives," in *Understanding Minority-Dominant Relations*, pp. 40–53, ed. F. James Davis. Arlington Heights, Ill.: AHM Corp.

MOORE, JOAN and HARRY PACHON (1976). *Mexican Americans* (2nd ed.). Englewood Cliffs, N.J.: Prentice-Hall, Inc.

MORALES, ARMANDO (1971). *Ando Sangrando! (I Am Bleeding)*. Los Angeles: Congress of Mexican American Unity.

NOSTRAND, RICHARD (1975). "'Mexican American' and 'Chicano': Emerging Terms for a People Coming of Age," in *The Chicano*, pp. 143–60, ed. Norris Hundley, Jr., Santa Barbara, Calif.: Clio Press.

PENALOSA, FERNANDO (1972). "The Changing Mexican-American in Southern California," in *Pain and Promise: The Chicano Today*, pp. 61–71, ed. Edward Simmons. New York: New American Library.

PITT, LEONARD (1966). *The Decline of the Californios: A Social History*. Berkeley: University of California Press.

RAMIREZ, MANUEL II (1970). "Identity Crises in the Barrios," *Music Educators Journal*, 5(57):69–70.

RAMIREZ, MANUEL II and CLARK TAYLOR, JR. (1971). "Mexican American Cultural Membership and Adjustment to School," *Developmental Psychology*, 4(2):141–48.

SALCIDO, RAMON (1977). "Utilization of Community Services and Immigration Experiences of Documented and Undocumented Mexican Families" (unpublished doctoral dissertation, University of California, Los Angeles).

SIMMONS, OZZIE (1972). "The Mutual Images and Expectations of Anglo-Americans and Mexican Americans," in *Pain and Promise: The Chicano Today*, pp. 106–18, ed. Edward Simmons. New York: New American Library.

TAYLOR, WILLIAM and ELLIOTT WEST (1975). "Patron Leadership at the Crossroads: Southern Colorado in the Late Nineteenth Century," in *The Chicano*, pp. 73–95, ed. Norris Hundley, Jr. Santa Barbara, Calif.: Clio Press.

TIRADO, MIGUEL DAVID (1970). "Mexican American Political Organization," *Aztlan*, 1(1):53–78. Los Angeles: University of California, Chicano Cultural Center.

The banner reads: PHILIPPINE COMMUNITIES EXECUTIVE COUNCIL, INC. FOUNDED 1951

ASIAN AMERICANS

Perhaps the least known and the most stereotyped of all American minorities are the Asian Americans. Although they possess a remarkable diversity in terms of nationality, language, and culture, to American eyes they must all look alike, so that Chinese, Japanese, Koreans, Pilipinos, and Vietnamese are often lumped together in one category.

What is known about them has been through essentially negative stereotypes such as the "yellow peril" and the pictures of the teeming masses of Asia, of coolie labor, of the cheapness of human life; of opium dens, of inscrutable faces, and of people who have difficulty pronouncing English.

The Far East was also the area for our brand of colonialism, and our allies were most often those rulers that we could bring under our control. American feelings can best be summarized by the phrase, "our little brown brothers" used in reference to our Pilipino allies, and the terms "gooks" and "slant eyes" for our antagonists. An additional factor has been that of Communism and the Communist menace. Thus, our perspectives on Asia have usually been biased.

Because most Asian Americans are concentrated on the West Coast and Hawaii (the 1970 census reported that 38 percent of the total Asian population resides in California and another 27 percent in Hawaii), few Americans have an opportunity for intimate social contact with Asian Americans. Therefore, their portrayal by the mass media takes on an exaggerated importance. We see Asians, if they are seen at all, as cooks, houseboys, exotic women, and camera-clicking tourists. But these current images may be an improvement over the sneaky, fanatic enemy of World War II (Japanese), the Korean War (Chinese and North Koreans), and the action in Vietnam (North Vietnamese).

The Asian Americans are one of the smallest ethnic minorities. The 1970 census established the following figures: Chinese, 435,062; Pilipinos, 343,060; and Japanese, 591,290. Together the three major Asian groups total 1,369,412 in a country of 203,211,926. The low figures are somewhat ironic, for it was not too long ago that white Americans feared the "yellow peril" and envisioned the United States being overrun by hordes of little yellow men. It is also a commentary on the rapidity of racial change, for the "yellow peril" is now the "model" minority (Kitano & Sue, 1973). The Asians are often cited as an example of good race relations in the United States, but a more realistic view is that this is only by comparison with the "unruly" minorities who are adapting with much less silence and conformity.

Although white America has continually regarded the Asians as a homogeneous group, nothing could be further from the truth. They represent different nationalities and cultures, and even within their own cultures there are wide disparities. One of the distortions of racism is to lump diverse groups into one category, or at best, into a few stereotypes: the Chinese laundryman, the Japanese gardener, and the Pilipino gambler.

If we look at the group more closely, we see problems that have hitherto been hidden by the stereotypes. The problems of unrest, the elderly (Kalish & Moriwaki, 1973), and the mentally ill (Berk & Hirata, 1973), are partially obscured because of the general adaptive style used by the Asian minorities in their quest for survival and acceptance in the white world. It would have been sheer folly for most Asians to challenge the power of the dominant culture; the small scattered Asian communities could not hope to survive by confronting and inviting the retaliation of the more powerful Americans. But even when they attempted to acculturate through invisibility, they were objects of attack. This is partly because racism sees anything but white faces as different and therefore, inferior—partly because of America's peculiar relationship with the countries of the Far East. Americans have so strongly associated Asian Americans with their home nations that even today, Asians three and four generations removed from the homeland of their forebearers are expected to be experts on China, Japan, or the Philippines.

The Asian experiences with the dominant culture are different from those of the blacks, Indians, and Chicanos, and are perhaps more similar to those of the European immigrants. First, much of their immigration was voluntary, which included a transient mentality with the possibility of returning to the home community. Second, their cultures were not systematically dismantled, and "normal" family life was allowed; economic opportunities were also developed by some of the Asian communities. Third, there was a tie with the home nation, which meant some degree of external support. Finally, most of the Asian groups were able to by-pass any significant dependency on the federal bureaucracy. But, in common with the blacks, native Americans, and Chicanos, they faced racism, discrimination, prejudice, and segregation; the Japanese even suffered a concentration camp experience.

The dominant-subordinate model is appropriate to Asians, yet the data in Chapter 7 on social inequality show that Asian American groups are not consistently below white male norms on all of the measures, as was true of the minorities previously discussed. Therefore, it is apparent that the models for explaining Asian-American interaction with the majority will be different from those for the blacks, Chicanos, and Indians.

We shall present the experiences of the Chinese and Japanese in greater detail than those of the Koreans, Samoans, Pilipinos. The reason for the emphasis is simple: there is much more available information on the Chinese and Japanese. It is hoped that the forthcoming *Harvard Ethnic Encyclopedia* will include much needed material on the other groups. We would also encourage scholars from neglected ethnic groups to conduct research and to publish their findings.

Before discussing the Chinese and Japanese, we will provide information on three often ignored Asian groups—the Koreans, the Pilipinos, and the Samoans.

THE KOREANS

A number of factors about the Korean immigration make them relatively unique among Asian groups. First, their early immigration was short-lived, from 1902 to 1905, at a time when the Japanese occupied their country, and they became a people without a country, unless they wanted to identify with Japan. Second, many of their immigrants were Christian, so that the Church has been and continues to be an important part of their community structure. Third, although the early immigrants generally settled in Hawaii and along the Pacific Coast, the post-World War II immigration was less limited, so that the Koreans are much more geographically dispersed than the Chinese and Japanese are. In addition, a new immigration is taking place, so that the number of Koreans recorded in the 1970 United States Census is deceptive. Finally, Korea was never an enemy nation, as were China and Japan, so its people were not predetermined stereotypes, although during the Korean War they were divided into the enemy (North) and the ally (South).

Early Immigration[1]   Korean immigration was formally acknowledged by the Shufeldt Treaty, which opened Korea to the Western world in 1882. The significant immigration took place between 1903 and 1905 with the arrival of 7,226 Koreans in Hawaii. In common with most immigrations, there were a number of pushes and pulls. The push was from home conditions: a cholera epidemic, a drought, a locust plague, famine, and generally poor economic conditions. The primary pull was from Hawaiian plantation owners who wished to limit the power of Chinese and Japanese workers through the importation of another national group of workers, and a desire on the part of the Korean government to gain a favorable image and support from the United States for their immigration policies.

Of the 7,226 immigrants who arrived as plantation workers in Hawaii between 1902 and 1905, over 6,000 were male adults. Less than 60 percent remained in Hawaii; some 1,000 returned to Korea, while another 2,000 moved on to the continental United States. An additional 1,033 were reported as immigrants to Mexico in 1905.

The Koreans were a heterogeneous group of male laborers, peasants, low-rank government officials, ex-soldiers, students, and political refugees. In 1905 pressure from Korean politicians, American missionaries, and most important, the Japanese government led to the cessation of immigration. Japan had started to exert its hegemony over Korea through the Treaty of Portsmouth at the conclusion of the Russo-Japanese war; by 1905 Korea was already a Japanese colony, although its official colonial status was not declared until 1910.

Most of the Korean emigrants left home with a weak national identification, but Korean identity, solidarity, and nationalism quickly grew in the United States. Although the Koreans were cut off from their homeland and were in danger of losing their national identity under Japanese rule, they maintained their "Koreanness" by politicizing their communities through involvement in the Korean independence movement. For example, between 1905 and 1907, the Koreans in Hawaii established more than twenty organizations that had as a central theme Korean solidarity and resistance to Japanese occupation. Most of them published their own mimeographed language newspapers. Yang (1979) found that there were over fifteen such publications during this period.

Christian churches also were numerous; there were thirty-one congregations serving 2,800 Koreans; there also was a similar number of Christian churches on the mainland (Lyu, 1976). Besides their ministerial functions for the Korean laborers, Korean pastors in Hawaii also served as interpreters, job placement officers, legal aid advisors, mediators,

---

[1] Much of the material in this section is drawn from Houchins & Houchins (1976) and Yang (1979).

marriage counselors, teachers, and community workers (Yang, 1979). The Koreans who migrated to the mainland were described as more educated and aggressive, and they set the tone for the community during this early era.

The major problems included the uncertainty of employment and the high proportion of unmarried males. One solution to the marital problem was through "picture brides"; marriages were arranged on the basis of an exchange of photographs and letters. A total of 1,066 picture brides emigrated to the United States before the 1924 immigration law closed the door to any further Asian immigration (Yang, 1979). But there remained a significant number of unmarried Korean males who eventually lost interest and contact with the fragmented Korean community.

Most of the immigrants had come for economic reasons and had thoughts of returning, but they could not because Korea was then a Japanese colony. A number of young intellectuals had also come to the United States before the Japanese annexation and with a few exceptions decided to remain in the United States and fight for Korean independence. Most prominent in this group were Ahn Chang-ho, who was a Korean community organizer; Syngman Rhee, who was to eventually return to Korea as the first president of the republic after World War II; and Park Yong-man, who created an armed Korean national brigade in Hawaii with the thought of a military reconquest.

The existence of numerous organizations whose leaders advocated a variety of tactics made it difficult to achieve an overall Korean community unity. Even today there is no central organization among Koreans; as Kim stated, "with new immigrants, new organizations are created, like mushrooms after a spring shower" (1977a:65). Much of the energy and finances of the Korean community during the early era were used to support the activities of Korean patriots and various governments in exile.

The irony of the confused situation involving the Japanese and the Koreans, in the context of American perceptions of the Asians, was described by Yang (1979) in the following incident. In 1913 a group of Korean laborers was attacked in Hemet Valley, California by a white mob that had mistaken them for Japanese workers. The Japanese consul general in Los Angeles stepped in to protect the Koreans by asking for compensation on behalf of "their nationals," but the Koreans rejected this offer because they had left Korea before the Japanese annexation and questioned the validity of being represented by Japanese officials.

The number of Koreans in America remained very small; both the 1920 and 1930 census showed less than 2,000 Koreans in California. Like the Chinese and Japanese who had preceded them to the United States, the Koreans pushed for educational achievement, if not for themselves, for their children. In 1938, when only one college-aged American out of 100 went to college, the rates for the young Korean was 1 in 59. But they faced the depressed economic conditions shared by everyone, compounded by racial discrimination, so that Korean college graduates could be found as waitresses, fruitstand workers, and herb sellers (Yang, 1979).

A study of Korean American stereotype of the 1940s was conducted by Vinacke (1949). He reported that although Koreans shared the image of being quiet, traditional, neat, and polite with their Chinese and Japanese peers in Hawaii, they were also viewed as hot-tempered, stubborn, independent, and outspoken. They were also the only group to describe themselves in negative terms.

There were other differences between this new generation of Korean Americans and their immigrant parents. The Korean Nisei, or second generation, spoke English and adhered more closely to American norms. Most of them were not interested in perpetuating the traditional Korean culture or in continuing the patriotic fight to liberate the homeland. The indifference of the young Koreans to the old community organizations and the stubbornness of the old leadership meant that the immigrant organizations did not gain new recruits and eventually faded away. There also was the gap between generations and the loss of parental control. One result of this conflict was the high rate of outmarriage in Hawaii, especially between Korean males and Japanese females (Yang, 1979).

Syngman Rhee returned to Korea as the new president in 1945 after the Allied victory over Japan. But it was to a divided Korea, separated at the thirty-eighth parallel between the North and the South. The conflict between the two eventually led to the Korean ''police action'' during President Harry Truman's term in office.

The New Immigration

It was only in 1970 that the United States Census took the Koreans out of the ''other'' category and placed them in a column of their own. In that year the 70,000 Koreans made them the fifth largest Asian group. Ryee (1977) estimated that in 1974 there were over 217,000 or about three times the number reported in the 1970 census. Other figures vary; Wagatsuma and Lee (1978) estimated that in 1978 there were approximately 70,000 Koreans living in Los Angeles County, whereas an article by Sherman in the *Los Angeles Times* (1979) talks about 150,000 to 170,000. The most reasonable generalization is that the Korean population in the United States is growing rapidly, but the exact numbers are unknown.

The reasons for immigration include better employment and educational opportunities and a chance to be reunited with family and other relatives (Kim & Condon, 1975). The immigrants arrive with little knowledge of America or the language, but with high expectations. They reflect the influence of the 1965 Immigration Act, which gives priority to those applicants with advanced education, training, and skills.

Adaptation

Hurh (1977) constructed a stage-by-stage model for analyzing the adaptation of the newcomer. Initially there is a feeling of satisfaction, accomplishment, and relief that the immigrant has finally reached the United States. They share a sense of excitement and enjoy the reunion with family, relatives, and friends. The newcomer is especially impressed by the material affluence of the new country. Many can scarcely believe that they are here.

This stage is generally short-lived, and by the end of the first year there is a feeling of disenchantment. The harsh realities of the language barrier, the difficulty of finding suitable employment, social isolation, and culture shock lead to doubts about ever adapting to the new country. There are feelings of homesickness and a possible change in expectations of America. Those who have a command of English are generally in much better shape to pass through this stage. Those who do not may remain at this stage for a long time.

The next phase is cultural assimilation: "the immigrant is now employed, his English is now improving, the family income is stable, and he may even own a car" (Hurh, 1977:90). There are signs of material affluence, self-confidence, and a desire to become American. The immigrants may take on American first names and have increased social contact outside the group. They want to validate their Americanism, and rates of naturalization are very high at this stage. Kim (1977) reported that Korean rates of naturalization are higher than those of other Asian American groups. This may be the final stage of "making it" for some. For others there is another stage in which there is the reawakening of an ethnic identity and a desire to know much more about the culture of Korea. This phenomenon is common among most immigrant groups and has sometimes been named the "Hansen effect," which refers to the rejection of the immigrant culture by the second generation and a reawakening interest by the third generation. There are no available data on the number of Koreans in each of the phases.

Current Data

The 1970 Census contains summary data on the Korean (*A Study of Selected Socio-Economic Characteristics*). In 1970, the Koreans were the second largest group of Asian immigrants (the Pilipinos were the first). They are more dispersed than the other Asians; 44 percent live in the West, 20 percent in the Northeast, 19 percent in the Midwest, and 17 percent in the South. The majority of the early immigrants is concentrated in Hawaii and California, but the more recent immigrants are more widely scattered. They are a young population, and over a third of the group under nineteen years of age was born in Korea.

They have high educational achievement. Perhaps the most impressive statistic is the number of college-educated individuals. Nationwide, 36 percent have a college education (mostly from Korea), compared to the United States norm of 11 percent. In New York City, 53 percent of immigrant Korean adults have had four or more years of college.

The census offers no data on occupational level, but of those Koreans who reported an occupation in the home country, the overwhelming majority (72 percent) had highly skilled backgrounds as professional, technical, and managerial workers.

Census data on the Koreans in Hawaii indicate that of all the racial subgroups living in that state, they have the highest rates of outmarriage. Koreans in Hawaii have a 50 percent intermarriage rate, primarily with whites and Japanese. The Korean rate of intermarriage is such that they could be assimilated into the larger local Hawaiian culture (a blend of Asian, Hawaiian and "old" white ways) before too many more generations pass.

Los Angeles. Los Angeles has had a rapid influx of Koreans. Much of the immigration has been invisible, since Los Angeles is composed of a large number of transient individuals. But in certain sections the Korean community is clearly visible, such as on Olympic Boulevard between Western and Vermont Avenues. Here there are many Korean shops, restaurants, night clubs, and a large Korean community building. Liquor stores, real estate offices, and service stations are popular; other business establishments include wig sellers, shoe repairs, small appliances, grocery stores, and other small businesses that Asian immigrants traditionally have entered. Kim and Wong (1977) pointed out that these small business enterprises often are a symbol of disguised poverty rather than of material success. The lack of alternatives has forced many Koreans into these small business ventures. There has been a high turnover rate and many business failures, caused by factors such as insufficient financial resources, signing long-term leases at high rates without adequate information, and entrance into high-risk enterprises.

The major problems are underemployment and low income. Many newcomers arrive in the country with a sufficient background of professional skills but face an uncertain job market. Underemployment is a severe problem, with about one-third employed as factory operators (garment workers). Of those with professional degrees such as physicians, pharmacists, and nurses, 49 percent were working as operatives, craftspeople, or salespeople. The situation is even worse for those professionally qualified in the liberal arts; only 7 percent were able to secure the kind of employment for which they were trained (Kim & Wong, 1977:231).

Income is generally low, although family income may be higher because more than one member may be working. For example, in a Los Angeles survey conducted in 1976, Kitano and Owan (in press) found that 49.9 percent of Korean respondents reported incomes below $10,000 (compared to only 12 percent of a Japanese sample).

But Yu (1979a), in a study of Los Angeles Koreans with the surname of Kim, reported median family incomes at the $19,000 level. Perhaps the most recent figure is the most accurate. He also found that the typical Korean family consists of hard-working, high-achievement-oriented individuals whose major life styles revolve around hard work. For example, in many families both father and mother work, sometimes including weekends. The children study hard and are very competitive in school. The major hindrance to their mobility and acceptance is related to problems with the English language.

Only about 10 percent of the newcomers speak English fluently; Korean is the primary language of 98 percent of Los Angeles's Koreatown residents. In the 1970 census, 76 percent of the national sample listed Korean as their native tongue; thus the lack of language facility is one barrier to educational and occupational mobility.

The recent immigrants from Korea face an overall much healthier situation than the hostility and overt discrimination that was the lot of the early Chinese and Japanese immigrants. They also arrive with many of the same characteristics of the previous Asian groups—high motivation to succeed in America, hard work, high educational aspirations, and a strong family orientation. Although there has never been a specific stereotype of Koreans, except for the general stereotypes of all Asians, influence peddling and the Koreagate scandals of 1978 may mark the beginning of one. In writing about the Koreans in the *Los Angeles Times* (1979), Sherman noted that the city now has the largest gathering of Koreans outside of the home country. They are described as affluent, well educated, aggressive, dynamic, and ruthless in their business dealings. The problem of discrimination, however, is not dead. Yu (1979b) observed that the longer the Korean lives and works in Los Angeles, the more likely he or she is to report instances of racial slurs.

The Korean Model

The model of Korean adaptation is different from that of domination and domestic colonialism. The first-generation Koreans retained their own culture with little attempt to acculturate and integrate, partly because they envisaged a triumphant return to their homeland. When that homeland was annexed by Japan, much of their energy was aimed at fostering and maintaining their lost identity, while developing a number of competing governments in exile. Perhaps the most appropriate title for this type of adaptation would be a "government-in-exile" model, in which groups see themselves as transients until such time that they can reconquer their homeland. The model is fairly prevalent: Latvians in the United States and the Chinese who fled to Taiwan are examples of the government-in-exile orientation that does not fit any of our traditional models.

The second generation of Koreans, without the emotional or structural ties to the "we shall return" orientation, followed a more traditional path toward acculturation and integration, although it should be noted that their primary outmarriage choices were not to the dominant Caucasians, but to other subordinated groups. It is our observation that the "exile" model usually lasts for only the original generation, unless there are unusual circumstances that keep the priorities at the forefront of the consciousness and concern of subsequent generations.

The new Korean immigrant also does not fit readily into any of the previously discussed models. Many have arrived in the United States with capital and high educational and skill levels. Some have started at the bottom in the dual labor economy as seamstresses and in sweat shops, but many others have gone into small business and into positions appropriate to a *middleman minority* position. By middleman, we refer to a group that is above the status of other minorities because of a competitive advantage or high adaptive capacity (Blalock, 1967:79–84), yet remains below the status of the dominant group. Bonacich (1973) and Kitano (1974) wrote about the Chinese and Japanese in the United States as other possible middleman groups.

The middleman model is based on a dominant-subordinate stratification system. There are basically two competing groups (whites and blacks), with the middleman minority serving as a mediating influence between the two power groups. Bonacich and Jung (1979), in surveying Korean small-business activity in Los Angeles, found it an appropriate model to explain current Korean adaptation. Based on middleman concepts, they hypothesized the following Korean economic activity: that Koreans would be overrepresented in the small business sector, particularly in retailing and small shops; that they would be concentrated in a narrow range of economic activities; that they would serve a Korean clientele and a substantial non-Korean clientele, particularly the poor and other minorities; that ethnicity would be vital to business development, including the generation of capital, circulating business information, and mutual aid; and that there would be a heavy reliance on a hard-working, loyal work force, including unpaid family members. The data on Korean businesses supported their predictions.

Middleman minorities often serve as buffers between dominant and subordinated groups and can become the targets and scapegoats for the stresses of that system (for example, Jews in Germany during the Nazi era). The pertinent question relates to the length of time a group may serve in that position. Will it become a semipermanent role for the Korean minority, or is it a passing phase in their interaction with the dominant and subordinated groups in our society? More or less permanent middleman positions occur because of a combination of external factors such as systematic, powerful discrimination (denial of citizenship) and internal factors such as cultural preferences and psychological identifications (feeling inferior to the dominant group but superior to the subordinated groups).

It is perhaps too early to predict, but it is probable that the Koreans may be the Asian group that will integrate most rapidly into the American system. They are still few in number and scattered, but there has been a strong motivation to become American. They are a well-educated group that greatly values education, and they have family solidarity coupled with a high degree of individualism and a hard-work ethic. The barriers of language and of underemployment may be temporary, and although they face the stresses and strains that are a part of all immigrant life, it appears that they have the perseverance to cope and to overcome. The major barrier is anti-Asian prejudice, which is currently not as formidable as it was in a previous era. Since their middleman orientations are probably not permanent, the Koreans may use these positions as steps toward higher mobility and dispersion.

THE FILIPINOS[1]

Early History

The Filipino followed the Chinese and Japanese immigration to America.[2] It was a largely male immigration, and the young men who came essentially filled the niche in the labor force that had been occupied by the Japanese, who by the 1920s were no longer available in significant numbers to work for Caucasian growers. Had Japanese immigration not been cut off, it is probable that the Filipino migration would not have been as large as it was. However, thanks to American imperialism, the Filipino enjoyed a different status than did other Asians. Like other Asians, Filipinos were not eligible for naturalization; but since the United States owned the Philippines, they were not aliens, but nationals. As such, they traveled under United States passports and could not be excluded from the United States. Congress eventually rectified this by passing the Tydings-McDuffie Act in 1935, which granted a deferred

[1] The current spelling of Pilipino is preferred by members of that group over the previous spelling, Filipino. There is no *F* sound in their speech, according to our informants. However, we will use the *F* throughout this chapter, primarily because our references and sources are still based on the old spelling.
[2] Much of the historical material is drawn from Daniels and Kitano (1970).

independence to the Philippines but imposed immediately a rigid quota of fifty a year, thus ending, for all practical purposes, Filipino immigration. Ironically, some of the leading anti-Filipino nativists in California were among the chief advocates of Philippine independence, since independence—or to be precise, the promise of independence—was the *sine qua non* of exclusion.

The major thrust of Filipino immigration lasted about ten years. In 1920 there were only 5,000 Filipinos in the whole country (3,000 in California); by the next census the figures had risen to 45,000 nationwide, with about 30,000 in California. Yet this tiny minority raised the hackles of the California exclusionists, who saw the Filipinos as yet another Asian horde about to overwhelm Caucasian California. A Sacramento exclusionist informed a national magazine audience that, since all American blacks were descended from a small slave nucleus, even this tiny group represented a danger. Ignoring the fact that very few women came from the Philippines, he insisted, with that mindless arithmetic that California exclusionists delighted in, that "Filipinos do not hesitate to have nine children . . . [which means] 720 great-grandchildren as against the white parents' twenty-seven" (Daniels and Kitano, 1970:67)

But the explosive nature of the Filipino problem was caused not by Filipino reproduction, but by Filipino sex. The sex bugaboo, the ravishing of pure white women by lascivious oriental men, had always lurked in the background of the antioriental movements in California. It had never become, overtly at least, a major factor, for the simple reason that sex relations between oriental men and occidental women had been all but nonexistent. (Intercourse between males of the majority race and females of the minority races aroused little opposition; Chinese and Japanese prostitutes had been a titillating feature of West Coast brothels since gold-rush days.) With the Filipinos, however, the sex issue became tangible. The Filipinos enjoyed and sought the companionship of Caucasian girls; and soon, in every major center of Filipino population in the state, special dance halls sprang up which catered exclusively to the Filipino trade, and a lucrative trade it was. The basic charge was ten cents a minute, and the places did a thriving business.

This kind of "free enterprise" was just too much for most Californians. The conservative *Los Angeles Times* railed against two such dance halls located just a few blocks from the newspaper's headquarters. One set of headlines read:

Taxi-Dance Girls Start Filipinos on Wrong Foot

Lonely Islanders' Quest for Woman Companionship Brings Problems of Grave National Moment

Mercenary Women Influence Brown Man's Ego

Minds Made Ripe for Work of Red Organizers (Daniels and Kitano, 1970:67)

Exclusionists suffered a further shock when the courts ruled that the state's miscegenation statute—which forbade marriages of white persons to "Negroes, Mongolians, or mulattoes"—did not apply to the Filipinos, who were considered Malayans. The California legislature quickly amended the law to extend the ban to "members of the Malay race."

In the meantime the alleged sexual aggressiveness of the Filipinos had set off much mob violence. (It could be argued that the Filipinos were merely conforming to the "melting pot" ideal and thus were more Americanized than other orientals, but this never occurred to California exclusionists.) In addition, the Filipinos who were often, they felt, exploited by Japanese and Chinese businesses in the United States, were much more prone to join unions and participate in strikes than earlier Asian immigrants had been, a propensity that caused them to be viewed with alarm in the America of Harding, Coolidge, and Hoover. Despite their willingness to be organized, the California trade-union hierarchy wanted little to do with them and participated almost as eagerly in the anti-Filipino movement as it had in previous antioriental crusades.

Bogardus (1929), in studying early white attitudes toward the Filipino, found that whites favored their educational ambition, willingness to do menial tasks, and courtesy and politeness while working in hotels and restaurants. But whites feared their economic competition, their inability to engage in heavy farm work, their propensity to strike and quarrel, and their forwardness with white girls. Filipinos were welcome if they remained in their place. Job discrimination sent them to the bottom of the economic scale, and housing discrimination segregated them into slums. It was inevitable that overt clashes would result. Melendy wrote:

California's first serious riot occurred at a carnival in Exeter on October 24, 1929, when a Filipino stabbed a white man. Prior to the incident, Filipinos had been abused in town, shoved off sidewalks, and molested by white transient workers. At the carnival, whites threw objects at Filipinos, particularly those in the company of white girls. This led to the stabbing. (Melendy, 1967:7)

The most explosive riot occurred in the Watsonville agricultural area in 1930. Anti-Filipino attitudes were set in motion by the chamber of commerce, which passed resolutions harassing Filipinos. The mobs followed suit, and for several days armed white hunting parties roamed the streets looking for Filipinos and invaded dance halls. The violence reached a climax with the killing of a Filipino, numerous assaults, and the burning of Filipino dwellings.

By World War II, attitudes toward Filipinos had changed. The "brave little brown brothers" who fought and died alongside the whites at Bataan and Corregidor became the new stereotype. Nonetheless, Filipinos were considered to be an invisible minority group that ranked very low in most ethnic classification schemes.

Visibility

Although they are most often classified as Mongolian and are therefore considered "yellow," Filipinos are of Malayan stock. They also often have Spanish surnames and can be mistaken quite easily for Puerto Ricans or Latin Americans. The 1970 Census listed 343,060 Filipinos in the United States, primarily on the West Coast, with 138,859 in California and 93,915 in Hawaii.

The Filipinos are by far the most disadvantaged Asian group. Their income is lower than that of the Chinese or Japanese; and in California, their annual income long has been the lowest of any ethnic group. They were also the lowest group in number of school years completed.

Groupings

The Filipinos, or Pinoys, can be divided into four main groups:

1. The first generation, which is composed primarily of males who immigrated in the 1920s. Most went into agricultural labor and retained their native Philippine dialect. Acculturation for them has been slow.
2. The second and third generations, who were born in America and who have very little contact with their native land, language, or culture.
3. The post-World War II arrivals, many of whom are veterans and war victims.
4. The new immigrants, which includes many professionals who have come under the liberalized immigration laws of 1965.

These various groupings provide a background for some of the problems facing the Filipinos. For example, the first-generation immigrants–mostly male, less educated, but hard working–have now grown old. Most of them have remained single and have no family ties. Long arduous lives as fruit pickers or laborers have not netted them much capital. Their isolation and poverty make them extremely vulnerable to changing conditions, especially as their earning power declines. Their last years are usually spent in dingy hotel rooms in California valley towns such as Stockton or in the blighted areas of San Francisco. The irony of their plight can be appreciated if we recall the one guiding ethic of their life: hard work.

The second generation. Racist barriers discouraged intermarriage for first-generation males, but many were able to find mates from both majority-group and other minority-group females. There are almost no empirical data on the number of these intermarriages; however, we would predict a relatively high proportion of separation and divorce, especially when compared to the rates for the other Asian populations. These higher rates of separation and divorce may be attributed to job discrimination, social isolation, subordinate status, as well as to cultural differences such as language and life styles.

The second generation and their children face many problems. Like most racial minorities, they share such problems as lack of social acceptance, low income, low educational achievement, and negative self-image. A special problem has been the lack of education, as summarized by Cordova et al:

1. There is an obvious lack of encouragement, either in the home or in the high schools, to go to college and succeed.
2. There is a noticeable absence of proper counseling to help young Filipinos choose between college or training school.
3. Many counselors lack the knowledge, experience, and rapport to deal adequately with Filipino-Americans.
4. Neither the colleges nor the high schools provide any courses in Filipino culture or history.
5. The future plans of many young Filipinos extend no further than the next day, the next month, or the next year.
6. The cost of education is beyond the reach of most Filipino families.

Predictably, there are very few Filipino college graduates. Only five Filipino-Americans graduated from the three major colleges in the Seattle area in 1971.

As with many of their peers in other ethnic communities, the second- and third-generation youngsters are unfamiliar with their native country. They generally know nothing of Philippine culture, except through the reminiscences of some older Filipinos with whom they might occasionally be in contact.

The Post-World War II veteran. A number of veterans came to the United States after World War II. Many of them had been in the Filipino Scouts; some brought their families and others came by themselves with the idea of sending for their families after finding jobs. The author remembers working with a large group of these veterans who immigrated to San Francisco in the 1950s. Many of them were middle-aged, generally unskilled (although they brought with them diplomas from unknown technical and vocational colleges in the Philippines), and quite thoroughly army disciplined. They shared a mixture of patriotism, naive belief of the wonders of the United States, and a hard-work ethic.

Although life was extremely difficult for them during the early months, the need for unskilled laborers was great, and most of them did make an adaptation to the new country. On occasional meetings in the Asian community, the war veteran can still be spotted by his military bearing and his reminiscences of Bataan and Corregidor.

Another group of veterans are the Filipinos who were in the United States Navy. Most of them served as officer's stewards, but in spite of the Navy's attempt to acculturate these sailors, they continue to retain close ties with the Philippines and to live within their own cultural network (Duff & Arthur, 1973).

The newly arrived. The immigration legislation of 1965 has contributed to a new and large Filipino migration. Before the passage of the law, Filipino immigration in 1965 was 2,545, whereas 25,417 entered the country in 1970. They are the fastest growing minority in cities such as San Francisco. There is also a corresponding increase in businesses catering to them—many Filipino restaurants, grocery stores, and movie houses.

There are several reasons for the large migration: an unstable economic and political situation in the native country, the expectation of better opportunities in the United States, and favorable immigration legislation.

The new immigrants are much different from the old-timers of many decades ago. There are many doctors, lawyers, engineers, teachers, and nurses, reflecting the policy of the new immigration legislation of bringing highly skilled and professional people to the United States. Most are well educated and speak English. However, "despite their professional education in the Philippines, [they] are finding difficulty in getting jobs that suit their occupational and educational levels. So Filipino lawyers work as clerks; teachers as secretaries; dentists as aides; engineers as mechanics; and many professionals work also as laborers and janitors" (Cordova, 1973:12). Still, a low-status job in the United States often pays better than a high-status job in the Philippines. As one interviewee related, "My one day earning here is more than my one month salary in Manila, especially when I do a plus eight (overtime)" (Munoz, 1971:29).

Munoz (1971:26) studied the transformation of some Filipinos as they perceived the opportunities in the United States. Whereas in the old country they may have been soft, easy going, even parasitic, indolent, and inefficient, in the new country they became work oriented with a vengeance. Many moonlight by taking on additional jobs in the evenings and weekends and place a high value on putting money in the bank and eventually returning to the Philippines to retire.

Although Los Angeles has become a major attraction for Filipino immigrants, they have not developed a cohesive, geographically tight community. Rather, they are widely scattered and are not without a number of problems. Morales (1974), a social worker, found that immigrants had problems with education, finances, unemployment, youth, family, and the elderly. Identity also becomes an issue in the context of culture shock and racism.

The Filipinos come from a diverse culture, representing a country with eighty seven major dialects. Although they are lumped together with Asians, their background is Malayan, so that they are closer to the Indonesians than they are to the Chinese, Japanese, and Koreans. The confusion is reflected in the lack of a clear-cut Filipino identity. They are constantly mistaken for being Japanese, Chinese, Hawaiian, American Indian, or Mexican, and there are many with Spanish surnames. Cordova (1973) referred to the Filipino as a "hidden minority."

Some recent data are available in a monograph entitled *A Study of the Socio-Economic Characteristics of Ethnic Groups Based on the 1970 Census.* By the mid-1970s, an estimated 90,000 Filipinos had immigrated to the United States; by the 1980 census, they may be the largest Asian group in this country. Most of the Filipinos reside in the West, with 40 percent in California and another 28 percent in Hawaii.

Generalizations about the group using variables such as income, occupation, and education are very deceptive since they vary widely according to age, sex, time of immigration, and geographic area of settlement. For example, the old-timer is usually a single male who has lived a life of hard work in low-paying jobs. His education, income, and life savings are meager, and he has generally resided in the least desirable parts of the city and in poor rural areas. On the other hand, the new immigrants, both males and females, arrive with a high level of educational achievement and professional backgrounds. Their main complaint may be about underemployment. These and other individuals of Filipino background are put together for national averages that show that less than half, or 49 percent, of Filipino males have finished high school (national norms are 54 percent), but 15 percent have completed college (national norms, 13 percent).

Similarly, 60 percent of the Filipino females have completed high school and 20 percent have completed college. The college completion figures appear to represent the new immigrants; American-born Filipinos are not attending at anywhere near that figure.

Twelve percent of all Filipino families live in poverty (United States average, 11 percent). In rural families the figure is 14 percent. The problem of poverty appears especially acute in families headed by females in which the poverty figure is 40 percent. The rates for female-headed families in poverty are especially high in Hawaii (43 percent), and in rural areas (48 percent). In 1969, 19 percent of Filipino families headed by males had incomes below the poverty line (compared to 13 percent of male-headed Anglo families). In 1976, these figures had dropped to 6 percent (compared to 9 percent for the majority group). The change is probably related to the influx of the highly educated and well-trained new immigrants even though there may be many instances of underemployment.

The Filipino Model

As with all of our previously discussed groups, there is no one model that can encompass the diversity within the Filipino population. The Filipinos represent another variation of the dominant-subordinate model. They emigrated from a country that had been under continuous colonial rule for over 400 years, first under the Spanish, then under the Americans, so that they were accustomed to a subordinated position in relation to white dominance. Cordova (1973) noted that one consequence of this type of association is that the natives are trained not to exceed or surpass the pace of their colonial benefactors.

A large group carried their subordinated position into the Navy, where they served their "superiors" with dedication and duty as stewards and attendants. Upward mobility in this hierarchical structure for Filipinos was extremely rare.

Many early immigrants were single, male laborers and, because of the lack of Filipino women, chose "American" wives (amalgamation) or remained single. The laborer was positioned in the lower half of the socioeconomic structure and never participated in the mainstream of the American culture.

The new immigrants, especially those with professional degrees, fill many middleman positions. There are a goodly number of nurses among Filipino females. Among male M.D.s, one would expect to find them serving in less prestigious and less affluent communities. For example, we have noticed a high proportion of foreign-trained doctors (including those with language problems) at the Martin Luther King Hospital in Watts (Los Angeles) and would expect a similar distribution in other cities.

In closing, the Filipinos are a direct product of American colonialism. Very few profited from this relationship; rather, discriminatory legislation controlled and shaped a male-only group with limited opportunities for normal family life. Recently, there has been a new immigration, and it is hoped that they would not replicate the experience of Carlos Bulosan, an early immigrant and writer. In his moving autobiography, *America Is in the Heart,* he described what it felt like to be a Filipino in California in the 1920s:

> . . . in many ways it was a crime to be a Filipino in California. I came to know that the public streets were not free to my people; we were stopped each time . . . patrolmen saw us driving a car. We were suspect each time we were seen with a white woman. And perhaps it was this narrowing of our life into an island, into a filthy segment of American society, that had driven [many] Filipinos inward, hating everyone and despising all positive urgencies toward freedom.

THE SAMOANS

The Samoans are a new immigrant group. Their significant immigration began in 1951, when the United States Navy, then the largest employer of Samoans, closed its base on the islands. A number of Samoan workers moved with the Navy and eventually settled around naval bases on the West Coast and Hawaii (Shu & Satele, 1977).

Prior to their emigration, Samoans were best known through the work of anthropologist Margaret Mead (1961), whose *Coming of Age in Samoa* was a standard reference for generations of American college students. It is difficult to assess the relationship between Mead's Samoans and the group today, except to note that South Sea Island culture and that of urban America is quite different.

The pushes and pulls of Samoan immigration are familiar. Lack of jobs and an attempt to break away from an overly strict social structure were among the pushes, while a chance for better education, employment, and upward mobility were among the pulls (Shu & Satele, 1977).

Much of the immigration was family- and kinship-based. As the original settlers became established, they sent for their families and relatives, who in turn sent for others, so that there has been a steady flow of Samoans since 1951. Current informal estimates place the Samoan population in southern California between 20,000 to 40,000 (Civil Rights Commission: 1975). Because Samoans were not classified separately in the 1970 census, it is difficult to obtain a more precise figure.

Western and American Samoa

The Samoans came from two regions: Western Samoa (at one time part of the British Commonwealth under the administration of New Zealand) and American Samoa, which was incorporated as a trust territory of the United States in 1904. Western Samoa became independent in

1962, and its citizens enter the United States as immigrants, whereas American Samoans are United States nationals, and therefore do not face any immigration restrictions. Although there had been a history of animosities between the Western and American Samoans, there is evidence that past rivalries are being forgotten as the groups find themselves living together and facing common problems (Shu & Satele, 1977).

They come from a culture that stresses the importance of kinship ties and minimizes individuality (Mead, 1961), and in which the organizational structure includes a *matai* (chief) who makes decisions and assumes responsibility for family members. The chiefs, in turn, sit on a village council and collectively recognize a high chief who presides over the entire village community. Observers have indicated that the matai system has been transplanted to the United States, but with important modifications. As Shu and Satele observed, immigration, the coming together of Western and American Samoans, and the attempt to fit into a new society have disrupted the matai system, so that it is similar to building "a jigsaw puzzle with some missing pieces" (1977:14). The increasing emphasis on individuality and the opportunity for individuals to exercise other options in the United States have modified the power and the authority of traditional chiefs.

Nevertheless, the extended Samoan family and kinship system remain central to the group. The family-bonding pattern provides socialization, affection, and identity; there is mutual helping and an interdependency among Samoan families. Problems are resolved and social control is exerted through this extended family system.

The Church also is important to the community. Affiliations are primarily Christian, including Congregational (London Missionary Society), Mormon, Methodist, and Catholic. In addition to its religious functions, the Church helps members to find jobs and raise funds, and it serves as a vehicle for acculturation to the new society. Consequently ministers also are prominent in the community.

Values

Like most Asian immigrants, the Samoans come from a vertically structured society in which prestige, status, and power are clearly demarcated. Females are subordinate to males; the young defer to the old; "the young are taught to respect their elders and never to talk back to them, and the men are expected to protect and to provide for the women" (Shu & Satele, 1977:21).

Charity and sharing are a part of the culture. A pride in self-sufficiency has developed, so that Samoans in need find it difficult to ask for outside help. They come from a culture more balanced than ours in terms of the role of work and leisure. Most arrive in America with a healthy self-concept; they possess the confidence of individuals who have achieved an identity through their families and extended kinship structures and who have strong feelings of loyalty and obligation to their social system.

Their entrance into the United States is through working-class communities in which the vast majority of residents is non-Samoan. Housing is overcrowded, and their job skills, education, and training are insufficient for higher level employment. Therefore, they fill the less desirable occupations, just as generations of immigrants from other cultures found their way into the lower status positions in the new country.

Despite the absence of a visible Samoan community, there remains a cultural network. Since most residents are of the immigrant or first generation, the Samoan language, culture, and customs provide strong ties. But what is comfortable for the first generation is often viewed by the second generation as too restrictive.

A survey by Shu and Satele (1977) showed a number of problems that face the Samoan community in the Los Angeles area. Housing is a major problem, for there are large households and overcrowded homes. Other problems are unemployment and low income, adjustment to the American schools, and the constant clash between the old Samoan ways and the urban, technologically oriented society. The ability of the Samoan family and community to aid in this transition is under constant strain.

Some factors that have caused school problems, such as aggression and physical contact, have helped individual Samoans achieve visibility in the larger society. Their aggressive behavior and their ability to handle physical force, coupled with their large body size, have led many to local fame as football players. This is in direct contrast to other Asian groups, whose participation and use of athletics as a source of upward mobility has been minimal.

Whether Samoans should ally themselves with other Asian-American groups or work toward an independent identity are issues yet unresolved. There are a number of important similarities among the various Asian groups, especially in the existence of an extended family and kinship system that encourages problem solving within their own structures. As long as the community copes with local issues, it remains functional; but larger problems such as unemployment, poverty, and culture clash may overwhelm existing resources. In addition, because the groups may be unwilling to bring their needs to the attention of the larger community, they may continue to suffer in silence. Therefore, needy groups of Samoans, such as the unemployed, the elderly, and those with school problems, are not receiving the necessary attention and help from appropriate community agencies. If the Samoans continue to be identified as

Asian Americans, their chances for receiving appropriate help will continue to be minimal since the general stereotype of Asians as having no problems remains strong.

The Samoan Model

A number of factors lead to a prediction of the acculturation, integration, and assimilation model for the Samoans. They are few in number and scattered, with no strong, visible community. Their cultural ties, including their language, are not functional in the context of trade or other benefits and, unless artificially supported, will probably soon disappear. Further, discrimination against them is not as widespread as with previous Asian immigrants, so that acculturation and integration should not take too long. As with many of subordinated groups, however, the integration will be with other subordinated groups, rather than with the dominant group.

OTHER ASIAN GROUPS

We are witnessing a new immigration from countries such as Vietnam, Cambodia, and Thailand. Many unknowns and differences affect these newcomers, including historic hostilities, conditions of immigration (group sponsors, initial landing in temporary centers), relatives and community support, and the state of the economy of the United States. It is our impression that most of the Asian immigrants possess some skills and education and are therefore likely to follow the acculturation-integration model, although their initial out-group interaction will probably be with other Asian-American groups.

BIBLIOGRAPHY

General

BERK, BERNARD and LUCIE HIRATA (1973). "Mental Illness among the Chinese: Myth or Reality," *Journal of Social Issues*, 29(2):149–166.

BLALOCK, HUBERT JR. (1967). *Toward a Theory of Minority Group Relations*. New York: John Wiley.

BONACICH, EDNA (1973). "A Theory of Middleman Minorities," *American Sociological Review*, 38:583–94.

KALISH, RICHARD and SHARON MORIWAKI (1973). "The World of the Elderly Asian American," *Journal of Social Issues*, 29(2):187–209.

KITANO, HARRY H. L. (1974). "Japanese Americans: The Development of a Middleman Minority," *Pacific Historical Review*, 43(4):500–19.

KITANO, HARRY H. L. and STANLEY SUE (1973). "The Model Minorities," *Journal of Social Issues*, 29(2):1–10.

KITANO, HARRY H. L. and TOM OWAN (1977). "Japanese and Korean Responses to Health Needs in Los Angeles" (unpublished paper).

LYN, KINGSLEY (1976). "Korean Nationalist Activities in Hawaii and America, 1901–1945," in *Counterpoint: Perspectives on Asian Americans*. Los Angeles: University of California, Asian American Center.

Koreans

BONACICH, EDNA and TAE HWAN JUNG (1979). "A Portrait of Korean Small Business in Los Angeles, 1977" (paper presented at the Korean Community Conference, sponsored by Koryo Research Institute; Los Angeles, March 10, 1979).

CHA, MARN J. (1977). "Political Orientation of Koreans in Los Angeles," in *The Korean Diaspora*, pp. 191–203, ed. Hyung-Chan Kim. Santa Barbara, Calif.: Clio Press.

DEARMAN, MARION and STEVE SHIM (1979). "Current Religious Dimensions of Korean Immigrant Community in Los Angeles Area" (paper presented at the Korean Community Conference, sponsored by Koryo Research Institute; Los Angeles, March 10, 1979).

GARDENER, ARTHUR (1977). "Notes on the Availability of Materials for the Study of Korean Immigrants in the United States," in *The Korean Diaspora*, pp. 247–57, ed. Hyung-Chan Kim. Santa Barbara, Calif.: Clio Press.

HAHN, MELANIE and FREDERICK DOBB (1975). "Lost in the System: Korean Students in San Francisco," *Integrated Education*, 13(4):14–16.

HONG, LAWRENCE (1979). "Family Profile and Marital Satisfaction of Koreans in the Los Angeles Metropolitan Area" (paper presented at the Korean Community Conference, sponsored by Koryo Research Institute; Los Angeles, May 10, 1979).

HOUCHINS, LEE and CHANG-SU HOUCHINS (1976). "The Korean Experience in America, 1903–1924," in *The Asian American*, pp. 129–56, ed. Norris Hundley. Santa Barbara, Calif.: Clio Press.

HURH, WON-MOO (1977). "Comparative Study of Korean Immigrants in the United States: A Typology," *Korean Christian Journal*, 2 (Special Spring Issue):60–69.

KIM, BOK-LIM C. and MARGARET E. CONDON (1975). "A Study of Asian Americans in Chicago: Their Socio-Economic Characteristics, Problems and Service Needs," *Interim Report to the National Institute of Mental Health*. Washington, D.C.: Department of Health, Education, and Welfare.

KIM, DAVID S. and CHARLES C. WONG (1977). "Business Development in Koreatown, Los Angeles," in *The Korean Diaspora*, pp. 229–245, ed. Hyung-Chan Kim. Santa Barbara, Calif.: Clio Press.

KIM, HYUNG-CHAN (1977a). "Ethnic Enterprises among Korean Immigrants in America," in *The Korean Diaspora*, pp. 85–107, ed. Hyung-Chan Kim. Santa Barbara, Calif.: Clio Press.

KIM, HYUNG-CHAN (1977b). "Korean Community Organizations in America: Their Characteristics and Problems," in *The Korean Diaspora*, pp. 65–83, ed. Hyung-Chan Kim. Santa Barbara, Calif.: Clio Press.

KIM, HYUNG-CHAN (1977c). "Some Aspects of Social Demography of Korean Americans," in *The Korean Diaspora*, pp. 109–26, ed. Hyung-Chan Kim. Santa Barbara, Calif.: Clio Press.

PATTERSON, WAYNE (1977). "Korean Laborers for Hawaii, 1896–1897," in *The Korean Diaspora*, pp. 9–31, ed. Hyung-Chan Kim. Santa Barbara, Calif.: Clio Press.

RYEE, JAI (1977). "Koreans in America: A Demographic Analysis," in *The Korean Diaspora*, pp. 205–38, ed. Hyung-Chan Kim. Santa Barbara, Calif.: Clio Press.

SHERMAN, DIANA (1979). "Korea Town's Extent, Population Grow Daily," *Los Angeles Times*, February 25, section 8, p. 1.

SUNOO, HAROLD H. and SONIA SHINN SUNOO (1977). "The Heritage of the First Korean Women Immigrants in the United States, 1903–1924," *The Korean Christian Journal*, 2:142–71.

SONG, JOHNG-DOO (1979). "Educational Problems of Korean Students" (paper presented at the Korean Community Conference, sponsored by Koryo Research Institute; Los Angeles, March 10, 1979.

VINACKE, EDGAR (1949). "Stereotyping among National Racial Groups in Hawaii: A Study in Ethnocentrism," *The Journal of Social Psychology*, 30:265–91.

WAGATSUMA, HIROSHI and LEE, CHANG-SOO (1978). "Settlement Patterns of Korean Immigrants in the Greater Los Angeles Area" (final report, University of California, Los Angeles, Asian American Study Center).

YANG, EUN-SIK (1979). "Korean Community, 1903–1970: Identity to Economic Prosperity" (paper presented at Korean Community Conference, sponsored by Koryo Research Institute; Los Angeles, March 10, 1979).

YU, CHAE-KUN (1977). "The Correlates of Cultural Assimilation of Korean Immigrants in the United States," in *The Korean Diaspora*, pp. 167–76, ed. Hyung-Chan Kim. Santa Barbara, Calif.: Clio Press.

YU, EUI-YOUNG (1979a). "Koreans in Los Angeles: Size, Distribution, and Composition" (paper presented at the Korean Community Conference, sponsored by Koryo Research Institute; Los Angeles, March 10, 1979).

YU, EUI-YOUNG (1979b). "Occupation and Work Patterns of Korean Immigrants in Los Angeles" (paper presented at the Korean Community Conference, sponsored by Koryo Research Institute; Los Angeles, March 10, 1979).

YUN, YO-JUN (1977). "Early History of Korean Immigration to America," in *The Korean Diaspora*, pp. 33–46, ed. Hyung-Chan Kim. Santa Barbara, Calif.: Clio Press.

Filipinos

A Study of Selected Socio-Economic Characteristics of Ethnic Minorities Based on the 1970 Census. Volume II: Asian Americans (n.d.). Arlington, Va.: Urban Associates. (Monograph prepared for the Department of Health, Education, and Welfare, HEW Publication no. (OS) 75-121.)

BULOSAN, CARLOS (1973). *America Is in the Heart*. Seattle: University of Washington Press.

CORDOVA, FREDERIC, PETER JAMERO, BARRETTO OGILVIE, ROBERT SANTOS, SILVISTRE TANGALAN, ANDRES TANGALIN, and DALE TIFFANY (n.d.). "Filipino-American Position Paper" (unpublished paper).

CORDOVA, FRED (1973). "The Filipino-American: There's Always an Identity Crisis," in *Asian Americans*, pp. 136–39, eds. S. Sue and N. Wagner. Palo Alto, Calif.: Science and Behavior Books.

DANIELS, ROGER and HARRY H. L. KITANO (1970). *American Racism: Exploration of the Nature of Prejudice*. Englewood Cliffs, N.J.: Prentice-Hall, Inc.

DUFF, DONALD and RANSOM ARTHUR (1973). "Between Two Worlds: Filipinos in the U.S. Navy," in *Asian Americans*, pp. 202–11, eds. S. Sue and N. Wagner. Palo Alto, Calif.: Science and Behavior Books.

MELENDY, H. BRETT (1967). "California's Discrimination against Filipinos," in *The Filipino Exclusion Movement, 1927/1935,* pp. 3, 10. Quezon City, Philippines: Institute of Asian Studies, University of the Philippines.

MORALES, ROYAL (1974). *Makibaba.* Los Angeles: Mountain View Publishers.

MUNOZ, ALFREDO (1971). *The Filipinos in the United States.* Los Angeles: Mountain View Publishers.

SANIEL, JOSEF, ED. (1967). *The Filipino Exclusion Movement, 1927/1935.* Quezon City, Philippines: Institute of Asian Studies, University of the Philippines.

Samoans

CIVIL RIGHTS COMMISSION (1975). "Asian Americans and Pacific People: A Case of Mistaken Identity."

MEAD, MARGARET (1961). *Coming of Age in Samoa.* New York: Morrow.

SHU, RAMSAY and ADELE S. SATELE (1977). *The Samoan Community in Southern California.* Chicago: Asian American Mental Health Research Center.

12

CHINESE AMERICANS

The Chinese were the first Asian immigrants to enter the United States in significant numbers. They came to the West Coast in the 1840s because of economic reverses, local rebellions, and social discontent in China (Purcell, 1965).

The Chinese have not been a very mobile people. They generally have preferred to stay in China, and the fear of them overrunning the earth has little basis in historical fact. China has not been an expansionist nation, especially when compared to the Western countries that have established and maintained far-flung empires and spheres of influence over the past several hundred years. Yet the European nations and the United States have constantly feared Chinese expansionism.

Most Chinese immigrants came from two Southern provinces, Fukien and Kwangtung—or more specifically, two villages in Kwangtung Province, Chung Shan (formerly Hsiang Shan) and Ssu Yi. (The Kwangtung area had had considerable contact with the Western world.)

EARLY YEARS[1]

At first the Chinese immigrants were well received in California. They were regarded as objects of curiosity, and because they were willing to provide supplementary rather than competing economic services, there

[1] Much of the historical material is from Roger Daniels and Harry H. L. Kitano, *American Racism: Exploration of the Nature of Prejudice* (Englewood Cliffs, N.J.: Prentice-Hall, Inc., 1970).

was little or no objection to them. In fact in August, 1850, when Chinese, on two occasions, participated in San Francisco civic ceremonies, their colorful costumes, according to a local chronicler, made "a fine and pleasing appearance." This warm reception can be better understood if the fantastic inflation that the gold rush produced in California is taken into account. In San Francisco in 1850 a common laborer received a dollar an hour; on the East Coast he would have received a dollar a day. A loaf of bread, priced at about a nickel elsewhere, cost fifty cents. Laundry rates were astronomical; prices as high as $20 per dozen items have been reported. Some Californians actually sent their dirty clothes to Honolulu and Canton. This inflation was a result of the gold strikes and the extreme shortage of women; those women who were in the labor force worked at more glamorous occupations than domestic service. The Chinese (and later, the Japanese) quickly filled the jobs that were generally regarded as women's work.

But most Chinese, like other Forty-niners, eventually made their way into the diggings, and it was in the lawless mining regions that anti-Chinese feeling broke out. By 1852 hostility toward the Chinese was already well developed and showed that curious mixture of class and race antagonism that was to be one of its hallmarks. One writer reports the following resolution passed by a miner's meeting:

> Be it resolved: That it is the duty of the miners to take the matter into their own hands . . . to erect such barriers as shall be sufficient to check this Asiatic inundation. . . . That the Capitalists, ship-owners and merchants and others who are encouraging or engaged in the importation of these burlesques on humanity would crowd their ships with the long-tailed, horned, and cloven-hoofed inhabitants of the infernal regions (if they could make a profit on it).

> Resolved: That no Asiatic or South Sea Islander be permitted to mine in this district either for himself or for others, and that these resolutions shall be a part and parcel of our mining laws. (Daniels and Kitano, 1970: 36)

Despite such resolutions, the Chinese population of California continued to grow: in 1852 there were perhaps 25,000 in the state; a decade later there were more than 50,000. Almost all were adult males. Among the Chinese migrants males outnumbered females by at least 15 to 1; among contemporary European immigrants the figure was about 2.5 to 1. Throughout the 1850s, sixties, and seventies, Chinese accounted for 10 percent or more of the California population. Despite virulent opposition, the economic opportunities for Chinese in California were so great that they continued to come for three decades. The hostility was more than verbal; first in the mining districts and then in the cities, Chinese were robbed, beaten, and murdered. These crimes were seldom punished because of the notorious laxity of law enforcement in California at the time. Whatever chance a Chinese might have had to obtain justice vanished because of a ruling that no Chinese could testify against a white person. An 1849 law had provided that "no Black, or mulatto person, or Indian, shall be allowed to give evidence in favor of, or against a white man." Five years later, the chief justice of the California Supreme Court, himself a member of the anti-immigrant "Know Nothing," or American Party, ruled that Chinese were included within the prohibition:

> The anomalous spectacle of a distinct people, living in our community, recognizing no laws of this State except through necessity, bringing with them their prejudices and national feuds, in which they indulge in open violation of the law; whose mendacity is proverbial; a race of people whom nature has marked as inferior, and who are incapable of progress or intellectual development beyond a certain point, as their history has shown; differing in language, opinion, color, and physical conformation; between whom and ourselves nature has placed an impassable difference, is now presented and for them is claimed, not only the right to swear away the life of a citizen, but the further privilege of participating with us in administering the affairs of our Government. (Daniels and Kitano, 1970: 37)

The chief justice was perhaps the first Californian to speculate publicly on the possibility of an Oriental inundation, a fantasy that would later grip the Western imagination under the rubric of the "Yellow Peril."

By the 1860s, anti-Chinese sentiment had developed to the point where it was political suicide for anyone to take their side. The presence of the Chinese promoted all white persons to a superior status. It also blurred differences within the white majority and solidified it to the extent that Jews and Catholics, who were usually scapegoats elsewhere, were more readily accepted in places like San Francisco and Los Angeles. Chinese competition also forced white workers to band together.

The Chinese issue smoldered in California during the late 1850s and early sixties; at the end of the 1860s, it burst into flame. The census of 1870, which probably underestimated their number, showed that a fourth of the state's 50,000 Chinese lived in San Francisco, which had become the undisputed center of anti-Chinese agitation. The situation in San Francisco was exacerbated by the constant influx of new immigrants (some 15,000 had arrived between 1870 and 1871), the continued expulsion of Chinese from the mining districts, and perhaps most crucial, the arrival of 10,000 Chinese laborers after the completion of the Central Pacific Railroad. The increase in Chinese population, together with a severe economic depression, produced an explosive situation throughout the state. In the sleepy village of Los Angeles, for example, some twenty Chinese were killed by gunfire and hanging on October 24, 1871—an outrage that must have involved, in one way or another, most of the adult male inhabitants. But it was in San Francisco in 1870 that the anti-Chinese movement came to a head.

Throughout California the Chinese lived in distinct communities, such as those who were clustered in the twelve-block confines of San Francisco's Chinatown. After the completion of the Central Pacific Railroad, the Chinese, who already dominated the laundry business and had filled most of the positions for domestic servants and menials, began to work in various manufacturing enterprises. In the shoe industry, for example, Chinese shoemakers soon outnumbered whites by four to one; in the process, wages fell from $25 to $9 per week. In the cigar industry their dominance was even more marked: 91 percent (1,657 workers) of all those employed were Chinese. In the textile industry the figure was 64 percent. In addition, Chinese operated many small retail and service shops. The economic competition that the Chinese offered to white workers in the 1860s and seventies was quite real and was resented more and more as the economic depression of the seventies worsened. By the mid-1870s the "sandlot," anti-Chinese meetings of the unemployed had already become a regular occurrence. Although the economic hardship of the 1870s was nationwide and its causes manifold, the working people of California tended to place most of the blame for it on the most obvious visible factor—the Chinese laborers and those who employed them. It apparently occurred to no one in the young California trade-union movement to try to include the Chinese in their organization (the color bar that was established then remains largely effective even today).

During the summer of 1870, anti-Chinese mass meetings flourished in San Francisco and other northern California cities, featuring slogans like:

We Want No Slaves or Aristocrats.

The Coolie Labor System Leaves Us No Alternative—Starvation or Disgrace.

Mark the Man Who Would Crush Us to the Level of the Mongolian Slave—We All Vote.

Women's Rights and No More Chinese Chambermaids.

These meetings were addressed by labor leaders and agitators; they passed resolutions demanding an end to Chinese immigration and calling for a battery of discriminatory acts against Asian immigrants.

State and local governments responded quickly to the voice of the people. The state legislature passed a patently unconstitutional act requiring a $500 bond for each Asian immigrant (regulation of immigration is exclusively a federal concern), while the city of San Francisco passed a number of frankly harassing ordinances to "drive [the Chinese] to other states." These included special taxes on Chinese laundries; a "cubic air" ordinance, enforced only in Chinatown, which jailed the tenants rather than the landlords of overcrowded slum dwellings (critics quickly pointed out that the city jail provided much less than the statutory 500 cubic feet per prisoner); and a "queue" ordinance, which placed a tax on pigtails. All of these invidious acts eventually were declared unconstitutional, thus adding to popular frustration.

By the mid-1870s, the California anti-Chinese agitation attracted a congressional investigating committee, which visited San Francisco in 1876. The testimony against the Chinese was blatantly racist: they lowered wages; they were unassimilable; they were heathens; they were disgusting and tended to debauch those around them. Their defenders emphasized their ability to work and their productivity.

In 1877—a year punctuated by labor violence, riots, and the use of state militia and federal troops throughout the country, during which many conservatives thought that the Paris Commune was being reenacted in America—the anti-Chinese movement found its most volatile leader in Denis Kearney, a San Francisco teamster and a recent immigrant from Ireland. Kearney, a born orator, kept reiterating an almost classic refrain—"The Chinese Must Go"—and embellished his tirades with incendiary slogans like "Every Workingman Should Get a Musket." For the despised Chinese capitalists he suggested "a little judicious hanging," and for San Francisco, where he and his "sandlotters" flourished, he sometimes suggested burning. Like most American demagogues, Kearney's bark was worse than his bite, but he was the spokesman for large groups—probably the majority—of the population who had legitimate grievances in the harsh depression decade of the 1870s.

The Workingmen's Party, which was an outgrowth of Kearneyism, had a lot more to it than its prominent anti-Chinese rhetoric. Its program, essentially a prelude to the populism of the 1890s, called for such basic and eventually forthcoming reforms as: the eight-hour day, direct election of United States senators, compulsory education, an improvement of the monetary system, an end to corruption in public serivce, regulation of banking and industry (especially the railroads), and a more equitable system of taxation. These demands, none of which was effectively realized at the time, were overshadowed by the simplistic and more easily realized cry for an end to Chinese immigration. A series of frightening (to conservatives) electoral victories for the Workingmen, including enough seats to hold the balance of power at the 1879 California Constitutional Convention, caused both major parties, first on the state and then on the national level, to embrace the anti-Chinese cause.

Accordingly, in 1882 Congress overwhelmingly passed a Chinese Exclusion Act, which prohibited Chinese immigration for ten years. The act was renewed for another decade in 1892 and made permanent in 1902.

California's nativist forces, in conjunction with racism in other parts of the country, were able to put into practice overt discriminatory laws. The American labor movement gave its support, but it is clear that political expediency rather than principle was responsible for many of the congressional votes. Within the state, the old demand that the "Chinese Must Go!" quickly lost most of its force. Within a few decades Californians, faced with a new threat of "yellow inundation" from the Japanese, were already remembering the Chinese with a trace of nostalgia that would have shocked both the Kearneyites and their hapless targets.

The anti-Chinese movement of the 1860s and seventies must be counted "successful," for it not only achieved an immediate goal, Chinese exclusion, but also helped to shape a restrictive pattern to which our immigration laws adhered for almost a century. Some historians have judged this democratic "antidemocratic" manifestation as an aberration from our popular heritage. Professor Charles A. Barker, for example, in his monumental biography of Henry George, claimed that his subject's "Californian attitude toward Chinese immigration" was an exception to his "Jeffersonian and Jacksonian principles." This is a basic misunderstanding of the period and of the relationship between popular feeling and race. Jefferson and Jackson shared and perpetuated the racist prejudices of their own times, and those who followed in their tradition have usually done the same. In ethnic, if not in economic matters, enlightenment has been more prevalent among the upper than the lower classes (Daniels & Kitano, 1970).

It is not surprising that this is so. In late nineteenth-century California, anti-Chinese attitudes were part and parcel of the struggle for the rights of labor. One can be repelled by the racist views expressed by George and other spokesmen for the working class and still realize that, within the context of their times, they could hardly be otherwise. With the closing of the frontier (and the California frontier, in the Turnerian sense, closed in the 1860s), free and unlimited immigration had become primarily a source of cheap industrial labor. Therefore, some kind of immigration restriction was almost a foregone conclusion, if organized labor was to grow and prosper. Few today can "approve" the racist and discriminatory forms that it took, but considering the times, it was to be expected.

Federal immigration restriction legislation, which first discriminated against Asians, was soon directed against southern and eastern Europeans, the "new" immigrants who began to dominate the national immigration statistics from the 1880s on. Had the frontier—whose disappearance is traditionally dated at 1890—been exhausted while the "old" immigration was still dominant, a more equitable restrictive law might have ensued. Immigration restriction was originally fostered by forces that are usually labeled progressive; by the 1920s, when it became law, it had attracted broad support from the most reactionary elements in our national life. Liberal historians (and most historians are now liberals) have been reluctant to come to grips with this essential paradox of American life: movements for economic democracy usually have been violently opposed to a throughgoing ethnic democracy. Nowhere can this strain of American racism be seen more clearly than in the anti-Chinese movement.

One other fact about the Chinese experience in the United States should be remembered. In the late 1930s and during World War II, the Chinese became our friends and allies, although the general tone of the friendship was condescending. Their peace-loving nature was emphasized; they had fought valiantly against the "sly, tricky Jap"; they were different from their more aggressive neighbor; and they were honest, hard-working, gentle, and compliant. In many ways, this praise alleviated the everyday humiliation, harassment, and deprivation faced by many Chinese, even with the relatively favorable attitude toward all Orientals (except the Japanese) at this time (Daniels & Kitano, 1970).

FAMILY AND KINSHIP PATTERNS

We will present a broad picture of the Chinese family, although there is no "typical Chinese family," just as there is no "typical American family." The variations within a culture may be as wide as between cultures, but generalizations based on family patterns are possible.

The changes in the structure and style of Chinese family life that the immigrants brought with them developed from acculturation, exposure to newer models, and challenges in the new country. As in the Japanese family, it is the interaction of the power, culture, and visibility of the ethnic community with the American culture that explains the development of the Asian family style in the United States.

One type of family was described by Hsu (1971). It is a cohesive, extended family structure and stresses duty, obligation, importance of family name and ancestor worship. Roles are clearly defined, with the father and eldest son having the most dominant. The duty of the woman is to please her husband, his family, and to provide sons. As with most such traditional family units across the world, there are definitions of good and bad children, attempts to arrange suitable marriages, and sacrifice of self for the larger family unit.

Relatives are essential to this family system. The widespread combining of families can be seen by the relatively small number of Chinese surnames (Hsu estimated a core of about 400 to 500) that provide the bulk of Chinese names.[2]

Hsu (1971) pointed out, some of the advantages of the extended kinship system. The Chinese way gives individuals a greater sense of

[2] The usual Chinese surname consists of three characters: the first, the surname; the second, indicating the man's generation in the clan; and the last, his own character.

security and a means of dealing with the world. Unattractive women do not have to become lonely old maids; men with less ability or motivation do not have to strive constantly for an individual identity; old people do not live in fear of being thrown out of the home as their productive years decline, to face their last years in a home for the aged. (There are risks and consequences in any type of family or kinship system, and preferring one over the other is essentially a matter of values.)

Most of the studies describe upper-class Chinese families, and one can only speculate on the family life of the peasants. For example, Tom (1971) viewed the Chinese-American heritage in terms different from those of most traditional writers. Rather than discussing the scholar-official class, which did not immigrate to the United States in any significant numbers, he focused on the powerless peasant and considered him to be major figure in Chinese immigration. The peasant was dominated by the psychology of survival; he minded his own business and took care of his own problems, expecting to be left alone. The peasant had little power to define culture, to control relationships, or to develop a vigorous individual identity; rather, his best chance for survival was to be ignored by those who were more powerful. Those were the conditions for most peasants in China, and the similarity of their treatment under California racism shaped a similar adaptation.

Changes in China   The picture of Chinese family life that we have presented is based on pre-World War II principles, and it is interesting to contrast that style of life with the view of Mao Tse Tung. We quote from selected articles of the marriage law of the people's republic, promulgated by the Central People's Government on May 1, 1950 (Yang, 1959).

> *Article 1.* The arbitrary and compulsory feudal marriage system, which is based on the superiority of man over woman and which ignores the children's interest is abolished.

> *Article 2.* Polygamy, concubinage, child betrothal, interference with the remarriage of widows and the exaction of money or gifts in connection with marriage shall be prohibited.

> *Article 7.* Husband and wife are companions living together and shall enjoy equal status in the home.

> *Article 8.* Husband and wife are duty bound to love, respect, assist and look after each other, to live in harmony, to engage in production, to care for the children and to strive jointly for the welfare of the family and for the building up of a new society.

> *Articles 9, 10, 11, 12.* Both husband and wife shall have the rights to free choices of occupations and free participation in work or in social activities . . . equal rights in the possession and management

of family property . . . right to use his or her own family name . . . right to inherit each other's property.

Article 15. Children born out of wedlock shall enjoy the same rights as children born in lawful wedlock.

Articles 17–18. Divorce shall be granted when both the husband and wife desire it.

As can be seen, the new marriage laws in China are quite different from the marriage customs in old China. The extremeness of the old norms, as seen by Mao, was one important factor in bringing about the changes.

Changes in the United States

The "ideal" family structure of China could never be duplicated in the United States. First, there were very few Chinese women among the early immigrants, as was pointed out before. Most able-bodied young immigrants had a transient mentality; they intended to return to China rather than to send for their wives and children. Finally, the old family system was more suited to an agricultural society and probably would never have survived in the rapidly changing, urbanized, and technology-oriented United States.

These conditions often led to what Sung called the *mutilated family*—a family united in bond, such as marriage, but separated physically. "In other words, the Chinese men in the United States were [often] family men without the presence of family members, which explains why there were four times as many married men as married women in the census of 1930" (Sung, 1967:155). Chinese tradition was certainly one bar to these families getting together; another was the discriminatory features of the Immigration Act of 1924, which made it practically impossible for a married Chinese man to send for his wife and family. The mutilated family was the predominant form of family life among the Chinese in the United States until more liberal legislation was passed after the end of World War II (Sung, 1967:156).

The mutilated marriage refers to cases in which men married in China before immigrating and left China without bringing their wives. After many years of separation, (for some as long as thirty years) there was the chance to rejoin their spouses again. These reunions tested the old phrase, "absence makes the heart grow fonder." The husband and wife were each brought up in a different culture under completely different circumstances. Sung (1967) described a number of marital failures arising from clashing expectations; Rose Hum Lee (1957) cited a divorce rate of 8.5 among the Chinese in San Francisco.

There was also another way of marrying. Although many of the Chinese immigrants remained bachelors during most of their lives in the

United States, the liberalization of immigration laws after World War II enabled many to go to Hong Kong in search of wives. The courtship was instantaneous, and complete strangers often found themselves married to each other. In many cases, older men, accustomed to a life of hardship in the United States, married younger, more "modernized" Chinese women. After marriage, they returned to the crowded, dilapidated quarters of the urban Chinatowns on the West Coast, and it is probable that many became seriously disillusioned.

But, as Sung found: "In spite of the stresses and strains borne by both husband and wife in the transition, the Chinese family usually remains intact. Discord and unhappiness are generally turned inward toward the self and are reflected in a higher suicide rate rather than divorce statistics" (1967:161–62). Suicide has been one form of protest for Chinese women caught in unbearable matrimonial situations.

Today, family patterns reflect age and class differences. The wide kinship patterns of old China are uncommon; Sung observed that the husband generally occupies a stronger position than the wife in the Chinese-American family. Unless the woman is an aristocrat, highly educated, or quite modern, she will tend to stay in the background.

Parents born in China tend to have more children than those born in America (Sung, 1967:165); "discipline is strict and punishment immediate in the Chinese household" (168). Deviant behavior is not a personal matter between an individual and his or her conscience but affects others, including family and loved ones upon whom dishonor and shame could fall.

Although there is much handling, hugging, and kissing when young, as the child grows older these overt expressions are often withdrawn. The child is shoved "firmly towards independence and maturity. Emulation of adult behavior is encouraged. The mother does not invite confidences nor direct talks and discussions. She commands and decides what is best for the children, and the children are expected to obey. Disobedience is not tolerated and corporal punishment is freely meted out" (Sung, 1967:169). The father plays a distant role in the family proceedings. He is the authority and maintains his superior position by means of a certain emotional distance.

Huang (1976) discussed both the Chinese ghetto family and the professional family. One type of ghetto family is composed of the hardworking but poorly paid Chinese male and his "imported," much younger wife from Hong Kong. The preference in this case seems to be for Chinese-born women, since the American-born woman is felt to be too "modern." Huang found that the professional Chinese male also rejects the Chinese-American woman in favor of Caucasian partners. One of her respondents joked about awarding a fifty-dollar prize to the first member of his group who married a Chinese American. She offered no information about the marital preferences of the Chinese-American female.

Data from the U.S. census for 1970 showed a very high rate of Chinese in-marriage; 87 percent of all Chinese men and 88 percent of all Chinese women married within the group. Marriage out of the group is reported as increasing sharply in the younger age groups.

**School
Experiences**

Most teachers comment on the delightful qualities of Chinese children. Liu (1950) compared teacher's perceptions of Caucasian and Chinese children and found that teachers remarked on the better behavior, obedience, and self-reliance of Chinese-American youngsters. The Chinese, like their Asian counterparts, the Japanese, have done very well in the American educational system and rank as one of the highest educated of the minority groups.

Conflict may arise when Chinese youngsters perceive the different styles of their Caucasian peers. They see the informal and casual relationships that Americans have with their parents and are often apt to wonder whether the American model is more desirable. As with most children of immigrant parents, they see their own hard-working but poor parents, their restricted life styles, the frugality, and the limited English in the home. The comparison may cause them to be ashamed of their parents, family, and ethnic group.

The educational picture based on the 1970 census shows a population of disparate attainments. There is a large proportion who have not gone beyond elementary school (23 percent, compared to the United States national average of 27 percent), but the Chinese also show the highest proportion of any group with college degrees (25 percent, as compared to the United States national average of 13 percent).

The college-enrollment figures for college-age populations are as follows: 71 percent of Chinese males and 58 percent of Chinese females are enrolled. This compares to the national average of 37 percent males and 27 percent females. It is also interesting to note that, despite the high proportion attending American institutions of higher learning, 70 percent of the second-generation children under fourteen years of age speak Chinese in their homes.

In our data on inequality (Chapter 7), both male and female Chinese are revealed competitive with majority-group males. They showed superior attainment in every one of our educational variables in 1960, 1970, and 1976.

EMPLOYMENT

Employment characteristics are partially reflected in the educational patterns of the group. The largest category of employment among males is that of professional occupations (29 percent), but there is also a large number employed as service workers, and many still in the stereotyped

Chinese occupations of laundries and restaurants (24 percent). There also has been a large increase in working married women; only 13 percent of all Chinese wives worked in 1960, but in 1970 the figure was 48 percent.

Income levels of the Chinese do not reflect their high educational status. Of all Chinese men, 41 percent earned an annual income of less than $4,000 (there are serious problems of poverty among older Chinese and new immigrants). It should also be noted that 60 percent of Chinese families have more than one wage earner (compared to 51 percent in the total population), which may be one reason why family income looks high but obscures a large number of very badly paid individuals.

In our data on inequality (Chapter 7) Chinese males and females had higher rates of unemployment than majority-group males did in all of the comparison years, 1960, 1970, and 1976. The degree of occupational segregation of Chinese males was especially high, as was their lower chances for occupational mobility.

Income and Housing

Data from Chapter 7 indicate that the college-trained Chinese earn less than majority-group males with the same education; their median household incomes are lower; their mean earnings are lower; and their poverty rates are higher. Chinese housing patterns for the comparison years of 1960, 1970, and 1976 also show less owner occupancy, more overcrowding, and less complete facilities than housing for the majority group does.

In terms of inequality, the Chinese are more than equal in education, but their employment, income, and housing figures reflect inequality.

SOCIAL PROBLEMS

Rates of problem behavior among the Chinese such as crime and delinquency have historically been low (Beach, 1932), although there is current concern about the rise in delinquency. Part of the explanation for these low rates can be attributed to strong family controls, to life styles that encourage the individual to internalize problems, and to a cohesive community that prefers to handle problems in its own way. Much deviant behavior may remain hidden from official sources. There has been a recent influx of many young immigrants from Hong Kong, with minimal English skills, whose lack of opportunity for absorption into the Anglo and ethnic communities can be hypothesized as one source of potential strain that might lead to a rise in problem social behavior.

Official rates of mental illness (with their limitations) indicate that the Chinese currently have a high rate (Kitano, 1969; Berk & Hirata, 1973). Berk and Hirata, tracing mental illness historically among the Chinese in California, showed that the increase in mental hospital commitments cannot be attributed solely to the demographic composition (old, single males) of the population. They hypothesized that the rise may be due to a reduction in the cohesion of the Chinese community, the loss of alternative institutions to cope with increasing problem behavior, and the source of social control moving from the ethnic to the large community. In any case, the Chinese are beginning to become much more visible to the institutions of social control and prevention.

CHINESE ORGANIZATIONS IN AMERICA

Since emigration generally meant leaving kinship ties at home, groupings along several lines developed in the United States. They included family-name associations along the old kinship models and locality organizations based on previous village ties. Hsu (1971) commented on the relative fluidity of such organizations, thus making it difficult to assess their size accurately. Kinship and locality ties tend to be highly binding.

One important factor is that older Chinese organizations are very specific, limited in scope and membership, and conservative. Recruitment and socialization techniques are predicated on concrete relationships. These organizations seldom have links with other organizations, nor are they apt to be "cause" oriented. Very few old organizations are involved in charitable causes or focus on social welfare activities. It is just not their style.

Organizations such as the Six Companies in San Francisco gained an inordinate amount of power through a variety of means. The restricted opportunities in a racist structure limited the alternatives for most Chinese; the clan and kinship systems ensured a solid membership loyalty. Under these conditions, the Chinese could exploit members of their own group, especially new immigrants with no English or vocational skills, who were highly dependent on ethnic organizations.

New organizations are more apt to reflect the American pattern. Golf clubs and service organizations such as the Chinese Lions Clubs are symptomatic of the influences of acculturation, although their membership is limited to a select group. In spite of these changes, Hsu (1971) feels that the kinship and locality organizations will persist for a very long time; that the American-born Chinese will be slow in initiating or joining cause-oriented organizations, especially of an abstract nature; and finally, in the long run, that newer associations will tend to reflect social and professional interests, although the type, extent, and ethnicity of their membership will be highly dependent on the area of residence and the opportunities available in the dominant culture. Up to now, the Chinese have had no national organization and their organizations appear to wield little power in the outside community.

Religion

The Chinese attitudes toward religion reflect the spirit of the culture. Since the Chinese have been nonexpansionist and nondenominational, they have neither sent their missionaries forth to proselytize the world nor have they been divided by conflicts between sects and denominations. Instead, they have kept a relaxed and polite distance and have incorporated foreign gods and respected all varieties of supernatural belief. Organized religion, ritualistic attendance, and loyalty to one church have not been the pattern; there are few membership drives, and selective membership, tithing, and the like are not common. Relationships with family and kin tend to have a higher priority than those with gods and temples.

Hsu feels that among the Chinese in Hawaii roughly one-third are Christian. But their Christianity includes many Chinese ways. For example, except for directly church-sponsored events, very few meetings open or close with a prayer. There is a tendency to reduce rather than to increase the influence of the church.

Other Patterns in the Chinese Community

Friendship patterns in the Chinese community often are secondary to family and kin relationships. Therefore, Chinese individuals are unable to move about as freely as their American counterparts can. They are part of a much larger human network and have less need to go outside it. They do try to bring outsiders into the network; and in this sense, friendships could be labeled "additive," whereas American patterns could be called "replacements."

Several consequences can be deduced from this type of friendship, kinship, and locality network. Helping others within the network is common and includes what could be regarded as intrusion and intervention into family disputes. (Most Americans would be disturbed over this kind of "meddling.") Friendships also tend to be of long duration and are not like the short-lived, "brittle" American kind. Even business relationships, so sacred to the American system, are secondary to the other links; charges of nepotism and reverse discrimination often are hurled at Chinese establishments. Acculturation has changed some Chinese patterns. Many have taken the American business model to heart and give high priority to economic matters; but in their social dealings, they may still retain the ethnic network.

PERSONALITY

A study by Sue and Kirk (1972) of Chinese American students at the University of California, Berkeley, tested personality differences of Chinese students and those of other ethnic backgrounds. The test results indicated the following: (1) Chinese students score higher on quantitative sections and lower on verbal sections of ability tests; (2) they are more interested in physical sciences, applied technical fields, and business occupations, and are less interested in social sciences, aesthetic and cultural fields, and verbal and linguistic vocations; (3) they prefer more concrete and tangible approaches to life and are more conforming and less socially extroverted compared to other students.

Sue and Kirk offered several cultural explanations for Chinese-American students' lower verbal and higher quantitative scores. First is their bilingual background and insufficient knowledge of English. Second, Chinese-American families restrain strong feelings, which inhibits communication. Third, higher quantitative scores could indicate compensatory means of expression. Fourth, quantitative activity by nature emphasizes a "structured, impersonal, and logical approach"—attributes found most desirable to Chinese-American students. Finally, early immigrants may have encouraged their children to enter vocations that would maximize economic and social mobility. Vocations in the physical sciences instead of in the social sciences seemed most conducive to this goal, since the latter required skills in written and oral communication and an understanding of Western culture.

Analysis of the family structure further explained the differences in test results. For example, family emphasis on tradition, established rules for behavior, conformity, respect for authority, and submergence of individuality help to explain the discomforts of Chinese-American students in new situations and also their tendency to show greater anxiety and less tolerance for ambiguity. Their great emphasis on family loyalty and their distrust of those outside the family contribute to the impression of their lack of concern for the welfare of others. The Chinese tend to "control" their behavior through guilt and shame; they worry over the conflict between their culture and the dominant one; and they feel acute discomfort when communicating outside the family. All these factors result in greater emotional distress.

Sue and Kirk warned that their results may be exaggerated because many Chinese Americans are leaving their families and subculture for the first time. To be independent in a new social setting requires a greater degree of adjustment for people who are used to prolonged family dependency and obligation. They concluded that care must be taken in cultural interpretations of traits in terms of values. For example, some Westerners consider being inhibited undesirable because they favor spontaneity. But the Chinese consider the former characteristic to be a sign of self-control and maturity and the latter to be an indication of bad manners. However, Tom (1971) cited a number of limitations in using psychological tests and models on Chinese Americans. He feels that it is a mistake to judge Chinese Americans by white Anglo-Saxon personality typologies.

CHINATOWNS

The Chinese in the United States represent a compact, urbanized population with large clusters in Hawaii, San Francisco, Los Angeles, and New York. In these "Chinatowns" one can hear different languages and music (from atonal Chinese classics to modern rock); one can taste unusual foods, investigate small shops, choose from a staggering number of restaurants, behold natives, newcomers, old, and young intermingling with the tourists (especially on weekends) and breathe the odors of barbecued pork, ginger, and soy sauce. Other streets have the quiet, residential air of a typical middle-class community. Yet the temptation to stereotype this diversity is so strong that mention of the word "Chinese" usually elicits images of "opium dens, Tong wars, coolie labor, the yellow peril, highbinders, hatchetmen, laundries, waiters, houseboys, slave wages, unassimilable aliens, and so on" (Sung, 1967:1–2).

These stereotypes survive because there has been no adequate information. As Sung observed: "From 1909 when Professor Mary Coolidge's book, *Chinese Immigration,* was published, to 1960, when Professor Rose Hum Lee's book, *The Chinese in the United States of America,* was imported from Hong Kong, no serious work about this neglected minority appeared in the United States" (1967:2). The void was filled by Hollywood movies, newspaper articles, and novels that up until World War II portrayed the Chinese as variations of Fu Manchu and the Dragon Lady.

Overcrowded Chinatowns are not conducive to good health. The tuberculosis rate among Chinese in San Francisco was 104 per 100,000, compared to 49.6 among the whites. Tuberculosis is often equated with poverty, poor diet, and unsanitary, overcrowded facilities (Chin, 1965).

Housing for many Chinese is old and poor; crime is on the increase, and employment under sweat shop conditions is not unusual. The Chinese garment shops in San Francisco are notorious for long hours and meager compensation. Upward mobility into supervisorial and administrative positions remains difficult (Chin, 1965).

For a long time, Chinatowns, whether in New York, Los Angeles, or San Francisco, were highly dependent on tourism. One consequence was the image of law and order and a safe place to be. But the wave of recent new immigrants has strained the meager resources, so that unemployment, welfare, and other, more familiar symptoms of overcrowded ghetto living are becoming visible. There is now a high potential for protest and violence, especially among the younger generations, who are less tolerant of depressed conditions. A high proportion of men can find employment only in Chinese restaurants and an even higher proportion of Chinese women can find work only in the garment industry (Light & Wong, 1975).

Jung (1976), in writing about the Philadelphia Chinatown, emphasized the lack of sufficient recreational, social welfare, and therapeutic resources (as do Sue and Sue, 1973), the high potential for gang conflict, the lack of upward mobility, especially among the newer immigrants, inadequate housing, the lack of adequate care for the elderly, and the encroachment of urban blight. The old agencies such as the YMCAs and YWCAs and the Chinese Benevolent Associations can no longer handle Chinatown's problems without additional assistance.

Kendis and Kendis (1976) examined delinquent Chinese youth gangs in Boston. These youths have rejected both the Chinese and the American identities and have acquired a "street-boy" image. Peer-group orientation is paramount, partly because both parents are unavailable to transmit the ethnic culture because of long working hours in Chinese restaurants.

Wong (1976) stratified the New York Chinatown into four groups. The leaders are the successful businessmen, generally of the immigrant generation, who have accumulated wealth and are active in family and village associations. The majority of this group is anticommunist and pro-Taiwan, although the establishment of formal relationships between the United States and the People's Republic in 1978 may have an effect. Then there are the recent immigrants, who consider themselves sophisticated and urbane but who tend to have a lower economic status. The American-born Chinese (Nisei) are often college educated and have professional status. Many from this group do not speak Chinese, and the more successful are apt to move to the suburbs. The fourth group includes illegal aliens, such as sailors who have jumped ship. Therefore, a legitimate question is raised by Chu (1977): "Who speaks for Chinatown?"

As with most immigrant groups, the transfer of power from one generation to another has not been without considerable stress. Because the traditional power elite and the Chinese civic associations have been unwilling to include the younger generations in decision making, many of the younger groups have formed dissident groups independent of the social control of the old community (Lee, 1973).

The new immigrants who are already in their teens face an especially difficult task. Many are trapped in sociocultural conditions that are considered classic in terms of producing problem behavior. They arrive in the country with little knowledge of English and with minimal occupational skills. They face a cultural discontinuity with broken and disorganized families. They live in overcrowded Chinatowns where rates of disease and poor health conditions are high. They face poverty, rejection, discrimination, and unemployment. Their situation is further exacerbated by the relative affluence of those who have achieved professional status but who show little sympathy toward or recognition of the plight of the newcomers. Many feel exploited, both by the larger society and by their own ethnic community. It is no surprise that destructive gang activity and other forms of deviant behavior are occurring in areas like San Francisco's overcrowded Chinatown.

THE CHINESE MODEL

The diversity of the Chinese group is such that a number of models may be necessary to chart their experience. The melting pot is still not taking place; Lyman (1975) found that the Chinatowns, whether in the United States, Manila, Bangkok, Calcutta, or Liverpool, have a remarkable similarity. The one common denominator is their resistance to "melting." The Indonesian government questions their loyalty and the Malaysians resent their own poverty and the commercial affluence of the Chinese. In most countries, the Chinese are urged to abandon their exclusiveness and become a part of the community, but a combination of discrimination, institutional racism, and cultural factors appears to reinforce the continued existence of the pluralistic structure.

Lyman (1974) noted that the move to suburbia by the Chinese who have acquired professional status has not "melted" them into white, middle-class suburbans. Rather, there has been an attempt to constitute a community that may be likened to the suburban Jews in the Chicago area, who also have maintained a sense of community. Rather than assimilation for this highly assimilable group, there has been a continuation of cultural pluralism.

Part of the reason for the continuing pluralistic structure has been the historical occupational and residential segregation that has resulted in effective seclusion from the American mainstream. Very few cross-ethnic or horizontal alliances were established between the Chinese and their non-Chinese counterparts, whether owners, entrepreneurs, or laborers; the Chinese achieved a vertical integration among their own. Antagonism and discrimination reinforced this parallel structure (Hraba, 1979:305).

One possible resolution for the Chinese in the United States is that of bicultural individuals who acculturate to a certain extent. They see the value of learning the American way, especially in the systems of higher education. But they do not wish to assimilate completely because they see the value of retaining much of their ethnic heritage and culture, especially its language and life styles. Yet they cannot be completely satisfied in being only "ethnic."

A bicultural adaptation is not totally new, but its being deliberate and voluntary may be. Previously, minorities such as the Chinese were forced into biculturalism through discrimination, living in ethnic ghettos, and a transient's orientation. But now it is legitimate to want to retain one's own culture; the *Lau* v. *Nichols* decision in San Francisco supported the teaching and use of the Chinese language in public schools.

The problems of a bicultural adaptation are familiar. Immigrants have always had this problem, but it has somehow been given minor attention as a viable model. One group deems it "schizophrenic," and another deems it "un-American" or "Uncle Tom." Language is one of the more prominent features of bicultural adaptation; it also includes a selective preference for social and cultural relationships from both cultures. However, it may be one of the most appropriate models for a multi-ethnic society such as that of the United States, although the equality of the cultures and their relative power have to be considered.

The other model that seems appropriate for special groups of Chinese is that of a middleman minority. The Chinese small businessman and trader has had such a role in the Philippines, Malaysia, and in the Mississippi Delta. Loewen (1971) studied the delicate accomodations required of the upwardly mobile Chinese in Mississippi who were playing the middleman between the whites and blacks of that region. They avoided group conflict, retained the Chinese culture, but also adopted functional white ways, while still serving as grocers and small businessmen to a predominently black population.

The Chinese in the United States are just beginning to be known to the rest of the country. As more information becomes available, the tremendous diversity among the people of this country gradually will be revealed. The most visible and the best known Chinese (the highly educated intellectuals) comprise only one small part of this group, as do the stereotyped coolies.

New situations further expose this diversity. In the early 1970s, when the San Francisco schools began to integrate by busing, the Chinese formed a major opposition group. Some mounted a boycott and started their own freedom schools; yet other Chinese actively worked with the school system in its integration plans. The Chinese had many reasons to resist busing. There was undoubtedly a degree of racism, but they also wanted local autonomy and control: They felt that many Chinese who were less skilled in the English language faced unfair competition.

The stressful conditions faced by many members of this group—overcrowded quarters in cramped Chinatowns, the constant flow of new immigrants, and the lack of opportunities—cannot be ignored much longer. To assume that "all Asians have made it" will only add to the discontent. Unless some attention is paid to their needs and problems, another group will face the discrepancy between American ideals and racial realities.

BIBLIOGRAPHY

A Study of Selected Socio-Economic Characteristics of Ethnic Minorities Based on the 1970 Census. Volume II: Asian Americans (n.d.) Arlington, Va.: Urban Associates. (Monograph prepared for Department of Health, Education, and Welfare.)

BONACICH, EDNA (1973). "A Theory of Middleman Minorities," *American Sociological Review,* 38:583–94.

BEACH, W. C. (1932). *Oriental Crime in California*. Stanford, Calif.: Stanford University Press.

BERK, BERNARD and LUCIE HIRATA (1973). "Mental Illness among the Chinese: Myth or Reality?" *Journal of Social Issues*, 29(2):149–166.

CHANG, LILY and others, ed. (1971). *Asian Women*. Berkeley, Calif.: University of California Press.

CHIN, JAMES WILBUR (1965). "Problems of Assimilation and Cultural Pluralism among Chinese Americans in San Francisco: An Exploratory Study" (unpublished master's thesis, University of the Pacific).

CHOW, WILLARD (1975). "Reviving the Inner City: the Lessons of Oakland's Chinatown," *Public Affairs Report*, 16(4):1–7.

CHU, ERNEST (1977). "The Two Faces of Chinatown," *The Journal of Philanthropy*, 18(2): 18–26.

COOLIDGE, MARY ROBERTS (1909). *Chinese Immigration*. New York: Henry Holt.

DANIELS, ROGER AND HARRY H. L. KITANO (1970). *American Racism: Exploration of the Nature of Prejudice*. Englewood Cliffs, N.J.: Prentice-Hall, Inc.

FUJITOMI, IRENE and DIANE WONG (1973). "The New Asian American Woman," in *Asian Americans*, pp. 252–63, eds. S. Jue and N. Wagner. Palo Alto, Calif.: Science and Behavior Books.

GEE, EMMA and others (1976). *Counterpoint: Perspectives on Asian America*. Los Angeles: Asian American Studies Center, Resource Development and Publications.

HUANG, LUCY JEN (1976). "The Chinese American Family," in *Ethnic Families in America*, pp. 124–45, eds. Charles Mendel and Robert Haberstein. New York: Elsevier.

HRABA, JOSEPH (1979). *American Ethnicity*. Itasca, Ill.: F. E. Peacock.

HSU, FRANCIS L. K. (1971). *The Challenge of the American Dream: The Chinese in the United States*. Belmont, Calif.: Wadsworth.

JUNG, MARSHALL (1976). "Characteristics of Contrasting Chinatowns," *Social Casework*, 57(3):149–54.

KALISH, RICHARD and SHARON MORIWAKI (1973). "The World of the Elderly Asian American," *Journal of Social Issues*, 29, 2:187–209.

KENDIS, KAORU and RANDALL KENDIS (1976). "The Street-boy Identity: An Alternate Strategy of Boston's Chinese-Americans," *Urban Anthropology*, 5(1):1–17.

KINGSTON, MAXINE HONG (1976). *The Woman Warrior*. New York: Vintage Books.

KITANO, HARRY H. L. (1969). "Japanese-American Mental Illness," in *Changing Perspectives on Mental Illness*, pp. 256–84, eds. Stanley Plog and Robert Edgerton. New York: Holt, Rinehart & Winston.

KITANO, HARRY H. L. and AKEMI K. MANNING (1973). "The Japanese-American Family," in *Ethnic Families in America*, eds. Charles Mivdele and Robert Hanbenstein. New York: Elsevier.

KITANO, HARRY H. L. and STANLEY SUE (1973). "The Model Minorities," *Journal of Social Issues*, 29(2):1–9.

LAI, HIM MARK and PHILIP CHOY (1973). *Outlines: History of the Chinese in America*. San Francisco: Chinese American Studies Planning Group.

LEE, ROSE HUM (1960). *The Chinese in the United States*. Hong Kong: Hong Kong University Press.

LEE, RUSSELL (1973). "Patterns of Community Power: Tradition and Social Change in American Chinatowns," in *Ethnic Conflicts and Power: A Cross National Perspective,* eds. Donald E. Gelfaud and Russell Lee. New York: John Wiley.

LEVINE, GENE and DARREL MONTERO (1973). "Socioeconomic Mobility among Three Generations of Japanese Americans," *Journal of Social Issues,* 29(2):33–48.

LIGHT, IVAN and CHARLES WONG (1975). "Protest or Work: Dilemmas of the Tourist Industry in American Chinatowns," *American Journal of Sociology,* 80(6):134–68.

LIU, CHING HO (1950). "The Influence of Cultural Background on the Moral Judgment of Children" (unpublished doctoral dissertation, Columbia University).

LOEWEN, JAMES (1971). *The Mississippi Chinese between Black and White.* Cambridge, Mass.: Harvard University Press.

LYMAN, STANFORD (1975). "Contrasts in the Community Organization of Chinese and Japanese in America," in *Majority and Minority* (2nd ed.), pp. 285–96, eds. Norman Yetman and C. Hoy Steele. Boston: Allyn Bacon.

LYMAN, STANFORD M. (1977). *The Asian in North America.* Santa Barbara, Calif.: Clio Press.

NEE, G. VICTOR and BRETT DE BARY NEE (1973). *Longtime Californio.* New York: Random House.

PURCELL, VICTOR (1965). *The Chinese in Southeast Asia* (2nd ed.), Ch. 2. London: Oxford University Press.

SANDMEYER, ELMER C. (1973). *The Anti-Chinese Movement in California.* Urbana: University of Illinois Press. (Foreword by Roger Daniels).

SAXTON, ALEXANDER (1971). *The Indispensable Enemy.* Berkeley: University of California Press.

SUE, DERALD and B. KIRK (1972). "Psychological Characteristics of Chinese American College Students," *Journal of Counseling Psychology,* 19:471–478.

SUE, STANLEY and DERALD W. SUE (1973). "Chinese American Personality and Mental Health," in *Asian Americans,* pp. 111–24, eds. S. Sue and N. Wagner. Palo Alto, Calif.: Science and Behavior Books.

SUE, STANLEY and HARRY H. L. KITANO (1973). "Stereotypes as a Measure of Success," *Journal of Social Issue,* 29(2):83–98.

SUNG, BETTY LEE (1967). *Mountain of Gold.* New York: Macmillan.

SUNG, BETTY LEE (1976). *A Survey of Chinese-American Manpower and Employment.* New York: Praeger.

TOM, BEN (1971). "The Ghetto of the Mind: Notes on the Historical Psychology of Chinese America," *Amerasia Journal,* 1(3):1–31.

WOLFE, TOM (1969). "The New Yellow Peril," *Esquire Magazine,* December, pp. 190–200.

WONG, BERNARD (1976). "Social Stratification, Adaptive Strategies and the Chinese Community of New York," *Urban Life,* 5(1):33–52.

WU, CHENG-TSU (1972). *Chink.* New York: World Publishing.

YANG, C. K. (1959). *The Chinese Family in the Communist Revolution.* Cambridge: Technology Press, Massachusetts Institute of Technology.

13

JAPANESE AMERICANS

In many ways, the history of the Japanese Americans is similar to that of the Chinese, except that they arrived later. The initial group was made up primarily of young males, many of whom intended to return to Japan. They were imported for their labor; they faced many of the barriers and restrictions erected for the Chinese; they looked alike ("Can you tell them apart?"), at least to the majority; and most important, they quickly became the main targets for racism in California and the West Coast.

But the Japanese and Chinese are different, not only in nationality and culture, but also in other ways. For example, Lyman (n.d.) contrasted the community organizations of the two groups and described how each represents different needs. The Japanese came from a developing industrial nation, whereas the Chinese were from a primarily agricultural one. The Japanese used their embassy and consular officials as resources, whereas the Chinese depended on informal organizations. Many Japanese brought their wives with them and started families almost immediately, whereas the Chinese often left their wives in China: therefore, there were important differences in sexual and recreation patterns. Because their children were born in America, the Japanese were immediately concerned about acculturation, whereas this stage was delayed among the first Chinese immigrants because they had so few children. Each of these factors is important in explaining some of the patterns of differential adaptation, and only under the incredible stereotyping of racism do the Chinese and the Japanese appear identical. As with all of our ethnic groups, the individual differences within the group are so wide that any generalizations have to be carefully limited.

EARLY HISTORY

The Issei

The first-generation immigrants, known as the *Issei,* were relatively homogeneous: most of them were young and had had four to six years of schooling; most were male; and most had come from rural Japan. The Issei came primarily from southern Japan, particularly the prefectures of Hiroshima, Fukuoka, Kumamoto, Wakayama, and Yamaguchi.

The bulk of their immigration took place between 1870 and 1924, after which time the United States immigration laws prohibited the permanent immigration of any Japanese nationals (as well as of all Asians). Not even a token quota was assigned to them.

The immigrants found employment as agricultural laborers, in small business, or as service workers, often working with or for other Japanese; they also established small shops of their own. Japanese tend to be interdependent and segregated housing patterns served to reinforce the existing ethnic network.

Some Issei returned to Japan in those early days, considering themselves ''successful'' and hoping to lead a more leisurely life in the home country; others returned as ''failures.'' Those who remained in the United States sent to Japan for women in order to marry and raise children. This practice made their communities in the United States more permanent. Men and women were brought together through an exchange of photos, and many young women were called ''picture brides.''

The Issei brought with them the behavioral orientations of Meiji Japan (1867–1912), although it was probably a tentative, day-by-day reaction rather than a codified set of values to be rigidly memorized. It also should be emphasized that the Issei came from a vertically stratified society, and behaviors were closely linked to rank, status, and position. Very few of the immigrants came from the upper class. Conversely, because of a degree of selectivity by the Japanese immigration officials, the Issei also were not from the bottom of the class structure. There was an emphasis on deference, especially to those perceived to be in positions of power and authority, on duty and obligation, and on the importance of the family, the community, and larger groups over the individual. Connor (1977) reported that according to a recent survey, most surviving Issei still retain these orientations, athough they also had acquired certain American orientations, such as individualism and self-reliance. Connor's sample included three generations of Japanese Americans and a Caucasian sample drawn from Sacramento, California.

The Issei lived their lives segregated from the American mainstream, and their major interactions revolved around their families and their community. Most of them acquired just enough knowledge about America in order to function but left the major task of acculturation and a more secure existence to their American-born children.

The Nisei

The children of the Issei, or *Nisei,* were generally born between 1910 and 1940, and by the 1970s were in their middle years. Although they were influenced by their parents, they became more acculturated to America than the Issei did. Discrimination and prejudice caused many Nisei to lower their expectations and life styles in order to make a living in the United States. One writer called them the "quiet generation" (Hosokawa, 1969), and although there was a minor furor in the ethnic community over the title, it is a reasonable description.

Life was particularly difficult for this group in the 1920s and 1930s because of discrimination, prejudice, and segregation, especially since the majority of Nisei identified with the country and wished to be treated as American citizens. The plight of the Nisei was such that in 1929, the Carnegie Corporation financed a study at Stanford University that was eventually reported by Strong (1934) under the title *The Second Generation Japanese Problem.* Interviews with the Nisei indicated doubts about their employment, concern over their low status in American society, ambivalence about possibly seeking a future in Japan, and overall insecurity and anxiety about their future in the United States. The objective findings of the study indicated that the Nisei were as bright as the Caucasian as measured by IQ tests; their rates of crime and delinquency were very low; and their school achievement was high. Strong's conclusion was that racial prejudice lay at the root of the "Nisei problem."

In terms of behavioral orientations, the Nisei have moved away from the Issei toward more American norms. Connor (1977) saw less deference and diminished importance of duty and obligation, but the Nisei generally fall in between the Issei and the third, or Sansei, generation on most measures.

The Sansei and Other Generations

The *Sansei,* or third generation, were born after World War II and by the 1970s were in high school, college, or the work force. The differences within this group are perhaps the greatest and reflect the vast changes and stratifications of the youngest generations of American society. For example, older Sansei may still retain the values and styles of their Nisei parents, but the younger groups are often radical and militant.

Sansei differences are especially noticeable according to area of settlement; the Midwesterner and the Easterner are more likely to reflect the orientations of those areas, rather than a Japanese community norm. The one Sansei student attending a high school in Michigan or New Jersey will have very little in common with the Sansei attending Mc-Kinley High School in Honolulu (where there is a high proportion of Japanese Americans), except that of physical likeness.

In terms of Japanese behavioral orientations, Connor (1977) found that the Sansei were closer to the American norms of deference, duty and obligation, and collective orientation when compared to the Issei and Nisei, but still were not identical to their Caucasian peers.

There are other important Japanese groups, such as the transient businessman (kaisha), the student, the tourist, and the new immigrants; but the basic group of Japanese immigrants has been the Issei, Nisei, Sansei, and Yonsei (fourth generation).[1]

THE WARTIME EVACUATION

Japanese Americans came into negative prominence during World War II. The evacuation has been variously termed as America's "greatest wartime mistake" and "America's day of infamy." It is the main subject of recent books by Daniels (1971), Girdner and Loftis (1969), Myer (1971), Bosworth (1967), Fisher (1965), Spicer and others (1969), and Weglyn and Zeller (1969). Earlier books are by Eaton (1952), Grodzins (1949), Leighton (1945), Okubo (1946), Thomas, Kikuchi, and Sakoda (1952), Thomas and Nishimoto (1946), and Tenbroek and others (1954). Many government documents and articles and most books on Japanese Americans discuss the subject.

However, the evacuation has remained relatively obscure to most Americans; practically every non-Japanese the author has ever met has been ignorant of this event, but sympathetic when told about it. "If we only knew," is the usual reply, with its brave but futile implication that things would have been different. But empirical evidence from the wartime years does not present a reassuring picture. For example, Bloom and Riemer (1945) surveyed various student campuses in 1943; 63 percent on the West Coast and 73 percent in the Midwest felt that the handling of the Japanese during this period was correct. A more recent survey in

---

[1] There also are other Japanese groups that should be mentioned: The Kibei were born in the United States of Issei parents but were sent back to Japan for much of their upbringing—primarily in the 1930s; Japanese businessmen have constantly visited this country, except during World War II; there were an estimated 25,000 war brides by 1960. New immigrants began to arrive from Japan from 1954 on and represent a new Issei.

conjunction with the Japanese American Research Project at UCLA in 1969 (approximately twenty-five years after the evacuation) indicated that over 48 percent of California respondents surveyed felt that the evacuation was justified.

Prejudice, Discrimination, and Segregation

   The necessary conditions for placing groups behind barbed wire (or for more severe actions, such as extermination and genocide) are shaped by prior circumstances, especially by prejudice, discrimination, and segregation (Daniels & Kitano, 1970). Prejudice, usually maintained by stereotyping, leads to the avoidance of a group; discrimination and segregation, maintained by laws, customs, and norms, foster disadvantage and isolation. For a group so cut off, stereotypes become the operating reality, since there is no way of effectively correcting the biased information. If certain incidents crystallize the already negative sentiments, more permanent solutions (concentration camps, exile, isolation, and extermination) may be instituted.

   For example, before 1954, the Issei could not become United States citizens; therefore certain basic civil rights had never been a part of their expectations. They were the targets of stereotyping and legal harassment. Issei could neither vote nor own land; nuisance laws prevented them from employing white women, and the price of their California state fishing licenses were set deliberately high. Antimiscegenation laws discouraged the Issei from believing that they were equal to white people. Stereotyped as less than human and placed at a competitive disadvantage by laws and customs, they were limited in their opportunities for any kind of equal status contact.

   The Nisei had been segregated into Little Tokyos and Osakas, usually in the older and less desirable areas of the cities. These Japanese communities were able to maintain effective social control over their members, and there were none of the usual signs of social disorganization, such as high rates of crime and delinquency.

   But segregated ethnic groups lack any equal-access contact and are subject to ethnic stereotypes by the dominant group. The problem is not solely with dominant group perceptions; other minorities may see the stereotypes as the reality, and even members of the target group may turn on each other—those with the "desired" qualities (who are more acculturated) may reject their peers. As a consequence, target minorities often find themselves stereotyped, isolated, avoided, and fighting among themselves. The Japanese in the United States at the time of Pearl Harbor were victims of all of the boundary-maintenance mechanisms; the Pilipinos, Chinese, and Koreans had turned against them; most of the majority group thought in terms of the stereotype of the "sly, sneaky, tricky, Jap"; and politicians and journalists played upon popular anti-Japanese sentiments. The group itself was divided by generation (Issei, Nisei, Kibei) and by American and Japanese loyalties.

The "Trigger" and its Effects

Action against the Japanese was triggered by the attack on Pearl Harbor. But plans for the "final solution" were never clear. The momentum was established by a series of actions. The cumulative effect of many decisions, past feelings and actions of prejudice, discrimination, and segregation, panic, racism, and the wartime atmosphere all combined to shape the eventual decision to evacuate and incarcerate the entire Japanese population along the West Coast, whether citizen or alien.

Immediately after December 7, 1941, the FBI rounded up selected enemy aliens, including 2,192 Japanese. Even this roundup, which was logical enough at the time, had its ludicrous moments. The arrested were those who had contributed money to Japan, who had achieved some degree of prominence, or who belonged to certain organizations. (My father was taken away initially on the charge of possessing illegal contraband—which turned out to be several flashlights and a knife).

Pressure Grows

The incarceration of only selected aliens did not satisfy the Hearst press. The cry, "Japs Must Go," was echoed by the syndicated Hearst columnist Henry McLemore when he wrote on January 29, 1942:

> I am for the immediate removal of every Japanese on the West Coast to a point deep in the interior . . ., let 'em be pinched, hurt, and hungry. Personally, I hate Japanese. And that goes for all of them. (Kitano, 1976:70)

Those advocating the removal of the Japanese included individuals such as then California Attorney General Earl Warren, "liberal" columnist Walter Lippman, and civil-rights fighter Carey McWilliams; the usual patriotic and right-wing organizations; farm and labor groups; the press; local and national magazines and newspapers. Most organizations usually alert to cases of blatant discrimination remained silent.

In chronological sequence, the following events occurred: On January 29, 1942, United States Attorney General Francis Biddle established security areas along the Pacific Coast from which all enemy aliens were to be removed. On February 19, 1942, President Franklin Roosevelt signed Executive Order 9066, which designated restricted military areas and authorized the building of "relocation camps." The ten camps were scattered over California, Arizona, Idaho, Wyoming, Colorado, Utah, and Arkansas.

In March 1942, the evacuation of persons of Japanese ancestry, defined as anyone with as little as one-eighth Japanese blood, began. By November, more than 110,000 West Coast Japanese, most of them American citizens, were behind barbed wire. The rapid, smooth, and efficient evacuation was aided by the cooperation of the Japanese people themselves. They responded to posted notices to register, voluntarily assembled at designated points, and marched off to the trains and buses sent to haul them to the camps.

Beneath this accommodating facade lay the disruption of years of effort. Homes and possessions were abandoned; personal treasures were sold for a fraction of their value or were stolen; farms and gardens were ruined; families disintegrated. Few of the Japanese seemed to expect fair play or justice. The evacuation was justified "for the good of the Japanese themselves." (It is this kind of thinking that encouraged the United States to bomb villages and hamlets in Southeast Asia "for the good of the inhabitants.")

Although there were riots (Kitano, 1976:34), draft-dodging (Daniels, 1971), and other acts of resistance, most Japanese accepted it, or were resigned to it (*shikataganai*). Several individual cases were brought to the Supreme Court (Kitano, 1976:39–40); although there was no direct ruling on the evacuation, the decisions supported the legality of the action. In all of its phases, the forced evacuation and incarceration of the Japanese, whether citizens or aliens, was legally sanctioned.

The evacuation ended in 1944 as it started, on a legal note, when the Supreme Court ruling on the Endo case revoked the West Coast exclusion orders. Effective January 2, 1945, the Japanese were no longer under forcible detention (Kitano, 1976:40).

Although there were problems in getting some Japanese to leave, by June 1946 the concentration camps were closed. There were incidents of vandalism and terrorism against the Japanese when they returned to their homes on the West Coast, but these soon ended. Some Japanese moved to the Midwest and to the East Coast, but many returned to California and by 1970, the majority were again on the West Coast.

Racism

The most reasonable conclusion is that racism was the primary factor in the removal of the Japanese. The definition of who was Japanese was based on "blood," and the presumption of guilt by ancestry condemned the entire race to incarceration. As Daniels and Kitano (1970) pointed out, the actions of Germans was attributed to evil and sick *individuals*, but the actions of the Japanese were attributed to an evil *race*.

If the Japanese were a menace to the West Coast, then they should have been even more of a menace to Hawaii. But there was no mass jailing of Japanese on the much more vulnerable islands, and this fact supports the belief that West Coast racism was primarily responsible for the concentration camps. Although Hawaii was not free of racial prejudice and discrimination, it was a racial paradise compared to California. Further, the Japanese were vital to Hawaii's economy (resource power); there were many more Japanese in Hawaii (numerical power); and the commander of the area was a much more enlightened man than his counterpart on the West Coast.

Was there a possibility that the Japanese Americans could have suffered the same treatment in America as the Jews did in Germany? Could the Japanese have been placed in death ovens? Were they ever faced with the danger of extermination? Before answering these questions, a series of other events bearing on this issue will be described.

Daniels (1971) observed that when the decision to move the Japanese into the interior was planned, the Army called a special meeting of governors of western states in Salt Lake City on April 7, 1942. Milton Eisenhower was asked to present information to the select group, and one of the basic questions was what would happen to the "Japs" after the war. The United States administration wanted to handle the evacuees with some degree of restraint; there were ideas of homesteading and the like, but the hostility of the western governors soon quelled any liberal approach. Cries that no state should be a "dumping ground for California's problems" were typical, and there was almost no alternative but to build settlements on the model of concentration camps with barbed-wire fences and armed guards. The paranoia and fear caused by the Japanese stereotype was powerful indeed.

A government that could herd a race of people into concentration camps could probably also exterminate them. For example, if the Japanese had invaded Hawaii and were threatening the West Coast, passions might have run even higher. Or, if the Japanese actually had been dropping bombs on United States cities, the administration might have used the ultimate retaliation against the Japanese Americans behind barbed wire. The extermination of a group, of course, does not necessarily mean only overt violence. Inadequate diets, the separation of sexes, and sterilization all were mentioned as "solutions" for the Japanese at one time by members of the United States Congress. The important point is that the momentum acquired through prejudice, stereotyping, discrimination, segregation, and the neutralization of the human qualities of the target group ("tricky, sneaky yellow dogs") sets the stage for more dramatic solutions. Other processes then take over. Organizational roles ("I was just doing my duty") can assume such high priority that placing innocent people behind barbed wire is simple. The colonel who was in charge of putting the Japanese into the camps received high commendation for the effectiveness of his operation. There is little question that if orders were given for more drastic solutions, they would have been dispatched with the efficiency and speed of a people proud of their organizational ability and their reputation for following through on "orders."

The 1970 Census reported 591,290 Japanese in the United States. The two most populous states for the Japanese are Hawaii (217,307) and California (213,280). Nationally, the Japanese represent but 0.02 percent of the United States total of over 203 million. Although there are Japanese scattered throughout the United States, they are mainly in the coastal states. In Hawaii they represent one of the largest ethnic units and have achieved some political power.

The Japanese are a physically visible population, although their Asian features are similar to those of the Chinese and the Korean, at least to the white majority. Their life styles are less visible; they live quiet lives; and their dress and their consumption patterns do not stand out. Like their Asian neighbors, they do not quite fit into the black or white categories. In South Africa, they may be classified for business purposes as "white," but not on a social level. In the South during World War II they were considered white, and therefore the color classification of the Japanese is not an absolute. However, their distinctive oriental features, including their smaller, slanted eyes, their shorter physical stature, and straight black hair, make them easily identifiable ethnics.

One of the techniques adopted by many Japanese was to become less visible. The life styles of most Japanese did not reflect their social class; they consistently lived below the average non-Japanese individual of a similar class position.[2] Actions that might bring attention to them, especially of a negative nature, were discouraged. Loud talking, loud clothes, big cars, and fancy houses were thought to present a negative image and so were generally discouraged as popular models. To be quiet, to conform, to be modest, and to refrain from actions of a deviant nature were strong role prescriptions.

Conversely, visibility in terms of wearing clean and conservative clothes, getting good grades, and belonging to "good" organizations (YMCA, Scouts) was strongly encouraged. Some attempted to pass by

[2] This is still true of many Japanese Americans today, although many Sansei of our acquaintance are beginning to react to the conservative style of their parents. They want the most expensive things from the most prestigious stores; they dress to draw attention; and they constantly clash with their parents over consumption patterns.

having eye operations and adopting Anglo names,[3] but the proportion has been extremely low. Perhaps the model choice for handling the problem of visibility has been *psychological passing*—identifying and acquiring the American culture at such a rapid rate that the Japanese have been termed America's model minority.

Social Class   Whatever power the Japanese Americans have acquired is due to their educational and occupational achievement. They are one of the best educated groups in the United States, and their school achievement remains consistently high. Their incomes are among the highest of all ethnic groups; many have become professionals; their housing pattern reflects a middle-class status; very few would be considered "poor" (Kitano, 1976). Although the first Issei group started on a relatively homogeneous lower-class level, by the 1970s there was sufficient differentiation to support a wider class structure. There are millionaires (usually land investors), many professionals (such as doctors, lawyers, dentists, optometrists, and pharmacists), and many teachers, nurses, and engineers. There also are the familiar gardeners and many farmers who own their land. Many also are civil service employees.

Occupational mobility and educational achievement are closely related. Levine and Montero (1973), in a study analyzing three generations of Japanese, found that the higher the education level of the Issei, the more likely that their sons would be in high status occupations. They also reported that a large proportion of the Nisei (71 percent) had white-collar jobs. The higher status Nisei differed from the blue-collar Nisei in that they (1) intended to live in primarily white neighborhoods; (2) were less adamant about their children marrying within the ethnic group; (3) were less involved in the ethnic community, including the Buddhist church; and (4) were less likely to speak or read Japanese as fluently or as well. It is interesting to note that 15 percent of the blue-collar workers had incomes of $10,000 per year or more (this reflects the income of the independent Japanese gardener).

The Levine and Montero findings can be questioned as to their sample. It was a three-generational study with the original sample chosen from Issei lists compiled primarily from Japanese community organization rosters. Therefore, as the authors emphasized, there was a bias against the peripheral and unaffiliated Issei, and the bias may have been compounded by restricting the subsequent interviews to the progeny of the original sample. Despite these biases, the movement toward college and professionalization is strong and is supported by independent observation.

A summary of the Japanese American according to the 1970 Census

---

[3] A common compromise in terms of names is for a very Anglicized first name with ethnic surname and sometimes an ethnic middlename.

indicates that 70 percent have finished high school and 19 percent have completed college—well above national norms of 54 percent and 13 percent. Similarly, 67 percent of Japanese women have completed high school, compared to the national norm of 55 percent. The number completing college, 11 percent, is also greater than the national average of 8 percent.

There are occupational differences between Japanese males born in Japan and those born in the United States. Forty-five percent of foreign-born Japanese are in upper-status, white-collar occupations such as professionals and managers, whereas slightly less than 33 percent of American-born Japanese are in this category. Conversely, a third of American-born Japanese are in skilled and blue-collar jobs, while only 13 percent of the foreign born are in this category.

In spite of their high educational and occupational achievement, there is evidence that the Japanese are underemployed. "The proportion working in higher status white collar jobs has not kept up with the proportion who are college educated" (A Study of Selected Socio-Economic Characteristics, 1970).

It is interesting to note the income distribution of Japanese males: one-third is in the middle and upper-income groups, but another one-third is also among the low-income groups in the United States. As in most Asian groups in America, family income is dependent on more than one worker; over 50 percent of Japanese families include working wives and husbands, compared to 39 percent of such combinations in the total population. It also should be noted that over a third of the Japanese live in Hawaii, where the cost of living is at least 25 percent higher than in the rest of the United States (A Study of Selected Socio-Economic Characteristics, 1970).

Nationally, the rate of poverty among Japanese families is 6 percent, compared to the United States average of 11 percent. However, the rate of poverty among Japanese families outside Hawaii and California is 11 percent. The major poverty group is the elderly; 20 percent of Japanese sixty-five years and older are poor. Many of them are widows who reside by themselves.

More recent data are indicated in our analysis of social inequality in Chapter 7. The Japanese (along with the Chinese on selected items) are the one minority group that consistently surpasses white male norms on most of our measures of inequality for 1976, especially in the area of educational achievement.

THE FAMILY

Analyzing the Japanese family will add to our understanding of its acculturation to the United States and help identify some of the variables that may have slowed this process. The power of the ethnic community and ethnic visibility are variables that help explain differential rates of acculturation. For example, the Japanese in Hawaii are much more apt to retain elements of the Japanese culture than are Japanese families living in Connecticut (Kitano & Kikumura, 1973).

Another important factor is the Japanese work ethic. It is such an integral part of their system that one Japanese professor wrote: "Japanese work as if they were addicted to it" (*Japan Times,* 1973:3). The roots of the work orientation can be traced as far back as the teachings of Confucius and Buddha; the familiar Protestant work ethic is a recent borrowing by Europeans of something that has existed in Asia for many centuries (Kitano & Kikumura, 1973).

The Issei immigrants brought their work ethic to the United States. For many, hard work and effort were desirable goals in themselves. We know of surviving Issei who remain uncomfortable with many of the modern, work-saving appliances because they entail so little time, effort, and expenditure of energy.

Although there are difficulties in assessing the culture that the Japanese brought to the United States, Nakane (1965, 1972) presented a framework that is helpful in understanding the Japanese family in Japan. She stressed the importance of situational membership and the role of the *ie* or traditional family unit in socializing family members and in providing the major reference group. Marriages were between *ies* rather than individuals, and "good" *ies* trained their men and women for appropriate roles in the Japanese social system. Group power and group control were paramount in shaping the attitudes and behaviors of individuals. Group needs had a higher priority than individual needs and desires. Relationships within the ethnic community were mostly noncontractual, and socialization was toward a narrow living range and dependency. In general, we now see the Japanese-American family as follows:

1. It has remained an intact family unit with low rates of separation and divorce, although there are changes towards a more American model. The low past rates of divorce (1.3 percent) are probably rising (Kitano, 1976).

2. The structure of the family initially was vertical, with father and males on top. It could be compared to a traditional family model, in contrast to the modern urban American family. Entertainment and recreation often take place in the family and extended family units. Families are larger, and problems often are handled within the unit. The use of outside professionals is a last resort.

3. The *ie* unit was adopted in America to incude larger units, including village, *ken,* and even the entire Japanese community. It serves as an effective social control device and provides socialization opportunities through ethnic language schools and cultural and recreational opportun-

ities. The Japanese community is a reference group; its functions are similar to those of an *ie*.

4. Socialization and child rearing take into account minority-group position, power, and the perpetuation of the Japanese culture. Those values, norms, and behaviors most likely to persist are those of the Japanese culture that interact with the power position of the Japanese in the United States and their visibility in a race-conscious society. Many of these behaviors also are reinforced by the majority group, so that they become stereotypes of the Japanese. These include quietness, conformity, loyalty, diligence, maximum effort, good citizenship, high school achievement, and group orientation.

5. The situational orientation is an important part of Japanese-American behavior. Learning how to behave to those above, below, and equal has meant learning appropriate styles. As Kitano stated:

> There are elements of a "schizophrenic adaptation" on the part of the Japanese to life in the United States. But most physically identifiable groups are also faced with the same problem—the how-to-behave problem when interacting with the majority and the behaviors when with one's own group. Therefore, within one individual there is often the many personalities—the "Uncle Tom" to the white man, deferential and humble; the "good son" to his parents, dutiful and obedient; and the "swinger" to his peers, wise-cracking, loud, and irreverent. And all of these behaviors are real so that none can be said to give a truer picture except in terms of time, place, and situation. (1976:106–7).

The situational approach is intimately related to power. The less powerful have to learn many adaptations; those with power can afford to use one style. Americans expect others to adapt to them and, with their power, they can often command or buy this recognition. Americans even assume that there are social science universals—"the personality" and "the truth"—whereas the search may be more a reflection of a power position than a social scientific reality.

6. Acculturation has been the most powerful single influence on Japanese behavior, but it has not been a simple linear movement. The variables of power and visibility have shaped differential styles; Japanese Americans in Hawaii will be different in many instances from their peers along the Pacific and Atlantic seaboards. There is a current reawakening of an ethnic identity and a militancy among the Sansei (Kitano, 1972; Maykovich, 1973) that may slow the trend toward acculturation.

One of the most influential events hastening acculturation was the evacuation of the Japanese during World War II. It broke up the power of the Issei and the ethnic ghettos, altered family life, scattered Japanese throughout the United States through resettlement, sent many males into the armed forces and overseas, and made many renounce everything Japanese (Kitano, 1976).

7. Japanese child-rearing techniques involve less direct confrontation than American techniques do. Parents attempt to provide outside stimuli, divert a child's attention, elicit cooperation, and shape a child's behavior through the force of "others." The fear of being ridiculed, being made to look foolish, and bringing shame on the family are primary sanctions in obtaining desired behavior.

Similar behavior characterizes husband-wife interaction, with much more indirect communication, inferences, and unstated feelings, and less direct interaction (loud arguments).

It is our interpretation that Japanese normalize interaction through acknowledgment of differing power positions. As Nakane (1965) pointed out, the Japanese social system can be seen as a series of parallels. Each individual is in a set position and has to learn how to interact with those above and those below; escape from the structure is extremely limited. It therefore would be difficult to collide head on continually with those within the system, and various techniques have been developed to handle power, dependence, and potential disruptive conflict.

8. Social class has always been a factor in the Japanese culture, but it is difficult to transcribe into the American scene. The *ies* tried to make appropriate matches, and "good" families were class conscious. Although most of the immigrants started at the bottom of the American class structure, they did not identify with the life styles of the lower classes. Rather, they brought with them many of the values associated with the middle class: high educational expectations for their children, respect for those in authority (including the police), desire to own property, emphasis on banking and savings, and a future orientation (Kitano, 1976). They seldom fully adopted a lower-class style, even though their incomes and housing were clearly in the ghetto areas.

There is increasing heterogeneity in the Japanese-American community and the development of a more formal social class system (debutantes, professional organizations). With continued differences in education and income, the system may soon become much more crystallized.

Finally, it is important to emphasize that there is no one American culture, just as there is no one Japanese or Japanese-American culture. Therefore, acculturation means different things to different families, and this variety is reflected in their attitudes and behaviors. Perhaps the most appropriate generalization is that the Japanese families in the United States were different to begin with and that length of time in the United States has been just one of the many influences leading to further change. But despite these differences there appears to be enough of a thread so that it is still possible to talk of a Japanese-American subculture (Kitano & Kikumura, 1973).

The old ghetto communities have undergone vast changes. Although there are still recognizable Japanese clusters (''J''-towns), they may be much smaller than before and are usually business centers. The acculturated have moved into better housing, but the predicted demise of the ethnic community has not taken place. Instead, there are continuing attempts to rebuild and uplift the old Japanese communities, often with capital from Japan, as well as with federal funds.

There are several hypothesized reasons for this rebirth. Part of the motivation comes from business—J-towns are centrally located, are tourist attractions, and do a thriving business. Furthermore, there has been a constant flow of new Japanese immigrants over the past decade, and many of these newcomers feel comfortable in an ethnic community. Then there is the ever-increasing group of businessmen from Japan, as well as Japanese tourists who also enjoy the ethnic communities. Finally, there are many older Issei, especially of limited economic means, who prefer to spend their last years among their ethnic group.

The Japanese business structure was an important factor in building the Japanese community. Both the Chinese (*hui*) and the Japanese (*tanomoshi*) used a rotating credit system which makes a pool of money available for investment and credit purposes (Light, 1972). The system also aided community cohesion.

Further, as Light found, membership in oriental organizations, being ascriptive, provided group identity, enforced ethnic honor and pride, and motivated members toward achievement that they probably would not have sought otherwise. In contrast, Light argued that black organizations draw on a culturally undifferentiated mass, which includes a high proportion of poor people who do not tend to participate in voluntary organizations. Because there is often a ''What's in it for me?'' attitude, the organizational elites are forced to spend much of their time working for popular support.

About the Japanese community one could say generally:

1. It is much more scattered and dispersed than in earlier times. Business rather than residential centers are more common.
2. Many organizations serve the ethnic community and are modeled after American patterns (Boy and Girl Scouts, the Y's, the Lions, and other service clubs), but they reflect a structural pluralism.
3. Many ethnic professionals (doctors, lawyers, pharmacists) are available to the community.
4. The use of majority social service and psychiatric facilities has, until recently, been low due to the availability of ethnic resources within the Japanese community. However, as the ethnic

community changes and can no longer provide adequate resources for itself, more Japanese Americans will be dependent on larger community services; or, alternatively, larger community (including federal) financing may be necessary to support ethnic institutions.

5. The ethnic family is still more or less dependent on the community. The Japanese are able to rely on themselves in solving most of their problems, but not all.[4]

6. Japanese communities are not problem-free, contrary to the popular stereotype. Aside from problems common to any community, such as communication, economic well-being, and the like, there are acute problems of the aged, parent-child relationships, and drugs.

Choices Affecting Japanese Behavior

The following four cases indicate the pressures of the dominant culture on immigrant groups and help explain the influence of broader variables such as race, color and nationality on personality.

Two Hawaiian Issei in the 1920s—Fred Makino, the editor of a newspaper, *Hawaiian Hochi,* and Takie Okumura, a Christian missionary—were described by Jacobs and Landau (1971); both were sincerely interested in their ethnic group, but each used quite divergent strategies in his adaptation to the new country.

Fred Makino. Fred Makino was a model for those Issei who actively retained their ethnic identity.[5] He came to Hawaii from Japan in 1899 and soon began to perceive some of the problems that faced his ethnic group. He saw the Japanese being exploited by white Hawaiian plantation owners, whereupon he helped the Japanese workers organize their own unions. He started lawsuits against discriminatory practices and was willing to go to jail for his convictions. He felt that the best protection for a relatively small, powerless minority group was to organize and fight *actively* to protect its own interests, rather than to fade quietly into the background.

Makino's main emphases were on heightening ethnic awareness, promoting ethnic identity, and fostering group cohesion. Consequently, one of the main tenets in his program was to open and maintain Japanese language schools. Here the Issei and their children could learn their native language, understand their own culture, and resist the attempts of the Americans to "rob" them of their native heritage. He felt that it was

[4] For example, there has been a rise in adolescent drug use among Japanese in Los Angeles. The ethnic community was tapped for funds and raised enough to start a self-help drug center. However, the continuing rise in drug use may force the Japanese to seek help from the larger community.
[5] We have taken some liberties with Makino's life in order to formulate a model for this category (Kitano, 1972).

important that the Japanese build up pride in their ethnicity, that Japanese values (of the Meiji era) be held superior to those of the American culture, and that Japanese institutions and styles be preferred and maintained. He advocated political organization—"bloc" power—and felt that pressure was the most effective means of dealing with the white man.

Takie Okumura. Another Issei living in Hawaii at the same time as Makino was Takie Okumura. He perceived the problems of the ethnic community differently and advocated an active, acculturative position— that is, that Japanese should acquire American culture. Okumura felt that the maintenance of Japanese culture was one of the major barriers towards acceptance by the white group. He felt that ethnic living conditions, manners, habits, and customs should be discarded, such as smelly foods, noisy festivals, loud conversation in Japanese, and prominent Japanese architecture. Any behavior (especially in public) that offended Americans should be controlled or eliminated.

Okumura thought of the Japanese as "visitors" or "guests" in the United States and felt that they should conduct themselves accordingly. They should do nothing to alienate their hosts; they should go to American schools and be taught and trained as Americans; they should avoid such unpopular acts as labor strikes and slowdowns; they should continue to work loyally for their employers, no matter what the provocation.

Okumura felt that if Japanese expected to be Americans, then they must be American in every way. They must associate with them, learn their language, and go to their schools. The only way for a small minority to become successful was to merge with the host culture. Okumura's advice to the Japanese colony was, "above everything else remember that you are guests of this land and be very careful in everything you do" (Jacobs and Landau, 1971:213).

Senator S. I. Hayakawa. There is little question that the appointment of Dr. S. I. Hayakawa to the presidency of San Francisco State College would have been greeted with unanimous acclaim by the ethnic community during the prewar days, for he epitomizes the idea of integration: he has a Ph.D., is married to a Caucasian wife, and retired as the president of a large educational institution.

Even today he is probably a hero to many Japanese—but it is not quite unanimous. In Disneyland in April 1969, a large group of Japanese assembled to pay him honor. Inside the auditorium, over 500 people greeted him with a standing ovation. But while the older Nisei were applauding, a smaller, younger group gathered outside waving signs such as "Hayakawa Is a Banana—Yellow Skin but White Inside" or "Hayakawa Is Not Our Spokesman." Such overt expressions would have been rare several years previously and impossible decades before.

In 1976 Hayakawa was elected to the United States Senate from

California, a rather unbelievable turnabout for a state that "invented" the "yellow peril," that passed laws to get "rid of the Japs," and that was instrumental in placing the Japanese behind barbed wire during World War II. In 1978, the Japanese American Citizen's League (JACL) passed a resolution calling for redress for this incident; the Senator's response was that the evacuation was a "good thing" for the Japanese American and that it had been an act of protection.

Hayakawa's election and his position on redress for the evacuation illustrate the changes that have occurred in California and the wide diversity among Japanese Americans. In 1979, California also had two Japanese Americans in the United States House of Representatives, Norman Mineta and Robert Matsui.

Dr. Thomas Noguchi. The case of Dr. Noguchi, County Coroner of Los Angeles, also occurred in 1969. Dr. Noguchi was dismissed from his position by the Los Angeles County Board of Supervisors on numerous charges that ranged from drug taking to mental illness, to incompetence. In a previous era, he would have quietly resigned and accepted an alternate position. The ethnic community would have been embarrassed by the whole affair and would have preferred the physician to remain quiet and to accept the demotion.

But instead, Noguchi chose to challenge his dismissal. Even more important, the ethnic community supported him. They quickly raised over $40,000 for a defense fund. The large number of small contributors indicated that many Japanese felt that they too had been ignored or passed over in their own job situations. Dr. Noguchi was eventually reinstated as county coroner. The Japanese were exhibiting atypical "Japanese behavior"; rather than accepting and accommodating, they were challenging and confronting. Noguchi's support came from *all* generations.

Overt Dissent

Why, after decades of acceptance, accommodation, assimilation, and inward aggression, did overt dissent appear in the Japanese community in the latter 1960s, especially when things were going so well?

First, there are several social-psychological explanations. One relatively consistent social science finding is that periods of dissent, strain, and rebellious behavior often occur when social conditions are improving, whereas extreme deprivation is usually associated with apathy. Concern for sheer survival takes precedence under completely depressed conditions and is accompanied by low expectations and a feeling of hopelessness. Conversely, as opportunities increase, expectations rise more quickly than actual improvements in social conditions, which produces strain and dissatisfaction. For example, the women's liberation movement is strongest in the United States, where women are perhaps more liberated than in most other countries; the Watts riots occurred in Los Angeles, where the treatment of the blacks has been presumably better than in other sections of the country.

Another reason is that new generations have found newer ways of being "Asian." For example, by the end of the 1960s, groups with titles such as the Asian-American Political Alliance, the Council of Oriental Organizations, the Yellow Brotherhood, the Third World Liberation Front, and the Red Guards were emerging from the Asian communities. The Asian-American Political Alliance stated: "The crucial question facing us today is not that of integration. Now there is the more compelling question. . . . What is this society which we have sought, too often with ludicrous fever, to become integrated into [sic]?" (*Gidra*, 1969).

Racism and discrimination are concerns central to most of these newer groups, who have shifted away from an accomodationist-acceptance mode toward ethnic identity and autonomy. A newspaper entitled *Gidra*, produced by Sansei of the college-age generation, challenged the local Japanese, Chinese, and other Asian establishments by advocating stands on such controversial issues as student demonstrations, yellow identity, and yellow power.

Coalitions are beginning to be established among all Asian groups, whereas in the past, nationality differences prevented an overall Asian identity. It is difficult to ascertain the number, representation, and power of these groups, but perhaps the differences among Asian groups are disappearing in the push toward Pan-Asian identity. There is little question that earlier generations of Chinese, Japanese, Koreans, and Pilipinos would have been greatly disturbed by this effort.

Another important reason for the increased conflict has been the change in goals. Becoming 100 percent American is no longer the ultimate desire for a great many; once this drive is modified, previous patterns of accommodation, ritualism, and retreat will change.

The World War II Soldier

The exploits of Japanese Americans during World War II influenced American public opinion toward a more favorable view of the group. The 442nd combat team and the 100th battalion, composed mainly of Nisei (under Caucasian officers) suffered more than 9,000 casualties, had more than 600 killed in action, and became known as the most decorated unit in American military history (Kitano, 1976:82). Japanese Americans also played a key role in the Pacific, especially in interpreting, translating, and intercepting Japanese codes.

But Shibutani (1978) examined another group of Nisei soldiers who earned the dubious distinction of being one of the worst companies in World War II. Although they were from the same ethnic group and had the potential to become excellent soldiers, discrimination, poor leadership, inept communication, unclear goals, and the failure of the leadership to acknowledge Nisei norms lead to low morale, excessive drinking, violence, insubordination, sloppiness, and disruptiveness. The study is important since it shows how poor organization and leadership can turn potentially constructive groups into disorganized, alienated units with high rates of deviant behavior.

Generational Change

Perhaps the greatest change can be labeled as *generational*, since it is the Sansei and Yonsei (third and fourth generations) who are at the forefront of the new movement. Given the unequal power relationships, previous generations developed "indirect styles" as a reasonable strategy. Many Sansei prefer direct confrontation and are impatient with the older Japanese-American ways.

One of the most drastic changes has been interracial marriage. Levine and Montero (1973) found that only 8 percent of the Nisei in their study had interracial marriages, whereas about 33 percent of the Sansei married out of the group. A more comprehensive study by Kikumura and Kitano (1973) revealed in 1971 and 1972 the Japanese-American rates of interracial marriage were near 50 percent. This is true in areas as diverse as San Francisco, Fresno, Los Angeles, and Hawaii, and is primarily a Sansei phenomenon since interracial marriages in these areas over a decade ago were below the 20 percent level.

This move toward the melting pot is occurring at the same time that others are advocating a strong ethnic identity and pluralism. It may presage an interesting pattern of multiple Japanese-American adjustments, which is perhaps the healthiest state since it indicates that both the ethnic and the dominant communities are no longer as "closed" as they once used to be.

THE JAPANESE MODEL

As with all of our groups, there are several models to explain the Japanese. One pattern has been the European one of immigration, acculturation, integration, and assimilation, albeit somewhat delayed because of racial discrimination. Perhaps this development is the most surprising, considering the early history of the group, which emphasized their unassimilability and culminated in their forced evacuation into concentration camps. But the recent high rates of intermarriage, especially by the newer generations, indicates that some "melting" is taking place.

The Japanese also fit into Park's cyclical model: contact, competition, accomodation, and assimilation. They have not adapted in a purely

"Japanese" way; rather, they have assimilated into the mainstream but also have maintained some of their own cultural styles (Montero & Tsukashima, 1977).

Another pattern has been that of acculturation and a bicultural adaptation, based partly on the barriers of racism and partly on the strength of the Japanese culture. One interesting variation of the bicultural model has been the rejection of the "old" Japanese culture on the part of some. Instead, there is an emphasis on the experiences of the group in America as the starting point for the development of an ethnic identity. One interesting consequence is that Caucasians who marry into the group often know more about the history, language, and culture of Japan than do the Sansei or Yonsei, who are in turn much more conversant with the wartime evacuation and the history of anti-Japanese activity in America.

Another pattern involves the Japanese business people and traders, who bring with them a transient's orientation. Most stay close together. Their primary relationships are business based; they are highly visible in areas such as New York and Los Angeles, and they represent a high degree of economic power. Then there are the Japanese tourists, most often seen in groups, who provide another picture of who the Japanese are. Both of these groups retain a cultural and structural pluralism.

The situation in Hawaii provides another contrast. In that state, the Japanese are one of the more powerful groups. For example, in 1978 the governor and the two United States senators were of Japanese-American ancestry, and the local culture of the islands has a definite oriental flavor. Acculturation to Hawaii often means taking on some Japanese ways (food, taking off one's shoes in the house). Professor Seymour Lutzky, Chairman of the Department of American studies at the University of Hawaii, in a personal conversation also saw the state's social welfare system as reflecting Japanese values such as obligation and paternalism. Hawaii provides an example of a minority group that has achieved power, and the Japanese in that state retain a strong bicultural orientation. Non-Japanese in Hawaii may have to acculturate to that model.

Some Japanese on the mainland may fit the middleman minority model (Kitano, 1974). They have achieved a degree of mobility from the bottom but are having difficulty in achieving leadership positions.

The Japanese still remain stereotyped, even though the characteristics of the image are more favorable. They are no longer "Japs"; they are Japanese (Ogawa, 1971). But as with all stereotypes, they remain less than human. The "successful" label has made it difficult to probe for the many problems that lie within this ethnic group. Because there remains a stereotype that associates the Japanese in America with the Japanese in Japan, many Japanese Americans fear that they may once again become targets of American aggression should relations between America and Japan ever become strained.

BIBLIOGRAPHY

A Study of Selected Socio-Economic Characteristics of Ethnic Minorities Based on the 1970 Census. Volume II: Asian Americans (n.d.). Arlington, Va.: Urban Associates. (Monograph prepared for Department of Health, Education, and Welfare.)

ARKOFF, ABE (1959). "Need Patterns in Two Generations of Japanese Americans in Hawaii," *Journal of Social Psychology,* 50:75–79.

BLOOM, LEONARD and RUTH RIEMER (1945). "Attitudes of College Students toward Japanese Americans," *Sociometry,* 8(2):157–173.

BOSWORTH, ALLAN P. (1967). *America's Concentration Camps.* New York: W. W. Norton & Co., Inc.

CONNOR, JOHN (1977). *Tradition and Change in Three Generations of Japanese Americans.* Chicago: Nelson-Hall.

CONROY, FRANCIS HILARY and T. SCOTT MIYAKAWA, eds. (1972). *East Across the Pacific.* Santa Barbara, Calif.: American Bibliographical Center, Clio Press.

DANIELS, ROGER (1968). *The Politics of Prejudice.* New York: Atheneum.

DANIELS, ROGER (1971). *Concentration Camps U.S.A.: Japanese Americans and World War II.* New York: Holt, Rinehart & Winston.

DANIELS, ROGER and HARRY H. L. KITANO (1970). *American Racism: Exploration of the Nature of Prejudice.* Englewood Cliffs, N.J.: Prentice-Hall, Inc.

EATON, ALLEN H. (1952). *Beauty behind Barbed Wire: The Arts of the Japanese in Our War Relocation Camps.* New York: Harper & Row, Pubs.

FISHER, A. R. (1965). *Exile of a Race.* Seattle: Ford T. Publishers.

Gidra (Los Angeles, Cal.), August, 1969.

GIRDNER, AUDRIE and ANN LOFTIS (1969). *The Great Betrayal.* New York: Macmillan.

GRODZINS, M. (1949). *Americans Betrayed.* Chicago: University of Chicago Press.

HOSOKAWA, WILLIAM (1969). *Nisei: The Quiet Americans.* New York: Morrow.

ICHIHASHI, YAMATO (1969). *Japanese in the United States.* New York: Arno.

IWASA, DAVID (1976). "The Japanese in Southern Alberta," *Alberta History,* 24(3):5–19.

JACO, DANIEL and GEORGE WILBER (1975). "Asian Americans in the Labor Market," *Montly Labor Review,* 98(7):33–38.

JACOBS, PAUL and SAUL LANDAU (1971). *To Serve the Devil,* pp. 166–270. New York: Vintage Books.

Japan Times. 1973. Editorial, p. 3.

KIKUMURA, AKEMI K. and HARRY H. L. KITANO (1973). "Interracial Marriage: A Picture of the Japanese Americans," *Journal of Social Issues,* 29(2):67–81.

KITANO, HARRY H. L. (1972). "Japanese American Dissent," in *Seasons of Rebellion,* eds. R. Rosenstone and J. Boskin. New York: Holt, Rinehart & Winston.

KITANO, HARRY H. L. (1976). *Japanese Americans: The Evolution of a Subculture* (2nd ed.). Englewood Cliffs, N.J.: Prentice-Hall, Inc.

KITANO, HARRY H. L. (1974). "Japanese Americans: The Development of a Middleman Minority," *Pacific Historical Review,* 43(4):500–19.

KITANO, HARRY H. L. and AKEMI KIKUMURA (1973). "The Japanese-American Family," in *Ethnic Families in America,* pp. 41–60, eds. Charles Mindel and Robert Habenstein. New York: Elsevier.

LEIGHTON, ALEXANDER (1945). *The Governing of Men,* p. 344. Princeton, N.J.: Princeton University Press.

LEVINE, GENE and DARREL M. MONTERO (1973). "Socioeconomic Mobility among Three Generations of Japanese Americans," *Journal of Social Issues,* 29(2):33–48.

LIGHT, IVAN (1972). *Ethnic Enterprise in American Business and Welfare among Chinese, Japanese, and Blacks.* Berkeley: University of California Press.

LYMAN, STANFORD (n.d.). "Contrasts in the Community Organization of Chinese and Japanese in North America" (unpublished paper, Sonoma State College).

MAYKOVICH, MINAKO (1973). "Political Activation of Japanese American Youth," *Journal of Social Issues,* 29:167–68.

MONTERO, DARREL and RONALD TSUKASHIMA (1977). "Assimilation and Educational Achievement: The Case of the Second Generation Japanese-American," *Sociological Quarterly,* 18:490–503.

MYER, DILLON (1971). *Uprooted Americans.* Tucson: University of Arizona Press.

NAKANE, CHIE (1972). *Japanese Society.* Berkeley: University of California Press.

OGAWA, DENNIS (1971). *From Japs to Japanese.* Berkeley: Calif.: McCutchan Publishing Co.

OKIMOTO, DANIEL I. (1971). *American in Disguise.* New York: Walker Weatherhill.

OKUBO, MINE (1946). *Citizen 13660.* New York: Columbia University Press.

PETERSEN, WILLIAM (1971). *Japanese Americans.* New York: Random House.

SPICER, EDWARD H., ASAEL T. HANSEN, KATHERINE LUOMALA, and MARVIN K. OPLER (1969). *Impounded People.* Tucson: University of Arizona Press.

TACHIKI, AMY and others (1971). *Roots: An Asian American Reader.* Los Angeles: Continental Graphics.

TENBROEK, JACOBUS, EDWARD N. BARNHART, and FLOYD W. MATSON (1970). *Prejudice, War and the Constitution.* Berkeley: University of California Press.

THOMAS, DOROTHY S., CHARLES KIKUCHI, and JAMES SAKODA (1952). *The Savage.* Berkeley: University of California Press.

THOMAS, DOROTHY S. and RICHARD NISHIMOTO (1946). *The Spoilage.* Berkeley: University of California Press.

TINKER, JOHN (1973). "Intermarriage and Ethnic Boundaries," *Journal of Social Issues,* 29(2):49–65.

SHIBUTANI, TAMOTSU (1978). *The Derelicts of Company K.* Berkeley: University of California Press.

STRONG, EDWARD K. (1934). *The Second Generation Japanese Problem.* Stanford, Calif.: Stanford University Press.

WEGLYN, MICHI (1976). *Years of Infamy.* New York: Morrow.

ZELLER, WILLIAM D. (1969). *An Educational Drama.* New York: American Press.

14

PUERTO RICANS

The Puerto Rican migration is still in progress; therefore, many of the observations about them are tentative because of the scarcity of data. The majority of Puerto Ricans reside in New York, which has been the host to several generations of immigrants—the Irish, Italians, and Jews, to name but a few. The Puerto Ricans are entering the city when symptoms of social disorganization are especially prominent. Large cities have always been plagued by outbreaks of violence and disorder, and residents have constantly feared for their personal safety, but such anxieties appear to have reached a zenith in present-day New York.

Further, the changes in our economic system have been such that unskilled immigrants may no longer be able to follow the models of "success" laid down by earlier immigrant groups, even though they may arrive with a strongly internalized work ethic. For as Padilla (1977) pointed out, Puerto Rican concepts of work are historically linked to agrarian, colonial experiences and reflect obligation, family background, and personal worth. Despite this value placed on work, Puerto Ricans in New York, especially those with nontransferable or inadequate skills, face unemployment or employment in the least desirable jobs, and welfare. Prejudice and discrimination exacerbate the situation, but the fundamental problem may lie in the structural conditions of our economy, which has attracted a large number of displaced people to our urban ghettos.

BACKGROUND

Puerto Rico was ruled by Spain for over four hundred years. The Spanish-American War and the Treaty of Paris in 1898 ceded the islands to the United States, and formal interaction between the two countries is acknowledged from that year. The significant migration of Puerto Ricans to the United States, however, did not take place for several decades. World War I and the need for labor provided the impetus for a small migration; and by 1930, approximately 53,000 Puerto Ricans were residing on the mainland. But the depression years and World War II brought a virtual halt to immigration.

The great migration came after World War II. There were several reasons for this: first, Puerto Ricans were U.S. citizens and were therefore under no quota restrictions; second, there was unemployment at home and employment on the mainland; third, there was cheap transportation; and finally, many had friends and relatives living in New York and elsewhere on the East Coast.

In 1960 the U.S. Census reported almost 900,000 Puerto Ricans living in the United States, and by 1970 there were 1,429,604 first and second generation Puerto Ricans in the Continental United States with almost one million in New York (Marden & Meyer, 1978:266).

The Puerto Rican immigration pattern is unusual because of its departure rate. Although figures for net migration are difficult to ascertain, in 1969 the Puerto Rican Planning Board reported 2,105,217 departures and 2,112,264 arrivals. There is of course no way of identifying how many Puerto Ricans were coming to the mainland for the first time, how many were tourists, or how many planned to stay permanently. However, migration back to the island has been heavy, and some even refer to the Puerto Ricans as "commuters."

From an analysis published in 1972 by the Puerto Rican Resources Center for the Federal Office of Civil Rights, Padilla noted that the Puerto Rican immigration may be a lengthy one because of the structural weakness of the Puerto Rican economy. The lack of integrated planning has led to the export of Puerto Ricans as the "only way of achieving economic growth" (1977:156). High island unemployment, which has remained at a constant 12 percent since 1947, and a natural population increase have meant a mass exodus of workers to the labor markets of the United States.

Contract Laborers   Many of the early Puerto Rican immigrants came to the United States as contract laborers. Such an arrangement was typical for non-whites; their labor was desired but not their permanent residence. The farm labor contracts in the 1940s proved to be particularly attractive because they enabled the laborer to find more than seasonal work. He could harvest in the United States through the summer and fall, then return to Puerto Rico in time to work on the sugar-cane plantations. But migrant labor conditions were generally far from ideal, and the Puerto Rican government had to supervise constantly in order to ensure the fulfillment of the contracts. By this means large numbers of Puerto Ricans were exposed to the American system, and much of the groundwork was laid for the subsequent large migration. Many Puerto Rican communities arose from groups of early contract laborers who remained on the mainland.

As with some of the Asian ethnic groups on the West Coast, Puerto Ricans were unwelcome on any permanent basis. Small, rural Southern towns were inhospitable to Puerto Ricans, since these communities were largely unprepared to deal with people who spoke a foreign language and whose culture was alien. Tensions mounted, especially in schools, employment, recreation, and housing.

The number of Puerto Ricans working as migrant laborers is difficult to estimate. The major stream of Puerto Rican migration, however, has flowed into New York City and other urban areas.

New York City

The rise of the Puerto Rican population in New York City has been dramatic. The 1920 census reported 7,365 persons; the 1940 figures were 61,463; in 1960, there were 612,574; and by 1971, it was at 1,000,000. The heaviest concentration of Puerto Ricans is now in the South Bronx, but the East Harlem community is considered to be the original barrio.

The Puerto Ricans have been a very mobile people. They have spread out rapidly in their search for better housing, not being content to stay long in one place. One consequence of their housing patterns (which is also due to overcrowded conditions in New York) has been the lack of a tightly knit, strong, physically contiguous ethnic community. They have not developed Little Italies or Chinatowns. Such self-contained ethnic enclaves (despite many of their handicaps) were often very functional: the culture could be maintained while the groups became familiar with the new country; friends and relatives could move in; ethnic blocs could wield a degree of political power; and a consensus of norms and a high degree of social cohesion served to control deviant behavior. The quick integration of the Puerto Rican (aided by the nondiscriminatory policies of the New York City Housing Authority) will probably hasten the acculturation of the group, but may also create many serious social problems.

**Color and
Visibility**

There are many contradictory findings concerning color prejudice in Puerto Rico, as there are in most Latin American countries. Some claim that Puerto Ricans are completely integrated and colorblind; others claim that they are highly but subtly stratified. Color does not seem to be as important an indicator of social status as social class is, but there is a correlation between darker skin color and low status. However, color is less a sign of pariah status among Puerto Ricans than among Americans.

There is a high degree of color integration in Puerto Rico. They did not develop the two-category, black-white structure found in the United States; rather, the differentiations of color were spread over a wider spectrum. For example, words such as *pardo, moreno, mulatto,* and *trigueño* classify a range of colors other than black and white. Terms such as *indio* and *grifo* denote other identifying characteristics. (The United States practices of segregation and antimiscegenation laws, were not a part of the Puerto Rican experience.)

Social class is an essential part of the Puerto Rican stratification system. Although whiteness may be considered desirable, an individual's status is more clearly demarcated by class position. Fitzpatrick quoted a saying that provides some insight concerning color and class: "In the United States, a man's color determines what class he belongs to; in Puerto Rico, a man's class determines what his color is" (1971:103). Therefore, living in a barrio is an indication of one's status, whether black, *trigueño,* or white, as is occupation, income, and education. Color is viewed within the context of other role signs and is not the sole criterion.

Fitzpatrick mentioned a number of cultural and historical factors in Puerto Rico that have contributed to their more tolerant racial attitudes (1971:103).

1. The long Spanish experience with people of dark skin color (Moors), including intermarriage.
2. Different experiences under slavery. In the wars of the Christians against the Moors and Saracens, captured whites also became slaves. Therefore there were attempts to protect slaves who were white, and such attitudes were carried over to the blacks.
3. Upper-class men in the Spanish colonies baptized and recognized their illegitimate children by colored women.
4. The practice of *compadrazgo,* in which outstanding white members of a community would frequently be the godparents of colored children at baptism. The "padrino" or "compadre" could become a significant person in a child's life, and although the real father might be obscure, the godparents would be well known.
5. The concept of a Puerto Rican community in which all, whether

rich or poor, white or colored, shared a sense of communal identity. Therefore all persons were conscious of having a place, especially during community events such as fiestas, religious processions, and public events.

As a consequence, color was not a strong barrier, and upward mobility under this more open system was a theoretical possibility. But Puerto Rico has advanced very rapidly in education, industry, government services, and the like, and a middle class has formed. Upward social and economic mobility complicates the role of color and class, and color prejudice is growing. For example, Fitzpatrick (1971:105) observed that societies and clubs are now not as open to people of color. Puerto Ricans quickly learn that color is an important role sign in the United States. They see that the two-category system has abolished the intermediate categories and that social acceptance and economic advantages are easier to obtain if one is white.

Perhaps the most difficult position is that of the *trigueños* of intermediate color. In one study (Padilla, 1958), they showed the least evidence of assimilation into the New York community. They were not accepted as white; many did not want to be classified as blacks and were therefore caught in a marginal position. Many responded by retaining a strong Puerto Rican identity. Another study (Berle, 1959) of twenty young Puerto Rican drug addicts showed that nineteen of them were the darkest members of their families.

Puerto Ricans are also visible on levels other than color. The Spanish language and their preference for more colorful clothing styles make them conspicuous as a group.

A major Puerto Rican problem is identity. For many years they were a part of the Spanish empire with Latin traditions; then suddenly they became a part of the United States. Currently, several different identifications have surfaced. For example, one group advocates complete autonomy and independence because they fear that they will lose their culture, language, and sense of independence if they maintain close relations with the United States. The advocates of statehood feel that only by becoming an integral part of the United States can Puerto Ricans achieve a true identity. Statehood would not necessarily mean the destruction of their culture; rather, the gains through political and economic stability would give them more freedom in shaping an identity. Then there are those who seek to maintain Puerto Rico as a "free associated state." They cite the current situation in which Puerto Ricans can maintain their own culture and identity while still benefiting from close ties with the United States.

The Problem of Identity

Puerto Ricans were able to express their preferences in the 1967 elections. The advocate for the free associated state won; he was followed by the advocate for statehood, while the independence candidate ran a poor third. But the intensity of the conflict represented "the anxiety and uncertainty of a people in danger of losing themselves, and seeking to discover the political and social institutions which will enable them to preserve a genuine sense of identity in the presence of rapid changes with which they seek to cope. Thus before any question of large-scale migration arose, the Puerto Ricans had been facing a crisis of national and cultural identity" (Fitzpatrick, 1971:46).

Integration

It is difficult to find consistent evidence on the extent of Puerto Rican intermingling in New York City. They have brought their more relaxed racial attitudes with them, and Puerto Rican gatherings present a wider range of color mixtures. But as they advance to middle-class status, they may become much more sensitive to American definitions of race.

The relations between Puerto Ricans and blacks have been strained. They are both involved in similar struggles for power and control and are sometimes pitted against each other. Among the more militant young there is some degree of cooperation.

There is evidence that the outmarriage rate of Puerto Ricans (7.8 percent in 1959) is higher than the general rates of such marriages in the United States. Fitzpatrick (1971:112) also noted that Puerto Ricans of different color were intermarrying at a high rate (26 percent) in New York City, but the marriage patterns in other areas would probably be different.

Role of the Church and Family

The Puerto Ricans come from a predominantly Roman Catholic country. Church membership there was somewhat different from the United States model of organized membership and a consistent church affiliation. Rather, they had a much more personalized spiritual relationship, and this often took place outside the organized church structure. Adherence to Roman Catholic practices was not so strict that native cult practices, spiritism, and other religious variations could not flourish. The Protestant religion was introduced by the United States, and by 1970 roughly 20 percent of the island's inhabitants were of that faith. Church influence is diffused in Puerto Rican life on the mainland. There are of course many parochial schools, but partly because of the distribution of the Puerto Ricans, it is difficult to assess the specific influence of religion in their lives.

The family structure in Puerto Rico was described by Fitzpatrick (1971:83) as falling into the following fourfold typology:

1. An extended family system. These families have strong bonds, and grandparents, parents, and children often may live together in the same household. It may include consensual unions as well as regular marriages.[1]

2. The nuclear family. The rise of the middle class has increased the number of families following the United States pattern of an independent unit of father, mother, and children.

3. Father, mother, their children, and children of another union or unions of husband and wife. This is not an uncommon pattern in Puerto Rico, with children of different names residing in the same household.

4. The mother-based family, with children of one or more men, but with no permanent male in the home.

All four typologies are present in the United States. The greatest white animosity is directed toward the Type 4 family unit, often found in welfare families. Pragmatic politicians are especially adept at laying the blame for much of society's ills on "those welfare chiselers," who, if one were to believe the claims, are the main contributors to the financial and moral crises of our time. Because certain ethnic groups are stereotyped in this fashion, prejudice and discrimination against them are strengthened.

Personalism. A number of values have been hypothesized to explain Puerto Rican behavior in a broad context. The most important is personalism, which Fitzpatrick described as "a form of individualism which focuses on the inner importance of a person . . . those inner qualities which constitute the uniqueness of the person and his goodness or worth in himself" (Fitzpatrick, 1971:90). This value derives its strength from the relatively rigid class structure in which individuals are respected if they know their position and behave with dignity and sensitivity. They take family obligations seriously.

Puerto Ricans have developed a strong sense of the hierarchical class structure. Lower and upper classes were taken for granted; therefore a person's personal worth was distinct from his or her position in the social class structure. The idea of upward mobility was not a common

Values

[1] Consensual unions have been recognized in Puerto Rico, although their number is declining.

one in Puerto Rico; rather, an acceptance of playing a designated role with dignity was valued highly.

Like other ethnic groups, Puerto Ricans have their own ideas of what constitutes a joke or is likely to cause embarrassment. The informal, offhand American manner may bring a different reaction from a Puerto Rican group. The behavior styles of various groups are an important aspect, especially those of older generations.

The Puerto Rican values of personalism conflict with American values. In the Latin system, the individual is to be trusted above all; life is a network of personal relationships, and a person's word, honor, and style are to be reckoned with and respected. In contrast, the American style of individualism emphasizes the ability to compete aggressively for social and economic gain. Americans have a high regard for systems, organizations, legal regulations, and efficiency; they become uneasy when the system fails. It is said, however, that Latin Americans become uneasy when the system works too well—they feel that impersonal elements have taken precedence over personal relationships.

The *padrino* system is another Puerto Rican structure which is related to personalism and reflects a rigid class structure. It involves "a person, strategically placed in a higher position of the social structure, who has a personal relationship with the poorer person in which he provides employment, assistance at times of need, and acts as an advocate if the poor person becomes involved in trouble" (Fitzpatrick, 1971:91). The *padrino* serves as an ombudsman who helps the less knowledgeable and unsophisticated in dealing with more powerful and influential individuals and institutions. Of course, these relationships are open to exploitation. Although the *padrinos* have been less evident in Puerto Rico, they are still sought out, especially in business affairs.

Machismo. Machismo is another aspect of personalism; it connotes masculinity and personal daring "by which one faces challenge, danger, and threat with calmness and self-possession; this sometimes takes the form of bravado" (Fitzpatrick, 1971:91). Associated attributes and qualities include personal magnetism, sexual prowess, and power over women, including the jealous protection of wife or sweetheart.

Materialism. The Latin feels that most Americans are grossly materialistic. Although it is highly debatable which culture places a greater value on the acquisition of material things, Latins emphasize that their fundamental concerns have nothing to do with worldly things or their tangible features. "He has a sense of spirit and soul as much more important than the body, and as being intimately related to his value as a person; he tends to think in terms of transcendent qualities, such as justice, loyalty, or love, rather than in terms of practical arrangements which spell out justice or loyalty in the concrete" (Fitzpatrick, 1971:91–92). He or she is more willing to sacrifice material satisfactions for ultimate or spiritual goals and does not emphasize mastering and subjecting the physical universe through continuous technological advancements.

Fatalism. The fatalistic attitude is best summed up by the phrase, *"Que, será, será"* ("Whatever will be, will be"). There is a strong sense that certain events are inevitable and are dictated by God. This modifies the impact of failure or success and the attendant sense of guilt or satisfaction because "God willed it."

Change of values. The values of the Puerto Rican, as described above, are not so different from those of many other immigrant groups, and they will probably handle their value conflicts in the same manner. These conflicts will be resolved or perpetuated by:

1. The cohesion and strength of the ethnic family and community system in order to reinforce their way of life.
2. The functional or dysfunctional actions of the values themselves, as well as their similarity and complementarity with those of the majority culture.
3. The potential for symbiotic interaction.
4. The strength of the competing socializing institutions in the United States.

It is anticipated that the heaviest burden of the conflict will be felt by the second-generation child—that is, the individual who is born of Puerto Rican immigrant parents in the United States. The stress, tension, and disorganization faced by Puerto Ricans are evident from their more visible social problems.

SOCIAL PROBLEMS

Education and the School System

The Puerto Rican Study, 1953–57 (Board of Education, 1958) pointed out some of the difficulties faced by Puerto Rican students in New York City. Special problems included the language handicap and the tenuous relationship between the school system and Puerto Rican parents. Subsequent studies have shown that these problems have grown progressively worse. Very few survive the competition to enter colleges and universities, although the open admissions policy in New York may increase Puerto Rican attendance in the city college and university system. The route to success by way of education, used by many other immigrant groups, remains an expectation rather than a reality for most Puerto Ricans.

One fundamental issue, difficult to resolve, centers on cultural pluralism in education. Bilingualism and English as a second language are unresolved issues, and the debate over the validity of various models continues. There are also the larger issues of the school strikes of 1968–69 and the decentralization controversy.

Cordasco (1975) found that in 1972 the high-school dropout rate for Puerto Ricans was 57 percent, compared to 46 percent for blacks and 29 percent for others in New York City. In the data on social inequality (Chapter 7), the Puerto Ricans were among the lowest in high school and college completion. For example, in 1976 the rate for males completing college was 82 percent below that of the majority group, while for females the rate was 88 percent lower.

Welfare

A special problem for the Puerto Ricans has been their relatively high numbers on public welfare. For example, one study estimated that as many as 35 percent of Puerto Rican families were receiving Aid to Families with Dependent Children (AFDC) benefits. Without going into the accuracy of these figures, it is of critical importance to understand that dependence on public welfare affects Puerto Rican adaptation to the United States. Although the goals of AFDC and other welfare programs are appealing and although the planners no doubt had the best intentions, the actual programs have become an embarrassment to the American public. It would be difficult to conceive of a worse institutionalized alternative to American life, considering the current American attitudes toward welfare recipients. The degradation of the recipients is a result of both inadequate resources and an unpopular program.

Mental Illness

Rogler and Hollingshead (1965) offered systematic data on mental illness in Puerto Rico and identified several contradictory strains that contributed to the problem. Girls were carefully protected from sexual experience, while boys were allowed great freedom; the housewife was expected to be submissive, while the husband had to embody all aspects of *machismo;* there was a great discrepancy between expected and achieved standards of living, and poverty exerted severe pressure on everyone's life.

Rates of mental illness are higher for the Puerto Ricans than for the general population. For example, Malzberg (1956) noted that the rate of first admissions for schizophrenia for Puerto Rican males in New York State was 122 per 100,000, as compared to the general population rate of 36.6 per 100,000. He could find no convincing reason for this differential, which is apparently related to such diverse variables as the experience of migration, language difficulties, occupational problems, and segregation into areas that have a high incidence of mental illness. A major problem, of course, is that the poor have little access to health services because of high cost and superstition.

The Midtown Manhattan Study (Langner & Stanley, 1963) also noted a high incidence of mental illness among Puerto Ricans, mostly because of the shortage of Spanish-speaking professionals, the lack of communication and understanding, and other cultural disparities.

In spite of certain biases in the statistics on mental illness, the available evidence indicates that the stress and tension of migration and urban living have exacted a high toll in mental illness from Puerto Ricans. The question now is whether this is a preliminary adaptive stage for any newly arrived immigrant group, and whether it is followed by another stage.

There is also evidence of high drug use in certain census tracts in New York City. These areas are also characterized by poverty and by a large proportion of blacks and Puerto Ricans. The relationships among poverty, drug use, and ethnicity should be targets for future research.

The major problem for the Puerto Ricans is the lack of economic resources:

Occupations, Income, Housing

> Puerto Ricans living in New York City had a median family income of $5575, 43 percent lower than the $9,682 median family income for the entire city. Nearly 30 percent . . . had annual incomes of less than $3000. . . . Nearly one third of the heads of . . . households were unemployed. . . . Only 4.5 percent . . . earned $15,000 or more . . . only 15 percent of adults had a high school diploma, and 1.5 percent had completed college. (Padilla, 1977:159)

More recent data on social inequality (Chapter 7) show that in 1976 Puerto Ricans ranked among the most unequal. Their incomes were low; their unemployment was high; their occupational prestige was low; their rates of poverty were high; and their housing conditions were among the poorest. They are caught in a cycle of poor jobs, lack of skills, low education, poor housing, discrimination, and an ever-increasing population.

THE PUERTO RICAN MODEL

Rosenberg and Lake (1976), in analyzing the 1960–1970 census data in the New York Metropolitan Statistical Area, commented that neither the melting pot nor the black model can be used for the Puerto Rican.

They cited the competition between the Puerto Rican and the larger, more established black population as one factor, and the constant return to Puerto Rico as another that has to be considered in any model.

The persistence of the Spanish language is another factor. Most social planners assumed that the Puerto Ricans (as well as other Hispanics from the Dominican Republic, Peru, Colombia, and Ecuador) would become mainstream Americans over a period of time, but an estimated 70 to 80 percent still rely on Spanish as their primary language (Cowan, 1977). They find it both comfortable and functional; they can read their home town newspapers flown in from Latin America and live their lives in a Hispanic atmosphere.

The Puerto Ricans are clearly demarcated by social inequality (Chapter 7). They form a large part of New York's unskilled labor force. They face discrimination by the unions, in licensing procedures, in the courts, and in housing (Marden & Meyer, 1978:271). They form an underclass but have retained a pluralistic community with their own cultural system based on language, family and kinship patterns, and Hispanic values. Along with the Pilipino on the West Coast, they were also products of Spanish and American colonialism.

The Puerto Rican model appears closest to a bicultural adaptation in the subordinated sector of the stratification system. The bicultural mode is strengthened by the proximity of the Islands and the high flow (both ways) between the United States and Puerto Rico. There is very little information available on the adaptation of Puerto Ricans outside New York City, but it would be reasonable to hypothesize a pattern of acculturation and integration in areas in which their population is much more scattered and distant from the home islands. Because of their Spanish surnames, they may find it easier to identify and to integrate with Hispanics from other countries.

BIBLIOGRAPHY

BERLE, BEATRICE (1959). *Eighty Puerto Rican Families in New York City*. New York: Columbia University Press.

BOARD OF EDUCATION (1958). *The Puerto Rican Study, 1953–57*. New York.

BURKEY, RICHARD (1978). *Ethnic and Racial Groups*. Menlo Park, Calif.: Cummings Publishing.

CHEIN, ISADORE (1964). *The Road to H*. New York: Basic Books.

CORDASCO, FRANCESCO (1975). "Spanish Speaking Children in American Schools," *International Migration Review*, 9(3):379–82.

COWAN, PAUL and RACHEL COWAN (1977). "For Hispanics It's Still the Promised Land," in *Uncertain Americans*, pp. 307–16, eds. Leonard Dinnerstein and Frederic Jaher. New York: Oxford University Press.

ELMAN, RICHARD (1966). *The Poorhouse State*. New York: Pantheon.

FITZPATRICK, JOSEPH P. (1971). *Puerto Rican Americans*. Englewood Cliffs, N.J.: Prentice-Hall, Inc.

GOLDEN, HILDA and CURT TAUSKY (1977). "Minority Groups in the World of Work," in *American Minorities and Economic Opportunity,* pp. 10–49 ed. H. Roy Kaplan. Itasca, Ill.: F. E. Peacock.

HANSON, EARL P. (1955). *Transformation: The Story of Modern Puerto Rico*. New York: Simon & Schuster.

LANGNER, THOMAS S. and MICHAEL T. STANLEY (1963). *The Midtown Manhattan Study*. New York: Free Press.

MALZBURG, BENJAMIN (1956). "Mental Illness among Puerto Ricans in New York City, 1949–51," *Journal of Nervous and Mental Disease*, 123:457–65.

MARDEN, CHARLES and GLADYS MEYER (1978). *Minorities in American Society* (5th ed.). New York: D. Van Nostrand.

PADILLA, ELENA (1958). *Up from Puerto Rico*. New York: Columbia University Press.

PADILLA, ELENA (1977). "Concepts of Work and Situational Demands on New York City Puerto Ricans," in *American Minorities and Economic Opportunity,* pp. 148–69, ed. H. Roy Kaplan. Itasca, Ill.: F. E. Peacock.

PODELL, LAWRENCE (1968). *Families on Welfare in New York City*. New York: City University, Center for the Study of Urban Problems, Bernard Baruch College.

ROGLER, LLOYD H. and AUGUST B. HOLLINGSHEAD (1965). *Trapped: Families and Schizophrenia*. New York: John Wiley.

ROSENBERG, TERRY and ROBERT LAKE (1976). "Toward a Revised Model of Residential Segregation and Succession: Puerto Ricans in New York," *American Journal of Sociology*, 81:1142–50.

OVERVIEW

It is easy to criticize America's race relations. The discrepancies between ideals, as embodied in our slogans of justice and equality, and reality, as demonstrated by our racial boundaries and inequities, are plainly visible. But the step from criticism to a search for solutions is a difficult one, and we have yet to achieve any consensus in terms of adequate programs.

One problem is that of conflicting goals. We cannot evaluate the success of any program unless there are clearer ideas of where we are and where we should be going. We currently have a wide variety of purported goals, each expressing different perspectives and solutions to our racial problems. Consider the following, drawn from common sentiments that are expressed daily: "Why don't they work hard and become more like us, then they'll be accepted." "We only want an equal chance, nothing more, nothing less." "Why don't they go back to where they came from?" "Let each group develop its own culture and leave us alone." "Let them prove themselves." "If they act like animals, let them be treated like animals." "Get rid of the hyphenated American and we'll see a real America." These and countless other expressions reflect the lack of consensus and the difficulty in establishing any kind of rational program with much support.

Perhaps this multiplicity of goals is one reason why the search for solutions for race relations has instead concentrated on the means and processes of human relations. By means and processes we refer to programs such as human relations workshops, group encounters, therapy, and the like, which are geared to treating people as individuals, observing and dealing with racial sensitivities and stereotypes, and feeling good about individual and racial differences. Many of these programs have been effective in achieving their limited goals, but very few have succeeded in addressing the social conditions behind the problem.

The current issues in race relations are different from those of a previous era, when the goal of forming a "melting pot" was reasonably clear but the access to the goal was blocked. The barriers to persons who belonged to a racial minority—that is, those not white, Anglo-Saxon, and Protestant—were so formidable that achieving the goal was not possible. The basic strategies in this era included Americanization (quite successful for certain groups) and discarding the immigrant culture. The problems of prejudice, discrimination, and segregation, however, were not directly addressed, and we ended up with a dominant-dominated stratification system.

When we talk about current goals and the means for achieving them, at least three major points of view should be considered. One perception is that of the dominant, white majority. Although there are many viewpoints within this body, majority-group values and majority-group culture have long been equated with being American and have been primary in shaping the country's race relations. After the dominant group conquered, overwhelmed, outfought, and outdealt the natives for this land, they forced some nonwhites to join them as slaves and invited others to work as cheap labor. For these people of color, almost impassable barriers to any degree of upward mobility were erected, and the means of becoming like the dominant group were denied. The white majority holds the power in our society; therefore it is imperative that its definitions of success and its expectations in regard to race relations be considered a significant factor.

The second perception is that of the dominated ethnics, and here, too, there are varied opinions. They are the victims of racism, and they lack the resources and the power of the majority group. Their goals, their expectations, and their solutions have been ignored too long. They have suffered under prejudice, discrimination, and segregation; they have felt the effects of incarceration, concentration camps, and genocide; and most are no longer content to remain victims of the social system. Unless the majority group desires to erect new barriers or to use its power to eliminate the minorities, there is no alternative but to begin discussions with ethnics about goals and means.

The third perspective, which draws from various sectors but primarily from the dominant group, includes scholars, professionals, and those who are in a position to shape government policy. The major tasks for this heterogeneous group include theory and model building, continued research, and the formulation and implementation of programs.

The task is complicated by the interdisciplinary nature of the problem, for as Van den Berghe (1967) emphasized, race and racism are empirical data that can be used by all the behavioral sciences. To the physical anthropologist, race in the genetic sense may be a subspecification of *homo sapiens*; to the social psychologist, it may be a special instance of prejudice; to the political scientist, a special kind of political idealogy; to the sociologist, a form of stratification; to the historian, a by-product of slavery and colonial expansion; and to the economist, a nonrational factor influencing economic behavior.

OVERALL MODEL

Our presentation has emphasized the following factors:

1. Reasons and conditions of migration
2. Background, culture, and power of the minority group
3. Initial contact and reception by the dominant culture
4. Goals—as shaped by the dominant group, the minority group, and their interaction
5. Placement of the group in the stratification system and the various models for explaining their historical and current status
6. Effects of acculturation
7. Effects of prejudice, discrimination, and segregation
8. Minority group adaptation
9. Development and maintenance of an ethnic identity

Our overall generalization was that the racial minorities started out in, and continue to remain in, the subordinated sector of the stratification system. Therefore, the most important single issue facing minority groups is that of *inequality*. The various models and goals of society, ranging from pluralism to amalgamation, are all defensible, given equality; but all turn out to be less than ideal under conditions of inequality.

The most common American model has been that of acculturation, integration, and assimilation. But as Hraba (1979:356) noted, under conditions of inequality, acculturation can be to a "culture of poverty" which has been handed down from generation to generation, or it can be to a subordinated position in the stratification system. One can learn to be an "inferior" as readily as one can learn to be an "equal" or a "superior."

Feagin (1978:370) also commented on the weakness of acculturation models to deal with the notion that the process can occur at the lower end of the stratification system. The acculturation, integration, assimilation sequence assumes an "open" system whereby individuals and groups can find their appropriate levels, but does not take into account the presence of discrimination and other barriers that interrupt the process. It also minimizes the possibility that the dominant group may consciously want to retain subordinated groups at the bottom of the system as an adequate source of labor available to fill the less desirable and unwanted jobs in the system.

Greeley (1974) used the term *ethnogenesis* to amplify the meaning of acculturation. He rejected the notion that acculturation inevitably leads to Anglo conformity; rather, he saw at least three parts to acculturation. One part is that of Anglo conformity, or conformity to whatever part of the host society one is supposed to become acculturated (including the unequal part of the system); another part is the immigrant, or the "root" culture; the third and most important part is the "unique adaptive culture;" which is the result of the interaction of the first two factors. It is this interaction that makes for the hyphenated American—whether black, Asian, or of Spanish surname—and why they are both different and similar to their brethren who have remained in the homeland. This interaction explains why the Japanese or Chinese scholar from Asia or the black from an African country sees a certain familiarity among Chinese, Japanese, and black Americans, and yet finds it difficult to fully understand them. This interaction also helps to explain why Ogawa (1978) claimed that the Japanese in Hawaii were different from those from the mainland, and why Kitano (1976) wrote of the differences among Japanese Americans growing up in various sections of the country.

Resources and Power of the Minorities

Minorities have had, and will continue to have, differential resources and power as they attempt to adapt to the American system. Blacks and Chicanos have the power of numbers; the Chinese and Japanese have cohesive units; still other groups may be concentrated for effective political participation.

Probably because of their cultural values, the Chinese and Japanese have used an educational elitist strategy (college education, professional degree). Some groups have used politics, entertainment, or athletics as primary means of upward mobility. The problem with elitist approaches is that they do little for the large numbers who do not possess these special abilities and qualities.

There are other factors in ethnic-group cohesion. Some ethnic groups (Chinese and Japanese) have developed a parallel opportunity structure and are less dependent on the dominant group for economic support, whereas others have had to deal with unemployment and financial need through government programs.

Color is another variable that affects ethnic-group cohesion. Groups with a wide range of color will tend to adopt a color stratification system within their own group which tends to be divisive, whereas groups with a higher degree of color homogeneity will tend to be less divided.

The similarity or congruence of the ethnic culture with that of the dominant culture also can aid group cohesion. Those subcultures (Chinese, Japanese) whose values are congruent with those of the dominant group will tend to retain their ethnic culture. Factors such as geographic and cultural isolation will not affect this adaptation. Conversely, those subcultures at variance with the American system (Mexican Americans and Indians) may find it difficult to retain their own ways comfortably when forced to interact with the dominant group. *Culture conflict* is one hypothesized result. Furthermore, geographic and cultural isolation may exacerbate the culture conflict because the differences will be maintained.

Many of the generalizations concerning power cut across ethnic lines. Much minority-group adaptation can be attributed to coping from weaker power positions, and their adaptation is often independent of their culture. The same holds true for the majority group, whose behavior may be based more on their dominant position and not their culture.

For example, during the Revolutionary War, Americans used guerilla tactics. Our heroes, with names such as the "Swamp Fox," used a strategy of retreat and avoided direct conflict. The British generals probably felt that this realistic adaptation to superior forces was tricky and sly and that Americans never stood up and fought in the open like "real men." But technological advances have made us the most powerful nation, and it is now we who now question the masculinity of foes who prefer to hit and run, rather than to face us like "real men."

Similarly, minority-group adaptation has been a matter of survival in a powerless position. All of our ethnic groups have developed their own etiquette for dealing with the dominant group. Either because of naivete or the arrogance that often accompanies power, the dominant group has been blind to the feelings behind the etiquette. Only when violence erupts, such as at Watts, is there some awareness that everything is not quite right.

Yet, powerless groups learn that they would be risking mass suicide if they consistently attempted to meet issues head-on with the group in power. Young militants have learned this lesson the hard way. The majority group controls the courts, the law-enforcement system, the political and economic system, and the overall resources. Its power remains so disproportionate that the probabilities of effecting any significant change through a direct challenge is totally unrealistic. The system can be disrupted, but only temporarily.

Attitudes
of the Majority

In spite of the uniqueness of each ethnic group, the overriding factor in a group's ability to cope has been, and will continue to be, their reception by the majority group. In one sense all nonwhites were considered to be pariahs and therefore unacceptable, except under certain conditions. But there were gradations of acceptability based on variables such as time, place, and circumstances, as well as power threat and cultural styles.

There are several interrelated factors that influence the effect of the discriminatory attitudes and practices of the dominant group on the minority. These include frequency, depth, length of time, and universality. Groups that are victimized the most, over a long period of time by almost all members of the dominant group, would be the ones most likely to feel unwanted and isolated and to acquire a pariah identity. Part of the "success" of the Chinese and Japanese came about when previous negative stereotypes changed—the Chinese became our allies during World War II and the Japanese during the post-World War II era. The behavior of the target minorities in these instances probably changed less than the attitudes of the majority did. These two Asian groups also never experienced the universal hostility that has been the experience of the blacks—even during World War II, Japanese Americans relocating to the Midwest and the East found that not all Americans shared the anti-Japanese feelings of the West Coast.

PLURALISM

The development of pluralistic systems in America is not difficult to trace. The country is composed of groups with obvious physical differences, dissimilarities in habits and life styles, and variations in language and nationality. Social hostility, discrimination, prejudice, and economic necessity tended to shape segregated living patterns with various degrees of isolation and separation. Differentiated opportunities restricted the mobility of selected populations. Therefore, a variety of pluralistic structures, based on such variables as nationality, ethnicity, religion, culture, and race, developed.

Various forms of pluralism can be ranked according to rigidity, voluntarism, and permanence. From this perspective, racial pluralism is the most rigid, involuntary, and permanent. Other forms of pluralism are much less so; for example, cultural pluralism and nationality groupings can be temporary (participating in the yearly ethnic festival) and voluntary. Although there are periodic efforts to revive ethnic identity among some European groups, most have acculturated and intermarried to the point where their nationality and ethnic differences have virtually disappeared.

Racial pluralism is the most extreme form, since it is generally reinforced by the majority group in power, which elects to maintain social and psychological distance. The institutions that maintain segregation are among the most powerful; discriminatory laws, although changing, and lack of opportunity combine to force people of color to attend separate and unequal schools; (moves toward school desegregation are among the most fiercely resisted). In the past, there were attempts to maintain total structural differentiation based on race: schools for blacks, Asians, Indians, and Chicanos, separate eating and recreational facilities, and specified low-status occupational roles. Current housing segregation has encouraged this historical tradition. The general effect has been restrictive racial pluralism that has kept large proportions of minority individuals separated and in lower-class positions.

Even though separated, most ethnics are exposed to the society and learn how to be American. Although there are qualitative differences in school systems, the language, the curriculum, the goals, and the expectations are typically American, to the extent that racial pluralism has not carried over too deeply into the cultural areas of minority groups. Most ethnic groups, although structurally separated, are American by culture; but because so many are caught in lower-class positions, their pervading life styles are heavily influenced by lower-class perspectives.

Factors such as cultural drift, stereotypical interaction, differential goals, experiences, opportunities, and individual differences have encouraged other kinds of pluralism. The term *bicultural* refers to one such variation. It is a partial integration of the ethnic and the dominant culture that is neither fully one nor the other. It also may include individuals whose parents are of different races, or the "marginal person" as described by Park.

Gordon (1987:88–89) differentiated between *liberal pluralism* and *corporate pluralism*. Liberal pluralism is characterized by the absence of any legal or governmental recognition of different groups so that ethnicity is voluntary, and ethnic criteria are not used for special or favored treatment. Corporate pluralism, on the other hand, formally recognizes ethnic groups as legally constituted entities with official standing. Economic and political rewards are distributed on the basis of variables associated with ethnicity (for example, affirmative action that takes into account past discrimination and attempts to correct the underutilization of specific groups, including women).

Many of the current conflicts over programs and policies reflect the liberal versus the corporate approach. For example, the liberal approach discourages ethnic quotas, views ethnicity as a crutch, and advocates "objective standards" over situational factors. Conversely, the corporate approach views ethnic (and female) mobility as of the highest priority and pushes toward a better ethnic and sex distribution throughout the economic system. At the present time, the disadvantaged groups are more likely to favor the corporate approach, whereas the advantaged ones advocate the liberal definition; still others favor a racial status quo or may even support a regression to a clearly dominant, subordinate relationship.

One effect of these different positions is through their relationship to voluntary and involuntary pluralism. The liberal position encourages voluntary ethnic pluralism; the corporate encourages structural pluralism; the reactionary position insists upon racial pluralism.

The Role of Goverment

The historical role of government in supporting and expanding corporate pluralism can be seen by a short review of presidential executive orders.[1]

1941. President Roosevelt issued Executive Order 8802. This order mandated the right to be employed in defense industries regardless of race, creed, color, or national origin. It did not define discrimination nor provide means for enforcement. In 1943, the President extended the coverage to all government contracts. This order can be interpreted as a liberal approach.

1951. President Truman issued Executive Order 10308. The order established the Committee on Government Contract Compliance (CGCC).

1953. President Eisenhower issued Executive Order 10479. This order abolished CGCC and established a new government committee, that heard discriminatory complaints but had no authority to impose sanctions on violators. It relied on persuasion and conciliation.

1961. President Kennedy issued Executive Order 10925 creating the President's Committee on Equal Opportunity. It functioned as an enforcement agency and issued rules and imposed sanctions, such as contract cancellation or debarment. The order required government contractors to take affirmative action to insure that employees and applicants were treated without regard to race, color, creed, or national origin. Coverage was extended to federal and federally assisted construction in 1962.

1965. President Johnson issued Executive Order 11246, which delegated enforcement responsibility to the Secretary of Labor. The Office

---

[1] Presidential executive orders can be a two-edged sword. The Japanese Americans were placed in their concentration camps by Executive Order 9066 signed by President Franklin Roosevelt in 1942.

of Federal Contract Compliance was created in October 1965 to implement this responsibility.

1967. President Johnson issued Executive Order 11367, which amended 11246 to require that federal contractors take affirmative action to insure equal employment opportunity without regard to race and sex (Federal Contract Compliance Manual, 1978). This order can be interpreted as a corporate approach to race and sex equality.

More recent additions to affirmative action have included Vietnam era veterans and disabled and handicapped individuals.

Affirmative action programs have come under attack from dominant-group individuals. There have been accusations of racial quotas, reverse discrimination, the placement and advancement of unqualified minorities, and emphasis on equality of condition rather than on equality of opportunity.

Minority groups have also been critical of affirmative action. The program is accused of being more interested in processes and procedures than in outcomes, of moving too slowly, of skimming the "cream" off the top but having little effect on the average and below-average minority group member, and of encouraging expectations without delivering substantive change.

The most important feature of affirmative action is its symbolic value, since it places the government, however modestly, on the side of groups who, up to now, have been receiving less than their equal share of America's economic benefits.

Values, Goals, and Life Styles

Cultural pluralism is generally characterized by the coexistence of several value systems, differential goals, and a variety of life styles. Shared values lead to social integration, and in culturally pluralistic societies such consensus is often difficult to obtain. It is our judgment that in the past, the United States, despite its diverse ethnic and other groups, was characterized by remarkably homogeneous goals, values, and life styles. Public schools, the widespread mass communication network, and the effectiveness of advertising have led to relatively high consensus in values.

Nevertheless, our racial stratification system has produced subcultures with their own values, goals, and life styles. But, our analysis of various ethnic groups indicates that what is often labeled cultural pluralism may be the culture of survival, the culture of poverty, and the culture of a lower-class life style. These are natural consequences of the white-nonwhite stratification system that was extremely effective in restricting the educational, occupational, and social mobility of the ethnics. Generally, as jobs become steadier and incomes rise, minority-group values and life styles show a corresponding change. Majority-group observers may comment on the "success" of those who have become more like them, while members of ethnic organizations may call these same individuals "Uncle Toms."

Individual Perceptions

Even though there may be institutions and organizations that shape behavior and a legal system that enforces and provides sanctions, the individual may still move back and forth through structural and cultural space. The current emphasis on all people "doing their own thing" reflects an individualistic approach that can lead to serious conflict. In a more rigidly stratified system that allowed for little individuality (for example, feudal Japan), individual perceptions, needs, and goals had a lower priority than group expectations. But an individual emphasis, as opposed to a group emphasis, can work in multiple directions. The individual who feels that it is his or her "right" to discriminate can remain a major stumbling block to racial harmony, especially since that individual will find group support for such a position.

But individualism may also provide one "solution" to our racial problems. The relative openness of certain institutions, especially in educational fields, and the chance for upward mobility are developing a melting pot at a surprising time. A study (Kikumura & Kitano, 1973) on Japanese-American interracial marriage in areas as diverse as Honolulu, Los Angeles, San Francisco, and Fresno showed a high rate of approximately 50 percent. In view of the low rates of interracial marriage for Japanese in the past, this study indicated that one of the most rigid strictures in race relations has begun to erode. The change is hypothesized as stemming primarily from an individual orientation.

A brief review of the Japanese experience will serve to illustrate this change. The Issei, or immigrant first generation, came from a culture that emphasized group solidarity and did not allow much freedom in marital choice. A language barrier, few opportunities to interact with majority-group females, discrimination, prejudice, and a strong desire for in-group marriage limited interracial unions. Estimates of interracial marriage for this group are below 10 percent.

The second-generation Nisei were highly acculturated but lived in a structurally pluralistic system. Their closest friends were fellow Nisei, and social interaction was generally limited to their own ethnic group. Despite mobility for some through higher education and entrance into the professions, this was still the era of rampant discrimination (antimiscegenation laws), and in-group social pressure encouraged marriages to other Japanese. The group orientation remained strong, and estimates of interracial marriage for the Nisei were around 20 percent.

The third-generation Sansei are much more individualistic and are less tied to ethnicity or to the Japanese culture. The American expectation of freedom of choice is their current model. Even though 98 percent of their Nisei parents prefer that they marry other Japanese (Kitano, 1976), the Sansei are deciding for themselves. Many come from families of high status, most are in college, and few ethnic institutions control their social interaction. Conversely, the attitudes held by members of the dominant culture also have changed; race prejudice and discrimination have diminished, and there are better occupational and social opportunities for the Sansei. A social-class bias has become more common, and Nisei parents now ask their Sansei children, "What does he do?" rather than "Is he Japanese?" Issues of love and happiness are taking precedence over duty and obligation; individual needs and perceptions are of primary importance. One out of every two Sansei are marrying out of the group. Our analysis indicates that, especially for women, marital choice means a degree of upward mobility. The majority of Sansei marriages are with Caucasians (Kikumura & Kitano, 1973).

We hypothesize that the rates of intermarriage for other ethnic groups may be even higher than for the Sansei, since the Japanese have been one of the most exclusive groups. For example, Adams recognized "that they [the Japanese] marry within their own group in higher proportion than any other of the peoples in Hawaii" (1937:160).

Some Melting

It is ironic that at a time when ethnic awareness and solidarity are being promoted, other forces are pushing toward consolidation—the melting pot. The "melting" is occurring gradually because the organizations and institutions most concerned with racial separateness have changed. For example, our marital customs have stressed free individual choice; our educational institutions have opened up, albeit slowly; and hiring practices have absorbed many more minorities, although not quickly enough.

It is difficult to appreciate the relative openness of American society unless one has spent some time abroad. Most other countries do not automatically grant citizenship to "foreigners," and their educational institutions remain either principally for the wealthy, for those from proper family backgrounds, or for the few who can pass a number of examinations. Rather than weakening it, marriage generally strengthens the existing stratification scheme.

Although there is no standard American model of marriage in the United States, there is less emphasis today on family name, family background, and parental wishes. Looks, personality, ability, and potential are given a higher priority. Therefore, as ethnics achieve a degree of upward mobility, they become more attractive and may be more attracted to others of a similar disposition. Although interracial marriage used to be prohibited by law (sixteen states still retain antimiscegenation statutes that are constitutionally illegal), it can be argued that, racist as it was, the attitude behind this law also was heavily class oriented, since most ethnics were in the lower classes.

The major reason for the delay in achieving a true melting pot of races, then, has been the barriers of racial prejudice, discrimination, and segregation. The major effect has been the restricted mobility of non-whites, so that significant proportions have occupied the lower positions in our social structure.

As ethnics rise in status, mutual acceptability also has risen, and with it, more intimate social interaction. The answer to the classic racist question, "Do you want your daughter to marry one?" has changed from an outright "No" to "Well, if he's wealthy (or handsome, or intelligent, or a professional, or if it's love)."

RACIAL PROBLEMS AND SOCIAL CLASS

It is difficult to argue against the hypothesis that our racial problems are tied basically to social class. At one stage the close correlation between the two variables made the difference difficult to detect because the great majority of ethnics were also in the lower classes, and even now the proportions are unequal. It may be most accurate to describe America's racial problem as that of disadvantaged social classes, compounded by the factor of race.

Previous studies of miscegenation (whites with Indians or blacks) indicate very little change in the attitudes toward these pariah groups, probably because most of these marriages were between powerless groups, such as the marginals and the lower classes. However, as miscegenation begins to occur in the higher social strata, it may begin to affect racial attitudes.

The problem would be primarily racial if *all* avenues of mobility were closed on the basis of race alone. It remains a matter of degree; some ethnic groups, such as the Asians, currently have a higher rate of mobility. The barriers are like sieves or filters that permit upward mobility only for some. It is among those who have been upwardly mobile—the better educated, more acculturated, and more affluent—that interracial marriage and equal-status contacts have occurred more frequently.

The problem of upward mobility is, therefore, not strictly a racial one. If the racial stratification system worked "perfectly," all whites would be at the top and all colored minorities would remain at the bottom. Although many barriers are racial, there are other barriers that make mobility difficult for those individuals and groups of any color less motivated to compete in the system. As we indicated earlier, although 4.3 million blacks were receiving public assistance, so were 6.5 million whites. But racial pluralism has been one strong factor in minimizing any significant alliance among groups caught in a residual position.

Sometimes there is the temptation to romanticize poverty and equate it with purity. This is a fantasy that only those who are not poor can afford. There is a vast difference between the voluntary poor and the involuntary poor; the latter are caught in a web of poverty, alienation, hopelessness, and suffering from which there is little escape. Exhortations to work hard or threats to cut off welfare are poor substitutes for providing better opportunities in a more open society.

For the ethnics, as well as for members of the underclass, the highest priority should be given to maximizing the means for achieving economic independence so that they may create their own goals. Steady incomes, better education, and decent housing have transformed some of our former pariah groups into "model minorities," and similar predictions may be made for other groups. It does not mean that life will then become problem free, for all positions in a social structure have their advantages and disadvantages. But for the minorities, the achievement of some degree of control over their daily lives is a dream that has eluded them for so long that any further delay will be critical to their own lives and may even prove fatal to the entire society.

BIBLIOGRAPHY

ADAMS, ROMANZO (1937). *Interracial Marriage in Hawaii.* New York: Macmillan.

FEAGIN, JOE (1978). *Racial and Ethnic Relations.* Englewood Cliffs, N.J.: Prentice-Hall, Inc.

Federal Contract Compliance Manual (1978). U.S. Department of Labor, Office of Federal Contract Compliance Programs.

GORDON, MILTON (1978). *Human Nature, Class and Ethnicity.* New York: Oxford University Press.

GREELEY, ANDREW (1974). *Ethnicity in the United States.* New York: John Wiley.

HRABA, JOSEPH (1979). *American Ethnicity.* Itasca, Ill.: F. E. Peacock, Inc.

KIKUMURA, AKEMI K. and HARRY H. L. KITANO (1973). "Interracial Marriage: A Picture of the Japanese," *Journal of Social Issues,* 29(2):67–81.

KITANO, HARRY H. L. (1976). *Japanese Americans.* Englewood Cliffs, N.J.: Prentice-Hall, Inc.

KITANO, HARRY H. L. and AKEMI I. KIKUMURA (1976). "The Japanese American Family," in *Ethnic Families in America,* pp. 41–60, eds. Charles Mindel and Robert Habenstein. New York: Elsevier.

OGAWA, DENNIS (1978). *Kodomo No Tame Ni.* Honolulu: University of Hawaii Press.

PARK, ROBERT E. (1950). *Race and Culture.* New York: Free Press.

VAN DEN BERGHE, P. (1967). *Race and Racism.* New York: John Wiley.

INDEX

NAME INDEX

SUBJECT INDEX